OXFORD WORLD'S CLASSICS

THE ESSENTIAL WRITINGS

MOHANDAS KARAMCHAND ('Mahatma') GANDHI was born in 1869 in Porbandar, in western India. As was customary, he was married very young, at the age of 13, to Kasturbai Makanji, and they had four sons (she died in 1944). After the death of his father Gandhi went to England in 1888 to study law, returning to India in 1891. Having failed as a lawyer in India, he went to South Africa, where he stayed until 1914. Here he became a successful lawyer and increasingly turned to political activity and journalism to fight discrimination against Indians, eventually organizing civil resistance. Early in the twentieth century he experienced a deepening religious and social vision and in 1906 took a vow of celibacy as part of his new dedication to public service. He simplified his personal life, and founded two communities modelled on a Hindu *ashram*. He became critical of Western civilization and its impact on India, which found expression in his piece of writing, *Hind Swaraj* (Indian Home Rule), 1909.

He returned to India in 1915 and soon became involved in India's nationalist movement against British rule, becoming the dominant personality in the politics of the Indian National Congress. He believed passionately in non-violence and led several major non-violent movements of civil resistance to the British Raj, which led to his own imprisonment and that of many of his followers on numerous occasions. At the end of his life he was saddened by the widening gulf between Hindus and Muslims which culminated in the partition of the country when the British left in 1947. Ironically, he was assassinated at a prayer meeting in January 1948 by a Hindu who thought he was responsible for the partition. India was plunged into shocked mourning and his close ally, now Prime Minister, Jawaharlal Nehru, spoke of a light going out of their lives at his death. He remains a revered figure in India and a global source of inspiration to those who believe in non-violence and who see him as a man whose simplicity of life and compassion prefigured a more just and peaceful society.

JUDITH M. BROWN is Beit Professor of Commonwealth History at the University of Oxford. Her many publications include *Gandhi's Rise to Power: Indian Politics 1915–1922* (1972), *Gandhi and Civil Disobedience: The Mahatma in Indian Politics 1928–34* (1977), *Gandhi: Prisoner of Hope* (1989), *Nehru: A Political Life* (2003), and *Global South Asians: Introducing the Modern Diaspora* (2006).

OXFORD WORLD'S CLASSICS

MAHATMA GANDHI

The Essential Writings

New Edition

Edited with an Introduction and Notes by
JUDITH M. BROWN

OXFORD
UNIVERSITY PRESS

OXFORD
UNIVERSITY PRESS

Great Clarendon Street, Oxford ox2 6DP

Oxford University Press is a department of the University of Oxford.
It furthers the University's objective of excellence in research, scholarship,
and education by publishing worldwide in

Oxford New York

Auckland Cape Town Dar es Salaam Hong Kong Karachi
Kuala Lumpur Madrid Melbourne Mexico City Nairobi
New Delhi Shanghai Taipei Toronto

With offices in

Argentina Austria Brazil Chile Czech Republic France Greece
Guatemala Hungary Italy Japan Poland Portugal Singapore
South Korea Switzerland Thailand Turkey Ukraine Vietnam

Oxford is a registered trade mark of Oxford University Press
in the UK and in certain other countries

Published in the United States
by Oxford University Press Inc., New York

First published as an Oxford World's Classics paperback 2008

British Library Cataloguing in Publication Data

Data available

Library of Congress Cataloging in Publication Data

Data available

Typeset by Cepha Imaging Private Ltd., Bangalore, India
Printed in Great Britain by
Clays Ltd., St. Ives plc.

ISBN 978-0-19-280720-5

2

PREFACE

It has been a challenge and a pleasure to work on a new edition of *The Essential Writings of Mahatma Gandhi*, first published by the Clarendon Press in 1986–7. I would like to thank my editor at OUP, Judith Luna, for first suggesting the project and masterminding it to its conclusion. To Mrs Stephanie Jenkins in the History Faculty, University of Oxford, I owe thanks for her technical skills in helping to prepare the documents for inclusion in the selection. To the Navajivan Press and to Oxford University Press I am indebted for permission to use much of the material included here.

It is appropriate here to comment on the principles behind this new selection. The first edition of the *Essential Writings* was prepared by the late Professor Raghavan Iyer, whose discipline was political science. It was based upon his much larger, three-volume collection of Gandhi's moral and political writings published by OUP in 1973 (*The Moral and Political Thought of Mahatma Gandhi*). The volumes were subtitled 'Civilization, Politics, and Religion', 'Truth and Non-Violence', and 'Non-violent Resistance and Social Transformation'. Although this worked well for an extended collection, and the volumes remain a valuable source for students of Gandhi's thought, the use of the same sub-divisions in the much smaller *Essential Writings*, intended for a rather different audience, possibly unfamiliar with the disciplines of political science and philosophy, works less well, and in particular leads to the omission of extracts from some of Gandhi's most critical writings, for example *Hind Swaraj* (1909), the *Autobiography* (1927), and the *Constructive Programme* (1941). I have therefore built on parts of Professor Iyer's selection but worked with a completely different structure which has required many new documents. At the start of the twenty-first century there is considerable interest in Gandhi, among students and the lay public, many of whom may not have much knowledge of Gandhi's life and work in India and South Africa, and may not be familiar with philosophical concepts. This selection is designed for them, as an interpretive starting point. Those who wish to pursue their interest further can proceed to Iyer's three-volume selection, or to the great corpus of Gandhi's

Collected Works and his individual books and pamphlets. In the Introduction I place Gandhi in his particular time and multiple geographical locations, showing the challenges and resources available to him. I suggest that we should see him not as a systematic or trained thinker, or a professional intellectual, but as a pilgrim figure, someone who was forced to consider big philosophical and political issues and profound human dilemmas by the life he led as a social and political activist. His thinking and writing were essentially responses to the specific challenges he faced, and his written works were therefore much more likely to be short ephemera than lengthy sustained arguments. I then discuss some of the core and interlocking beliefs which over time came to make up his thinking. The selection of documents reflects this approach to Gandhi. They start with the influences on him and how he saw himself and his work. They continue with three sections which reflect Gandhi's ideas about radical change, starting with the individual, proceeding to the level of society, and only then to the level of the politics, in particular the specific problems of India under British rule and the meaning of and creation of *swaraj*, self-rule. The final section concentrates on the hallmark of Gandhi's life and thought, the centrality of non-violence and its use in the arena of politics. I hope, as did Raghavan Iyer before me, that the selection will introduce more people in the English-speaking world to Gandhi's life and thought, and to his responses to profound issues which are still significant at the start of a new millennium, over half a century after his death.

Judith M. Brown
Oxford, 2007

CONTENTS

THE ESSENTIAL WRITINGS

I. GANDHI, HIS MISSION, AND THE INFLUENCES ON HIM

II. AUTHENTIC HUMAN LIFE AND THE TRANSFORMATION OF THE INDIVIDUAL

III. TRANSFORMING SOCIETIES

IV. INDIA UNDER BRITISH RULE: MAKING A NEW NATION

V. NON-VIOLENCE AS POLITICAL ACTION

INTRODUCTION

MOHANDAS KARAMCHAND GANDHI, later in life known as 'Mahatma' or Great Soul, was a most unusual public figure. He became, somewhat reluctantly, a notable leader in the Indian nationalist movement, particularly associated in his lifetime and subsequently with the practice of non-violent civil resistance. He was also a profound and original thinker, although it would be wrong to think of him primarily as a philosopher. There was no dichotomy between Gandhi the activist and Gandhi the thinker: rather, in his life there was a symbiotic relationship between thought and action. Almost always he felt compelled by particular events and challenges to think deeply about issues relating to the nature and worth of the individual, what should be humanity's central values, and the right form of human society and polity. Nor was he primarily a writer, although he probably wrote more during his life than many professional authors. He wrote when he felt he had to, in response to particular issues or situations. Another unusual aspect of Gandhi the thinker was the fact that he was completely self-taught. By profession a lawyer, he never formally studied philosophy, politics, or theology, which might have been routes into structured thinking about political and philosophical issues. However, he read copiously and eclectically; he responded to the people he met and felt he could learn from; he observed human kind in action; and he drew inspiration from many of the world's great religious traditions as he came across them. With the aid of these infinitely varied resources he slowly built up for himself a world view and a philosophy of action which had an inner coherence, though he disliked and denied the idea that he was the founder of 'Gandhism' as a school of thought. Although Gandhi's thinking had an inner coherence, it was not always consistent. In his view, consistency was not a particular virtue, because he believed that he should primarily be a pilgrim, someone who was seeking truth, but who at no time would ever see the totality of truth. He was therefore always intellectually and spiritually on the move, learning as he went along, expanding his understanding of truth, and being prepared to leave behind visions of truth he came to feel were too narrow. Consequently, to understand Gandhi's thinking we have to engage with his life, to see both the roots of much of his thought as well as the shifting context of his life which was constantly challenging him to refine his ideas about ultimate goals as well as immediate problems.

Gandhi's Life: Challenges—Opportunities—Resources

Gandhi was born in 1869 in western India, in the area now known as Gujarat. Some would have called it a backwater. His early life was spent in small princely states, in whose service his father worked. The surviving Indian princes were subsidiary clients of the British rulers of the subcontinent, who governed two-thirds of it directly but left one-third under loyal princes whose modes of rule were often far more traditional and where there was far less direct British influence. Even here modern communications and the presence of the British Raj on the subcontinent were opening doors to new political and social ideas, new opportunities and new senses of Indian identity. Gandhi's family recognized the significance of these new life chances. Although they were from a middle-ranking, *bania* or merchant caste, his father was a government official, and they wished to equip their son with the skills necessary for success in a changing India. They sent the young man first to school and then to an English-medium college, though as a native speaker of Gujarati he struggled with education in the strange language of the imperial rulers. On the death of his father the family sent him to England to study law, in the hope of making him into a successful, modern professional man who could, on his return, support his wider family as well as Kasturbai, the bride he had married, as was quite usual at the time, at the age of 13. Although this trajectory was one he shared with many successful contemporaries as well as Indian young men of a later generation such as Jawaharlal Nehru, in Gandhi's case it did not deliver the success story his family had hoped for. He had initially in London tried to mould himself into a modern, cosmopolitan young man (even taking music, elocution, and dancing lessons), but he soon realized he could not afford such an experiment and lived a frugal life, reflecting the vow made to his mother before leaving home that he would protect his moral and ritual status by avoiding wine, women, and meat.[1]

---

[1] On Gandhi's early life and his wry recollections of his time as a student in London, see M. K. Gandhi, *An Autobiography: The Story of My Experiments with Truth* (1927), part I.

Although he was a diligent student in London his achievements were not remarkable; he was diffident and shy, and did not have the connections or self-confidence to make his way in the law on his return to India. Nor was there any intimation that this struggling lawyer was going to make his mark in public life and politics, become a notable leader and a subtle thinker. He had been brought up in an orthodox Vaishnava Hindu family, where his father was unusual in that he had close contacts with people of other religious traditions. But there was no hint in Gandhi's own young life that Hinduism meant much to him (see I. 19 and 20[2]), or that this was a man who would become a Mahatma, someone who would strive with all his energy towards a spiritual goal which would encompass his whole life. To rescue himself from his apparent personal and professional failure he took the lifeline offered in 1893 of a one-year contract as a lawyer in South Africa, working for a Gujarati trading firm which needed a lawyer who spoke English and Gujarati.

What had been intended as a year's visit turned into a sojourn which lasted until 1914, when Gandhi finally left South Africa to make his home in India. These two decades were the making of him. They were the truly formative years when he grew to maturity as a person, first as a family man and then as a celibate by choice, a man of deepening spiritual vision and conviction, and one who acquired the inner and external resources to deal with the huge challenges posed by the position of the Indian minority in South Africa. By 1914 the failed lawyer had become a public figure and political activist, known in England, India, and South Africa. The South African authorities were glad to see the back of this troublesome 'saint' who had taken to the politics of civil resistance,[3] while the Government of India bestowed on him the Kaiser-i-Hind gold medal, a formal honour for his work amongst Indians overseas, and seemed to have little idea that this was a man who would work radical change in Indian politics.

[2] References in this form refer to the numbered extracts in the present selection.

[3] This was the opinion of J. C. Smuts in August 1914: see Judith M. Brown, *Gandhi's Rise to Power: Indian Politics 1915–1922* (Cambridge: Cambridge University Press, 1972), 3. On Gandhi's work in South Africa, see Judith M. Brown, *Gandhi: Prisoner of Hope* (New Haven and London: Yale University Press, 1989), chs. 2 and 3; M. Swan, *Gandhi: The South African Experience* (Johannesburg: Ravan Press, 1985); R. A. Huttenback, *Gandhi in South Africa. British Imperialism and the Indian Question, 1860–1914* (Ithaca and London: Cornell University Press, 1971).

In South Africa, Gandhi was challenged in various ways by his new environment to refine his thinking on almost every aspect of private and public life. Here he was exposed to many opportunities made possible by belonging to a cosmopolitan imperial world, so different from the comparative isolation of his home region of India. One aspect of this new world of opportunity was exposure to a wide range of religious and philosophical positions, enabled by a range of personal connections and friendships, and by wide reading of a sort he had never done before. He was in a position to work and ultimately live in close proximity to Europeans and make friendships (such as those with Henry Polak, Albert West, and Hermann Kallenbach) which would have been impossible in India in the early twentieth century, where close relationships across racial boundaries were rare. In this context he was also opened to a wide range of religious and secular literature which he would probably never have encountered in India. In England he had had early encounters with devout people of various traditions who had tried to influence the young student from abroad. Two Theosophists introduced him to a translation of an important Hindu scriptural text, the *Bhagavad Gita*, which he had never read before but which was to become a core spiritual resource for him (see I. 24 and 26). He also attempted to read the Bible for the first time, but fell asleep reading the Old Testament. He later admitted frankly that he could make no sense of it; but the New Testament made a profound impression on him (see I. 27).[4] In Africa he was exposed more fully to Christianity, its scriptures and theology, by devout evangelical friends, as well as to Islam, as many of the more educated and successful Indians among whom he worked were Muslims from his home region of India. He also explored more deeply the resources of Hinduism, which had meant little to him as a youth, under the mentorship of the remarkable Jain, Raychandbhai (see I. 21–3). Through the written word he encountered some of the deepest critics of Western civilization, including the Russian, Leo Tolstoy (see I. 31 and 32) and the British author John Ruskin (see I. 29 and 30). Tolstoy, as he said, 'overwhelmed' him, while Ruskin's *Unto this Last*, given to him by his Jewish friend Henry Polak, 'gripped' him and led to profound changes in his personal way of life.

---

[4] Gandhi, *An Autobiography*, part I, chap. XX.

During his time in South Africa Gandhi was also confronted with practical political problems which raised profound moral issues. Nearest to hand was the discrimination and ill-treatment experienced by the Indian minority in South Africa at the hands of the local white population, who were prompted by a sense of racial superiority over all non-white peoples, as well as by fear of the rapidly growing number of Indians in the country. By the time Gandhi reached South Africa, in Natal Indians were numerically outstripping the white population. The Indian community was itself diverse; it was composed partly of free traders who came for business and were known as 'Arabs' because many of them were Muslims, partly of indentured labourers imported from India to work on the sugar plantations of Natal, and partly of the free children of indentured labourers. Discrimination took many forms, ranging from the discourtesies and social prohibitions of daily life, to legislation designed to prevent Indians from settling or working freely, denial of the franchise, and even the non-recognition of marriages conducted by rites which were not Christian, thereby impugning the morals of Indian women and the legitimacy of their children. Discrimination touched the lives of educated and relatively wealthy free immigrants, like Gandhi himself, as well as the poorest indentured labourers. Famously, Gandhi's own acute introduction to discrimination was on an early journey from the port of Durban to Pretoria. He had booked a first-class ticket but was thrown off the train when a white passenger objected to sharing a compartment with him. The train was standing at Pietermaritzburg station, and after his unceremonious removal Gandhi spent the night there in the bitter winter cold of an unlit waiting room.[5] This experience and, increasingly, his knowledge of the plight of his compatriots persuaded Gandhi to stay on in South Africa and fight discrimination.

Gandhi's subsequent career in South Africa forced him to consider the very nature of the British Empire, and the worth of citizenship within that Empire to Indians since they were so clearly unequal compared with white citizens. He remained loyal to the Empire throughout this time, even being prepared to offer his services to the local colonial government as the leader of an Indian ambulance party in the Boer War and Zulu rebellion. As he wrote of the former,

[5] See Gandhi's own account of this event, ibid., part II, chap. VIII.

'I felt that, if I demanded rights as a British citizen, it was also my duty, as such, to participate in the defence of the British Empire.'[6] Gandhi's work to gain Indians redress and rights as British subjects on such issues as the franchise, a tax on indentured labourers and their children, and prohibition on movements within the provinces of South Africa, made him learn many of the skills of organization and communication essential to successful political campaigning, and to overcome his inherent shyness in public. He began his own newspaper, *Indian Opinion*, as a method of spreading news about the growing struggle and to educate Indians about a wide range of social and political issues. He organized petitions to the local government and the imperial government in London (even returning there twice to lobby himself), and helped to found a political organization, the Natal Indian Congress, named after the Indian National Congress, which back in India was becoming the mouthpiece of a new sense of nationalism. Ultimately the political struggle for rights brought Gandhi to an awareness of the potential power of peaceful resistance to wrong, and to experiments with this form of political action which were later to become his hallmark. The major step towards civil resistance occurred in 1906, against the hated 'Black Act' of the Transvaal legislature, which insisted that any Indian wishing to reside and work legally there had to have a valid registration certificate. In a mass meeting of Indians one present suggested that they should refuse to obey the new law, and Gandhi took up the proposal. But he admitted that at this stage his response was pragmatic and limited in its understanding of the potential of non-violent resistance. 'But I must confess that even I myself had not then understood all the implications of the resolutions I had helped to frame; nor had I gauged all the possible conclusions to which they might lead.'[7] From then onwards he experimented with various forms of non-violent resistance to the evil of discrimination, accepting that breaking the law meant suffering the penalty even if that meant imprisonment. He himself spent time in prison, and even encouraged women to participate in the struggle and go to jail, though this would have been anathema to women of good morals and social status in India. He also tried to find an appropriate word for their resistance, believing that

[6] Gandhi, *An Autobiography*, part III, chap. X.

[7] M. K. Gandhi, *Satyagraha in South Africa* (Ahmedabad: Navajivan, 1928), 102.

the common English designation, passive resistance, did not do justice to their actions. Eventually he called it *satyagraha*, or 'truth-force' (see V. 212 and 213), and from then onwards throughout his life he refined both his understanding of the nature and significance of non-violent resistance, as also its practical manifestations (see Section V). For Gandhi, *satyagraha* seemed to be not only a practical way of responding to wrong, but also a mode of action which would solve the problem of ends and means. He believed that good means inevitably achieve good ends, while evil means can only generate further evil. *Satyagraha* was not only good in itself, but inevitably productive of good results. Moreover, as *satyagraha* seemed to achieve some practical political success in South Africa, even though it was in retrospect not a lasting success, by the time Gandhi returned to India he was convinced that he had discovered a means of political action which would be of profound consequence to his compatriots there.

By his South African campaigning and the connections it gave him with Indian politics and politicians, particularly the remarkable western Indian politician, G. K. Gokhale (see I. 34), Gandhi was brought to consider the nature of India's own civilization, society, and polity. His reflections were to set him apart from most of his Indian contemporaries in South Africa and also, on his return, in India itself. The results of the challenges, opportunities, and resources which South Africa had offered Gandhi were clear by the end of the first decade of the twentieth century. Now approaching the age of 40, Gandhi was clearly a changed man compared with the struggling, insignificant lawyer who had left India on a year's contract. At the heart of this change lay a profound religious awakening and a deep personal transformation. He had come to a sense of an overarching and underpinning Truth, a divine power and nature beyond any vision of God as seen within a particular religious tradition. He believed that this Truth had called him (and indeed called all men and women), and that he had to follow that call, not through a life of meditation and withdrawal from the world, but through an active life of service to humanity (see I. 3, 5 and 12). Social and political action were central to such a life, and active engagement with social and political problems demanded a simple self-disciplined life which shed the ties of normal human love as well as attachment to possessions and status. Gandhi's wife had joined him in South Africa and

they now had four sons. But as a result of his new sense of vocation
he took a vow of celibacy in 1906. Although he had not apparently
consulted her first, she remained his loyal companion right up until
the time of her death when she was in prison with him in 1944, putting up with his increasingly simple lifestyle and his absorption in
public affairs, only sometimes complaining how different her life had
become from that expected by an Indian married woman.[8]

Gandhi expanded his own family community to include many people
of different backgrounds who would share a simple, self-sufficient
life, on the pattern of a Hindu *ashram* or religious community gathered round a spiritual leader. Leaving behind the Westernized
lifestyle of the successful professional man he had become, he set up
his home at Phoenix Settlement near Durban, and then at Tolstoy
Farm outside Johannesburg (see III. 87), communities which became
experiments in new forms of simple, egalitarian society as well as the
powerhouses of his political campaigns. Gandhi's personal transformation also reflected a growing unease with the whole style of life
developing in the apparently successful Western world, built on
industrialized economies, which as early as 1903 he condemned as
'tinsel splendour' (see III. 78). By 1909 his ideas had crystallized, as
he showed in a letter from London to his close friend Henry Polak
and in his seminal work on Indian Home Rule, *Hind Swaraj*, written
soon afterwards on board the ship taking him back to South Africa
(see III. 79 and 80). Now he believed that this so-called modern civilization was fundamentally wrong. It seemed to him to be built on
false ideas of wealth and achievement, denying the fundamentally
spiritual nature of humankind, and leading men and women into
lifestyles which set individuals and groups against each other and
generated violence. Not only did he attempt to withdraw himself and
his close associates from the corroding influence of such 'civilization'. He also preached a vision of an India which would throw off
the moral ills which were infecting India as a result of British rule and
the values it brought with it from the West, in which to their shame
Indians educated in Western style were complicit (see IV. 122).

[8] See the biography of his grandmother by Arun Gandhi, *Kasturba: A Life* (New
Delhi: Penguin Books India, 2000). It is noteworthy that their eldest son, Harilal, was
deeply resentful of his father's lifestyle and work and himself lived a life which caused
them considerable embarrassment. The youngest son, Devadas, became a journalist
working in the cause of nationalism.

For his inspiration he looked back to a rural India, where people inter-acted in small-scale societies and economies, and where he believed a spiritual vision of life had not been corrupted by materialism. Whether or not such an India had ever really existed, Gandhi used this vision as the basis for a view of freedom, *swaraj*, which was far more radical than those of most Indians active in politics, who saw a free India in terms of a polity in which Indians, rather than the British, held the reins of power and governance. For him, *swaraj* meant a new polity, founded on a society where individuals treated each other as equals in the search for Truth and reconstructed their social and political arrangements on this basis. Consequently the Gandhi who returned to India was a skilled and experienced polit-ician, who had a vision of India and a way of public action which marked him out from those he was to join in the struggle to create a nation and a nation state in the context of British imperial rule on the subcontinent.

Gandhi's return to India confronted him with new challenges rooted in the realities of Indian society and the nature of imperialism and the polity emerging under its sway. Although he was middle aged he rose to these challenges, and was effectively a lifelong learner in new contexts, or as he would have put it, a pilgrim after Truth. It was back in India that Gandhi became known as 'Mahatma', and to be seen in some senses as a Hindu holy man. He began to dress very simply, almost like an Indian peasant, identifying with the poor, and looked and lived in a way most unlike other educated political leaders. He founded two *ashram* communities, the first in his native western India in Ahmedabad, and the second deep in the heart of rural central India at Sevagram near Wardha (see III. 114–21). Here he practised a life of extreme simplicity and of daily prayer and religious devotion, and created new forms of social interaction unfettered by existing conventions of caste, gender, and religious difference. For example, one of the principles of *ashram* life from the outset was not to observe untouchability: and he admitted an untouchable family into the *ashram* at Ahmedabad (see IV. 156), thus breaking the con-vention that those who were considered ritually impure at the base of society should not touch those of higher caste, let alone live closely with them. Women were also members of the *ashram* communities as equals with men, and not subjected to patriarchal authority as they would have been in family homes in most of India. People of all religious traditions were welcome in the *ashrams*, and in the regular prayer sessions he drew on the scriptural and devotional resources of many traditions. From this experimental social base Gandhi became a serious and radical commentator on contemporary social practices such as the practice of untouchability (see IV. 155–74) and aspects of the treatment of Indian women—including conventions of *purdah* or seclusion, child marriage, and consequent child widowhood as widow remarriage was deeply frowned upon (see IV. 175–91). Through his struggles with the competing pressures of religious traditions, the complexity of scriptural sources, and the demands of reason and conscience, he began to challenge contemporary religious authorities and to preach and practise a spirituality beyond any specific religious tradition which drew on many sources for its inspiration and expected people of all faiths to live together in harmony as truth-seekers.

India also threw up the political challenges which made Gandhi the most notable and influential politician of his day in the context of a nationalist movement, and possibly the most controversial figure in Indian public life. On his return to India in 1915 it was clear to him that despite the organization of the Indian National Congress, the idea of an Indian nation was confined mainly to an educated elite who shared English as a common language, and was open to contestation and division on many grounds, including the presence of significant religious minorities on the subcontinent, among them Muslims, Christians, and Sikhs. Not only did Gandhi call for a unified and composite Indian nation, rising above divisions of region, language, and religion, he also believed that the nation had to be created from the grass roots upwards, and should be a community which offered equality of status to all its citizens and addressed their real problems. His fundamental critique of British rule in India was that it denied Indians freedom to achieve real *swaraj* and to solve their own problems according to the principles of their ancient civilization. For him, as he had indicated in *Hind Swaraj* (1909), true *swaraj* or freedom was not a matter of driving out the British and stepping into their shoes, but a condition which had to be created by working for true freedom through attention to India's internal social and economic problems. Consequently much of his teaching about *swaraj* related to very practical problems and very down-to-earth solutions (see Section IVc). For him, unity among different religious groups, particularly Hindus and Muslims, the abolition of untouchability, and the end to conventions which trapped women in a lower status than men were all essential for the achievement of real freedom. So was the socio-economic issue of fostering *swadeshi*, the use of goods made in one's own country (see IV. 191–201). Refusing to use foreign goods would help to undermine the economic roots of imperialism, and it would throw Indians back on their own small-scale production rather than relying on factory production for a mass market. In particular, he preached the importance of *khadi*, hand-spun clothing, which would undermine visual signs of class and caste, would draw people together in the use of the *charkha* or spinning-wheel, and would help to erode the value of the cotton trade for factory owners in England. Gandhi loosely referred to socio-economic prescriptions for the making of *swaraj* as his constructive programme—what had to be done to construct true freedom. He made his fullest exposition of this in a pamphlet of 1941 entitled *Constructive Programme: Its Meaning and Place* (see IV. 139). It ranged from communal unity, the removal of untouchability, the treatment of women, through observance of *khadi*, encouragement of village industries, necessary reform of education, to village health and sanitation. It was little wonder that few people shared the breadth of his vision of reconstruction in India, and he sadly recognized that more often than not his fellow Congressmen left his ideas about the Constructive Programme lying on the floor at their meetings rather than taking them seriously.

Gandhi seems to have had no plans for an all-India political career on his return from South Africa, but rather to have envisaged a role for himself as a social reformer in his own region. However, he was soon drawn into wider public life because of his growing reputation, not least as a practitioner of *satyagraha*, which offered his compatriots a new way of dealing with public conflicts. Initially, in 1917–18 the causes with which he was involved were particular local ones, such as the condition of indigo cultivators in a district of Bihar right across the country from his own Gujarat, and later the wages of industrial workers in Ahmedabad or the land revenue demand in Kaira district, both of which were in Gujarat.[9] However, in the aftermath of the First World War he rose rapidly and unexpectedly to all-India

[9] On these early local campaigns in 1917–18, see Brown, *Gandhi's Rise to Power*, chap. 3.

political prominence. The Indian nationalist movement had been rad-
icalized by the significant contribution India had made to the British
war effort, in terms of manpower, goods, and money. Not surprisingly, its leaders in the Indian National Congress claimed as a result
a greater political role in the governing of their country and movement towards political freedom. The British responded by accepting
in 1917 that there should be increasing association of Indians in every
part of government and the development of self-governing institutions, with a view to India gradually reaching self-government within
the Empire. As a consequence they embarked on constitutional reform
which devolved considerable power in the provinces of British India
to legislatures composed of elected Indian politicians. Gandhi still
maintained some sense of loyalty to the Empire, and indeed had par-
ticipated in a recruiting drive for Indian soldiers, arguing in the same
way as he had about his own contributions during the Boer War and
Zulu rebellion a decade earlier. However, by 1920 he had come to
feel that the British Raj in India was incapable of reform (although he
retained an affection for Britain and British people). The reasons for
this change of heart were partly his support for Indian Muslims in
their campaign (the so-called Khilafat campaign) to sustain the
Sultan of Turkey as the worldwide Khalifah of Muslims after his
defeat at the hands of Britain and her allies, and the outrage he shared
with thousands of his compatriots over the massacre of unarmed
Indians at Jallianwalla Bagh in the Punjab town of Amritsar in 1919
and the apparent 'whitewash' of the official inquiries into the incident. In the face of these insults to Indian opinion and sensitivities,
the constitutional reforms of 1919 seemed worthless. In response he
offered to the country and to Congress the strategy of non-cooperation
with the British.

As we have seen, Gandhi was very different from most other
Indian politicians—in his lifestyle, and in his core vision of India's
future. Many of the most Westernized could not understand why
he should have abandoned all the trappings and rewards of a successful legal career, and were fearful of the possible repercussions of
civil resistance and law-breaking. Yet he increasingly exhibited a
charisma which many found compelling; and more particularly he
offered in *satyagraha* a mode of direct action against the Raj which
excited them and seemed to liberate them from fear of the imperial
ruler. Jawaharlal Nehru, a sophisticated young lawyer educated at

Harrow School in London, Cambridge University, and the Inns of Court, testified to the electrifying effect of Gandhi on many of his generation.[10] Non-violent resistance to the British also made considerable sense. Gandhi had recognized by the time he wrote *Hind Swaraj* that British rule depended fundamentally on the collaboration of a wide range of Indians, from the remaining princes to those in British India who worked in the army, the police, the legal system, and the civil government. Apart from those who were employed directly by the Raj, millions of others were implicated in the system of rule and the civil society which was growing up under its aegis: those who worked in the courts, and the growing number of educational institutions, merchants, investors and shopkeepers who kept the economy going, doctors, dentists, bankers, and building contractors, and all those who paid their taxes. Any large-scale withdrawal of essential cooperation would fundamentally weaken the Raj because there were only tiny numbers of British people in India who manned the top levels of the civil machinery, the army, and the police, while the whole governmental machine was financed by the Indian taxpayer. Moreover, non-violence (if it could be achieved) would help to claim for nationalist resistance the high moral ground in the eyes of Indians, the British public at home, and a wider international audience. By contrast, as Indians had discovered in the past, violent resistance was something the British were able and willing to control. In Gandhi's hands non-violent campaigns of resistance could be carefully designed to offer opportunities to a wide range of participants, including those beyond the educated elite, women as well as men, to withdraw their cooperation from the British rulers and their system, and to make claims for the Indian nation on moral grounds, thus weakening the ideological as well as the practical foundations of British imperial rule. For example, in 1920–2 one of the main strategies of the campaign was the return of honours (including Gandhi's own), withdrawal from the law courts and from government educational institutions, as well as refusal to seek election to the reformed legislatures or to work within them. A decade later in the movement of civil disobedience Gandhi inaugurated the campaign with the carefully choreographed march to the seashore at Dandi on the west coast of India to make salt in defiance of the government monopoly of salt, thus choosing an

---

[10] J. Nehru, *An Autobiography* (London: The Bodley Head, 1936).

issue which would unite Indians across region, community, and class, in a visual demonstration of peaceful resistance which was unlikely to stir up violence. Later aspects of the campaign included the boycott of shops selling foreign cloth and liquor (another government monopoly)—often done by women *satyagrahis*.

Although the Indian National Congress voted to accept Gandhi's strategy of non-cooperation in 1920, thereby marking his emergence in a unique position of leadership, from then until his assassination in 1948 his role in the party and in the broader nationalist movement was always ambiguous. Because many did not share his vision of a new India and saw non-violent action as a temporary and useful tool in particular circumstances, rather than as a permanent commitment to non-violence rooted in a particular way of life, for much of the time the party engaged in the politics of the existing political system, collaborating in the imperial legislatures and profiting from the opportunities to use the various levels of devolved political power. Only at specific times when these types of politics seemed temporarily unproductive because of British policy did the party formally adopt the strategy of *satyagraha*, principally in the great campaigns of 1920–2, 1930–4, and 1942.[11] Gandhi recognized his ambiguous political position, despite his growing and unprecedented public image at home and abroad. He was therefore always prepared to advise the end of non-violent campaigns if he sensed that participants were violent in mind and increasingly in practice. This occurred most dramatically in 1922 when a crowd nominally pursuing non-cooperation attacked and burnt down a police station at Chauri Chaura, killing 22 Indian policemen inside it. Rather than continue campaigns in such circumstances which undermined his commitment to non-violence, he would fall back on his *ashram* communities, and work at his plans for radical socio-economic reform, believing that these were the long-term means to the achievement of his vision of *swaraj* or true freedom.

Perhaps the aspect of his position which caused him the most anguish was his failure to bring together Muslims and Hindus in a common sense of identity and purpose as he had done in South Africa, despite his personal practice and teaching about the nature of

---

[11] For two detailed studies of all-India *satyagraha* movements, the circumstances leading up to them, and their repercussions, see Brown, *Gandhi's Rise to Power*; Judith M. Brown, *Gandhi and Civil Disobedience: The Mahatma in Indian Politics 1928–34* (Cambridge: Cambridge University Press, 1977).

real religion and the reality of an Indian nation above divisions of creed. A deepening rift opened up in politics between Muslims and Hindus who were in a considerable majority in India as a whole. This hostility had roots often going back to local socio-economic conflicts, but increasingly the minority feared for its position as the British devolved power to elected politicians, even though Muslims (and other minority communities and groups) had gained from the start of the century what were called 'reserved seats' in the legislatures to protect their position. Ironically, Gandhi's own image as a Mahatma, and the way many of his followers thought of and portrayed him as a Hindu holy man, confirmed the fears of many Muslims that Congress was essentially a Hindu party. When it was clear after the Second World War that the British, having been fundamentally weakened by the war, were soon leaving India, the political leaders could reach no peaceful resolution of the problem of how to create a united India in the wake of the Raj, and they eventually agreed to the partition of the country into India and Pakistan. This occurred in August 1947 in circumstances of escalating violence and the demographic disaster of mass displacement of people who fled to what they hoped would be the safe side of the new international border. Gandhi supported the idea of partition with extreme reluctance, seeing it as the vivisection of India, an unnecessary and tragic rift between brothers, and he believed that in this context independence was not true *swaraj*. He was assassinated in January 1948 as he walked to preside at his daily prayer meeting in Delhi, at the hand of a young Hindu who held him responsible for the partition of what he saw as a Hindu national homeland. Yet the influence of this immensely creative man, from such unprepossessing beginnings, who had used the opportunities and resources offered to him to dream of a new India and to experiment with different ways of achieving his dream, did not end with his death. He was to remain an icon in his own country, a reminder of how men of vision and faith could behave in public life: while abroad, he became an inspirational figure associated with non-violence as a means of tackling some of the most fundamental problems of the twentieth century.

Gandhi the Author

Even a brief examination of Gandhi's life shows how his thought and action were symbiotic. His deepest thinking occurred in response to some of the greatest challenges he encountered in his very varied life. It is also important to understand how Gandhi came to be such a prolific author, and to recognize the nature of his writings, because they are very different from those of many other recognized thinkers. Gandhi was not a trained philosopher or even a systematic thinker: his written works grew out of his life and his need to communicate for very practical purposes. Although his collected works stretch to 90 volumes, many of his writings were ephemeral, composed hurriedly in the course of a busy life in response to specific needs and situations. Into this category fall his many personal letters, in a number of languages, to an international range of correspondents, covering issues as varied as key political problems, religious matters, or the personal dilemmas which faced individuals in their family and individual lives. He wrote so much that sometimes he could not use his right hand and had to use his left; or he would dictate to his friend and secretary, Mahadev Desai, who was also a key figure in the production of his longer pieces of writing. Other ephemera include his many press articles on key religious, social, and political issues. In order to give himself a mouthpiece through the press he acquired control of a number of periodicals, such as *Indian Opinion* in South Africa and *Young India* and *Navajivan* in India. Sometimes he would write an extended series of articles on such key problems as the abolition of untouchability, but more often he dealt briefly with matters which had arisen over the past days and weeks and which he wanted to bring to the attention of his readers in order to teach them moral or political lessons.

The didactic nature of all his writing was even clearer in his larger works. These included his seminal book, *Hind Swaraj*, written in 1909 during a sea voyage between England and South Africa, in which he expounded his vision of true Indian freedom in the form of a dialogue between a reader and himself as editor. His two autobiographical works, *An Autobiography: The Story of My Experiments with Truth* (1927) and *Satyagraha in South Africa* (1928), were also written with the present moment in view, particularly the development of non-violent resistance in India itself. Even when he was writing in his autobiography about his own personal transformations and struggles, his aim was to teach his readers. He wrote, 'It is not my purpose to attempt a real autobiography. I simply want to tell the story of my numerous experiments with truth', because he hoped this would 'not be without benefit to the reader'; particularly as he was now gaining such a wide reputation.[12] As he became more notable and politically active he had little time for concentrated writing. Much of his account of *satyagraha* in South Africa was written during the enforced rest of a prison sentence. More often his larger works originated in serial form, written piecemeal for publication as distinct articles. This was the original form of his *Autobiography* and also his 1908 Gujarati paraphrase of *Unto this Last*, the book by John Ruskin which had helped to transform his personal life. The nearest he came to a theological work, his discourses on the *Bhagavad Gita*, originated as talks for the members of his *ashram* in 1926. After the 1920s he rarely wrote at length, and even then only in time snatched on journeys and between meetings. His pamphlet in which he drew together his views on the Constructive Programme and its fundamental role in the gaining of freedom, was written in December 1941 while he was travelling on a train between Wardha in central India and Bardoli in Gujarat for a meeting of the Congress Working Committee.

Although Gandhi was a self-taught author, writing under pressure, responding to the problems of the moment in varied written forms, his readers, then and now, find him wrestling with huge issues which have perplexed and occupied trained thinkers who have had far more leisure to write. He grappled with the meaning of human life, concluding that to be truly human meant to recognize the spiritual nature of life and to pursue the spiritual truth at the core of life. This led him to ponder the nature of religious traditions and their claims to truth, and to conclude that all traditions had but partial glimpses of truth. Consequently for him the truth-seeker should be open to the insights of all traditions, and should view all with benign tolerance. For him, true religion was not about theology, the construction of belief systems, but about morality, the practical business of following after truth in daily life and interactions. This led him to consider the problems of ends and means and to conclude that they were like a seed and a tree—only good means could deliver good ends, and vice versa. In situations of conflict this involved adherence to non-violence, lest one should violate another's integrity and sense of truth. Gandhi also pondered the relation of the individual to

[12] Gandhi, *An Autobiography*, introd.

society, and the individual's rights and duties in relation to other individuals and also to the state within which he or she lived. He addressed issues of citizenship and the right of the citizen to disobey the law in the pursuit of a higher truth and a greater moral obligation, while being prepared to suffer the legal penalty.

An Approach to Gandhi's Thought

Recognizing the breadth of Gandhi's thought, subsequent writers have developed many different approaches to him. As in his lifetime, there are many Gandhis, as people find in him different types of inspiration, or seek to portray his thought to illuminate specific issues and approaches to problems which they bring to the study of him. In this volume, the organizing approach reflects what I understand as Gandhi's own sense of the need for radical transformations in human lives, relationships, and organizations, and his view of the interconnectedness of these. Although he recognized that his vision of the good life and the right social and political order was applicable outside his own country, he wrote primarily about India and its particular problems. He felt that his mission was first and foremost to India, dealing with his immediate environment, and intervening where he had some realistic hope of influence: in the words of the Victorian Christian hymn he used to quote, 'one step enough for me'. For him, at the root of real change was the individual, and everything else grew from this. So the selection begins with Gandhi himself and the influences he felt most important in his own life and thought. There follow some of Gandhi's writings on the authentic human life as a spiritual life in search of God or Truth, practising a religion beyond any particular religious creed or tradition, and the transformation of the individual person through non-violence, self-discipline, and service to mankind. Section III includes writings which show his exposition of a vision of necessary change in the social order, and his own experiments in this field as he created his *ashram* communities. In his view, these were the necessary preconditions for real *swaraj* or self-rule, and it was only in the context of this type of change that he could proceed to contemplate India's political problems in relation to imperial rule and the way a new nation could be constructed. Making a new nation and dealing with the problem of British rule thus forms the subject of Section IV. The final section focuses on what was for

Gandhi the key role of non-violence in all these interacting levels of change.

At the root of Gandhi's vision was the sense of the individual as an autonomous and responsible being. Each man and woman, to be truly human, needs to recognize that a divine, spiritual reality undergirds all life and gives it meaning, and must follow after that reality for him- or herself. Gandhi chose to call this divine reality Truth rather than God, to challenge the notion of a god encapsulated in specific religious traditions and encourage people to search for a truth beyond the inevitably limited and partial vision of truth and the divine held by any particular tradition. If the authentic human life is a pilgrim life, then individuals must adopt a lifestyle of self-discipline, spiritual devotion, and non-attachment which will free them to listen to the voice of conscience, revelation, and reason. In particular, Gandhi, drawing on Hindu tradition, felt that the non-attachment involved in sexual restraint would help the individual develop his or her spiritual vision and power as well as the capacity for public service. As in his view all people are interconnected, so an individual's life must always be conducted in such a way as to enhance the lives of others: in particular this means simplicity rather than over-consumption at the expense of others, charitable service rather than personal self-regard and aggrandizement. In the service of the poorest the truth-seeker will find the face of the divine. Moreover, as there was no distinction in Gandhi's mind between the public and the private, no possibility of different standards in different spheres of life, so the personal transformation of individuals became the more urgent in pursuit of a far wider public good.

As Gandhi sought to engage himself in the work of personal transformation, he recognized the need to create a social environment in which this sort of disciplined personal life and consequent transformed personal relationships could flourish. With this in mind he experimented with new forms of community life based on the pursuit of truth in his *ashram* communities in South Africa and then in India. They were to be the powerhouses of political and social service to the wider community, but at their heart they were experiments in living by people who tried to share his vision of authentic human life and the disciplines which enabled it, hence the simplicity of food and possessions, the times for prayer and physical labour, and the commitment to treating all members as equal, regardless of caste, creed, race, or gender.

Gandhi believed that his *ashrams* were his best creations, whatever their failures in practice and the tensions between people within them which occurred from time to time. But he also preached and campaigned for the principles elaborated in the *ashrams* to be observed in daily social life in India, tackling specific social customs as well as refining and publicizing his constructive programme as an overall blueprint for social transformation. The key principle of the desirable social order was the recognition that all people were of intrinsic and equal worth, despite long-standing social conventions often strengthened by or rooted in religious tradition. So he battled against aspects of Indian society which enshrined inequality. Most obvious was his long-term campaign against the practice of treating those at the base of Hindu society as untouchable. He never launched a head-on attack on caste itself, though it became obvious that he increasingly found the actual practice of caste deeply disturbing and destructive of a sense of human equality, even though he accepted the need for the division of labour in society. He also campaigned to end many of the customs which demeaned women and denied their intrinsic worth. Deeply ashamed at his own teenage marriage, he campaigned for the end of child marriage and its correlate, child widowhood, which he felt to be an abomination, called for the end of *purdah*, and argued that this was unnecessary if men developed sexual restraint in the way they looked on women, and learnt to value them as they would their own mothers and sisters. Moreover, he insisted that girls as well as boys should be educated, and that women should be encouraged to play their part in the making of a new India, including participation in politics and particularly in some manifestations of *satyagraha*, such as enforcing a ban on foreign cloth or liquor.

Gandhi's understanding of religion as the search for truth, and the moral life required for such a search, led him to a profound sense of the revelation and insights present in many religious traditions while at the same time concluding that no tradition was perfect or infallible. He consequently called for tolerance between people of different traditions as brothers. He believed that, without such mutual tolerance and respect bigotry and hostility to others on grounds of religious difference would destroy India's fundamental identity. But despite his pleas for tolerance, his personal example, his fasts for unity, this was an aspect of Indian social and public life he was least able to change—to his great distress. Another crucial aspect of his vision of social transformation which many of his compatriots failed to share was his understanding of the appropriate economic order which should underpin the good society. Condemning on moral grounds industrial and urban transformation of once essentially rural economies in the West, and increasingly in parts of India, he appealed to Indians to recognize that their civilization should be built on the small-scale interactions of village society, in particular on agriculture and the small-scale production of essential goods, on village industries which would provide employment, food, and clothing. This would provide for the needs of all, while preventing the accumulation of wealth and goods that he saw as inevitable in industrial society, and would be on a human scale, encouraging everyone to see others as fellow humans worthy of care and compassion, rather than as cogs in some vast economic machine where they would lose their identity and essential humanity. In particular, he preached and practised the importance of the *charkha* (spinning-wheel) as an emblem of and means to this new economic order.

In Gandhi's thinking, the political order was intimately tied to underlying social and personal relations. Consequently the reach of his thinking and action was much broader than that of many of his contemporaries. For him, spinning and public hygiene were, for example, far more important than using the political system, with its opportunities for exercising power. It is hardly surprising that many Indians found him politically incomprehensible, even when they recognized his power as a public leader. Indeed part of his political strength was the belief by many politicians that he had a particular ability to connect with a wider audience and to generate the mass following that was needed if the nationalist movement was to uphold its claim to speak for the whole nation. Jawaharlal Nehru certainly felt this way and stayed with his allegiance to Gandhi, despite the many differences in their values and attitudes. Gandhi, like many of his contemporaries, was brought up to value the political arrangements of Western democracies. However, by the time he wrote *Hind Swaraj* in 1909 it was clear that he was fundamentally disillusioned with such assumptions about what was politically desirable. He never wrote a coherent political treatise on the state or on different political systems, but from many hints it seems that he was close to being what many political thinkers would call an anarchist. He did not

accept the morality or necessity of the modern state, but believed
that small-scale communities should govern and defend themselves,
a view which reflected his vision of the inherent morality of the
small-scale, rural society. However, the circumstances of his life
meant that he had to address more pressing political concerns, particularly the nature of British imperial rule, its impact on India, and
what should replace it in the event of freedom. For him, the problem
of British imperialism in India was fundamentally a moral one: that
British rule was the harbinger of values and institutions that were at
odds with the core values of an older, spiritual Indian civilization,
and that the British in alliance with their Western educated Indian
allies were fundamentally damaging India's polity and society. He
lamented in *Hind Swaraj* that his educated compatriots could not see
this and when they spoke of freedom merely envisaged a change in
the ruling personnel, a chance to step into British shoes: they wanted
the 'tiger's nature' without the tiger (see IV. 122). He argued that
true *swaraj* was far deeper than political freedom, and had to be created by Indians through a series of interrelated personal and social
transformations, but he recognized that as an interim measure freedom from imperial rule would be the best course. He was prepared
to support the idea of an Indian democratic nation state as the
replacement for an imperial state (see IV. 125 and 126), though he
believed that India also needed men and women who would shun
politics and work quietly with local communities towards long-term
radical change. To this end, in 1948 he even suggested that the
Congress should disband itself as a political party and become an
organization of social servants of the country.

One constant motif runs through all Gandhi's mature thought,
from his ideas about the properly human life, to his vision of the
good society, to his practical opposition to British rule: the supreme
value of non-violence, *ahimsa*. This was a significant aspect of Hindu
thinking, particularly among the Jain sect who had so influenced
Gandhi's own spiritual development. But in his thought and action
it became an essential aspect of the way a truth-seeker should engage
in the public world and should conduct himself in all situations of
tension and conflict. For him, only non-violence would safeguard the
integrity of those who encountered each other in conflict, and safe-
guard against physical, social, political, or emotional violence. He
also believed that non-violence was a creative and transformative

force, which by its very action could change and heal situations of conflict and human nature itself. This was particularly demonstrated in 1946 when Gandhi insisted in walking unarmed in areas of eastern India torn by communal conflict, to identify with those who had suffered violence.

However, Gandhi also saw himself as a scientist in the matter of non-violence, experimenting with different kinds of *satyagraha*, and carefully calibrating its nature and operation in particular situations. This was clear in his all-India movements, where he chose types of non-violent protest which would undermine the imperial rulers at their most vulnerable points, would guard as much as possible against the outbreak of inadvertent violence, and would bind Indians together in new senses of common identity and obligation. Gandhi was aware that he could not turn people into *satyagrahis* overnight: the ability to behave non-violently and to accept the physical hurts and legal penalties which might be imposed on the protester had to be nurtured through a life of discipline, self-denial, and non-attachment. So he argued the need for personal transformation as a precondition for the practice of *satyagraha*, and was prepared on some occasions to select for his campaigns only those whom he could trust to stick with non-violence, at whatever cost to themselves. However, the reverse of this total belief in the moral and transformative nature of non-violence was that he could not believe that non-violence would ever fail. When confronted by manifest failure, particularly in the 'Quit India' movement of 1942, when the government clamped down on the leadership and the rank and file of the movement took to unprecedented violence and destruction of government property, he argued that *satyagraha* itself had not failed, but that his compatriots had never really been *satyagrahis*, and had used non-violent campaigns as temporary tools without believing in the core principles of non-violent behaviour and protest. As a result he was not prepared to ask hard questions about the circumstances in which *satyagraha* might or might not work in the practical terms of daily power politics.

Gandhi's life was marked by many ambiguities and sometimes inconsistencies in his actions and in his thinking. In his lifetime people understood and interpreted him in many ways, often making him into an image very different from the man himself. Later interpreters have also reinvented him in ways to suit their own ideals and purposes.

However, an attempt to engage with his thinking shows him to be a man in a specific time and place, with the resources and limitations of his particular environment, who grappled with the moral dilemmas of public activism, and who pursued a life of action informed by moral beliefs and principles rather than in pursuit of personal status and gains. In wrestling with underlying philosophical issues, made urgent for him in his personal work of private and public transformation, he came to be a serious thinker who saw life as a whole rather than in compartments, and who came to a vision of essential and radical change at the different but interconnected levels of the individual, society, and the political order. He created no system of thought, no 'Gandhism', despite the wishes of some of his admirers. His creativity as a thinker lay in the breadth of his concerns and thinking, his understanding of the interconnectedness of what appeared to be very different issues, and his attempt to understand and refine non-violence as a moral good and as a uniquely creative means of conducting oneself in public and private life.

The legacy of Gandhi as an activist is widespread but ambiguous. Historically, his decades of campaigning in South Africa left little lasting improvement in the place of Indians in the polity and society, as the development of the apartheid regime was to show. In India itself, his *satyagraha* campaigns were only one element in the success of the campaign for independence. They never succeeded in bringing the British Raj to a halt, as insufficient numbers of the Raj's core collaborators were willing to withdraw their services or their acquiescence. When the British did eventually decide to 'quit India' after the Second World War it was the long-term repercussions of that war which were the main determinants of that departure. However, Gandhi's unique style of leadership, his success in spreading ideas of freedom more broadly and deeply than most of his contemporaries in politics, and his insistence on non-violence did much to deepen the nationalist movement on the subcontinent and to ensure that its conduct helped to lead to a comparatively peaceful resolution of the issue of freedom in relation to the imperial rulers. From the perspective of those who feared an India dominated by a Hindu majority, particularly many of India's Muslims, this very success was deeply threatening and was an element in the mixture of fear, misunderstanding, and ambition which led to the partition of the country.

After his death Gandhi has lived on, his influence enhanced by the manner of his dying. In India itself he is a national icon, his name and image used (and perhaps abused) in national discourse and rhetoric. Although so many Indians did not share his vision of India, he is still in many ways a touchstone for the national polity, a figure by which people and practices in public life and society may still be judged. Further afield, his experiments in making non-violent resistance a practical proposition in modern politics have proved inspirational, not least in the American civil rights campaign. However, it is important to recognize that although Gandhi experimented with many aspects of non-violent resistance, he was at heart not a political analyst but a moralist: when *satyagraha* seemed to fail in a particular context he blamed the attitudes of the protagonists rather than enquiring whether there were particular political circumstances which were hospitable to non-violent protest and others which were not. Such enquiry is essential if non-violence is to be a viable political *modus operandi* in circumstances very different from that of British imperial rule in India. So, half a century after his death Gandhi remains more an inspirational figure than a practical guide in the world of politics. Serious engagement with his life and thought, however, is a way to contemplate some of the profoundest problems humans face in their lives as individuals and as communities, and to recognize that there are resources on which men and women can draw to help them fashion modes of resolving conflicts which enhance rather than threaten to destroy the human race.

SELECT BIBLIOGRAPHY

PRIMARY SOURCES

Published collections of works by Gandhi

The Collected Works of Mahatma Gandhi, 90 vols. (New Delhi: Publications Division of the Government of India, Navajivan, 1958–84).

The Essential Writings of Mahatma Gandhi, ed. R. N. Iyer (New Delhi: Oxford University Press, 1993).

The Moral and Political Writings of Mahatma Gandhi, ed. R. N. Iyer; vol. i: *Civilization, Politics, and Religion* (Oxford: Clarendon Press, 1986); vol. ii: *Truth and Non-Violence* (Oxford: Clarendon Press, 1986); vol. iii: *Non-violent Resistance and Social Transformation* (Oxford: Clarendon Press, 1987).

'My Dear Child': Letters from M. K. Gandhi to Esther Faering, ed. A. M. Barnes (Ahmedabad: Navajivan, 1956).

The Removal of Untouchability, compiled and ed. B. Kumarappa (Ahmedabad: Navajivan, 1954).

Individual works by Gandhi

Sarvodaya (paraphrase of John Ruskin, *Unto this Last*), published in 1908 in a series of articles in *Indian Opinion*; available in *CWMG*, vol. viii, and in *MPWMG*, vol. iii, pp. 410–33.

Hind Swaraj (1909), available in *CWMG*, vol. x, pp. 6–68. For the best modern edition see *Gandhi: Hind Swaraj and Other Writings*, ed. A. J. Parel (Cambridge: Cambridge University Press, 1997).

An Autobiography: The Story of My Experiments with Truth, trans. Mahadev Desai (Ahmedabad: Navajivan, 1927; available in several modern editions).

Satyagraha in South Africa, trans. V. G. Desai (Ahmedabad: Navajivan, 1928).

'History of the Satyagraha Ashram' (1932), published as *Ashram Observances in Action*, trans. V. G. Desai (Ahmedabad: Navajivan, 1955; available in *MPWMG*, vol. ii, pp. 559–612).

Constructive Programme: Its Meaning and Place (Ahmedabad: Navajivan, 1941; available in *CWMG*, vol. lxxv, pp. 146–66).

Journals edited by M. K. Gandhi

Indian Opinion (Natal, South Africa, 1903–14).
Young India (Ahmedabad, India, 1919–32).

Navajivan (Ahmedabad, India, 1919–31).
Harijan (Ahmedabad, India, 1933–48).

Many of Gandhi's articles from these journals are available in the appropriate chronological volumes of *CWMG*.

SECONDARY WORKS

Contemporary writings on Gandhi

Ambedkar, B. R., *What Congress and Gandhi have done to the Untouchables* (Bombay: Thacker & Co., 1945).

Andrews, C. F., *Mahatma Gandhi's Ideas* (London: George Allen, 1929).

—— *Mahatma Gandhi: His Own Story* (New York: Macmillan, 1930).

—— *Mahatma Gandhi at Work* (New York: Macmillan, 1931).

Balvantsinha, *Under the Shelter of Bapu* (Ahmedabad: Navajivan, 1962).

Birla, G. D., *In the Shadow of the Mahatma* (Bombay: Orient Longman, 1955).

Bose, N. K., *My Days with Gandhi* (Calcutta: Orient Longman, 1974).

Desai, Mahadev, *The Story of Bardoli: Being a History of the Bardoli Satyagraha of 1928 and Its Sequel* (Ahmedabad: Navajivan, 1929).

—— *The Diary of Mahadev Desai*, trans. and ed. V. G. Desai (Ahmedabad: Navajivan, 1953).

Doke, J. J., *M. K. Gandhi: An Indian Patriot in South Africa* (London: The London Indian Chronicle, 1909).

Elwin, V., *Mahatma Gandhi* (London: Golden Vista Press, 1932).

Fischer, L., *The Life of Mahatma Gandhi* (New York: Harper & Brothers, 1950).

Gregg, R. B., *The Power of Non-Violence* (Ahmedabad: Navajivan, 1938).

Krishnadas, *Seven Months with Mahatma Gandhi: Being an Inside View of the Indian Non-Co-operation Movement of 1921–22*, abridged and ed. R. B. Clegg (Ahmedabad: Navajivan, 1951).

Nehru, Jawaharlal, *An Autobiography* (London: The Bodley Head, 1936).

Prasad, R., *Satyagraha in Champaran* (Ahmedabad: Navajivan, 1949).

Pyarelal, *The Epic Fast* (Ahmedabad: M. M. Bhatt, 1932).

—— *Mahatma Gandhi: The Early Phase* (Ahmedabad: Navajivan, 1965).

—— *Mahatma Gandhi: The Last Phase*, 2 vols. (Ahmedabad: Navajivan, 1956–8).

Radhakrishnan, S. (ed.), *Mahatma Gandhi: Essays and Reflections* (London: Allen & Unwin, 1938).

Rolland, R., *Mahatma Gandhi: The Man who Became One with the Universal Being*, trans. C. D. Groth (London: George Allen & Unwin, 1924).

Spratt, P., *Gandhism: An Analysis* (Madras: Huxley Press, 1939).

Later studies and assessments

(a) Introductions

Arnold, D., *Gandhi*, Profiles in Power series (Harlow and London: Pearson Education Ltd., 2001).

Copley, A., *Gandhi: Against the Tide* (Oxford: Basil Blackwell, 1987).

Parekh, B., *Gandhi*, Past Masters series (Oxford and New York: Oxford University Press, 1997).

(b) Biographies

Brown, Judith M., *Gandhi: Prisoner of Hope* (New Haven and London: Yale University Press, 1989).

Nanda, B. R., *Mahatma Gandhi: A Biography* (London: George Allen & Unwin, 1958).

Tendulkar, D. G., *Mahatma*, 8 vols. (New Delhi: Publications Division of the Government of India, 1951–4).

(c) Studies of particular aspects of Gandhi's life, thought, and work

Alter, J. S., *Gandhi's Body: Sex, Diet and the Politics of Nationalism* (Philadelphia: University of Pennsylvania Press, 2000).

Bondurant, J. V., *Conquest of Violence: The Gandhian Philosophy of Conflict* (revised edn., Berkeley and Los Angeles: University of California Press, 1969).

Borman, W., *Gandhi and Non-Violence* (Albany: State University of New York Press, 1986).

Brown, Judith M., *Gandhi's Rise to Power: Indian Politics 1915–1922* (Cambridge: Cambridge University Press, 1972).

—— *Gandhi and Civil Disobedience: The Mahatma in Indian Politics 1928–34* (Cambridge: Cambridge University Press, 1977).

—— 'Gandhi—a Victorian Gentleman: An Essay in Imperial Encounter', in R. D. King and R. W. Kilson (eds.), *The Statecraft of British Imperialism: Essays in Honour of Wm. Roger Louis* (London and Portland: Frank Cass, 1999).

—— and Prozesky, M. (eds.), *Gandhi and South Africa: Principles and Politics* (Pietermaritzburg: University of Natal Press, 1996).

Chatterjee, M., *Gandhi's Religious Thought* (London and Basingstoke: Macmillan, 1983).

Dalton, D., *Mahatma Gandhi: Nonviolent Power in Action* (New York: Columbia University Press, 1993).

Dasgupta, A. K., *Gandhi's Economic Thought* (London and New York: Routledge, 1996).

Erikson, E. H., *Gandhi's Truth: On the Origins of Militant Nonviolence* (London: Faber & Faber, 1970).

Hardiman, D., *Gandhi in His Time and Ours: The Global Legacy of His Ideas* (London: Hurst & Co., 2003).

Hick, J., and Hempel, L. C. (eds.), *Gandhi's Significance for Today* (Basingstoke and London: Macmillan, 1989).

Huttenback, R. A., *Gandhi in South Africa: British Imperialism and the Indian Question, 1860–1914* (Ithaca and London: Cornell University Press, 1971).

Iyer, R. N., *The Moral and Political Thought of Mahatma Gandhi* (New York: Oxford University Press, 1973).

Johnson, R. L. (ed.), *Gandhi's Experiments with Truth: Essential Writings by and about Mahatma Gandhi* (Lanham, Md.: Lexington Books, 2006).

Kumar, R. (ed.), *Essays on Gandhian Politics: The Rowlatt Satyagraha of 1919* (Oxford: Clarendon Press, 1971).

Mehta, V., *Mahatma Gandhi and His Apostles* (New York: Viking Press, 1976).

Nanda, B. R., *Gandhi and His Critics* (Delhi: Oxford University Press, 1985).

Parekh, B., *Gandhi's Political Philosophy: A Critical Examination* (Basingstoke and London: Macmillan, 1989).

—— *Colonialism, Tradition and Reform: An Analysis of Gandhi's Political Discourse* (revised edn., New Delhi, Thousand Oaks, Calif., and London: Sage Publications, 1999).

Parel, A. (ed.), *Gandhi, Freedom, and Self-Rule* (Lanham, Md.: Lexington Books, 2000).

—— *Gandhi's Philosophy and the Quest for Harmony* (Cambridge: Cambridge University Press, 2006).

Rudolph, L. I., and Rudolph, S. H., *The Modernity of Tradition: Political Development in India* (Chicago and London: University of Chicago Press, 1967) (see in particular Part Two: 'The Traditional Roots of Charisma: Gandhi').

Sharp, G., *Gandhi as a Political Strategist* (Boston: Porter Sargent, 1979).

Swan, M., *Gandhi: The South African Experience* (Johannesburg: Ravan Press, 1985).

Further Reading in Oxford World's Classics

The Bhagavad Gita, trans. W. J. Johnson.
Empire Writing, ed. Elleke Boehmer.
Ruskin, John, *Selected Writings*, ed. Dinah Birch.

A CHRONOLOGY OF MAHATMA GANDHI

1869 2 October: Mohandas Karamchand Gandhi born, Porbandar, Kathiawar, Gujarat, son of Karamchand and Putlibai.

1876 Moves to Rajkot with family; attends primary school there.

1882 Marries Kasturbai Makanji.

1885 Death of father.

1888 Goes to England to study law; enrols in the Inner Temple, London.

1890 Joins the London Vegetarian Society.

1891 June: called to the Bar and returns to India.

1893 April: leaves India for South Africa on a one-year contract with the firm of Dada Abdullah & Co., after failing to establish legal practice in India. June: thrown off a train at Pietermaritzburg station, Natal: a critical experience of discrimination.

1894 Helps found the Natal Indian Congress, and enrols as barrister in the High Courts of Natal and Transvaal.

1895 Begins major publicity for Indian rights, including a pamphlet, *The Indian Franchise: An Appeal to Every Briton in South Africa*.

1896 June–November: visits India and brings his family to South Africa.

1897 January: attacked by mob in Durban on his return but declines to prosecute his attackers.

1899 Boer War; organizes Indian Ambulance Corps.

1901 October: returns to India with his family, intending to stay. Meets Indian politicians.

1902 Visits G. K. Gokhale. November: returns with his family to South Africa to fight for Indian rights in the Transvaal.

1903 Sets up legal practice in Johannesburg. Launches *Indian Opinion*.

1904 Reads John Ruskin, *Unto this Last*: establishes Phoenix Settlement near Durban.

1906 June–July: Zulu Rebellion. Does ambulance work. Takes vow of celibacy. September: addresses mass meeting at Empire Theatre in Johannesburg when a large number of Indians agree to resist the proposed Asiatic Registration Bill, the 'Black Act'. October–December: visits London to campaign for Indian rights in South Africa.

1907 Start of passive resistance, called *satyagraha* from 1908.

1908 January and October–December: imprisoned.

1909 February–May: imprisoned.

June–November: visits England. Writes *Hind Swaraj* on return voyage.

1910 Establishes second community at Tolstoy Farm, near Johannesburg.

1911 Agreement with J. C. Smuts leads to suspension of *satyagraha*.

1912 Visit to South Africa by G. K. Gokhale.

1913 Renews *satyagraha*. Women join the struggle, including Kasturbai, who is imprisoned. November–December: Gandhi imprisoned for fourth time.

1914 January: reaches agreement with Smuts and suspends *satyagraha*. July: leaves South Africa finally and sails to London. August: outbreak of First World War. In London he is clearly ill after his work and periods in prison in South Africa. Helps to organize Field Ambulance Training Corps for Indian students in London to help the Empire at war and particularly Indian soldiers wounded in Europe. December: sails for India.

1915 January: arrives in India. Death of Gokhale; Gandhi decides not to join his Servants of India Society. May: founds *ashram* at Ahmedabad. Awarded the Kaiser-i-Hind gold medal for services to Indians in South Africa.

1917 April: begins working on problems of farmers growing indigo in Champaran, Bihar: leads to individual *satyagraha*.

1918 February–March: leads *satyagraha* on behalf of millworkers, Ahmedabad. March–June: leads *satyagraha* in Kaira district, Gujarat, on the issue of land revenue. November: end of First World War.

1919 6–18 April: leads all-India *satyagraha* against the Rowlatt legislation and suspends it after outbreaks of violence: admits to a 'Himalayan miscalculation'. 13 April: massacre at Jallianwalla Bagh, Amritsar, in Punjab province. Becomes editor of *Navajivan* and *Young India*. Becomes involved in the issue of the Khilafat (the post-war future of the Sultan of Turkey). December: advises Congress to respond to the Royal Proclamation and cooperate with the reforms provided for by the 1919 Government of India Act: he regards this as marking his real entry into Congress politics.

1920 Advises non-cooperation with the government on the issues of the Punjab and the Khilafat. September: special session of Congress at Calcutta accepts the programme of non-cooperation, and this is confirmed by the December session at Nagpur. Congressmen in significant numbers boycott elections to the new legislatures in November.

1920–2 Non-cooperation movement (withdrawal of lawyers from courts, students from government schools, return of titles, *swadeshi*, etc.).

1921 August: rebellion in Malabar, south-west India. October: Gandhi vows to spin daily. December: preparations for civil disobedience under strict conditions.

1922 4 February: massacre of policemen in Chauri Chaura, UP (United Provinces). Gandhi fasts in protest against violence and calls off civil disobedience. March: is arrested, pleads guilty to inciting disaffection towards the government, and is jailed until February 1924.

1923 Begins writing *Satyagraha in South Africa*.

1924 January: operated on for appendicitis and released in February. Supports *satyagraha* in Vaikom, Travancore, to allow untouchables to use roads around temples. September: three-week fast for Hindu–Muslim unity.

1925 Acts as Congress President for the year. Founds All-India Spinners' Association.

1926 Spends a year in the Ahmedabad *ashram*.

1927 Extensive tours publicizing *khadi*. Serious ill-health from overwork. Publishes *Autobiography*, initially in a series of newspaper articles.

1928 February–August: *satyagraha* in Bardoli district, Gujarat, on issue of land revenue, led by Vallabhbhai Patel under Gandhi's direction. Publishes *Satyagraha in South Africa*. Moves resolution at Calcutta Congress in favour of independence if dominion status is not granted by the end of 1929 (having in previous years opposed the idea of a resolution supporting complete independence).

1929 Declines Congress presidentship and suggests Jawaharlal Nehru instead. Tours rural India to publicize *khadi*. The Viceroy, Lord Irwin, announces dominion status as goal for India, offering Round Table Conference in London as first step: but negotiations between Gandhi, Congressmen, and Moderates to accept this prove abortive. Gandhi frames main resolution passed at Congress session in Lahore, calling for independence, and also boycott of the legislatures and civil disobedience.

1930 26 January: declaration of independence (prepared by Gandhi) proclaimed. Gandhi plans forthcoming civil disobedience movement which begins with his march (12 March–6 April) from the Sabarmati *ashram* to Dandi on the west coast to make salt illegally, thus launching civil disobedience on 6 April. Imprisoned May 1930–January 1931. Round Table Conference in London leads to hope of a major political advance; the British Government wishes to include Congress in subsequent discussions if possible.

1931 26 January: Gandhi and other Congress leaders released. Gandhi negotiates a settlement with the Viceroy, to end civil disobedience: their 'Pact' signed on 4 March. September–December: Gandhi is in England for the second session of the Round Table Conference. Stays at Kingsley Hall in Bow, in the East End of London. Apart from attending the conference and its committee work, he visits several important places where there are groups of people he wishes to influence, including Lancashire, Oxford, Cambridge, and Eton. He also meets a wide range of Christian leaders.

1932 Civil disobedience resumed; and Gandhi is arrested and imprisoned in Yeravda jail, Poona, from January 1932 to May 1933. September: Gandhi begins a fast to the death, on the issue of separate electorates for untouchables provided for in the British 'Communal Award', after Congress and the minorities fail to reach agreement at the Second Round Table Conference. Gives up his fast after a compromise worked out with untouchable leaders, the so-called Poona Pact.

1933 Founds Harijan Sevak Sangh and new paper, *Harijan*. May: three-week fast: released from prison. Announces disbanding of Ahmedabad *ashram*. August: rearrested but released after less than a month. Begins extensive tour on the Harijan cause; tour lasts from November 1933 to June 1934.

1934 April–May: suggests suspension of civil disobedience and revival of work in the legislatures by those Congressmen who wish to. June: escapes bomb attempt on his life. September: announces decision to retire from politics and engage in rural development, work for Harijans, and new forms of education. Inaugurates All-India Village Industries Association and resigns from Congress.

1935 Government of India Act provides for provincial autonomy and plans for India's future as a dominion, bringing together British India and the Princely states. (The latter part of the plan is never achieved because of the outbreak of war in 1939; the first part comes into force after elections to the new legislatures in 1937.)

1936 April: settles at Sevagram, near Wardha, Central Provinces, making his *ashram* there his home and headquarters.

1937 October: presides over Educational Conference in October at Wardha and sets out a scheme of Basic Education. Congress becomes government in seven provinces in British India following elections.

1939 Early March: fasts in protest at ruler of Rajkot's refusal to reform his administration. September: outbreak of Second World War. October: Congress withdraws from cooperation in provincial government, reflecting Gandhi's wishes. Gandhi becomes central again in Congress politics.

1940 March: Congress at Ramgarh demands independence and a Constituent Assembly to frame a new constitution; announces that it plans to embark again on civil disobedience. Muslim League at Lahore demands 'Pakistan' for Muslims at independence. October: Gandhi launches individual *satyagraha* by handpicked volunteers to protest against cooperation in the war effort.

1941 December: the Japanese attack Pearl Harbor and begin their drive through Burma. America enters the war. Gandhi writes *Constructive Programme: Its Meaning and Place*.

1942 February: fall of Singapore. March–April: mission of Sir Stafford Cripps to India on behalf of British Government, offering an elected body after war to frame a new constitution for India, and, during the war, Indian participation in government. This proposal envisages India as a dominion after war but with the implication that secession from the Empire–Commonwealth would also be possible, and also assumes that no part of India could be forced to join a dominion, thus opening path to some form of partition. Congress and League reject the Cripps offer. August: Congress launches 'Quit India' movement of civil disobedience. It is declared an unlawful organization, leaders are imprisoned, and violence firmly controlled. Gandhi is imprisoned from August 1942 to May 1944. During this prison term Mahadev Desai dies (1942) as does Kasturbai (1944).

1944 May: released from prison because of ill-health. September: abortive talks with Jinnah on future of Indian Muslims.

1945 May: surrender of Germany and end of war in Europe. June–July: Gandhi attends conference at Simla as Viceroy Wavell attempts to restart the political process by reconstituting his Executive Council from among Indian politicians. Conference fails. August: surrender of Japan and end of war in Asia.

1946 March–June: Cabinet Mission, sent by the new Labour government, visits India, in an attempt to achieve political settlement. Gandhi meets members of the mission. Congress and League both reject Cabinet Mission Plan. Severe communal violence in Bengal and Bihar; Gandhi tours area on foot for four months from November.

1947 Communal situation deteriorates as there is no political agreement and British authority wanes. February: Prime Minister Attlee announces that the British will leave India by June 1948 and sends Mountbatten to India as Viceroy to replace Wavell. June: Mountbatten announces plan of partition of India at independence and the British intention to withdraw in August 1947. Gandhi deeply distressed at plan for partition but does not block it. His political influence is clearly waning. 15 August: the subcontinent attains independence and is partitioned into India and Pakistan. Violence breaks out, particularly in the Punjab, and mass migrations of people occur as they attempt to move to the side of the border where they think they will be safe, Muslims to Pakistan, and Hindus and Sikhs to India. Congress becomes the party of government in India and Jawaharlal Nehru becomes India's first Prime Minister. September: Gandhi fasts in Calcutta for communal peace.

1948 13–18 January: Gandhi fasts in Delhi for communal unity. Writes document advising Congress to disband as a political organization and devote itself to social service. 30 January: Gandhi is assassinated by a Hindu man who confronts him as he is walking to a prayer meeting in grounds of Birla House, New Delhi.

ABBREVIATIONS

CW	Archives of the Office of the Collected Works of Mahatma Gandhi, New Delhi
CWMG	*The Collected Works of Mahatma Gandhi*
EWMG	*The Essential Writings of Mahatma Gandhi*
G.	originally written or spoken in Gujarati
GN	Gandhi Memorial Museum and Library, New Delhi
H.	originally written or spoken in Hindi
MPWMG	*The Moral and Political Writings of Mahatma Gandhi*
RU	*The Removal of Untouchability*
SN	Sabarmati Sangrahalaya, Ahmedabad

Further details of published works can be found in the Select Bibliography. The source of each document in the present selection is given at the end of the item, together with its original title, where there is one. An asterisk in the text signals an explanatory note at the back of the book.

I · GANDHI, HIS MISSION, AND THE INFLUENCES ON HIM

a. Gandhi reflects on himself

1. The nature of my life

It is not my purpose to attempt a real autobiography. I simply want to tell the story of my numerous experiments with truth, and as my life consists of nothing but those experiments, it is true that the story will take the shape of an autobiography. But I shall not mind, if every page of it speaks only of my experiments. I believe, or at any rate flatter myself with the belief, that a connected account of all these experiments will not be without benefit to the reader. My experiments in the political field are now known, not only in India, but to a certain extent to the 'civilized' world. For me, they have not much value; and the title of *Mahatma* that they have won for me has, therefore, even less. Often the title has deeply pained me; and there is not a moment I can recall when it may be said to have tickled me. But I should certainly like to narrate my experiments in the spiritual field which are known only to myself, and from which I have derived such power as I possess for working in the political field. If the experiments are really spiritual, then there can be no room for self-praise. They can only add to my humility. The more I reflect and look back on the past, the more vividly do I feel my limitations.

What I want to achieve—what I have been striving and pining to achieve these thirty years—is self-realization, to see God face to face, to attain *Moksha*.* I live and move and have my being in pursuit of this goal. All that I do by way of speaking and writing, and all my ventures in the political field, are directed to this same end. But as I have all along believed that what is possible for one is possible for all, my experiments have not been conducted in the closet, but in the open; and I do not think that this fact detracts from their spiritual value. There are some things which are known only to oneself and one's Maker. These are clearly incommunicable. The experiments I am about to relate are not such. But they are spiritual, or rather moral; for the essence of religion is morality.

Only those matters of religion that can be comprehended as much by children as by older people, will be included in this story. If I can narrate them in a dispassionate and humble spirit, many other experimenters will find in them provision for their onward march. Far be it from me to claim any degree of perfection for these experiments. I claim for them nothing more than does a scientist who, though he conducts his experiments with the utmost accuracy, forethought and minuteness, never claims any finality about his conclusions, but keeps an open mind regarding them. I have gone through deep self-introspection, searched myself through and through, and examined and analysed every psychological situation. Yet I am far from claiming any finality or infallibility about my conclusions. One claim I do indeed make and it is this. For me they appear to be absolutely correct, and seem for the time being to be final. For if they were not, I should base no action on them. But at every step I have carried out the process of acceptance or rejection and acted accordingly. And so long as my acts satisfy my reason and my heart, I must firmly adhere to my original conclusions.

If I had only to discuss academic principles, I should clearly not attempt an autobiography. But my purpose being to give an account of various practical applications of these principles, I have given the chapters I propose to write the title of *The Story of My Experiments with Truth*. These will of course include experiments with non-violence, celibacy and other principles of conduct believed to be distinct from truth. But for me, truth is the sovereign principle, which includes numerous other principles. This truth is not only truthfulness in word, but truthfulness in thought also, and not only the relative truth of our conception, but the Absolute Truth, the Eternal Principle, that is God. There are innumerable definitions of God, because His manifestations are innumerable. They overwhelm me with wonder and awe and for a moment stun me. But I worship God as Truth only. I have not yet found Him, but I am seeking after Him. I am prepared to sacrifice the things dearest to me in pursuit of this quest. Even if the sacrifice demanded be my very life, I hope I may be prepared to give it. But as long as I have not realized this Absolute Truth, so long must I hold by the relative truth as I have conceived it. That relative truth must, meanwhile, be my beacon, my shield and buckler. Though this path is strait and narrow and sharp as the razor's edge, for me it has been the quickest and easiest. Even my Himalayan blunders have seemed trifling to me because I have kept strictly to this path. For the path has saved me from coming to grief, and I have gone forward according to my light. Often in my progress I have had faint glimpses of the Absolute Truth, God, and daily the conviction is growing upon me that He alone is real and all else is unreal. Let those, who wish, realize how the conviction has grown upon me; let them share my experiments and share also my conviction if they can. The further conviction has been growing upon me that whatever is possible for me is possible even for a child, and I have sound reasons for saying so. The instruments for the quest of truth are as simple as they are difficult. They may appear quite impossible to an arrogant person, and quite impossible to an innocent child. The seeker after truth should be humbler than the dust. The world crushes the dust under its feet, but the seeker after truth should so humble himself that even the dust could crush him. Only then, and not till then, will he have a glimpse of truth. . . .

If anything that I write in these pages should strike the reader as being touched with pride, then he must take it that there is something wrong with my quest, and that my glimpses are no more than a mirage. Let hundreds like me perish, but let truth prevail. Let us not reduce the standards of truth even by a hair's breadth for judging erring mortals like myself.

I hope and pray that no one will regard the advice interspersed in the following chapters as authoritative. The experiments narrated should be regarded as illustrations, in the light of which everyone may carry on his own experiments according to his own inclination and capacity. I trust that to this limited extent the illustrations will be really helpful; because I am not going either to conceal or understate any ugly things that must be told. I hope to acquaint the reader fully with all my faults and errors. My purpose is to describe experiments in the science of *Satyagraha*, not to say how good I am. . . . For it is an unbroken torture to me that I am still so far from Him, who, as I fully know, governs every breath of my life, and whose offspring I am. I know that it is the evil passions within that keep me so far from Him, and yet I cannot get away from them.

Gandhi, *An Autobiography*, Introduction

2. The ochre robe?

Some friends suggested to me that I should become a *sannyasi.** However, I have not become one. My conscience did not approve of such a step then and does not do so today. I am sure you will not believe that the reason for my not doing so is love of enjoyments. I am struggling to the best of my ability to conquer the desire for them. But in the very process of struggling, I see that I am not worthy of the ochre robe. I cannot say I always practise truth, non-violence and *brahmacharya** in action, speech and thought. Whether I want or no, I feel attachments and aversions, feel disturbed by desire; I try to control them with an effort of mind and succeed in repressing their physical manifestation. If I could practise them to perfection, I would be in possession today of all the supernatural powers they speak of; humble myself, the world would be at my feet and no one would ever want to laugh me out or treat me with contempt.

Speech at meeting, Vadtal (G.). *Navajivan*, 23 Jan. 1921

3. Life in South Africa

If I found myself entirely absorbed in the service of the community, the reason behind it was my desire for self-realization. I had made the religion of service my own, as I felt that God could be realized only through service. And service for me was the service of India, because it came to me without my seeking, because I had an aptitude for it. I had gone to South Africa for travel, for finding an escape from Kathiawad intrigues and for gaining my own livelihood. But as I have said, I found myself in search of God and striving for self-realization.

Gandhi, *An Autobiography*, part II, chap. XXII

4. Striving after *moksha*

1 November 1921

The fact is that I am not more than an aspirant after *moksha*. But I am not yet fit for *moksha* in this life. My *tapascharya** is not intense enough. I can control my passions no doubt, but I have not yet become completely free of them. I can control the palate, but the tongue has not yet ceased relishing good food.

He who can restrain the senses is a man of self-control; but the man whose senses have become, through constant practice, incapable of enjoying their objects has transcended self-control, has in fact attained *moksha*. I would not be tempted to give up my striving after *moksha* even for the sake of *swaraj** . . .

Letter to Mathurdas Trikumji (G.). *Bapuni Prasadi*, pp. 38–9. *EWMG*, pp. 28–9

5. Political vocation

I do not consider myself worthy to be mentioned in the same breath with the race of prophets. I am a humble seeker after truth. I am impatient to realize myself, to attain *moksha* in this very existence. My national service is part of my training for freeing my soul from the bondage of flesh. Thus considered, my service may be regarded as purely selfish. . . . For me the road to salvation lies through incessant toil in the service of my country and therethrough [*sic*] of humanity. I want to identify myself with everything that lives. In the language of the *Gita** I want to live at peace with both friend and foe. Though, therefore, a Mussalman or a Christian or a Hindu may despise me and hate me, I want to love him and serve him even as I would love my wife or son though they hate me. So my patriotism is for me a stage in my journey to the land of eternal freedom and peace. Thus it will be seen that for me there are no politics devoid of religion. They subserve religion. Politics bereft of religion are a death-trap because they kill the soul.

'My Mission'. *Young India*, 3 Apr. 1924

6. One step enough for me

21 December 1925

This physical frame which God has given us is a prison, but it is also the door leading to deliverance and, if we wish that it should serve only that purpose, we should understand its limitations. We may well desire to clutch the stars in the heavens, but we should note that it is beyond our power to do so; for our soul is imprisoned in a cage, its wings, therefore, have been clipped and it cannot fly as high as it would. It can secure a great many occult powers, but it will fail in its aim of winning deliverance if it goes after such powers. Hence, the kind of abstract questions which were put to me the other day should be avoided—in the conviction that in the course of time the soul will become strong enough and know the answers to them.

Instead of discussing such abstract questions, we should follow the advice of the poet: 'Let us spend today to some purpose, for who knows what tomorrow will bring?' This line may seem to come from the pen of Charvak, who also says: 'Live in ease while you live, drink ghee even if you have to borrow money for it, for the body will never return to life after it is cremated.' But the line is not by Charvak. Its author was a devotee and, when he advised us to spend today profitably, he meant that we should discharge the duty which lies before us today. We do not know if we shall be alive tomorrow, though a little later he says that we shall be born again. This duty is what was explained by Vinoba* the other day, 'ending the misery of all creatures that suffer', destroying the chain of ever-recurring birth and death. The only means for this is *bhakti*.* An Englishman named Newman,* a great devotee, wrote in a poem of his 'One step enough for me.'

This half line is the quintessence of all philosophy. That one step means patient, unswerving *bhakti*. If a sick person gets up and tries to walk down a staircase, he would feel giddy and fall. If we do not understand our limitations and try to get knowledge which is beyond us, we would not only not be able to digest it but would be sick with surfeit.

We should, therefore, cure ourselves of the disease of asking abstract questions, should attend to the immediate duty before us today and leave these questions for some other day. The couplet from a *bhajan** which was sung here today teaches us the very same thing, that instead of talking about *mukti** all the time we should spend our time in *bhakti*. Without *bhakti* there can be no deliverance. Only he, therefore, wins deliverance who is devoted to duty and fills his heart with love of God—he alone wins deliverance who never thinks about it.

Bhakti, moreover, does not imply ineptitude in practical affairs. That which produces such ineptitude cannot be called *bhakti*. It may, of course, be that, looking at the way we conduct our affairs, people will think of us as simpletons. A true devotee, though fully attentive to practical affairs, brings the spirit of *bhakti* into them. His conduct will always be in harmony with *dharma*.*

Speech at Wardha *ashram* (G.). *Navajivan*, 27 Dec. 1925

7. Teaching my message in India first

It is not without deep sorrow that I am now able to announce that the much-talked-of visit of mine to Europe is not to come off this year at any rate. To those in Austria, Holland, England, Scotland, Denmark, Sweden, Germany and Russia who had sent me kind invitations I can only say that their disappointment will be no greater than mine.

Somehow or other I dread a visit to Europe and America. Not that I distrust the peoples of these great Continents any more than I distrust my own, but I distrust myself. I have no desire to go to the West in search of health or for sightseeing. I have no desire to deliver public speeches. I detest being lionized. I wonder if I shall ever again have the health to stand the awful strain of public speaking and public demonstrations. If God ever sent me to the West, I should go there to penetrate the hearts of the masses, to have quiet talks with the youth of the West and have the privilege of meeting kindred spirits—lovers of peace at any price save that of Truth.

But I feel that I have as yet no message to deliver personally to the West. I believe my message to be universal but as yet I feel that I can best deliver it through my work in my own country. If I can show visible success in India, the delivery of the message becomes complete. If I came to the conclusion that India had no use for my message, I should not care to go elsewhere in search of listeners even though I still retained faith in it. If, therefore, I ventured out of India, I should do so because I have faith, though I cannot demonstrate it to the satisfaction of all, that the message is being surely received by India be it ever so slowly.

'To European friends'. *Young India*, 26 Apr. 1928

8. The call to lead

1 November 1928

I could still lead India. I shall only lead India when the nation comes to me to be led, when there is a national call.

I shall not go before then. I shall not go unless I am certain of my power over the masses. I could not lead India again until I realized that they are numerous enough to pursue a policy of non-violence, nor until I could control them.* But I see nothing on the horizon at the moment. That would not make me at all anxious to take that position. Perhaps it will not be in my lifetime. It may be in the time of my successor.

I cannot name one at this moment. There must be one who could lead India today but I cannot name him.* Truly I should be ashamed to remain inactive but it may be necessary in my lifetime. It may be there will come a man, but not now.

Interview with *Civil and Military Gazette. Hindustan Times*, 3 Nov. 1928. *EWMG*, p. 39

9. My life is my message

On or before 30 May 1945

QUESTION. Gandhiji, is there any special message you would care to send to the Negro people of America?

ANSWER. My life is its own message. If it is not, then nothing I can now write will fulfil the purpose.

Interview with Denton J. Brooks.* *The Hindu*, 15 June 1945. *EWMG*, p. 40

10. An activist, not an academic

A friend suggests that I should resume writing my autobiography from the point where I left off and, further, that I should write a treatise on the science of *ahimsa*.*

I never really wrote an autobiography. What I did write was a series of articles narrating my experiments with truth which were later published in book form.* More than twenty years have elapsed since then. What I have done or pondered during this interval has not been recorded in chronological order. I would love to do so but have I the leisure? I have resumed the publication of *Harijan** in the present trying times as a matter of duty. It is with difficulty that I can cope with this work. How can I find time to bring the remainder of my experiments with truth up to date? But if it is God's will that I should write them, He will surely make my way clear.

To write a treatise on the science of *ahimsa* is beyond my powers. I am not built for academic writings. Action is my domain, and what I understand, according to my lights, to be my duty, and what comes my way, I do. All my action is actuated by the spirit of service.

'Two Requests' (G.). *Harijan*, 3 Mar. 1946

11. The value of critics

20 October 1947

Perhaps you don't know that I greatly value people who abuse me. Thereby their anger is spent and their hearts are cleansed. I like such critics a thousand times better than those who worship me, applaud me, but at the same time commit murders and disregard what I say. For those who abuse me are candid and if I can convince them they work wonders. In my life I have often had such experience.

Note to Manu Gandhi* (G.). *Dilhiman Gandhiji*, vol. i, pp. 124–5. *EWMG*, p. 43

12. Saint or politician?

The critic* regrets to see in me a politician, whereas he expected me to be a saint. Now I think that the word 'saint' should be ruled out of present life. It is too sacred a word to be lightly applied to anybody, much less to one like myself who claims only to be a humble searcher after truth, knows his limitations, makes mistakes, never hesitates to admit them when he makes them, and frankly confesses that he, like a scientist, is making experiments about some of 'the eternal verities' of life, but cannot even claim to be a scientist because he can show no tangible proof of scientific accuracy in his methods or such tangible

results of his experiments as modern science demands. But though
by disclaiming sainthood I disappoint the critic's expectations, I would
have him to give up his regrets by answering him that the politician
in me has never dominated a single decision of mine, and if I seem
to take part in politics, it is only because politics encircle us today
like the coil of a snake from which one cannot get out, no matter
how much one tries. I wish therefore to wrestle with the snake, as
I have been doing, with more or less success, consciously since 1894,
unconsciously, as I have now discovered, ever since reaching the
years of discretion.

Quite selfishly, as I wish to live in peace in the midst of a bellow-
ing storm howling round me, I have been experimenting with myself
and my friends by introducing religion into politics. Let me explain
what I mean by religion. It is not the Hindu religion, which I certainly prize above all other religions, but the religion which tran-
scends Hinduism, which changes one's very nature, which binds
one indissolubly to the truth within and which ever purifies. It is
the permanent element in human nature which counts no cost too
great in order to find full expression and which leaves the soul
utterly restless until it has found itself, known its Maker and appre-
ciated the true correspondence between the Maker and itself.

'Neither a Saint nor a Politician'. *Young India*, 12 May 1920

13. Identification with labour

8 August 1925

As you know I am a labourer myself, I pride myself on calling myself
a scavenger, weaver, spinner, farmer and what not, and I do not feel
ashamed that some of these things I know but indifferently. It is a
pleasure to me to identify myself with the labouring classes, because
without labour we can do nothing. There is a great Latin saying of
which the meaning is 'to labour is to pray', and one of the finest writers of Europe has said that a man is not entitled to eat unless he
labours, and by labour he does not mean labour with the intellect, but
labour with the hands. The same thought runs throughout Hindu
religion. 'He who eats without labour eats sin, is verily a thief.' This
is the literal meaning of a verse in *Bhagavad Gita*. I therefore pride

myself on the fact that I can identify myself with labour throughout the world.

It was my ambition to see one of the greatest—if not the greatest—Indian enterprises in India, and study the conditions of work there.* But none of my activities is one-sided, and as my religion begins and ends with truth and non-violence, my identification with labour does not conflict with my friendship with capital. And believe me, throughout my public service of 35 years, though I have been obliged to range myself seemingly against capital, capitalists have in the end regarded me as their true friend. And in all humility I may say that I have come here also as a friend of the capitalists—a friend of the Tatas. And here it would be ungrateful on my part if I do not give you a little anecdote about how my connection with the Tatas began.

In South Africa, when I was struggling along with the Indians there in the attempt to retain our self-respect and to vindicate our status, it was the late Sir Ratan Tata who first came forward with assistance. He wrote me a great letter and sent a princely donation—a cheque for Rs 25,000 and a promise in the letter to send more, if necessary. Ever since I have a vivid recollection of my relations with the Tatas and you can well imagine how pleasurable it has been for me to be with you, and you will believe me when I say that, when I part company with you tomorrow, I shall do so with a heavy heart, because I shall have to go away without having seen so many things, for it would be presumption on my part to say at the end of two days that I had really studied things here. I know well enough the magnitude of the task before one who wants to study this great enterprise.

I wish to this great Indian firm all the prosperity that it deserves and to this great enterprise every success. And may I hope that the relations between this great house and labourers who work here under their care will be of the friendliest character? At Ahmedabad* I have had much to do with the capitalists and workmen, and I have always said that my ideal is that capital and labour should supplement and help each other. They should be a great family living in unity and harmony, capital not only looking to the material welfare of the labourers but their moral welfare also—capitalists being trustees for the welfare of the labouring classes under them.

I am told that though so many Europeans and Indians live here, their relations are of a happy character. I hope the information is literally true. It is the privilege of both of you to be associated in this great enterprise and it is possible for you to give India an object-lesson in amity and goodwill. You will, I hope, have best relations with one another not only under the roofs of the huge workshops you work in, but you will also carry your amity outside your workshops and both of you will realize that you have come to live and work here as brothers and sisters, never regarding another as inferior, or oneself as inferior. And if you succeed in doing that you will have a miniature *swaraj*.

I have said that I am a non-co-operator, I call myself a civil resister—and both words have come to possess a bad odour in the English language like so many other English words—but I non-co-operate in order that I may be able to co-operate. I cannot satisfy myself with false co-operation—anything inferior to 24 carats gold. My non-co-operation does not prevent me from being friendly even to Sir Michael O'Dwyer and General Dyer.* It harms no one, it is non-co-operation with evil, with an evil system and not with the evil-doer.

My religion teaches me to love even an evil-doer, and my non-co-operation is but part of that religion. I am saying these things not to soothe the ears of any one—I have in my life never been guilty of saying things I did not mean—my nature is to go straight to the heart, and if often I fail in doing so for the time being, I know that truth will ultimately make itself heard and felt, as it has often done in my experience. The wish, therefore, that the relations between you should be of the friendliest character is a desire from the bottom of my heart. And it is my deep prayer that you may help in delivering India from evil and bondage and help her to give the message of peace to the outside world. For this meeting of Indians and Europeans in India must have or can be made to have a special meaning, and what can be better than that we two may live together so as to spread peace and goodwill on earth? May God grant that, in serving the Tatas, you will also serve India and will always realize that you are here for a much higher mission than merely working for an industrial enterprise.

Speech at Indian Association, Jamshedpur. *Amrita Bazar Patrika*,
14 Aug. 1925. *Young India*, 20 Aug. 1925

14. Service of India includes the service of humanity

It is a privilege for me to enjoy the friendship of so many unknown American and European friends. It pleases me to note that the circle is ever widening, perhaps more especially in America. I had the pleasure of receiving a warm invitation about a year ago to visit that continent. The same invitation has now been repeated with redoubled strength and with the offer to pay all expenses. I was unable then as I am now, to respond to the kind invitation. To accept it is an easy enough task, but I must resist the temptation, for I feel that I can make no effective appeal to the people of that great continent unless I make my position good with the intellectuals of India.

I have not a shadow of doubt about the truth of my fundamental position. But I know that I am unable to carry with me the bulk of educated India. I can therefore gain no effective help for my country from the Americans and Europeans so long as I remain isolated from educated India. I do want to think in terms of the whole world. My patriotism includes the good of mankind in general. Therefore, my service of India includes the service of humanity. But I feel that I should be going out of my orbit if I left it for help from the West. I must be satisfied for the time being with such help as I can get from the West, speaking to it from my smaller Indian platform. If I go to America or to Europe, I must go in my strength, not in my weakness, which I feel today—the weakness I mean, of my country. For the whole scheme for the liberation of India is based upon the development of internal strength. It is a plan of self-purification. The peoples of the West, therefore, can best help the Indian movement by setting apart specialists to study the inwardness of it.

Let the specialists come to India with an open mind and in a spirit of humility as befits a searcher after Truth. Then, perhaps, they will see the reality instead of a glorified edition that, in spite of all my desire to be absolutely truthful, I am likely to present if I went to America. I believe in thought-power more than in the power of the word, whether written or spoken. And if the movement that I seek to represent has vitality in it and has divine blessing upon it, it will permeate the whole world without my physical presence in its different parts. Anyway, at the present moment I see no light before me. I must patiently plod in India until I see my way clear for going outside the Indian border.

After pressing the invitation, the American friend puts a number of questions for my consideration. I welcome them and gladly take the opportunity of answering them through these columns. He says:

Whether you decide, now or later, to come here or not to come, I trust you will find the following questions worth considering. They have developed insistently in my mind for a long time.

His first question is:

Has the time arrived—or is it coming—when your best way to help India will be by moving the whole world—and especially England and America— to a new consciousness?

I have partly answered the question already. In my opinion the time has not yet arrived—it may come any day—for me to go out of India to move the whole world to a new consciousness. The process, how- ever, is even now indirectly and unconsciously going on though slowly.

Are not the present-day interests of all mankind, everywhere, so inextric- ably interwoven that no single country, like India, can be moved far out of its present relationships to the others?

I do believe with the writer that no single country can remain in isolation for any length of time. The present plan for securing *swaraj* is not to attain a position of isolation but one of full self-realization and self-expression for the benefit of all. The present position of bondage and helplessness hurts not only India, not only England, but the whole world.

Is not your message and method essentially a world gospel—which will find its power in responsive souls, here and there, in many countries, who will thereby, gradually, remake the world?

If I can say so without arrogance and with due humility, my mes- sage and methods are indeed in their essentials for the whole world and it gives me keen satisfaction to know that it has already received a wonderful response in the hearts of a large and daily-growing number of men and women of the West.

If you demonstrate your message in the language only of the East and in terms only of Indian emergencies, is there not grave danger that inessen- tials will be confused with fundamentals—that some features which cor- respond only to extreme situations in India will be wrongly understood to be vital in the universal sense?

I am alive to the danger pointed out by the writer, but it seems to be inevitable. I am in the position of a scientist who is in the midst of a very incomplete experiment and who, therefore is unable to forecast large results and larger corollaries in a language capable of being understood. In the experimental stage, therefore, I must run the risk of the experiment being misunderstood as it has been, and probably still is, in many places.

Ought you not to come to America (which in spite of all her faults is perhaps, potentially, the most spiritual of all living peoples) and tell the world what your message means in terms of Western, as well as Eastern, civilization?

People in general will understand my message through its results. The shortest way, therefore, perhaps of making it effectively heard is to let it speak for itself, at any rate for the time being.

For example, should the Western followers of your inspiration preach and practise the spinning-wheel?*

It is certainly not necessary for the Western people to preach and practise the spinning-wheel unless they will do so out of sympathy or for discipline or with a view to applying their matchless inventive faculty to making the spinning-wheel a better instrument while retaining its essential characteristic as a cottage industry. But the message of the spinning-wheel is much wider than its circumference. Its message is one of simplicity, service of mankind, living so as not to hurt others, creating an indissoluble bond between the rich and the poor, capital and labour, the prince and the peasant. That larger message is naturally for all.

Is your condemnation* of railroads, doctors, hospitals and other features of modern civilization essential and unalterable? Should we not, first, try to develop a spirit great enough to spiritualize the machinery and the organized, scientific and productive powers of modern life?

My condemnation of railroads, etc., whilst true where it stands, has little or no bearing on the present movement which disregards none of the institutions mentioned by the writer. In the present movement, I am neither attacking railroads nor hospitals; but in an ideal State they seem to me to have little or no place. The present movement is just the attempt the writer desires. Yet it is not an attempt to spiritualize the machinery—because that seems to me an impossible task—but to introduce, if it is at all possible, a human or the humane spirit among the men behind the machinery. Organization of machinery for the purpose of concentrating wealth and power in the hands of a few and for the exploitation of many I hold to be altogether wrong. Much of the organization of machinery of the present age is of that type.

The movement of the spinning-wheel is an organized attempt to displace machinery from that state of exclusiveness and exploitation and to place it in its proper state. Under my scheme, therefore, men in charge of machinery will think not of themselves or even of the nation to which they belong but of the whole human race. Thus Lancashire men* will cease to use their machinery for exploiting India and other countries but, on the contrary, they will devise means of enabling India to convert in her own villages her cotton into cloth. Nor will Americans under my scheme seek to enrich themselves by exploiting the other races of the earth through their inventive skill.

Is it not possible, in conditions so favourable as America's, to clarify and advance the evolution of the best human consciousness into such purpose and power, courage and beneficence, as shall liberate the souls of India's millions—and of all men everywhere?

It is undoubtedly possible. Indeed, it is my hope that America will seek the evolution of the best human consciousness; but that time is perhaps not yet. Probably it will not be before India has found her own soul. Nothing will please me more than to find America and Europe making the difficult path of India as easy as it is possible for them to do. They can do so by withdrawing the temptations in India's way and by encouraging her in her attempt to revive her ancient industries in her own villages.

Why is it that people like myself, in every country, are grateful to you and eager to follow you? Is it not for two reasons chiefly: first; Because the next [*sic*] and basic need throughout the world is for a new spiritual consciousness—a realization, in the thought and feeling of average people, of the equal divinity of all human beings and the unity, brotherhood, of all; second, because you, more than any other widely known man, have this consciousness—together with the power to arouse it in others?

I can only hope that the writer's estimate is true.

It is a world need—is it not?—to which you have the best answer that God has vouchsafed to man? How can your mission be fulfilled in India alone? If my arm or leg could be vitalized to an extent far beyond the balance of my body, would that make for my general health—or even for the permanent best good of the one favoured member?

I am fully aware that my mission cannot be fulfilled in India alone, but I hope I am humble enough to recognize my limitations and to see that I must keep for the time being, to my restricted Indian platform till I know the result of the experiment in India itself. As I have already replied, I would like to see India free and strong so that she may offer herself as a willing and pure sacrifice for the betterment of the world. The individual, being pure, sacrifices himself for the family, the latter for the village, the village for the district, the district for the province, the province for the nation, the nation for all.

May I even submit—with deep reverence for your message—that possibly your own vision and inspiration would benefit by adjustment to the world instead of only, or chiefly, to India?

I recognize the considerable force of the foregoing statement. It is not at all impossible that a visit to the West may give me not a wider outlook—for I have endeavoured to show that it is the widest possible but it may enable me to discover new methods of realizing the outlook. If such is my need, God will open the way for me.

Is the political form of government, in India or anywhere, so important as the average individual's soul-force—his courageous expression of the best inspiration he can derive from the divine spirit within and all about him?

The average individual's soul-force is any day the most important thing. The political form is but a concrete expression of that soul-force. I do not conceive the average individual's soul-force as distinguished and existing apart from the political form of government. Hence I believe that after all a people has the government which it deserves. In other words self-government can only come through self-effort.

Is not the basic need, everywhere, for the clarification and development of this soul-force in individuals—beginning, possibly, with a few people and spreading like a divine contagion to the many?

It is, indeed.

You teach, rightly, that the faithful development of such soul-force in India will assure India's freedom. Will it not everywhere shape all political, economic and international institutions including the issues of Peace or War? Can those forms of human civilization be made radically superior in India to the rest of the world—now, when all mankind are neighbours?

I have already answered this question in the preceding paragraphs. I have claimed in these pages before now that India's freedom must revolutionize the world's outlook upon Peace and War. Her impotence affects the whole of mankind.

You know, better than I or anyone, how all these questions should be answered. I chiefly seek to express my eager faith in your gospel, my hungry desire for your leadership in solving the urgent problems of America and of all mankind. Therefore, will you graciously remember that, if (or when) the time may come that India's progress in the directions you have so inspiringly outlined appears to pause—waiting for the Western world to come up alongside—then we of the West stand urging you to give us a few months of your time and your personal presence. My own feeling is that if you will call us and instruct us, we (your uncounted followers scattered obscurely over the wide earth) will join our lives to yours in the discovery and realization of a new and noble, worldwide Commonwealth of the Spirit in which man's age-old dreams of brotherhood, democracy, peace and soul progress shall characterize the daily life of average people—in India, England, America and everywhere.

I wish I had confidence in my leadership on the world platform. I have no false modesty about me. If I felt the call within, I would not wait a single second but straightway respond to an invitation so cordial as this. But with my limitations of which I am painfully conscious, I feel somehow that my experiment must be restricted to a fragment. What may be true of the fragment is likely to be true of the whole. It is true indeed that India's progress in the direction I desire seems to have come to a pause but I think that it only seems so. The little seed that was sown in 1920 has not perished. It is, I think, taking deep root. Presently it will come out as a stately tree. But if I am labouring under a delusion, I fear that no artificial stimulus that my visit to America may temporarily bring can revive it. I am pining for the assistance of the whole world. I see it coming. The urgent invitation is one of the many signs. But I know that we shall have to deserve it before it comes upon us like a mighty flood, a flood that cleanses and invigorates.

'To American Friends'. *Young India*, 17 Sept. 1925

15. Brotherhood of man

9 March 1929

I thank you for this warmth of reception and the kindly sentiments expressed in your address. I am not able just now to appropriate, much less to assimilate, all the compliments that you have paid me. But I could certainly claim two things of which you have made kind mention. The first thing is that my mission is not merely brotherhood of Indian humanity. My mission is not merely freedom of India, though today it undoubtedly engrosses practically the whole of my life and the whole of my time. But through realization of freedom of India I hope to realize and carry on the mission of brotherhood of man. My patriotism is not an exclusive thing. It is all-embracing and I should reject that patriotism which sought to mount upon the distress or the exploitation of other nationalities. The conception of my patriotism is nothing if it is not always in every case, without exception, consistent with the broadest good of humanity at large. Not only that but my religion and my patriotism derived from my religion embrace all life.

I want to realize brotherhood or identity not merely with the beings called human, but I want to realize identity with all life, even with such beings as crawl on earth. I want, if I don't give you a shock, to realize identity with even the crawling things upon earth, because we claim common descent from the same God, and that being so, all life in whatever form it appears must be essentially one. I can therefore safely claim all the credit that you may choose to give me in describing my mission of brotherhood of man. As a necessary corollary you may naturally mention, as you have kindly mentioned, untouchability. I have said times without number that untouchability is a serious blot on Hinduism and, I think, in the long run, in the race for life in which all the religions of the world are today engaged, either Hinduism has got to perish or untouchability has to be rooted out completely, so that the fundamental principle of Advaita Hinduism may be realized in practical life.

Speech at Public Meeting, Rangoon. *Amrita Bazar Patrika*, 10 Mar. 1929. *Young India*, 4 Apr. 1929

16. Universal message of non-violence

11 June 1937

I thank you for your letter of the 20th May last. I have no message to give except this that there is no deliverance for any people on this earth or for all the people of this earth except through truth and non-violence in every walk of life without any exceptions. And this is based on an unbroken experience extending practically over half a century.

Letter to Daniel Oliver in Hammana, Lebanon. *Pyarelal Papers*. *EWMG*, p. 60

17. Propounder of no ism

7 June 1946

I do not know myself who is a Gandhian. Gandhism is a meaningless word for me. An ism follows the propounder of a system. I am not one, hence I cannot be the cause for any ism. If an ism is built up it will not endure, and if it does it will not be Gandhism. This deserves to be properly understood.

Letter to Rameshwari Nehru (H.). CW 3110. *EWMG*, p. 62

b. Gandhi acknowledges the major influences on him

18. Mother's influence

The outstanding impression my mother has left on my memory is that of saintliness. She was deeply religious. She would not think of taking her meals without her daily prayers, Going to *Haveli*— the Vaishnava temple—was one of her daily duties. As far as my memory can go back, I do not remember her having ever missed the *Chaturmas*.* She would take the hardest vows and keep them without flinching.

Gandhi, *An Autobiography*, part I, chap. I

19. Introduction to devotion to the God Ram

Being born in the Vaishnava faith, I had often to go to the *Haveli*. But it never appealed to me. I did not like its glitter and pomp. Also I heard rumours of immorality practised there, and lost all interest in it. Hence I could gain nothing from the *Haveli*.

But what I failed to get there I obtained from my nurse, an old servant of the family, whose affection of me I still recall. I have said before that there was in me a fear of ghosts and spirits. Rambha, for that was her name, suggested, as a remedy for this fear, the repetition of *Ramanama*.* I had more faith in her than in her remedy, and so at a tender age I began repeating *Ramanama* to cure my fear of ghosts and spirits. This was of course short-lived, but the good seed sown in childhood was not sown in vain. I think it is due to the seed sown by that good woman Rambha that today *Ramanama* is an infallible remedy for me. . . .

What, however, left a deep impression on me was the reading of the *Ramayana** before my father. During part of his [final] illness my father was in Porbandar. There every evening he used to listen to the *Ramayana*. The reader was a great devotee of Rama . . . He had a melodious voice. He would sing the *Dohas* (couplets) and *Chopais* (quatrains), and explain them, losing himself in the discourse and carrying his listeners along with him. I must have been thirteen at that time, but I quite remember being enraptured by his reading. That laid the foundation of my deep devotion to the *Ramayana*. Today I regard the *Ramayana* of Tulsidas as the greatest book in all devotional literature.

Gandhi, *An Autobiography*, part I, chap. X

20. The Vaishnava ideal

A true *Vaishnava* is he
   Who is moved by others' sufferings;
Who helps people in distress,

And feels no pride for having done so.
Respectful to everyone in the world,
    He speaks ill of none;
Is self-controlled in action, speech and thought—
    Twice-blessed the mother who bore such a one.
He has an equal-seeing eye, and is free from all craving,
    Another's wife is to him a mother;
His tongue utters no untruth,
    And never his hand touches another's wealth.
Moha and *maya* have no power over him,
    In his mind reigns abiding detachment;
He dances with rapture to Rama's name—
    No centre of pilgrimage but is present in his person.
A man he is without greed and cunning,
    And purged of anger and desire;
Offering reverence to such a one, says Narasainyo,*
    Will bring release to seventy-one generations of one's forebears.

From the marks of a *Vaishnava* described by Narasinh Mehta we
see that he is a man who

1. is ever active in bringing relief to the distressed,
2. takes no pride in doing so,
3. is respectful to all,
4. speaks ill of none,
5. is self-controlled in speech,
6. in action and
7. in thought,
8. holds all in equal regard,
9. has renounced desires,
10. is loyal to one woman, his wife,
11. is ever truthful,
12. keeps the rule of non-stealing,
13. is beyond the reach of *maya*,
14. is, in consequence, free from all desire,
15. is ever absorbed in repeating Rama's name,
16. and, as a result, has been sanctified,
17. covets nothing,
18. is free from guile,
19. from the urge of desire and
20. from anger.

Here Narasinh, the best among the *Vaishnavas*, has given pride of place to non-violence. This means that a man who has no love in him is no *Vaishnava*. One who does not follow truth and has not acquired control over all his senses is not a *Vaishnava*.

'To Vaishnavas' (G.). *Navajivan*, 5 Dec. 1920

21. Meeting Raychandbhai in 1891

But the introduction* that I need particularly take note of was the one to the poet Raychand. . . . The thing that did cast its spell over me I came to know afterwards. That was his wide knowledge of the scriptures, his spotless character and his burning passion for self-realization. I saw later that this last was the only thing for which he lived. . . .

. . . He was a connoisseur of pearls and diamonds. No knotty business problem was too difficult for him. But all these things were not the centre round which his life revolved. That centre was the passion to see God face to face. . . . I never saw him lose his state of equipoise. There was no business or other selfish tie that bound him to me, and yet I enjoyed the closest association with him. I was but a briefless barrister then, and yet whenever I saw him he would engage me in conversation of a seriously religious nature. Though I was then groping and could not be said to have any serious interest in religious discussion, still I found his talk of absorbing interest . . . I must say that no one else has ever made on me the impression that Raychandbhai did. His words went straight home to me. His intellect compelled as great a regard from me as his moral earnestness, and deep down in me was the conviction that he would never willingly lead me astray and would always confide to me his innermost thoughts. In my moments of spiritual crisis, therefore, he was my refuge.

. . . Three moderns have left a deep impress on my life, and captivated me: Raychandbhai by his living contact; Tolstoy by his book, *The Kingdom of God is Within You*; and Ruskin by his *Unto this Last*.

Gandhi, *An Autobiography*, part II, chap. I

22. Raychandbhai: tolerance and non-violence

I came in touch with him in 1891 . . . I was much struck by his simplicity and independence of judgement. He was free from all touch of blind orthodoxy . . . Himself a Jain, his toleration of the other creeds was remarkable . . .

I have said elsewhere that in moulding my inner life Tolstoy and Ruskin vied with Kavi [Raychandra]. But Kavi's influence was undoubtedly deeper if only because I had come in closest personal touch with him. His judgement appealed to my moral sense in the vast majority of cases. The bedrock of his faith was unquestionably *ahimsa*. His *ahimsa* was not of the crude type we witness today among its so-called votaries who confine their attention merely to the saving of aged cattle and insect life. His *ahimsa*, if it included the tiniest insect, also covered the whole of humanity.

'A Great Seer'. *Modern Review*, June 1930. *MPWMG*, vol. i, p. 153

23. Raychandbhai: freedom from attachment

> When shall I know that state supreme,
> When will the knots, outer and inner, snap?
> When shall I, breaking the bonds that bind us fast,
> Tread the path trodden by the wise and the great?
>
> Withdrawing the mind from all interests,
> Using this body solely for self-control,
> He desires nothing to serve any ulterior end of his own,
> Seeing nothing in the body to bring on a trace of the darkness of
>   ignorance.

These are the first two verses of Raychandbhai's inspired utterance at the age of eighteen.

During the two years I remained in close contact with him, I felt in him every moment the spirit of *vairagya** which shines through these verses. One rare feature of his writings is that he always set down what he had felt in his own experience. There is in them no trace of unreality. I have never read any line by him which was written to produce an effect on others. He had always by his side a book on some religious subject and a note-book with blank pages. The latter he used for noting down any thoughts which occurred to him. Sometimes, it would be prose and sometimes poetry. The poem about the 'supreme state' must have been written in that manner.

Whatever he was doing at the moment, whether eating or resting or lying in bed, he was invariably disinterested towards things of the world. I never saw him being tempted by objects of pleasure or luxury in this world.

I watched his daily life respectfully, and at close quarters. He accepted whatever he was served at meals. His dress was simple . . . It was the same to him whether he squatted on the ground or had a chair to sit on. In the shop, he generally squatted on a *gadi*.*

He used to walk slowly, and the passer-by could see that he was absorbed in thought even while walking. There was a strange power in his eyes; they were extremely bright, and free from any sign of impatience or anxiety. They bespoke single-minded attention. The face was round, the lips thin, the nose neither pointed nor flat and the body of light build and medium size. The skin was dark. He looked an embodiment of peace. There was such sweetness in his voice that one simply wanted to go on listening to him. The face was smiling and cheerful; it shone with the light of inner joy. He had such ready command of language that I do not remember his ever pausing for a word to express his thoughts. I rarely saw him changing a word while writing a letter. And yet the reader would never feel that any thought was imperfectly expressed, or the construction of a sentence was defective or the choice of a word faulty.

These qualities can exist only in a man of self-control. A man cannot become free from attachments by making a show of being so. That state is a state of grace for the *atman*.*Anyone who strives for it will discover that it may be won only after a ceaseless effort through many lives. One will discover, if one struggles to get rid of attachments, how difficult it is to succeed in the attempt. The Poet made me feel that this state of freedom from attachment was spontaneous to him.

The first step towards *moksha* is freedom from attachment. Can we ever listen with pleasure to anyone talking about *moksha* so long as our mind is attached to a single object in this world? If at any time we seem to do so, it is only the ear which is pleased, in the same way, that is, as we may be pleased merely by the musical tune of a song without following its meaning. It will be a long time before such indulgence of the ear results in our adopting a way of life which could lead towards *moksha*. Without genuine *vairagya* in the mind, one cannot be possessed with a yearning for *moksha*. The poet was possessed by such yearning.

'*Vairagya*'. *Shrimad Rajchandra*, chap. 3. *EWMG*, pp. 80–1

24. Reading the *Gita* for the first time

Towards the end of my second year in England I came across two Theosophists, brothers, and both unmarried. They talked to me about the *Gita*.* They were reading Sir Edwin Arnold's translation—*The Song Celestial*—and they invited me to read the original with them. I felt ashamed, as I had read the divine poem neither in Sanskrit nor in Gujarati. I was constrained to tell them that I had not read the *Gita*, but that I would gladly read it with them, and that though my knowledge of Sanskrit was meagre, still I hoped to be able to understand the original to the extent of telling where the translation failed to bring out the meaning. I began reading the *Gita* with them. The verses in the second chapter

>   If one
> Ponders on objects of the sense, there springs
> Attraction; from attraction grows desire,
> Desire flames to fierce passion, passion breeds
> Recklessness; then the memory—all betrayed—
> Lets noble purpose go, and saps the mind,
> Till purpose, mind, and man are all undone.

made a deep impression on my mind, and they still ring in my ears. The book struck me as one of priceless worth. The impression has ever since been growing on me with the result that I regard it today as the book *par excellence* for the knowledge of Truth. It has afforded me invaluable help in my moments of gloom. I have read almost all the English translations of it, and I regard Sir Edwin Arnold's as the best. He has been faithful to the text, and yet it does not read like a translation. Though I read the *Gita* with these friends, I cannot pretend to have studied it then. It was only after some years that it became a book of daily reading.

Gandhi, *An Autobiography*, part I, chap. XX

25. The message of the *Gita*

23 October 1927

In declaring the *Gita* class open Mahatmaji advised the students to get up at 4 o'clock in the morning and regularly read the *Bhagavad Gita* daily. He was anxious that they should begin the study of the *Gita* in right earnest. If they could not read Sanskrit they could go in for a Tamil translation of the *Gita*, but not the English one, because the English rendering could not impart the true significance of the *Gita*. He said that the third chapter is an important one in the *Gita*.

The *Gita* contains the gospel of *karma* or work, the gospel of *bhakti* or devotion and the gospel of *jnana* or knowledge. Life should be a harmonious whole of these three. But the gospel of service is the basis of all, and what can be more necessary for those who want to serve the country than that they begin with the chapter enunciating the gospel of work? But you must approach it with the five necessary equipments, viz., *ahimsa* (non-violence), *satya* (truth), *brahmacharya* (celibacy), *aparigraha* (non-possession), and *asteya* (non-stealing). Then and then only will you be able to reach a correct interpretation of it. And then you will read it to discover in it *ahimsa* and not *himsa*, as so many nowadays try to do. Read it with the necessary equipment and I assure you you will have peace of which you were never aware before.

Speech to students, Tiruppur, reported in *The Hindu*, 25 Oct. 1927.
Young India, 3 Nov. 1927

26. An infallible guide

28 May 1927

I am glad you have intensified your devotions. I do not know what you are reading at present. And I do not know whether I told you that we must arrive at a time when we do not need the solace of many books but that we make one book yield us all we want. In the last stage, of course, when life becomes one of perfect surrender and complete self-effacement, the support of even one book becomes unnecessary. At the present moment, though I am reading many things, the *Bhagavad Gita* is becoming more and more the only infallible guide, the only dictionary of reference, in which I find all the sorrows, all the troubles, all the trials arranged in the alphabetical order with exquisite solutions.

Letter to Gulzarilal Nanda. CW 9641. *EWMG*, p. 172

27. A Christian friend in England introduces Gandhi to the Bible

About the same time* I met a good Christian from Manchester in a vegetarian boarding house. He talked to me about Christianity. I narrated to him my Rajkot recollections.* He was pained to hear them. He said . . . 'do please read the Bible.' I accepted his advice, and he got me a copy . . . I began reading it, but I could not possibly read through the Old Testament. I read the book of Genesis, and the chapters that followed invariably sent me to sleep. But just for the sake of being able to say that I had read it, I plodded through the other books with much difficulty and without the least interest or understanding. . . .

But the New Testament produced a different impression, especially the Sermon on the Mount which went straight to my heart. I compared it with the Gita. The verses, 'But I say unto you, that ye resist not evil: but whosoever shall smite thee on thy right cheek, turn to him the other also. And if any man take away thy coat let him have the cloke too' delighted me beyond measure . . . That renunciation was the highest form of religion appealed to me greatly.

Gandhi, *An Autobiography*, part I, chap. XX

28. Reading Thoreau

12 October 1929

Dear Friend,

I was agreeably surprised to receive your letter. Yes, indeed your book* which was the first English book I came across on vegetarianism was of immense help to me in steadying my faith in vegetarianism. My first introduction to Thoreau's* writings was I think in 1907 or later when I was in the thick of passive resistance struggle. A friend sent me Thoreau's essay on civil disobedience. It left a deep impression upon me. I translated a portion of that essay for the readers of *Indian Opinion* in South Africa which I was then editing and I made copious extracts from that essay for that paper. That essay seemed to be so convincing and truthful that I felt the need of knowing more of Thoreau and I came across your life of him, his 'Walden' and other short essays all of which I read with great pleasure and equal profit.

Letter to Henry S. Salt. SN 15663. *EWMG*, pp. 70–1

29. The impact of John Ruskin

He* came to see me off at the station, and left me with a book to read during the journey which he said I was sure to like. It was Ruskin's *Unto this Last*.*

The book was impossible to lay aside, once I had begun it. It gripped me. Johannesburg to Durban was a twenty-four hours' journey. The train reached there in the evening. I could not get any sleep that night. I determined to change my life in accordance with the ideals of the book.

This was the first book of Ruskin I had ever read. During the days of my education I had read practically nothing outside textbooks, and after I launched into active life I had very little time for reading. I cannot therefore claim much book knowledge. However, I believe I have not lost much because of this enforced restraint. On the contrary, the limited reading may be said to have enabled me thoroughly to digest what I did read. Of these books, the one that brought about an instantaneous and practical transformation in my life was *Unto this Last*. I translated it later into Gujarati, entitling it *Sarvodaya* (the welfare of all).

I believe that I discovered some of my deepest convictions reflected in this great book of Ruskin, and that is why it so captured me and made me transform my life. A poet is one who can call forth the good latent in the human breast. Poets do not influence all alike, for everyone is not evolved in an equal measure.

The teachings of *Unto this Last* I understood to be:

1. That the good of the individual is contained in the good of all.
2. That a lawyer's work has the same value as the barber's, inasmuch as all have the same right of earning their livelihood from their work.

3. That a life of labour, i.e., the life of the tiller of the soil and the handicraftsman, is the life worth living.

The first of these I knew. The second I had dimly realized. The third had never occurred to me. *Unto this Last* made it as clear as daylight for me that the second and the third were contained in the first. I arose with the dawn, ready to reduce these principles to practice.

Gandhi, *An Autobiography*, part IV, chap. XVIII

30. Ruskin on education

28 March 1932

John Ruskin was a great writer, teacher and religious thinker . . . I suppose most inmates of the Ashram know that one book* of his had a great effect on me and that it was this book which inspired me to introduce an important change in my life practically on the instant. He started in 1871 writing monthly letters addressed to factory workers. I had read praise of these letters in some article of Tolstoy, but I had not been able to secure them till now. . . . I have been reading the first part. The thoughts expressed in these letters are beautiful and resemble some of our own ideas, so much so that an outsider would think that the ideas which I have set forth in my writings and which we try to put into practice in the Ashram, I had stolen from these letters of Ruskin. I hope readers will understand what is meant by 'stolen'. If an idea or ideal of life is borrowed from somebody but is presented as one's own conception, it is said to be stolen.

Ruskin has discussed many matters. Here I will mention only a few of his ideas. He says that it is a sheer error to suppose, as is generally done, that some education however little or however faulty is better than no literary education at all. It is his view that we should strive for real education alone. And then he says that every human being requires three things and three virtues. Anyone who fails to cultivate them does not know the secret of life. These six things should therefore form the basis of education. Every child, whether boy or girl, should learn the properties of pure air, clean water and clean earth, and should also learn how to keep air, water and earth pure or clean and know their benefits. Likewise, he has mentioned gratitude, hope and charity as the three virtues. Anybody who does not love truth and cannot recognize goodness or beauty lives in his own self-conceit and remains ignorant of spiritual joy. Similarly, he who has no hope, who has, in other words, no faith in divine justice, will never be cheerful in heart. And he who is without love, that is, lacks the spirit of *ahimsa*, who cannot look upon all living things as his kith and kin, will never know the secret of living.

Ruskin has explained these ideas at great length in his wonderful language. I hope I shall be able to write about them some time in a language which all the inmates of the Ashram can understand. Today I rest content with the brief precis given above. But I will say one thing, that what Ruskin has explained in his finished and cultivated prose with English readers in view, is practically the same ideas which we discuss in our rustic language and which we have been trying to put into practice. I am comparing here not two languages, but two writers. I cannot hope to equal Ruskin's mastery of language. But a time will certainly come when the love of our language will have become universal and we shall have writers like Ruskin who will have dedicated themselves heart and soul to it and will write as powerful Gujarati as the English of Ruskin.

'Some Reflections on Education' (G.). *EWMG*, pp. 71–3.

31. Reading Tolstoy

I made too an intensive study of Tolstoy's books.* *The Gospels in Brief* . . . and other books made a deep impression on me. I began to realize more and more the infinite possibilities of universal love.

Gandhi, *An Autobiography*, part II, chap. XXII

32. Tolstoy on non-retaliation

18 November 1909

The letter* translated below calls for an explanation.

Count Tolstoy is a Russian nobleman. He has had his full share of life's pleasures, and was once a valiant soldier. He has no equal among European writers. After much experience and study, he has come to the conclusion that the political policies generally followed in the world are quite wrong. The chief reason for that, according to him, is that we are vengeful, a habit unworthy of us and contrary to the tenets of all religions. He believes that to return injury for injury does harm both to ourselves and to our enemy. According to him, we should not retaliate against anyone who may injure us, but reward him with love instead. He is uncompromising in his loyalty to the principle of returning good for evil.

He does not mean by this that those who suffer must seek no redress. He believes rather that we invite suffering on ourselves through our own fault. An oppressor's efforts will be in vain if we refuse to submit to his tyranny. Generally, no one will kick me for the mere fun of it. There must be some deeper reason for his doing so. He will kick me to bend me to his will if I have been opposing him. If, in spite of the kicks, I refuse to carry out his orders, he will stop kicking me. It would make no difference to me whether he did so or not. What matters to me is the fact that his order is unjust. Slavery consists in submitting to an unjust order, not in suffering ourselves to be kicked. Real courage and humanity consist in not returning a kick for a kick. This is the core of Tolstoy's teaching.

The letter translated below was originally written in Russian. It was rendered into English by Tolstoy himself and sent to the editor of *Free Hindustan* in reply to a letter of his. This editor holds different views from Tolstoy's and hence he did not publish the letter. It reached my hands and a friend asked me whether or not it should be published. I liked the letter. What I saw was a copy of the original letter. I sent it to Tolstoy and sought his permission to publish it, asking him at the same time whether the letter was in fact written by him. His permission having been received, both the English version of the letter and a Gujarati translation are being published in *Indian Opinion*.

To me Tolstoy's letter is of great value. Anyone who has enjoyed the experience of the Transvaal struggle will perceive its value readily enough. A handful of Indian *satyagrahis** have pitted love or soul-force against the might of the Transvaal Government's guns. That is the central principle of Tolstoy's teaching, of the teaching of all religions. Khuda-Ishwar has endowed our soul with such strength that sheer brute force is of no avail against it. We have been employing that strength against the Transvaal Government not out of hatred or with a view to revenge, but merely in order to resist its unjust order.

But those who have not known what a happy experience *satyagraha* can be, who have been caught up in the toils of this huge sham of modern civilization, like moths flitting round a flame, will find no interest in Tolstoy's letter all at once. Such men should pause for a moment and reflect.

Tolstoy gives a simple answer to those Indians who appear impatient to drive the whites out of India. We are our own slaves, not of the British. This should be engraved in our minds. The whites cannot remain if we do not want them. If the idea is to drive them out with firearms, let every Indian consider what precious little profit Europe has found in these.

Everyone would be happy to see India free. But there are as many views as men on how that can be brought about. Tolstoy points out a simple way to such men.

Tolstoy has addressed this letter to a Hindu and that is why it cites thoughts from Hindu scriptures. Such thoughts, however, are to be found in the scriptures of every religion. They are such as will be acceptable to all, Hindus, Muslims and Parsis. Religious practices and dogmas may differ, but the principles of ethics must be the same in all religions. I therefore advise all readers to think of ethics.

No one should assume that I accept all the ideas of Tolstoy. I look upon him as one of my teachers. But I certainly do not agree with all his ideas. The central principle of his teaching is entirely acceptable to me, and it is set out in the letter given below.

In this letter, he has not spared the superstitions of any religion. That is, however, no reason why any proud follower of Hinduism or of any other religion should oppose his teaching. It should suffice for us that he accepts the fundamental principles of every religion. When irreligion poses as religion, as it so often does, even true religion suffers. Tolstoy points this out repeatedly. We must pay the utmost attention to his thought whatever the religion we belong to.

In translating, I have endeavoured to use the simplest possible Gujarati. I have been mindful of the fact that readers of *Indian Opinion* prefer simple language. Moreover, I want Tolstoy's letter to be read by thousands of Gujarati Indians, and difficult language may prove tedious reading to such large numbers. Though all this has been kept in mind, slightly difficult words may have been occasionally used when simpler ones were not available, for which I apologize to the readers.

Preface to Leo Tolstoy's 'Letter to a Hindoo' (G.). *Indian Opinion*, 25 Dec. 1909

33. The influence of Naoroji

The birth anniversary of the Grand Old Man of India, Dadabhai Naoroji,* fell on 4th September; . . . I have many sacred memories of him. This Grand Old Man of India was, and continues to be, one of the great men who have moulded my life. I think the memories that I recounted before the sisters are worth being reported to the readers.

I had the privilege to see Dadabhai in 1888 for the first time. A friend of my father's had given me a letter of introduction to him, and it is worth noting that this friend was not at all acquainted with Dadabhai. He, however, took it for granted that anyone from the public could write to such a saintly person. In England, I found that Dadabhai came in contact with all students. He was their leader and attended their gatherings. Ever since, I have seen his life flowing in the same rhythm till the end. I was in South Africa for twenty years, and exchanged hundreds of letters with Dadabhai during the period. I was astonished at the regularity with which his replies came. My letters used to be typed, but I do not remember any typed reply from him. The replies were all in his own hand, and moreover, as I came to know subsequently, he would himself make copies of his letters on a tissue-paper book. I could find that most of my letters were replied to by the return of post. Whenever I met him I tasted nothing but love and sweetness.

Dadabhai would talk to me exactly like a father to a son, and I have heard from others that their experience was the same as mine. The thought uppermost in his mind all the time was how India could rise and attain her freedom. My first acquaintance with the extent of Indian poverty was through Dadabhai's book;* I learnt from that book itself that about three crores of men in our country are half-starved. Today this number has increased. His simplicity was without limit. It so happened that someone criticized him in 1908. I found it extremely intolerable and yet I was unable to prove that it was wrong. I was troubled by many doubts.

I thought that it was sinful to entertain doubts about a great patriot like Dadabhai. Therefore I sought an appointment and went to see him with the consent of the critic. That was the first time I went to his private office. It was made up of a very small room with only two chairs. I entered. He asked me to sit in a vacant chair but I went and sat near his feet. He saw distress on my face and questioned me, asking me to speak out whatever weighed on my mind. With great hesitation I reported to him the criticisms of his detractors and said, 'I was troubled by doubts on hearing these things and, because I worship you, I consider it a sin to keep them back.' Smilingly, he asked me, 'What reply do I give you? Do you believe this thing?' His manner, his tone and the pain that was so apparent in his words, were enough for me. I said, 'I do not now want to hear anything more. I have no trace of a doubt left in me.' Even then he told me many things relating to this matter, which it is not necessary to recapitulate here. After this event I realized that Dadabhai was an Indian living in the simple style of a *fakir*. A *fakir*'s style does not imply that a man should not have even a farthing; but Dadabhai had forsaken the luxuries and standards which other people of his stratum were enjoying during those days.

I myself and many others like me have learnt the lessons of regularity, single-minded patriotism, simplicity, austerity and ceaseless work from this venerable man. At a time when criticism of the Government was considered sedition and hardly anyone dared to speak the truth, Dadabhai criticized the Government in the severest terms and boldly pointed out the shortcomings of the administration. I have absolutely no doubt that the people of India will remember Dadabhai affectionately as long as India endures as an entity in the world.

'Birth Anniversary of Dadabhai Naoroji' (G.). *Navajivan*, 7 Sept. 1924

34. The message of Gokhale

20 February 1915

My one desire tonight is that my heart may reach your hearts and that there should be a real at-one-ment between us.

You have all learnt something about Tulsidas's *Ramayana*.* The most stirring part is that about the companionship of the good.

We should seek the company of those who have suffered and served and died. One such was Mr Gokhale.* He is dead, but his work is not dead, for his spirit lives.

The masses came to know of Gokhale's efficiency in work. All know Gokhale's life of action. But few know of his religious life. Truth was the spring of all his actions.

This was behind all his works, even his politics. This was the reason he founded the Servants of India Society, the ideal of which was to spiritualize the political as well as the social life of the nation.

It was fearlessness which ruled all the actions of his life. But as he was fearless he was also thorough. One of his favourite *shlokas** from the Shastras* says: Real wisdom is not to begin a thing but to see the thing through to the end. This characteristic of thoroughness may be seen from this incident. He once had to speak to a large audience and he spent three days in order to prepare a short speech for this meeting and he asked me to write out a speech for him. I wrote out the speech. He took it and smiled his heavenly smile, discussed it with me and said, 'Give me something better, rewrite it.' For three days he worried over it. When the speech was given, it thrilled the whole audience. He delivered his speeches without notes, but he did so, because he was so thorough, that one might say he wrote his speeches with his own blood. As he was thorough and fearless, so he was gentle. He was human from top to toe in all his dealings. He was sometimes impatient, but he would ask forgiveness, coming forward with his smile, whether to a servant or a great man, saying, 'I know you will forgive me, won't you?'

He had a great struggle during the latter days of his life, a struggle with his conscience. He had to decide whether he should continue to take part in a struggle at the expense of his health. His conscience ruled every action of his life. He did not wear it on his sleeve, he wore it in his heart. Therefore he is living still, and may we all have the strength to carry out his last wish. His last word to those members of the Servants of India Society who were with him were: 'I do not want any memorial or any statue. I want only that men should love their country and serve it with their lives.' This is a message for the whole of India and not only for them. It was through service that he learnt to know his own nature and to know his country. His love for India was truthful and therefore he wanted nothing for India which he did not want for humanity also. It was not blind love, for his eyes were open to her faults and failings. If we can love India in the same way that he did, we have done well in coming to Shantiniketan* to learn how to live our lives for India's sake. Copy the zeal which he showed in all he took up, the love that was the law of his life, the truthfulness which guided every action and the thoroughness which was characteristic of all his work.

Remember that our *shastras* teach us that these simple virtues are the stepping stones to the higher state of life, without which all our worship and works are useless.

I was in quest of a really truthful hero in India and I found him in Gokhale. His love and reverence for India were truly genuine. For serving his country, he completely eschewed all happiness and self-interest. Even while lying on his sick-bed, his mind was occupied in thinking about the welfare of India. A few days ago, when at night he was under the grip of a painful ailment, he called for some of us and began talking about the bright future of India, as envisaged by him. Doctors repeatedly advised him to retire from work but he would not listen to them. He said, 'None but death can separate me from work.' And death at last brought peaceful rest to him. May God bless his soul!

Speech at Shantiniketan on Gokhale's death. *The Ashram*, June–July 1915. *EWMG*, pp. 78–9

35. Reading in prison

As a boy I had not much taste for reading anything outside my school books. They alone gave me enough food for thought; for it was natural for me to reduce to practice what I learnt at school. For home reading I had an intense dislike. I used to labour through home lessons because I had to. During my student days in England too the same habit persisted of not reading outside the books for examinations. When however I began life, I felt I ought to read for the sake of gaining general knowledge. But at the earliest period of my life it became one of storm and stress . . . I had therefore not much time for literary pursuits. In South Africa for one year I had fair leisure in spite of the battle for freedom that faced me. The year 1893 I devoted to religious striving. The reading was therefore wholly religious. After 1894 all the time for sustained reading I got was in the jails of

South Africa. I had developed not only a taste for reading but for completing my knowledge of Sanskrit and studying Tamil, Hindi and Urdu. . . . The South African jails had whetted my appetite and I was grieved when during my last incarceration in South Africa I was prematurely discharged.

When the opportunity* came to me in India, I hailed it with joy . . . I therefore settled down to studies with the zest of a youth of twenty-four instead of an old man of fifty-four with a broken constitution.

'My Jail Experiences—XI'. *Young India*, 4 Sept. 1924

II · AUTHENTIC HUMAN LIFE AND THE TRANSFORMATION OF THE INDIVIDUAL

a. The truly human life

36. Man's core goodness

12 January 1910

The more I observe, the greater is the dissatisfaction with the modern life. I see nothing good in it. Men are good. But they are poor victims making themselves miserable under the false belief that they are doing good. I am aware that there is a fallacy underneath this. I who claim to examine what is around me may be a deluded fool. This risk all of us have to take. The fact is that we are all bound to do what we feel is right. And with me I feel that the modern life is *not* right. The greater the conviction, the bolder my experiments.

Letter to A. H. West.* CW 4413. *EWMG*, p. 165

37. Human perfectibility

13 January 1918

To say that perfection is not attainable on this earth is to deny God. The statement about impossibility of ridding ourselves of sin clearly refers to a stage in life. But we need not search scriptures in support of the assertion. We do see men constantly becoming better under effort and discipline. There is no occasion for limiting the capacity for improvement. Life to me would lose all its interest if I felt that I *could* not attain perfect love on earth. After all, what matters is that our capacity for loving ever expands. It is a slow process. How shall you love the men who thwart you even in well-doing? And yet that is the time of supreme test.

Letter to Esther Faering. Gandhi, '*My Dear Child*', pp. 24–5

38. Optimism and religious faith

Optimism indicates faith; only an atheist can be a pessimist. The optimist lives in fear of God, listens with humility to the inner voice, obeys its promptings and believes that God ordains everything for the best.

The pessimist vainly thinks that it is he who does everything. When he fails in some undertaking, he leaves himself out and blames others; indulges in vain prating about not being sure whether God exists and, finally, concluding that this world is worthless and he alone good, but that his merit is not recognized, puts an end to his life. If he does not do that, he merely endures an existence which is little better than death.

The optimist lives delighting in thoughts of love and charity and, since there is none whom he looks upon as his enemy, he moves without fear whether he is in the forest or in the midst of men. He has no fear of ferocious animals or equally dreadful men, for his soul cannot be bitten by snakes nor pierced by the sinner's sword. Such a one will not give too much thought to his body, will rather look upon it as a fragile vessel of glass which is fated to break some day and will not go roaming all over the world to preserve it in health. The optimist will not kill or harass any human being. With his inner ear ever attuned to the sweet music of his soul, he will live floating on an ocean of joy.

The pessimist, being himself a prey of violent attachments and dislikes, looks upon every person as his enemy and fears him. He has of course no such thing as the inner voice. Like the honey bee, he flits from pleasure to pleasure, daily tiring of them and daily seeking new ones and, finally, dies, unloved, unwept and unsung.

'Optimism' (G.). *Navajivan*, 23 Oct. 1921

39. Progress towards perfection

28 May 1927

Your description of a truly religious life is accurate. I have not a shadow of a doubt that this blessed state of inward joy and freedom from anxiety should last in the midst of the greatest trials conceivable. It admits of no exception whatsoever. Naturally, it is unattainable except by the very fewest. But that it is attainable by human beings,

I have also no doubt. That we do not find in history evidence regarding the existence of any such person merely proves to me that all the record that we have has been prepared by imperfect beings, and it is impossible for imperfect beings to give us a faithful record of perfect ones. The same may be said of our own experiences. We have to be very nearly perfect in order to meet perfect souls such as you have described. Nor need you think that I have laid down an absurd proposition inasmuch as it is incapable of being recorded, or being experienced by the average man. To raise such a doubt would be begging the question, for we are here picturing to ourselves extraordinary mortals, though mortals nevertheless, and surely extraordinary powers are required to find out these extraordinary mortals. This statement is true even of much lesser things, things almost ridiculous, and yet very difficult of accomplishment, such, for instance, as the discoveries of Sir J. C. Bose* or the finest paintings. Both these, we average beings will have to take on trust. It is only the privileged few who have got the special faculty for understanding and appreciating either those discoveries, or those paintings. These do not appear to us to be incredible and we are able to accept them on faith only because in favour of these we have the testimony of a larger number of witnesses than we can possibly have for the things of permanent value, such as human perfection of the utmost type. Therefore the limitation that you have accepted is quite a workable thing for the time being. For, even inside the limitation, there is ample scope for widening the field for the progress of the state of being and remaining unruffled in the face of the onslaught of sorrows and trials, which before regeneration would have paralysed us.

Letter to Gulzarilal Nanda. CW 9641. *EWMG*, pp. 171–2

40. The purpose of life

21 June 1932

The purpose of life is undoubtedly to know oneself. We cannot do it unless we learn to identify ourselves with all that lives. The sum total of that life is God. Hence the necessity of realizing God living within every one of us. The instrument of this knowledge is boundless selfless service.

A letter. *Mahadevbhaini Diary*, vol. i, pp. 242–3. *EWMG*, p. 175

41. Human potential

Not to believe in the possibility of permanent peace is to disbelieve the godliness of human nature. Methods hitherto adopted have failed because rock-bottom sincerity on the part of those who have striven has been lacking. Not that they have realized this lack. Peace is unattainable by part performance of conditions, even as a chemical combination is impossible without complete fulfilment of the conditions of attainment thereof. If the recognized leaders of mankind who have control over engines of destruction were wholly to renounce their use, with full knowledge of its implications, permanent peace can be obtained. This is clearly impossible without the great Powers of the earth renouncing their imperialistic design. This again seems impossible without great nations ceasing to believe in soul-destroying competition and to desire to multiply wants and therefore increase their material possessions. It is my conviction that the root of the evil is want of a living faith in a living God. It is a first-class human tragedy that peoples of the earth who claim to believe in the message of Jesus who they describe as the Prince of Peace show little of that belief in actual practice. It is painful to see sincere Christian divines limiting the scope of Jesus' message to select individuals. I have been taught from my childhood and tested the truth by experience that the primary virtues of mankind are possible of cultivation by the meanest of the human species. It is this undoubted universal possibility that distinguishes the humans from the rest of God's creation. *If even one great nation were unconditionally to perform the supreme act of renunciation, many of us would see in our lifetime visible peace established on earth.*

'Answer to *The Cosmopolitan*'. *Harijan*, 18 June 1938

42. The self

24 March 1945

Personality, i.e., the quality of being oneself, can be good or bad. If it is in conformity with the Self it is good and if it disregards the Self it is bad. It becomes good and develops by meditating on the Self and understanding its attributes.

Note to Gope Gurbuxani (H.). GN 1334. *EWMG*, pp. 176–7

43. Knowing the self

4 August 1932

I got your letter. My experience tells me that, instead of bothering about how the whole world may live in the right manner, we should think how we ourselves may do so. We do not even know whether the world lives in the right manner or in a wrong manner. If, however, we live in the right manner, we shall feel that others also do the same, or shall discover a way of persuading them to do so.

To know the *atman* means to forget the body, or, in other words, to become a cipher. Anybody who becomes a cipher will have realized the *atman*.

Letter to Babalbhai Mehta (G.). SN 9449. *EWMG*, p. 182

44. Realizing God in ourselves

8 April 1932

1 and 2. We must believe in God if we believe in ourselves. If living beings have existence God is the sum total of all life and this in my view is the strongest proof.

3. The denial of God is injurious in the same way as denial of ourselves. That is to say, to deny God is like committing suicide. The fact remains that it is one thing to believe in God and quite another to realize God emotionally and act accordingly. Truly, no one in the world is an atheist; atheism is merely a pose.

4. One can realize God only by ridding oneself totally of attachment, aversion, etc., and in no other way. I hold that one who claims to have realized God has not truly done so. Realization can be experienced, but is beyond description. Of this I have no doubt.

5. I can live only by having faith in God. My definition of God must always be kept in mind. For me there is no other God than Truth; Truth is God.

Letter to Hanumanprasad Poddar (H.). *Mahadevbhaini Diary*, vol. i, p. 82. *EWMG*, p. 156

b. The search for God

45. Truth and ethics

But one thing took deep root in me—the conviction that morality is the basis of things, and that truth is the substance of all morality. Truth became my sole objective. It began to grow in magnitude every day, and my definition of it also has been ever widening.

Gandhi, *An Autobiography*, part I, chap. X

46. Seeing God as Truth

8 June 1927

TRUTH and LOVE have been jointly the guiding principle of my life. If God who is indefinable can be at all defined, then I should say that God is TRUTH. It is impossible to reach HIM, that is, TRUTH, except through LOVE. Love can only be expressed fully when man reduces himself to a cipher. This process of reduction to cipher is the highest effort man or woman is capable of making. It is the only effort worth making, and it is possible only through ever-increasing self-restraint.

Letter to Basil Mathews, Editor, *World's Youth*. SN 12514. *EWMG*, pp. 230–1

47. The realization of Truth as God

22 July 1930

I deal first with truth, as the Satyagraha Ashram* owes its very existence to the pursuit and the attempted practice of truth.

The word *satya* is derived from *sat*, which means that which is. *Satya* means a state of being. Nothing is or exists in reality except Truth. That is why *sat* or *satya* is the right name for God. In fact it is more correct to say that Truth is God than to say that God is Truth. But as we cannot do without a ruler or general, the name God is and will remain more current. On deeper thinking, however, it will be realized that *sat* or *satya* is the only correct and fully significant name for God.

And where there is Truth, there also is knowledge which is true. Where there is no Truth, there can be no true knowledge. That is why the word *chit* or knowledge is associated with the name of God. And where there is true knowledge, there is always *ananda*, bliss. There sorrow has no place. And even as Truth is eternal, so is the bliss derived from it. Hence we know God as *Sat-chit-ananda*, one who combines in Himself Truth, knowledge and bliss.

Devotion to this Truth is the sole justification for our existence. All our activities should be centred in truth. Truth should be the very breath of our life. When once this stage in the pilgrim's progress is reached, all other rules of correct living will come without effort and obedience to them will be instinctive. But without Truth it is impossible to observe any principles or rules in life.

Generally speaking, observance of the law of Truth is understood merely to mean that we must speak the truth. But we in the Ashram should understand the word *satya* or Truth in a much wider sense. There should be Truth in thought, Truth in speech and Truth in action. To the man who has realized this Truth in its fullness, nothing else remains to be known, because, as we have seen above, all knowledge is necessarily included in it. What is not included in it is not Truth, and so not true knowledge; and there can be no real bliss without true knowledge. If we once learn how to apply this never-failing test of Truth, we will at once be able to find out what is worth doing, what is worth seeing, what is worth reading.

But how is one to realize this Truth, which may be likened to the philosopher's stone or the cow of plenty? By *abhyasa*, single-minded devotion, and *vairagya*, indifference to all other interests in life—replies the *Bhagavad Gita*. Even so, what may appear as truth to one person will often appear as untruth to another person. But that need not worry the seeker. Where there is honest effort, it will be realized that what appear to be different truths are like the countless and apparently different leaves of the same tree. Does not God Himself appear to different individuals in different aspects? Yet we know that He is one. But Truth is the right designation of God. Hence there is nothing wrong in every man following Truth according to his lights. Indeed it is his duty to do so. Then if there is a mistake on the part of anyone so following Truth, it will be automatically set right. For the quest of Truth involves *tapascharya*, self-suffering, sometimes even unto death. There can be no place in it for even a trace of self-interest. In such selfless search for Truth, nobody can lose his bearings for long. Directly he takes to the wrong path he stumbles, and is thus redirected to the right path. Therefore the pursuit of Truth is true *bhakti*, devotion. Such *bhakti* is 'a bargain in which one risks one's very life'. It is the path that leads to God. There is no place in it for cowardice, no place for defeat. It is the talisman by which death itself becomes the portal to life eternal. . . .

God as Truth has been for me, at any rate, a treasure beyond price. May He be so to every one of us.

Letter to Narandas Gandhi (G.). *EWMG*, pp. 231–3

48. Truth is God

21 March 1932

Do you remember my definition of God? Instead of saying that God is Truth, I say that Truth is God. I did not always think thus. I realized this only four years ago. But without knowing it I always acted as if it was so. I have always known God as Truth. There was a time when I doubted the existence of God, but even at that time I did not doubt the existence of Truth. This Truth is not a material quality but is pure consciousness. That alone holds the universe together. It is God because it rules the whole universe. If you follow this idea, it contains the answer to all your other questions. If you have any difficulty, however, put your question to me. For me this is almost a matter of direct experience. I say 'almost' because I have not seen face to face God Who is Truth. I have had only a glimpse of Him. But my faith is unshakeable.

Letter to boys and girls (G.). *Mahadevbhaini Diary*, vol. i, p. 27.
EWMG, pp. 233–4

49. Limited truth and absolute truth

Beyond these limited truths [of different religions], however, there is one absolute Truth which is total and all-embracing. But it is indescribable, because it is God. Or say, rather, God is Truth. All else is unreal and false. Other things, therefore, can be true only in a relative sense.

He, therefore, who understands truth, follows nothing but truth in thought, speech and action, comes to know God and gains the seer's vision of the past, the present and the future. He attains *moksha* though still encased in the physical frame. . . .

The word *satya* comes from *sat*, which means 'to be', 'to exist'. Only God is ever the same through all time. A thousand times honour to him who has succeeded, through love and devotion for this *satya*, in opening out his heart permanently to its presence. I have been but striving to serve that truth. I have, I believe, the courage to jump from the top of the Himalayas for its sake. At the same time, I know that I am still very far from that truth. As I advance towards it, I perceive my weakness ever more clearly and the knowledge makes me humble. It is possible to be puffed up with pride so long as one does not know one's own insignificance. But once a man sees it, his pride melts away. Mine melted away long ago. I can very well understand why Tulsidas* called himself a villain. This path is for the brave alone; the timid had better not tread it. He who strives for all the twenty-four hours of the day ever meditating on truth, whether eating, drinking, sitting, sleeping, spinning or easing himself, doing anything whatever, will certainly have his whole being filled with truth. And when the sun of truth blazes in all its glory in a person's heart, he will not remain hidden. He will not, then, need to use speech and to explain. Or, rather, every word uttered by him will be charged with such power, such life, that it will produce an immediate effect on the people. I do not have this truth in me.

'What is Truth?' (G.). *Navajivan*, 20 Nov. 1921

50. God is beyond perception

15 August 1932

I believe in both Gods,* the one that serves us and the one that we serve. It cannot be that we should render service and should not receive service of any kind. But both Gods are of our imagining. There is only one God who is real. The real God is beyond conception. He neither serves nor receives service. He cannot be described by any epithets, being not an external power but something dwelling in our heart. Since we do not understand the ways of God, we have necessarily to think of a power beyond our conception.

And the moment we think of it, the God of our imagining is born. The fact is that belief in God is a function not of the intellect but of faith. Reasoning is of little help to us in this matter and once we accept God the ways of the world cease to bother us. Then we have to accept that no creation of God can be purposeless. Beyond this I cannot go.

Letter to Bhuskute (H.). *Mahadevbhaini Diary*, vol. i, p. 364. *EWMG*, pp. 157–8.

51. An inner voice

25 May 1932

It is true that I do not depend upon my intellect to decide upon any action. For me the reasoned course of action is held in check subject to the sanction of the inner voice. I do not know if others would call it the mysterious power or whatsoever. I have never deliberated upon this nor analysed it, I have felt no need of doing so either. I have faith, and knowledge, too, that a Power exists beyond reasoning. This suffices for me. I am unable to clarify this any further as I know nothing more in the matter.

Letter to Bhuskute (H.). *Mahadevbhaini Diary*, vol. i, pp. 173–4. *EWMG*, p. 213

52. The call of the inner voice

Now for the fast.*

The first question that has puzzled many is about the voice of God. What was it? What did I hear? Was there any person I saw? If not, how was the Voice conveyed to me? These are pertinent questions.

For me the voice of God, of Conscience, of Truth, or the Inner Voice or the 'still small Voice'* mean one and the same thing. I saw no form. I have never tried, for I have always believed God to be without form. . . .

. . . The inspiration I got was this: The night I got the inspiration, I had a terrible inner struggle. My mind was restless. I could see no way. The burden of my responsibility was crushing me. But what

I did hear was like a Voice from afar and yet quite near. It was as unmistakable as some human voice definitely speaking to me, and irresistible. I was not dreaming when I heard the Voice. The hearing of the voice was preceded by a terrific struggle within me. Suddenly the Voice came upon me. I listened, made certain that it was the Voice and the struggle ceased. . . .

Could I give any further evidence that it was truly the Voice that I heard and that it was not an echo of my own heated imagination? I have no further evidence to convince the sceptic. He is free to say that it was all self-delusion or hallucination. It may well have been so. I can offer no proof to the contrary. But I can say this—that not the unanimous verdict of the whole world against me could shake me from the belief that what I heard was the true voice of God.

'All About the Fast'. *Harijan*, 8 July 1933

53. Fitness to listen and self-deception

23/24 September 1939

How I wish I had the same enthusiasm that fires you. Of course I have the experience of listening, not merely of trying to listen. The more I listen, the more I discover that I am still far away from God. While I can lay down rules, the observance of which is essential for proper listening, the reality still escapes me. When we say we are listening to God and getting answers, though we say it truthfully, there is every possibility there of self-deception. I do not know that I am myself altogether free from self-deception. People sometimes ask me if I may not be mistaken, and I say to them, 'Yes, very likely, what I say may be just a picture of my elongated self before you.'

And then see how one may claim to be God-guided in taking a particular course of action, and another may make the same claim in taking an opposite course of action. I will give you a good illustration. Rajaji, whom you know, at any rate whose name you have heard, is I think unsurpassed in godliness or God-mindedness. Now when I took the 21 days' purificatory fast in the Yeravda Jail in 1933 and proclaimed that it was in answer to a call from God, Rajagopalachari* came all the way from Madras to dissuade me. He felt sure that I was deluding myself and that I should probably die and, if I did not, I should certainly be demented. Well, you see that I am still alive and of a sound mind. And yet perhaps Rajaji still thinks I was deluded and it was by an accident that I was saved, and I continue to think that I fasted in answer to the still small voice within.

I say this in order to warn you how unwise it may be to believe that you are always listening to God. I am not at all against the endeavour, but I warn you against thinking that this is a kind of 'open sesame' which has just to be shown to the millions. . . .

This I know that all that glitters is not gold, and also that if a man has really heard the voice of God, there is no sliding back, just as there is no forgetting it by one who has learnt to swim. The listening in must make people's lives daily richer and richer.

Let me not appear to damp your enthusiasm; but if it is to be built on solid rock, it is better that listening in is also based on solid rock.

This listening in presupposes the fitness to listen, and the fitness is acquired after constant and patient striving and waiting on God.

Discussion with Members of Oxford Group. *Harijan*, 7 Oct. 1939

c. True religion and particular religious traditions

54. What is religion?

25 November 1932

What a joy it would be when people realize that religion consists not in outward ceremonial but an ever-growing inward response to the highest impulses that man is capable of.

Letter to S. E. Stokes. *Mahadevbhaini Diary*, vol. ii, p. 279. *EWMG*, p. 158

55. The root and equality of all religions

1 November 1945

Right from my childhood I have lived with Muslims and when I went to London Providence placed me in close association with Christians, Muslims and Parsis. Hindus of course were there. I came into contact with the intellectuals among them and that is how I read the holy books of all the four religions. . . . As a result I have realized that every religion contains both truth and untruth. The root of all religions is one and it is pure and all of them have sprung from the same source, hence all are equal.

Letter to Mahadevshastri Divekar (H.). *Pyarelal Papers. EWMG*, pp. 159–60

56. No need to leave one's own religion

Raychandbhai* used to say that the different faiths were like so many walled enclosures in which men and women were confined. He whose one aim in life is to attain *moksha* need not give exclusive devotion to a particular faith. . . .

. . . he was always bored by religious controversy and rarely engaged himself in it. He would study and understand the excellence of each faith and explain it to the followers of that faith. Through my correspondence with him from South Africa, too, this is the lesson which I learnt from him.

My own belief is that every religion is perfect from the point of view of its followers and imperfect from that of the followers of other faiths. Examined from an independent point of view, every religion is both perfect and imperfect . . . If we follow Raychandbhai's point of view, no one need give up his faith and embrace another. Everyone may, following his own faith, win his freedom, that is, *moksha*, for to win *moksha* means to be perfectly free from attachments and aversions.

'Dharma'. *Shrimad Rajchandra*, chap. 5. *MPWMG*, vol. i, p. 152

57. Proper religious education

To me religion means truth and *ahimsa* or rather truth alone, because truth includes *ahimsa*, *ahimsa* being the necessary and indispensable means for its discovery. Therefore anything that promotes the practice of these virtues is a means for imparting religious education and the best way to do this, in my opinion, is for the teachers rigorously to practise these virtues in their own person. Their very association with the boys, whether on the playground or in the class-room, will then give the pupils a fine training in these fundamental virtues.

So much for instruction in the universal essentials of religion. A curriculum of religious instruction should include a study of the tenets of faiths other than one's own. For this purpose the students should be trained to cultivate the habit of understanding and appreciating the doctrines of various great religions of the world in a spirit of reverence and broad-minded tolerance. This, if properly done, would help to give them a spiritual assurance and a better appreciation of their own religion. There is one rule, however, which should always be kept in mind while studying all great religions and that is that one should study them only through the writings of known votaries of the respective religions. . . . This study of other religions besides one's own will give one a grasp of the rock-bottom unity of all religions and afford a glimpse also of that universal and absolute truth which lies beyond the 'dust of creeds and faiths'.

Let no one even for a moment entertain the fear that a reverent study of other religions is likely to weaken or shake one's faith in one's own. The Hindu system of philosophy regards all religions as containing the elements of truth in them and enjoins an attitude of respect and reverence towards them all. This of course presupposes regard for one's own religion. Study and appreciation of other religions need not cause a weakening of that regard; it should mean extension of that regard to other religions.

In this respect religion stands on the same footing as culture. Just as preservation of one's own culture does not mean contempt for that of others, but requires assimilation of the best that there may be in all the other cultures, even so should be the case with religion. Our present fears and apprehensions* are a result of the poisonous atmosphere that has been generated in the country, the atmosphere of mutual hatred, ill-will and distrust. We are constantly labouring under a nightmare of fear lest someone should stealthily undermine our faith or the faith of those who are dear and near to us. But this unnatural state will cease when we have learnt to cultivate respect and tolerance towards other religions and their votaries.

'Religious Education'. *Young India*, 6 Dec. 1928

58. Spiritual growth in one's own religious tradition

Religious ideas like everything else are subject to the same law of evolution that governs everything else in the universe. Only God is changeless and as His message is received through the imperfect human medium, it is always liable to suffer distortion in proportion as the medium is pure or otherwise. I would therefore respectfully urge my Christian friends and well-wishers to take me as I am. I respect and appreciate their wish that I should think and be as they are even as I respect and appreciate a similar wish on the part of my Mussalman friends. I regard both the religions as equally true. But my own gives me full satisfaction. It contains all that I need for my growth. It teaches me to pray not that others may believe as I believe but that they may grow to their full height in their own religion. My constant prayer therefore is for a Christian or a Mussalman to be a better Christian and a better Mahomedan. I am convinced, I know, that God will ask, asks us now, not what we label ourselves but what we are, i.e., what we do. With Him *deed* is everything, *belief* without deed is nothing. With Him doing is believing.

'My Jail Experiences—XI'. *Young India*, 4 Sept. 1924

d. Seeking truth through non-violence, self-discipline, and service

59. Non-violence—unique to human kind

9 April 1926

I have your letter. I too have seen many a lizard going for cock-roaches and have watched cockroaches going for lesser forms but I have not felt called upon to prevent the operation of the law of the larger living on the smaller. I do not claim to penetrate into the awful mystery but from watching these very operations, I learn that the law of the beast is not the law of the Man; that Man has by painful striving to surmount and survive the animal in him and from the tragedy of the *himsa* which is being acted around him he has to learn the supreme lesson of *ahimsa* for himself. Man must, therefore, if he is to realize his dignity and his own mission, cease to take part in the destruction and refuse to prey upon his weaker fellow creatures. He can only keep that as an ideal for himself and endeavour day after day to reach it. Complete success is possible only when he has attained *moksha*, a state in which the spirit becomes and remains independent of physical existence.

Letter to V. N. S. Chary. SN 19438. *EWMG*, p. 170

60. Non-violence and truth

16 March 1922

As I proceed in my quest for Truth, it grows upon me that Truth comprehends everything. I often feel that *ahimsa* is in Truth, not vice versa. What is perceived by a pure heart at a particular moment is Truth to it for that moment. By clinging to it, one can attain pure Truth. And I do not imagine that this will lead us into any moral dilemma. But often enough, it is difficult to decide what is *ahimsa*. Even the use of disinfectants is *himsa*. Still we have to live a life of *ahimsa* in the midst of a world full of *himsa*, and we can do so only if we cling to Truth. That is why I can derive *ahimsa* from truth. Out of Truth emerge love and tenderness. A votary of Truth, one who would scrupulously cling to Truth, must be utterly humble. His humility should increase with his observance of Truth. I see the truth of this every moment of my life. I have now a more vivid sense of Truth and of my own littleness than I had a year ago.

The wonderful implication of the great truth *Brahma satyam jaganmithya** grows on me from day to day. We should therefore be always patient. This will purge us of harshness and make us more tolerant. Our lapses will then appear as mountains and those of others as small as mole-hills. The body exists because of our ego. The utter extinction of the body is *moksha*. He who has achieved such extinction of the ego becomes the very image of Truth; he may well be called the *Brahman*. Hence it is that a loving name of God is *Dasanudasa*.*

Wife, children, friends, possessions—all should be held subject to that Truth. We can be *satyagrahis* only if we are ready to sacrifice each one of these in our search for Truth. It is with a view to making the observance of this Truth comparatively easy that I have thrown myself into this movement and do not hesitate to sacrifice men like you in it. Its outward form is Indian *swaraj*. Its real inner form is the *swaraj* of particular individuals. This *swaraj* is being delayed because we have not found even one *satyagrahi* of that pure type. This, however, need not dismay us. It should spur us on to greater effort.

Letter to Jamnalal Bajaj. GN 2843. *EWMG*, pp. 226–7

61. Non-violence—the way to truth

7 November 1945

I write the truth as I personally see it. Absolute truth alone is God. It is beyond reach. At the most we can say it is *neti, neti.** The truth that we see is relative, many-sided, plural and is the whole truth for a given time. There is no scope for vanity in it and the only way of reaching it is through *ahimsa*. Pure and absolute truth should be our ideal. We can reach the ideal only by constantly meditating on it, and reaching it is attaining *moksha*. For the last sixty years I have been experiencing what I have said above. I am still experiencing it.

Letter to Vamanrao Joshi (H.). *Pyarelal Papers. EWMG*, p. 236

62. *Ahimsa* and the realization of truth

My uniform experience has convinced me that there is no other God than Truth. And if every page of these chapters [of his *Autobiography*] does not proclaim to the reader that the only means for the realization of Truth is *Ahimsa*, I shall deem all my labour in writing these chapters to have been in vain. And, even though my efforts in this behalf may prove fruitless, let the readers know that the vehicle, not the principle, is at fault. After all, however sincere my strivings after *Ahimsa* may have been, they have still been imperfect and inadequate. The little fleeting glimpses, therefore, that I have been able to have of Truth can hardly convey an idea of the indescribable lustre of Truth, a million times more intense than that of the sun we daily see with our eyes. In fact what I have caught is only the faintest glimmer of that mighty effulgence. But this much I can say with assurance, as result of all my experiments, that a perfect vision of Truth can only follow a complete realization of *Ahimsa*.

Gandhi, *An Autobiography*, 'Farewell'

63. Non-violence—the greatest force in the world

14 November 1924

My study and experience of non-violence have proved to me that it is the greatest force in the world. It is the surest method of discovering the truth and it is the quickest because there is no other. It works silently, almost imperceptibly, but none the less surely. It is the one constructive process of Nature in the midst of incessant destruction going on about us. I hold it to be a superstition to believe that it can work only in private life. There is no department of life public or private to which that force cannot be applied. But this non-violence is impossible without complete self-effacement.

Message to *World Tomorrow*. Mahadev Desai's diary (MSS). *EWMG*, p. 240

64. Non-violence and individual transformation

15 July 1926

Non-violence is the greatest force man has been endowed with. Truth is the only goal he has. For God is none other than Truth. But Truth cannot be, never will be, reached except through non-violence.

That which distinguishes man from all other animals is his capacity to be non-violent. And he fulfils his mission only to the extent that he is non-violent and no more. He has no doubt many other gifts. But if they do not subserve the main purpose—the development of the spirit of non-violence in him—they but drag him down lower than the brute, a status from which he has only just emerged.

The cry for peace* will be a cry in the wilderness, so long as the spirit of non-violence does not dominate millions of men and women.

An armed conflict between nations horrifies us. But the economic war is no better than an armed conflict. This is like a surgical operation. An economic war is prolonged torture. And its ravages are no less terrible than those depicted in the literature on war properly so called. We think nothing of the other because we are used to its deadly effects.

Many of us in India shudder to see blood spilled. Many of us resent cow-slaughter, but we think nothing of the slow torture through which by our greed we put our people and cattle. But because we are used to this lingering death, we think no more about it.

The movement against war is sound. I pray for its success. But I cannot help the gnawing fear that the movement will fail, if it does not touch the root of all evil—man's greed.

Will America, England and the other great nations of the West continue to exploit the so-called weaker or uncivilized races and hope to attain peace that the whole world is pining for? Or will Americans continue to prey upon one another, have commercial rivalries and yet expect to dictate peace to the world?

Not till the spirit is changed can the form be altered. The form is merely an expression of the spirit within. We may succeed in seemingly altering the form but the alteration will be a mere make-believe if the spirit within remains unalterable. A whited sepulchre still conceals beneath it the rotting flesh and bone.

Far be it from me to discount or under-rate the great effort that is being made in the West to kill the war-spirit. Mine is merely a word of caution as from a fellow-seeker who has been striving in his own humble manner after the same thing, may be in a different way, no doubt on a much smaller scale. But if the experiment demonstrably succeeds on the smaller field and, if those who are working on the larger field have not overtaken me, it will at least pave the way for a similar experiment on a large field.

I observe in the limited field in which I find myself, that unless I can reach the hearts of men and women, I am able to do nothing. I observe further that so long as the spirit of hate persists in some shape or other, it is impossible to establish peace or to gain our freedom by peaceful effort. We cannot love one another, if we hate Englishmen. We cannot love the Japanese and hate Englishmen. We must either let the Law of Love rule us through and through or not at all. Love among ourselves based on hatred of others breaks down under the slightest pressure. The fact is such love is never real love. It is an armed peace. And so it will be in this great movement in the West against war. War will only be stopped when the conscience of mankind has become sufficiently elevated to recognize the undisputed supremacy of the Law of Love in all the walks of life. Some say this will never come to pass. I shall retain the faith till the end of my earthly existence that it shall come to pass.

'Non-Violence—The Greatest Force'. *The Hindu*, 8 Nov. 1926. *EWMG*, pp. 241–2

65. *Ahimsa*: end and means

Let us first take the argument that we are justified in gaining our end by using brute force because the English gained theirs by using similar means. It is perfectly true that they used brute force and that it is possible for us to do likewise, but by using similar means we can get only the same thing that they got . . .

The means may be likened to a seed, the end to a tree; and there is just the same inviolable connection between the means and the end as there is between the seed and the tree.

Gandhi, *Hind Swaraj*, chap. XVI

66. Non-violence: both ends and means

4 August 1932

Non-violence for me is not a mere experiment. It is part of my life and the whole of the creed of *satyagraha*, non-co-operation, civil disobedience, and the like are necessary deductions from the fundamental proposition that non-violence is the law of life for human beings. For me it is both a means and an end and I am more than ever convinced that in the complex situation that faces India, there is no other way of gaining real freedom.

Letter to M. Asaf Ali. SN 19108. *EWMG*, p. 244

67. The importance of self-control

24 March 1932

In working out plans for self-restraint, attention must not for a single moment be withdrawn from the fact that we are all sparks of the divine and, therefore, partake of its nature, and since there can be no such thing as self-indulgence with the divine it must of necessity be foreign to human nature. If we get a hard grasp of that elementary fact, we should have no difficulty in attaining self-control, and that is exactly what we sing every evening.* You will recall that one of the verses says that the craving for self-indulgence abates only when one sees God face to face.

A letter. CW 8961. *EWMG*, p. 174

68. The need for self-purification

14 August 1932

One's respective *dharma* towards one's self, family, nation and the world cannot be divided into watertight compartments. The harm done to oneself or one's family cannot bring about the good of the nation. Similarly one cannot benefit the nation by acting against the world at large. Thus the purport is that we must sacrifice ourselves in the interest of the family, the family must do so for the nation and the nation for the world. But the sacrifice has to be pure. Therefore it all starts from self-purification. When the heart is pure, from moment to moment one's duty becomes apparent effortlessly.

A letter (H.). *Mahadevbhaini Diary*, vol. i, p. 362. *EWMG*, p. 183

69. Vows and self-discipline

14 October 1930

. . . I have dealt cursorily with the importance of vows, but it is perhaps necessary to consider at some length their bearing on a godly life. . . . A vow means unflinching determination, and helps us against temptations. Determination is worth nothing if it bends before discomfort.

The universal experience of humanity supports the view that progress is impossible without inflexible determination. There cannot be a vow to commit a sin. Such a vow represents a wicked nature. In the case of a vow first thought to be meritorious but later found to be sinful, there arises a clear necessity to give it up. But no one takes, or ought to take, vows about dubious matters. Vows can be taken only on points of universally recognized principles, which, however, we do not habitually act upon. The possibility of sin in such a case is more or less imaginary. A devotee of Truth cannot stop to consider if someone will not be injured by his telling the truth, for he believes that truth can never do harm. So also about total abstinence. The abstainer will either make an exception as regards medicine, or will be prepared to risk his life in fulfilment of his full vow. What does it matter if we happen to lose our lives through a pledge of total abstinence? There can be no guarantee that our lives will be prolonged by liquor, and even if life is thus prolonged for a moment, it may be ended the very next through some other agency. On the other hand, the example of a man who gives up his life rather than his pledge is likely to wean drunkards from liquor and thus become a great power for good in the world. Only they can hope some time to see God who have nobly determined to bear witness to the faith that is in them even at the cost of life itself.

Taking vows is not a sign of weakness but of strength. To do at any cost what one ought to do constitutes a vow. It becomes a bulwark of strength. It makes no difference whether such a resolve is called a vow or known by some other name. A man who says that he will do something 'as far as possible' betrays either his pride or his weakness, though he himself may attribute it to his humility. There is, in fact, not a trace of humility in such an attitude of mind. I have noticed in my own case, as well as in that of others, that the limitation 'as far as possible' provides a fatal loophole. To do something 'as far as possible' is to succumb to the very first temptation. There is no sense in saying that we will observe truth 'as far as possible'. Even as no business man will look at a note in which a man promises to pay a certain amount on a certain date 'as far as possible', so will God refuse to accept a promissory note drawn by a man who will observe truth 'as far as possible'.

God is the very image of the vow. God would cease to be God if He swerved from His own laws even by a hair's breadth. The sun is a great keeper of observances; hence the possibility of measuring time and publishing almanacs. He has created in us the faith that he always rises and will for ever continue to rise, and thereby given us a sense of security. All business depends upon men fulfilling their promises. There could be no commerce if merchants did not regard themselves as bound by their word to one another. We thus see that keeping a vow is a universal practice. Are such promises less necessary in character building or self-realization? We should, therefore, never doubt the necessity of vows for the purpose of self-purification and self-realization.

Letter to Narandas Gandhi (G.). *EWMG*, pp. 198–200

70. Discipline and the pursuit of non-violence

It takes a fairly strenuous course of training to attain to a mental state of non-violence. In daily life it has to be a course of discipline though we may not like it, like for instance the life of a soldier. But I agree that unless there is a hearty co-operation of the mind, the mere outward observance will be simply a mask, harmful both to the man himself and to others. The perfect state is reached only when mind and body and speech are in proper co-ordination. But it is always a case of intense mental struggle. It is not that I am incapable of anger, for instance, but I succeed on almost all occasions to keep my feelings under control. Whatever may be the result, there is always in me a conscious struggle to follow the law of non-violence deliberately and ceaselessly. Such a struggle leaves one stronger for it.

Non-violence is a weapon of the strong. With the weak it might easily be hypocrisy. Fear and love are contradictory terms. Love is reckless in giving away, oblivious as to what it gets in return. Love wrestles with the world as with itself and ultimately gains a mastery over all other feelings. My daily experience, as of those who are working with me, is that every problem would lend itself to solution if we are determined to make the law of truth and non-violence the law of life. For truth and non-violence are, to me, faces of the same coin.

Whether mankind will consciously follow the law of love I do not know. But that need not perturb us. The law will work, just as the law of gravitation will work whether we accept it or no. And just as a scientist will work wonders out of various applications of the laws of nature, even so a man who applies the law of love with scientific precision can work greater wonders. For the force of non-violence is infinitely more wonderful and subtle than the force of nature, like for instance electricity. The man who discovered for us the law of love was a far greater scientist than any of our modern scientists. Only our explorations have not gone far enough and so it is not possible for every one to see all its workings. Such, at any rate, is the hallucination, if it is one, under which I am labouring. The more I work at this law the more I feel the delight in life, the delight in the scheme of this universe. It gives me a peace and a meaning of the mysteries of nature that I have no power to describe.

'From S.S. Rajputana*—III'. *Young India*, 1 Oct. 1931

71. Cultivating inward purity

23 August 1932

It does not seem correct to me to say that it is part of man's nature to spend some time in idle thoughts. If there is a single exception to this, we cannot say that it is part of man's nature to do so. Actually, we find many exceptions. It is true that vast numbers of people are always busy thinking about all manner of things which they will do or will not do, and thus may be said to spend time in idle thoughts. If this were not so, it would not be necessary to emphasize the importance of concentration. What is important for us at present is this. We ourselves make all kinds of plans and resolutions, most of which we do not even remember after some time. All such thoughts are mental incontinence. Just as man dissipates his physical strength through ordinary incontinence, so he dissipates his mental strength through mental incontinence, and, as physical weakness affects the mind, so mental weakness affects the body. That is why I have defined *brahmacharya* in a wide sense and described even idle thoughts as violation of it.

By defining *brahmacharya* in a narrow sense, we have made it more difficult to observe. If we accept its wider definition and try to control all the eleven organs,* the control of the one most important organ would be much easier. You seem to believe in the heart of your hearts that physical activity prevents or hinders us from watching the progress of our inward purification. My experience is the opposite of this. Without inward purification, work cannot be done in a spirit of non-attachment. Hence the degree of inward purification can be judged mainly by the purity of our work. Anybody who tries to cultivate inward purity without doing work will more likely than not be in danger of falling into a delusion. I have seen many such instances.

Letter to Darbari Sadhu (G.). *Mahadevbhaini Diary*, vol. i, pp. 378–80. *EWMG*, pp. 202–3

72. The discipline of chastity

Chastity is one of the greatest disciplines without which the mind cannot attain requisite firmness. A man who is unchaste loses stamina, becomes emasculated and cowardly. He whose mind is given over to animal passions is not capable of any great effort. This can be proved by innumerable instances. What, then, is a married person to do is the question that arises naturally, and yet it need not. When a husband and wife gratify the passions, it is no less an animal indulgence on that account. Such an indulgence, except for perpetuating the race, is strictly prohibited. But a passive resister has to avoid even that very limited indulgence because he can have no desire for progeny. A married man, therefore, can observe perfect chastity.

Gandhi, *Hind Swaraj*, chap. XVII

73. The vow of *brahmacharya*

I pondered over *brahmacharya* and its implication, and my convictions took deep root. I discussed it with my co-workers. I had not realized then how indispensable it was for self-realization, but I clearly saw that one aspiring to serve humanity with his whole soul could not do without it. It was borne in upon me that I should have more and more occasions for service of the kind I was rendering,* and that I should find myself unequal to my task if I were engaged in the pleasures of family life and in the propagation of children.

In a word, I could not live both after the flesh and the spirit. On the present occasion, for instance, I should not have been able to throw myself into the fray, had my wife been expecting a baby. Without the observance of *brahmacharya* service of the family would be inconsistent with service of the community. With *brahmacharya* they would be perfectly consistent. . . .

I also took the plunge—the vow to observe *brahmacharya* for life. I must confess that I had not then fully realized the magnitude and immensity of the task I undertook. The difficulties are even today staring me in the face. The importance of the vow is being more and more borne in upon me. Life without *brahmacharya* appears to me to be insipid and animal-like. The brute by nature knows no self-restraint. Man is man because he is capable of, and only in so far as he exercises, self-restraint. What formerly appeared to me to be extravagant praise of *brahmacharya* in our religious books* seems now, with increasing clearness every day, to be absolutely proper and founded on experience.

Gandhi, *An Autobiography*, part IV, chap. XXV

74. Non-attachment

28 September 1929

It is quite true that there cannot be real non-attachment* without spiritual knowledge. Non-attachment does not include ignorance, cruelty and indifference. The work done by a person filled with the real spirit of non-attachment shines far more and succeeds better than that of a man who works with attachment. The latter may sometimes get upset and forget things because of worries; he may even feel ill-will and in the result may spoil the work. The man of non-attachment is free from all these defects.

Letter to Chhaganlal Joshi (G.). GN 5448. *EWMG*, p. 180

75. The necessity of service

1935

I have been asked by Sir S. Radhakrishnan* to answer the following three questions:

(1) What is your religion?
(2) How are you led to it?
(3) What is its bearing on social life?

My religion is Hinduism which, for me, is the religion of humanity and includes the best of all the religions known to me.

I take it that the present tense in the second question has been purposely used instead of the past. I am being led to my religion through Truth and Non-violence, i.e., love in the broadest sense. I often describe my religion as religion of Truth. Of late, instead of saying God is Truth I have been saying Truth is God, in order more fully to define my religion. I used at one time to know by heart the thousand names of God which a booklet in Hinduism gives in verse form and which perhaps tens of thousands recite every morning. But nowadays nothing so completely describes my God as Truth. Denial of God we have known. Denial of Truth we have not known. The most ignorant among mankind have some truth in them. We are all sparks of Truth. The sum total of these sparks is indescribable, as-yet-Unknown Truth, which is God. I am being daily led nearer to it by constant prayer.

The bearing of this religion on social life is, or has to be, seen in one's daily social contact. To be true to such religion one has to lose oneself in continuous and continuing service of all life. Realization of Truth is impossible without a complete merging of oneself in and identification with this limitless ocean of life. Hence, for me, there is no escape from social service; there is no happiness on earth beyond or apart from it. Social service here must be taken to include every department of life. In this scheme there is nothing low, nothing high. For all is one, though we *seem* to be many.

'Questions and Answers'. S. Radhakrishnan, *Contemporary Indian Philosophy*, 21. *EWMG*, pp. 158–9

76. Service of the lowliest

I am a humble seeker after Truth and bent upon finding It. I count no sacrifice too great for the sake of seeing God face to face. The whole of my activity, whether it may be called social, political, humanitarian or ethical, is directed to that end. And as I know that God is found more often in the lowliest of His creatures than in the high and mighty, I am struggling to reach the status of these. I cannot do so without their service. Hence my passion for the service of the suppressed classes.* And as I cannot render this service without entering politics, I find myself in them. Thus I am no master. I am but a struggling, erring, humble servant of India and therethrough [*sic*] of humanity.

Young India, 11 Sept. 1924. *CWMG*, vol. xxv, p. 117

77. Service includes politics

To see the universal and all-pervading Spirit of Truth face to face one must be able to love the meanest of creation as oneself. And a man who aspires after that cannot afford to keep out of any field of life. That is why my devotion to Truth has drawn me into the field of politics; and I can say without the slightest hesitation, and yet in all humility, that those who say that religion has nothing to do with politics do not know what religion means.

Gandhi, *An Autobiography*, 'Farewell'

a. Creating moral societies

78. 'Tinsel splendour'

The catastrophe at Paris* must have filled all the portions of the globe where the news reached with gloom. We can well imagine the feelings of the victims and the survivors. To us, these untoward happenings are not merely accidents but we look upon them as divine visitations from which we, if we chose, may learn rich lessons. To us, they show a grim tragedy behind all the tinsel splendour of the modern civilization. The ceaseless rush in which we are living does not leave any time for contemplating the full results of events such as have placed Paris in mourning for the time being. The dead will be soon forgotten, and in a very short time, Paris will again resume its usual gaiety as if nothing whatsoever had happened. Those, however, who will give the accident, if so it may be called, more than a passing thought, cannot fail to realize that behind all the splendour and behind all the glittering appearances there is something very real which is missed altogether. To us, the meaning is quite clear, namely, that all of us have to live the present life merely as a preparation for a future, far more certain and far more real. Nothing that the modern civilization can offer in the way of stability can ever make any more certain that which is inherently uncertain; that, when we come to think of it, the boast about the wonderful discoveries and the marvellous inventions of science, good as they undoubtedly are in themselves, is, after all, an empty boast. They offer nothing substantial to the struggling humanity, and the only consolation that one can derive from such visitations has to come from a firm faith not in the theory, but in the fact, of the existence of a future life and real Godhead. And that alone is worth having or worth cultivating which would enable us to realize our Maker and to feel that, after all, on this earth we are merely sojourners.

'Accident?', *Indian Opinion*, 20 Aug. 1903

79. The beginnings of a critique of modern civilization

14 October 1909

I think I should jot down the definite conclusions to which I have almost arrived after more matured observations made here.*

The thing was brewing in my mind, but there was no certain clear light. The heart and brain became more active after I accepted the invitation of the Peace and Arbitration Society to speak to them on 'East and West'. It came off last night.* . . . The following are the conclusions:

(1) There is no impassable barrier between East and West.

(2) There is no such thing as Western or European civilization, but there is a modern civilization, which is purely material.

(3) The people of Europe, before they were touched by modern civilization, had much in common with the people of the East; anyhow, the people of India and, even today, Europeans who are not touched by modern civilization are far better able to mix with the Indians than the offspring of that civilization.

(4) It is not the British people who are ruling India, but it is modern civilization, through its railways, telegraphs, telephones, and almost every invention which has been claimed to be a triumph of civilization.

(5) Bombay, Calcutta, and the other chief cities of India are the real plague spots.

(6) If British rule was replaced tomorrow by Indian rule based on modern methods, India would be no better, except that she would be able then to retain some of the money that is drained away to England; but, then, Indians would only become a second or fifth edition of Europe or America.

(7) East and West can only and really meet when the West has thrown overboard modern civilization, almost in its entirety. They can also seemingly meet when East has also adopted modern civilization. But that meeting would be an armed truce, even as it is between, say, Germany and England, both of which nations are living in the Hall of Death in order to avoid being devoured, the one by the other.

(8) It is simply impertinence for any man or any body of men to begin or contemplate reform of the whole world. To attempt to do so by means of highly artificial and speedy locomotion is to attempt the impossible.

(9) Increase of material comforts, it may be generally laid down, does not in any way whatsoever conduce to moral growth.

(10) Medical science is the concentrated essence of Black Magic. Quackery is infinitely preferable to what passes for high medical skill.

(11) Hospitals are the instruments that the Devil has been using for his own purpose, in order to keep his hold on his kingdom. They perpetuate vice, misery and degradation, and real slavery.

(12) I was entirely off the track when I considered that I should receive a medical training. It would be sinful for me in any way whatsoever to take part in the abominations that go on in the hospitals.

If there were no hospitals for venereal diseases, or even for consumptives, we should have less consumption, and less sexual vice amongst us.

(13) India's salvation consists in unlearning what she has learnt during the past fifty years.

The railways, telegraphs, hospitals, lawyers, doctors, and such like have all to go, and the so-called upper classes have to learn to live conscientiously and religiously and deliberately the simple peasant life, knowing it to be a life giving true happiness.

(14) Indians should wear no machine-made clothing, whether it comes out of European mills or Indian mills.

(15) England can help India to do this, and then she will have justified her hold of India. There seem to be many in England today who think likewise.

(16) There was true wisdom in the sages of old having so regulated society as to limit the material condition of the people: the rude plough of perhaps five thousand years ago is the plough of the husbandman today. Therein lies salvation. People live long, under such conditions, in comparative peace much greater than Europe has enjoyed after having taken up modern activity, and I feel that every enlightened man, certainly every Englishman, may, if he chooses, learn this truth and act according to it.

There is much more than I can write upon today, but the above is enough food for reflection. You will be able to check me when you find me to be wrong.

You will notice, too, that it is the true spirit of passive resistance that has brought me to the above almost definite conclusions. As a passive resister, I am unconcerned whether such a gigantic reformation, shall

I call it, can be brought about among people who derive their satisfaction from the present mad rush. If I realize the truth of it, I should
rejoice in following it, and, therefore, I could not wait until the whole
body of people had commenced. All of us who think likewise have to
take the necessary step; and the rest, if we are in the right, must
follow. The theory is there: our practice will have to approach it as
much as possible. Living in the midst of the rush, we may not be able
to shake ourselves free from all taint. Every time I get into a railway
car, use a motor-bus, I know that I am doing violence to my sense of
what is right. I do not fear the logical result on that basis. The visiting of England is bad, and any communication between South Africa
and India by means of Ocean's grey-hounds is also bad, and so on.
You and I can, and may, outgrow those things in our present bodies,
but the chief thing is to put our theory right. You will be seeing*
there all sorts and conditions of men. I, therefore, feel that I should
no longer withhold from you what I call the progressive step I have
taken mentally.

Letter to Henry Polak. SN 5127. *MPWMG*, vol. i, pp. 292–5

80. Modern civilization is irreligion

November 1909

CHAPTER VI. CIVILIZATION

READER.* Now you will have to explain what you mean by civilization.

EDITOR. It is not a question of what I mean. Several English
writers refuse to call that civilization which passes under that name.
Many books have been written upon that subject. Societies have been
formed to cure the nation of the evils of civilization. A great English
writer* has written a work called *Civilization: Its Cause and Cure*.
Therein he has called it a disease.

READER. Why do we not know this generally?

EDITOR. The answer is very simple. We rarely find people arguing
against themselves. Those who are intoxicated by modern civilization
are not likely to write against it. Their care will be to find out facts and
arguments in support of it, and this they do unconsciously, believing
it to be true. A man, whilst he is dreaming, believes in his dream; he
is undeceived only when he is awakened from his sleep. A man

labouring under the bane of civilization is like a dreaming man. What we usually read are the works of defenders of modern civilization, which undoubtedly claims among its votaries very brilliant and even some very good men. Their writings hypnotize us. And so, one by one, we are drawn into the vortex.

READER. This seems to be very plausible. Now will you tell me something of what you have read and thought of this civilization?

EDITOR. Let us first consider what state of things is described by the word 'civilization'. Its true test lies in the fact that people living in it make bodily welfare the object of life. We will take some examples. The people of Europe today live in better-built houses than they did a hundred years ago. This is considered an emblem of civilization, and this is also a matter to promote bodily happiness. Formerly, they wore skins, and used spears as their weapons. Now, they wear long trousers, and, for embellishing their bodies, they wear a variety of clothing, and, instead of spears, they carry with them revolvers containing five or more chambers. If people of a certain country, who have hitherto not been in the habit of wearing much clothing, boots, etc., adopt European clothing, they are supposed to have become civilized out of savagery. Formerly, in Europe, people ploughed their lands mainly by manual labour. Now, one man can plough a vast tract by means of steam engines and can thus amass great wealth. This is called a sign of civilization. Formerly, only a few men wrote valuable books. Now, anybody writes and prints anything he likes and poisons people's minds. Formerly, men travelled in wagons. Now, they fly through the air in trains at the rate of four hundred and more miles per day. This is considered the height of civilization. It has been stated that, as men progress, they shall be able to travel in airships and reach any part of the world in a few hours. Men will not need the use of their hands and feet. They will press a button, and they will have their clothing by their side. They will press another button, and they will have their newspaper. A third, and a motor-car will be in waiting for them. They will have a variety of delicately dished up food. Everything will be done by machinery. Formerly, when people wanted to fight with one another, they measured between them their bodily strength; now it is possible to take away thousands of lives by one man working behind a gun from a hill. This is civilization. Formerly, men worked in the open air only as much as they liked. Now thousands of workmen meet together and for the sake of maintenance work in factories or mines. Their condition is worse than that of beasts. They are obliged to work, at the risk of their lives, at most dangerous occupations, for the sake of millionaires.

Formerly, men were made slaves under physical compulsion. Now they are enslaved by temptation of money and of the luxuries that money can buy. There are now diseases of which people never dreamt before, and an army of doctors is engaged in finding out their cures, and so hospitals have increased. This is a test of civilization. Formerly, special messengers were required and much expense was incurred in order to send letters; today, anyone can abuse his fellow by means of a letter for one penny. True, at the same cost, one can send one's thanks also. Formerly, people had two or three meals consisting of home-made bread and vegetables; now, they require something to eat every two hours so that they have hardly leisure for anything else. What more need I say? All this you can ascertain from several authoritative books. These are all true tests of civilization. And if anyone speaks to the contrary, know that he is ignorant. This civilization takes note neither of morality nor of religion. Its votaries calmly state that their business is not to teach religion. Some even consider it to be a superstitious growth. Others put on the cloak of religion, and prate about morality. But, after twenty years' experience, I have come to the conclusion that immorality is often taught in the name of morality. Even a child can understand that in all I have described above there can be no inducement to morality. Civilization seeks to increase bodily comforts, and it fails miserably even in doing so.

This civilization is irreligion, and it has taken such a hold on the people in Europe that those who are in it appear to be half mad. They lack real physical strength or courage. They keep up their energy by intoxication. They can hardly be happy in solitude. Women, who should be the queens of households, wander in the streets or they slave away in factories. For the sake of a pittance, half a million women in England alone are labouring under trying circumstances in factories or similar institutions. This awful fact is one of the causes of the daily growing suffragette movement.

This civilization is such that one has only to be patient and it will be self-destroyed. According to the teaching of Mahomed this would be considered a Satanic Civilization. Hinduism calls it the Black Age. I cannot give you an adequate conception of it. It is eating into the vitals of the English nation. It must be shunned. Parliaments are really emblems of slavery. If you will sufficiently think over this, you will entertain the same opinion and cease to blame the English. They rather deserve our sympathy. They are a shrewd nation and I therefore believe that they will cast off the evil. They are enterprising and industrious, and their mode of thought is not inherently immoral. Neither are they bad at heart. I therefore respect them. Civilization is not an incurable disease, but it should never be forgotten that the English people are at present afflicted by it.

.   .   .

CHAPTER XIII. WHAT IS TRUE CIVILIZATION?

READER. You have denounced railways, lawyers and doctors. I can see that you will discard all machinery. What, then, is civilization?

EDITOR. The answer to that question is not difficult. I believe that the civilization India has evolved is not to be beaten in the world. Nothing can equal the seeds sown by our ancestors. Rome went, Greece shared the same fate; the might of the Pharaohs was broken; Japan has become westernized; of China nothing can be said; but India is still, somehow or other, sound at the foundation. The people of Europe learn their lessons from the writings of the men of Greece or Rome, which exist no longer in their former glory. In trying to learn from them, the Europeans imagine that they will avoid the mistakes of Greece and Rome. Such is their pitiable condition. In the midst of all this India remains immovable and that is her glory. It is a charge against India that her people are so uncivilized, ignorant and stolid, that it is not possible to induce them to adopt any changes. It is a charge really against our merit. What we have tested and found true on the anvil of experience, we dare not change. Many thrust their advice upon India, and she remains steady. This is her beauty: it is the sheet-anchor of our hope.

Civilization is that mode of conduct which points out to man the path of duty. Performance of duty and observance of morality are convertible terms. To observe morality is to attain mastery over our mind and our passions. So doing, we know ourselves.

Gandhi, *Hind Swaraj*

81. The evil spirit of modern civilization

10 May 1910

I have ventured utterly to condemn modern civilization because I hold that the spirit of it is evil. It is possible to show that some of its incidents are good, but I have examined its tendency in the scale of ethics. I distinguish between the ideals of individuals who have risen superior to their environment, as also between Christianity and modern civilization. Its activity is by no means confined to Europe. Its blasting influence is now being exhibited in full force in Japan. And it now threatens to overwhelm India. History teaches us that men who are in the whirlpool, except in the cases of individuals, will have to work out their destiny in it; but I do submit that those who are still outside its influence, and those who have a well-tried civilization to guide them, should be helped to remain where they are, if only as a measure of prudence. I claim to have tested the life which modern civilization has to give, as also that of the ancient civilization, and I cannot help most strongly contesting the idea that the Indian population requires to be roused by 'the lash of competition and the other material and sensuous, as well as intellectual, stimuli'; I cannot admit that these will add a single inch to its moral stature.

Letter to W. J. Wybergh.* *Indian Opinion*, 21 May 1910

82. 'Satanic'

1 December 1931

Western civilization is material, frankly material. It measures progress by the progress of matter—railways, conquest of disease, conquest of the air. These are triumphs of civilization according to Western measure. No one says, 'Now the people are more truthful or more humble.' I judge it by my own test and I use the word 'Satanic' in describing it. You set such store by the temporal, external things. The essential of Eastern civilization is that it is spiritual, immaterial. The fruits of Western civilization the East may approach with avidity but with a sense of guilt. Your idea is the more you want the better you are, and you don't fall far short in your belief. Your civilization has gone from one stage to another. There is no end to it. You are proud of your conquest over nature, but this makes no appeal to me. You might see me fly tomorrow, but I should be feeling guilty about it. Suppose all your London tubes and buses were taken away, I should say, 'Thank God I shall be able to walk to my quarters at Bow,* even if takes me three hours.'

Interview with journalists. *The Friend*, 11 Dec. 1931. *Reconciliation*, Jan. 1932. *MPWMG*, vol. i, p. 328

83. Experiments with simplicity

The tendency towards simplicity began in Durban.* But the Johannesburg house came in for much severer overhauling in the light of Ruskin's teaching.*

  I introduced as much simplicity as was possible in a barrister's house. It was impossible to do without a certain amount of furniture. The change was more internal than external. The liking for doing personally all the physical labour increased.

Gandhi, *An Autobiography*, part IV, chap. XXIII

84. Phoenix Settlement

The majority of the settlers at present established on the said settlement* joined the said settlement for the following objects and purposes . . .

(1) So far as possible to order their lives so as to be able ultimately to earn their living by handicraft or agriculture carried on without the aid so far as possible of machinery;

. . .

(3) To follow and promote the ideals set forth by Tolstoy and Ruskin* in their lives and works;

'The Phoenix Trust Deed'. *Indian Opinion*, 14 Sept. 1912

85. Renunciation

28 October 1930

It will perhaps be worthwhile further to consider a principle which has been created along with mankind. *Yajna* is duty to be performed, or service to be rendered, all the twenty-four hours of the day, and hence a maxim like 'The powers of the good are always exercised for a benevolent purpose' is inappropriate, if benevolence has any taste of favour about it. To serve without desire is to favour not others, but ourselves even as in discharging a debt we serve only ourselves, lighten our burden and fulfil our duty. Again, not only the good, but all of us are bound to place our resources at the disposal of humanity. And if such is the law, as evidently it is, indulgence ceases to hold a place in life and gives way to renunciation. For human beings renunciation itself is enjoyment. This is what differentiates man from the beast. Some object that life thus understood becomes dull and devoid of art, and leaves no room for the householder. But I think in saying this they misinterpret the word 'renunciation'. Renunciation here does not mean abandoning the world and retiring into the forest.

The spirit of renunciation should rule all the activities of life. A householder does not cease to be one if he regards life as a duty rather than as an indulgence. A cobbler, a cultivator, a tradesman or a barber may be inspired in their work or activities either by the spirit of renunciation or merely by the desire for self-indulgence. A merchant who carries on his business in a spirit of sacrifice will have crores passing through his hands, but he will, if he follows the law, use his abilities for service. He will, therefore, not cheat or speculate, will lead a simple life, will not injure a living soul and will lose millions rather than harm anybody. Let no one run away with the idea that this type of merchant exists only in my imagination. Fortunately for the world, he does exist in the West as well as in the East. It is true such merchants may be counted on one's fingers but the type ceases to be imaginary as soon as even one living specimen can be found to answer to it . . .

A life of sacrifice is the pinnacle of art and is full of true joy. Such life is the source of ever fresh springs of joy which never dry up and never satiate. *Yajna* is not *yajna* if one feels it to be burdensome or annoying. Self-indulgence leads to destruction and renunciation to immortality. Joy has no independent existence. It depends upon our attitude to life. One man will enjoy theatrical scenery, another the ever new scenes which unfold themselves in the sky. Joy, therefore, is a matter of education. We shall delight in things which we have been taught to delight in as children. And illustrations can be easily cited of different national tastes.

Again, many sacrificers imagine that they are free to receive from the people everything they need and many things they do not need, because they are rendering disinterested service. Directly this idea sways a man, he ceases to be a servant and becomes a tyrant over the people. One who would serve others will not waste a thought upon his own comforts, which he leaves to be attended to or neglected by his Master on high. He will not, therefore, encumber himself with everything that comes his way; he will take only what he strictly needs and leave the rest. He will be calm, free from anger and unruffled in mind even if he finds himself inconvenienced. His service, like virtue, is its own reward, and he will rest content with it.

Again, one dare not be negligent in service or be behindhand with it. He who thinks that he must be diligent only in his personal business, and unpaid public business may be done in any way and at any time he chooses, has still to learn the very rudiments of the science of sacrifice. Voluntary service of others demands the best of which one is capable, and must take precedence over service of self. In fact, the pure devotee consecrates himself to the service of humanity without any reservation whatever.

Letter to Narandas Gandhi (G.). *EWMG*, pp. 381–3

86. Voluntary poverty

23 September 1931

You will be astonished to hear from me that, although to all appearances my mission is political, I would ask you to accept my assurance that its roots are—if I may use that term—spiritual. It is commonly known, though perhaps not believed, that I claim that at least my politics are not divorced from morality, from spirituality, from religion. I have claimed—and the claim is based upon extensive experience—that a man who is trying to discover and follow the will of God cannot possibly leave a single field of life untouched. I came also, in the course of my service, to the conclusion that if there was any field of life where morality, where truth, where fear of God, were not essential, that field should be given up entirely.

But I found also that the politics of the day are no longer a concern of kings, but that they affect the lowest strata of society. And I found, through bitter experience that, if I wanted to do social service, I could not possibly leave politics alone.

Do not please consider that I want to speak to you tonight about politics and somehow or other connect voluntary poverty with politics. That is not my intention. I have simply given you an introduction how I came to believe in the necessity of voluntary poverty for any social worker or for any political worker who wanted to remain untouched by the hideous immorality and untruth that one smells today in ordinary politics. The stench that comes from that life has appeared to some to be so suffocating that they came to the conclusion that politics were not for a God-fearing man.

Had that been really so, I feel that it would have been a disaster for mankind. Find out for yourselves, in the light of what I am now saying, whether directly or indirectly every activity of yours today in this one of the greatest cities of the world is not touched by politics.

Well, then, when I found myself drawn into the political coil, I asked myself what was necessary for me in order to remain absolutely untouched by immorality, by untruth, by what is known as political gain.

In the course of my search, I made several discoveries which I must, for tonight, leave alone. But, if I am not mistaken, this necessity for poverty came to me first of all.

I do not propose to take you through all the details of that act or performance—interesting and, to me, sacred though they are—but I can only tell you that it was a difficult struggle in the beginning and it was a wrestle with my wife and—as I can vividly recall—with my children also.

Be that as it may, I came definitely to the conclusion that, if I had to serve the people in whose midst my life was cast and of whose difficulties I was witness from day to day, I must discard all wealth, all possessions.

I cannot tell you with truth that, when this belief came to me, I discarded everything immediately. I must confess to you that progress at first was slow. And now, as I recall those days of struggle, I remember that it was also painful in the beginning. But, as days went by, I saw that I had to throw overboard many other things which I used to consider as mine, and a time came when it became a matter of positive joy to give up those things. And one after another then, by almost geometric progression, the things slipped away from me. And, as I am describing my experiences, I can say a great burden fell off my shoulders, and I felt that I could now walk with ease and do my work also in the service of my fellow-men with great comfort and still greater joy. The possession of anything then became a troublesome thing and a burden.

Exploring the cause of that joy, I found that, if I kept anything as my own, I had to defend it against the whole world. I found also that there were many people who did not have the thing, although they wanted it; and I would have to seek police assistance also if hungry, famine-stricken people, finding me in a lonely place, wanted not merely to divide the thing with me but to dispossess me. And I said to myself: if they want it and would take it, they do so not from any malicious motive, but they would do it because theirs was a greater need than mine.

And then I said to myself: possession seems to me to be a crime. I can only possess certain things when I know that others, who also want to possess similar things, are able to do so. But we know—every one of us can speak from experience—that such a thing is an impossibility. Therefore, the only thing that can be possessed by all is non-possession, not to have anything whatsoever. In other words, a willing surrender.

You might then well say to me: but you are keeping many things on your body even as you are speaking about voluntary poverty and not possessing anything whatsoever! And your taunt would be right, if you only superficially understood the meaning of the thing that I am speaking about just now. It is really the spirit behind. Whilst you have the body, you will have to have something to clothe the body with also. But then you will take for the body not all that you can get, but the least possible, the least with which you can do. You will take for your house not many mansions, but the least cover that you can do with. And similarly with reference to your food and so on.

Now you see that there is here a daily conflict between what you and we understand today as civilization and the state which I am picturing to you as a state of bliss and a desirable state. On the one hand, the basis of culture or civilization is understood to be the multiplication of all your wants. If you have one room, you will desire to have two rooms, three rooms, the more the merrier. And similarly, you will want to have as much furniture as you can put in your house, and so on, endlessly. And the more you possess the better culture you represent, or some such thing. I am putting it, perhaps, not as nicely as the advocates of that civilization would put it, but I am putting it to you in the manner I understand it.

And, on the other hand, you find the less you possess the less you want, the better you are. And better for what? Not for enjoyment of this life, but for enjoyment of personal service to your fellow-beings; service to which you dedicate yourselves, body, soul and mind.

Well, here you find there is ample room for hypocrisy and humbug, because a man or a woman may easily deceive himself or herself and deceive his or her neighbours also, by saying: 'In spirit I have given up all possessions, and yet externally I am possessing these things; you must not examine my deed, you must examine my intention; and of my intention only I must remain the sole witness.' That is a trap, and a death trap. How are you then to justify the possession even of a piece of cloth two or three or four yards, say, in length and a yard in width? How can you justify even the possession of that piece of cloth in order to cover your body somewhat, when you know that, if you left that piece of cloth alone, even that would be taken over by someone—not maliciously again—but because he would want it for he has not even so much as that piece of cloth? I am witness, eye-witness, of millions of human beings who have not even so much as that piece of cloth. How are you then to justify your act of possessing this thing with your intention not to possess anything at all?

Well, there is a remedy provided for this dilemma, this difficulty, this contradiction in life—that if you must possess these things, you must hold them at the disposal of those who want them. What happens is that, if somebody comes and wants your piece of cloth, you are not going to keep it from him, you are not going to shut any doors, you are certainly not going to the policeman to ask him to help you to keep these things.

And you have also got to be content with what the world will give you. The world may give you that piece of cloth or may not because, if you do not possess anything, naturally you do not possess the token coin with which you may buy clothing or food. You have got then to live purely on the charity of the world. And even when charitable people give you something, that something does not become your possession. You simply retain it with the fullest intention of that thing being surrendered to anybody who wishes to take it. If somebody comes and uses force against you to dispossess you, you may not go and report to the next policeman you meet and say you have been assaulted. You will not have been assaulted.

Well, that, to my mind, is the meaning of voluntary poverty . . .

. . . I can only throw out this hint to those who can appreciate the necessity of voluntary poverty for service. I have not tonight presented this blessed thing for the acceptance of all: though let me add that, in the innermost recesses of my heart, I feel that the world would not go all wrong, would not become a world of idiots, if all of us took the vow of voluntary poverty. But I know that this is almost an impossible thing. Everything is possible for God but, humanly speaking, it is wise to say that it is an impossible thing. But it is not an impossible thing; indeed, I hold it to be absolutely indispensable that those who give themselves wholly to the service of their fellow-beings must take the vow of voluntary poverty.

Speech at Guildhouse church, London. *The Guildhouse*, 23 Sept. 1931. *EWMG*, pp. 115–23

87. Tolstoy Farm—self-reliance

Upon the Farm oranges, apricots and plums grew in such abundance that during the season the Satyagrahis could have their fill of the fruit and yet have a surplus.

The spring was about 500 yards away from our quarters, and the water had to be fetched on carrying poles.

Here we insisted that we should not have any servants either for the household work or as far as might be even for the farming and building operations. Everything therefore from cooking to scavenging was done with our own hands . . .

As I have already stated, we wanted to be self-reliant as far as possible even in erecting buildings . . .

Every one had to go to Johannesburg on some errand or other. Children liked to go there just for the fun of it. I also had to go there on business. We therefore made a rule that we could go there by rail only on the public business of our little commonwealth, and then too travel third class. Any one who wanted to go on a pleasure trip must go on foot, and carry home-made provisions with him. No one might spend anything on his food in the city. Had it not been for these drastic rules, the money saved by living in a rural locality would have been wasted in railway fares and city picnics. The provisions carried were of the simplest: home-baked bread made from coarse wheat flour ground at home, from which the bran was not removed, ground-nut butter also prepared at home, and home-made marmalade. We had purchased an iron hand-mill for grinding wheat. Groundnut butter was made by roasting and then grinding groundnuts, and was four times cheaper than ordinary butter. As for oranges, we had plenty of them on the Farm . . .

A paragraph may be devoted to our sanitary arrangements. In spite of the large number of settlers, one could not find refuse or dirt any-where on the Farm. All rubbish was buried in the trenches sunk for the purpose. No water was permitted to be thrown on the roads. All waste water was collected in buckets and used to water the trees. Leavings of food and vegetable refuse were utilized as manure. A square pit one foot and a half deep was sunk near the house to receive the nightsoil, which was fully covered with the excavated earth and which therefore did not give out any smell. . . . A small spade is the means of salvation from a great nuisance. Leaving nightsoil, cleaning the nose or spitting on the road is a sin against God as well as human-ity and betrays a sad want of consideration for others.

M. K. Gandhi, *Satyagraha in South Africa*, chap. XXXIV

88. Self-reliance—*swadeshi*

14 February 1916

After much thinking, I have arrived at a definition of *swadeshi** that perhaps best illustrates my meaning. *Swadeshi* is that spirit in us which restricts us to the use and service of our immediate surroundings to the exclusion of the more remote. Thus, as for religion, in order to satisfy the requirements of the definition, I must restrict myself to my ances-tral religion. That is the use of my immediate religious surroundings. If I find it defective, I should serve it by purging it of its defects. In the domain of politics, I should make use of the indigenous institutions and serve them by curing them of their proved defects. In that of eco-nomics, I should use only things that are produced by my immediate neighbours and serve those industries by making them more efficient and complete where they might be found wanting.

Speech on *swadeshi* at Missionary Conference, Madras. *The Hindu*, 28 Feb. 1916. *Young India*, 21 June 1919

89. Eradicating machinery

READER. When you speak of driving out Western civilization, I suppose you will also say that we want no machinery.

EDITOR. . . . It is machinery that has impoverished India. It is difficult to measure the harm that Manchester has done to us. It is due to Manchester that Indian handicraft has all but disappeared.

But I make a mistake. How can Manchester be blamed? We wore Manchester cloth and this is why Manchester wove it. I was delighted when I read about the bravery of Bengal.* There were no cloth-mills in that Presidency. They were, therefore, able to restore the original hand-weaving occupation. It is true Bengal encourages the mill-industry of Bombay. If Bengal had proclaimed a boycott of *all* machine-made goods, it would have been much better.

Machinery has begun to desolate Europe. . . . Machinery is the chief symbol of modern civilization; it represents a great sin.

The workers in the mills of Bombay have become slaves. The condition of the women working in the mills is shocking. When there were no mills, these women were not starving. If the machinery craze grows in our country, it will become an unhappy land. It may be considered a heresy, but I am bound to say that it were better for us to send money to Manchester and to use flimsy Manchester cloth than to multiply mills in India. By using Manchester cloth we only waste our money; but by reproducing Manchester in India, we shall keep our money at the price of our blood, because our very moral being will be sapped, and I call in support of my statement the very mill-hands as witnesses. And those who have amassed wealth out of factories are not likely to be better than other rich men. It would be folly to assume that an Indian Rockefeller would be better than the American Rockefeller. Impoverished India can become free, but it will be hard for any India made rich through immorality to regain its freedom. I fear we shall have to admit that moneyed men support British rule; their interest is bound up with its stability. Money renders a man helpless. The other thing which is equally harmful is sexual vice. Both are poison. A snake-bite is a lesser poison than these two, because the former merely destroys the body but the latter destroy body, mind and soul. We need not, therefore, be pleased with the prospect of the growth of the mill-industry.

READER. Are the mills, then, to be closed down?

EDITOR. That is difficult. It is no easy task to do away with a thing that is established. We, therefore, say that the non-beginning of a thing is supreme wisdom. We cannot condemn mill-owners; we can but pity them. It would be too much to expect them to give up their mills, but we may implore them not to increase them. If they would be good they would gradually contract their business. They can establish in thousands of households the ancient and sacred handlooms and they can buy out the cloth that may be thus woven. Whether the mill-owners do this or not, people can cease to use machine-made goods.

READER. You have so far spoken about machine-made cloth, but there are innumerable machine-made things. We have either to import them or to introduce machinery into our country.

EDITOR. Indeed, our goods even are made in Germany. What need, then, to speak of matches, pins and glassware? My answer can be only one. What did India do before these articles were introduced? Precisely the same should be done today. As long as we cannot make pins without machinery, so long will we do without them. The tinsel splendour of glassware we will have nothing to do with, and we will make wicks, as of old, with home-grown cotton and use hand-made earthen saucers for lamps. So doing, we shall save our eyes and money and support *swadeshi* and so shall we attain Home Rule.

It is not to be conceived that all men will do all these things at one time or that some men will give up all machine-made things at once. But, if the thought is sound, we shall always find out what we can give up and gradually cease to use it. What a few may do, others will copy; and the movement will grow like the cocoanut of the mathematical problem. What the leaders do, the populace will gladly do in turn. The matter is neither complicated nor difficult. You and I need not wait until we can carry others with us. Those will be the losers who will not do it, and those who will not do it, although they appreciate the truth, will deserve to be called cowards.

READER. What, then, of the tram-cars and electricity?

EDITOR. This question is now too late. It signifies nothing. If we are to do without the railways we shall have to do without the tram-cars. Machinery is like a snake-hole which may contain from one to a hundred snakes. Where there is machinery there are large cities; and where there are large cities, there are tram-cars and railways; and there only does one see electric light.

English villages do not boast of any of these things. Honest physicians will tell you that where means of artificial locomotion have increased, the health of the people has suffered. I remember that when in a European town there was a scarcity of money, the receipts of the tramway company, of the lawyers and of the doctors went down and people were less unhealthy. I cannot recall a single good point in connection with machinery. Books can be written to demonstrate its evils.

READER. Is it a good point or a bad one that all you are saying will be printed through machinery?

EDITOR. This is one of those instances which demonstrate that sometimes poison is used to kill poison. This, then, will not be a good point regarding machinery. As it expires, the machinery, as it were, says to us: 'Beware and avoid me. You will derive no benefits from me and the benefit that may accrue from printing will avail only those who are infected with the machinery-craze.'

Do not, therefore, forget the main thing. It is necessary to realize that machinery is bad. We shall then be able gradually to do away with it. Nature has not provided any way whereby we may reach a desired goal all of a sudden. If, instead of welcoming machinery as a boon, we should look upon it as an evil, it would ultimately go.

Gandhi, *Hind Swaraj*, chap. XIX

90. The monster-god of materialism

22 December 1916

Before I take you to the field of my experiences and experiments, it is perhaps best to have a mutual understanding about the title of this evening's address: *Does economic progress clash with real progress?* By economic progress, I take it, we mean material advancement without limit and by real progress we mean moral progress, which again is the same thing as progress of the permanent element in us. The subject may therefore be stated thus: 'Does not moral progress increase in the same proportion as material progress?' I know that this is a wider proposition than the one before us. But I venture to think that we always mean the larger one even when we lay down the smaller. For we know enough of science to realize that there is no such thing as perfect rest or repose in this visible universe of ours. If therefore material progress does not clash with moral progress, it must necessarily advance the latter. Nor can we be satisfied with the clumsy way in which sometimes those who cannot defend the larger proposition put their case. They seem to be obsessed with the concrete case of thirty millions of India stated by the late Sir William Wilson Hunter* to be living on one meal a day. They say that before we can think or talk of their moral welfare, we must satisfy their daily wants. With these, they say, material progress spells moral progress. And then is taken a sudden jump: what is true of thirty millions is true of the universe. They forget that hard cases make bad law. I need hardly say to you how ludicrously absurd this deduction would be. No one has ever suggested that grinding pauperism can lead to anything else than moral degradation. Every human being has a right to live and therefore to find the wherewithal to feed himself and where necessary to clothe and house himself. But, for this very simple performance, we need no assistance from economists or their laws.

'Take no thought for the morrow'* is an injunction which finds an echo in almost all the religious scriptures of the world. In well-ordered society, the securing of one's livelihood should be and is found to be the easiest thing in the world. Indeed, the test of orderliness in a country is not the number of millionaires it owns, but the absence of starvation among its masses. The only statement that has to be examined is whether it can be laid down as a law of universal application that material advancement means moral progress.

Now let us take a few illustrations.

.   .   .

I should not have laboured my point as I have done, if I did not believe that, in so far as we have made the modern materialistic craze our goal, in so far are we going downhill in the path of progress. I hold that economic progress in the sense I have put it is antagonistic to real progress. Hence the ancient ideal has been the limitation of activities promoting wealth. This does not put an end to all material ambition. We should still have, as we have always had, in our midst people who make the pursuit of wealth their aim in life. But we have always recognized that it is a fall from the ideal. It is a beautiful thing to know that the wealthiest among us have often felt that to have remained voluntarily poor would have been a higher state for them. That you cannot serve God and Mammon is an economic truth of the highest value. We have to make our choice. Western nations today are groaning under the heel of the monster-god of materialism. Their moral growth has become stunted. They measure their progress in

£.s.d. American wealth has become standard. She is the envy of the other nations. I have heard many of our countrymen say that we will gain American wealth but avoid its methods. I venture to suggest that such an attempt if it were made is foredoomed to failure.

We cannot be 'wise, temperate and furious'* in a moment. I would have our leaders teach us to be morally supreme in the world. This land of ours was once, we are told, the abode of the gods. It is not possible to conceive gods inhabiting a land which is made hideous by the smoke and the din of mill chimneys and factories and whose roadways are traversed by rushing engines dragging numerous cars crowded with men mostly who know not what they are after, who are often absent-minded, and whose tempers do not improve by being uncomfortably packed like sardines in boxes and finding themselves in the midst of utter strangers who would oust them if they could and whom they would in their turn oust similarly. I refer to these things because they are held to be symbolical of material progress. But they add not an atom to our happiness.

Speech at Muir College Economic Society, Allahabad. *The Leader*, 25 Dec. 1916. *EWMG*, pp. 94–8

91. Industrialism not inevitable

Of course, industrialism is like a force of Nature, but it is given to man to control Nature and to conquer her forces. His dignity demands from him resolution in the face of overwhelming odds. Our daily life is such a conquest . . .

What is industrialism but a control of the majority by a small minority? There is nothing attractive about it, nor is there anything inevitable about it. If the majority simply wills to say 'no' to the blandishments of the minority, the latter is powerless for mischief.

'Snares of Satan'. *Young India*, 6 Aug. 1925

92. A humanitarian industrial policy—hand-spinning

A humanitarian industrial policy for India means to me a glorified revival of hand-spinning, for through it alone can pauperism, which is blighting the lives of millions of human beings in their own cottages in this land, be immediately removed. Everything else may thereafter be added, so as to increase the productive capacity of this country. I would therefore have all the young men with a scientific training to utilize their skill in making the spinning-wheel, if it is possible, a more efficient instrument of production in India's cottages.

'A Student's Questions'. *Young India*, 17 Dec. 1925

93. Appropriate mass production

16 October 1931

QUESTION. Then do you not envisage mass production as an ideal future of India?

ANSWER. Oh yes, mass production, certainly, but not based on force. After all, the message of the spinning-wheel is that. It is mass production, but mass production in people's own homes. If you multiply individual production to millions of times, would it not give you mass production on a tremendous scale? But I quite understand that your 'mass production' is a technical term for production by the fewest number through the aid of highly complicated machinery. I have said to myself that that is wrong. My machinery must be of the most elementary type which I can put in the homes of the millions. Under my system, again, it is labour which is the current coin, not metal. Any person who can use his labour has that coin, has wealth. He converts his labour into cloth, he converts his labour into grain. If he wants paraffin oil, which he cannot himself produce, he uses his surplus grain for getting the oil. It is exchange of labour on free, fair and equal terms—hence it is no robbery. . . .

Look, again, at another advantage that this system affords. You can multiply it to any extent. But concentration of production *ad infinitum* can only lead to unemployment. You may say that workers thrown out of work by the introduction of improved machinery will find occupation in other jobs. But in an organized country where there are only fixed and limited avenues of employment, where the worker has become highly skilled in the use of one particular kind of machinery, you know from your own experience that this is hardly possible.

Interview with an American correspondent. *Harijan*, 2 Nov. 1934

94. Alternative to industrialization

25 August 1946

I do not believe that industrialization is necessary in any case for any country. It is much less so for India. Indeed, I believe that Independent India can only discharge her duty towards a groaning world by adopting a simple but ennobled life by developing her thousands of cottage industries and living at peace with the world. High thinking is inconsistent with complicated material life based on high speed imposed on us by Mammon worship. All the graces of life are possible only when we learn the art of living nobly.

'Alternative to Industrialism'. *Harijan*, 1 Sept. 1946

95. Real India is in its villages

18 April 1947

I will have no regrets if the money invested in these machines is reduced to dust. True India lies in its seven *lakh** villages. Do you know that big cities like London have exploited India and the big cities of India in turn have exploited its villages? That is how palatial mansions have come up in big cities and villages have become impoverished. I want to infuse new life into these villages. I do not say that all the mills in cities should be demolished. But we should be vigilant and start afresh wherever we happen to make a mistake. We should stop exploiting the villages and should closely examine the injustice done to the villages and strengthen their economic structure.

Talk with Manu Gandhi (G.). *Biharni Komi Agman*, pp. 220–1.
MPWMG, vol. iii, p. 532

96. The importance of physical labour

QUESTION. Do you think that all should earn their livelihood by the sweat of the brow?

ANSWER. Certainly. Everyone does not do so and that is why dire poverty has arisen in the world and especially so in India. This is also the main cause of ill-health and the immense greed for acquisition of wealth. If all earned their livelihood by physical work, greed would decrease And much of the power to acquire wealth would weaken automatically. If physical labour is done, ill-health will almost disappear and the greatest gain will be the complete obliteration of the distinction between high and low in society.

'*Varnadharma* and the Duty of Labour—I' (H.). *Hindi Navajivan*, 6 Feb. 1930

97. Duty of bread labour

Mere mental, that is, intellectual labour is for the soul and is its own satisfaction. It should never demand payment. In the ideal State, doctors, lawyers and the like will work solely for the benefit of society, not for self. Obedience to the law of bread labour* will bring about a silent revolution in the structure of society. Man's triumph will consist in substituting the struggle for existence by the struggle for mutual service. The law of the brute will be replaced by the law of man.

Return to the villages means a definite voluntary recognition of the duty of bread labour and all it connotes.

'Duty of Bread Labour'. *Harijan*, 29 June 1935

98. The well-being of all

14 October 1946

Man should earnestly desire the well-being of all God's creation and pray that he may have the strength to do so. In desiring the well-being of all* lies his own welfare; he who desires only his own or his community's welfare is selfish and it can never be well with him.

Written message to prayer meeting. *Harijan*, 20 Oct. 1946

99. Rights flow from duties

I want to deal with one great evil that is afflicting society today. The capitalist and the zamindar* talk of their rights, the labourer on the other hand of his, the prince of his divine right to rule, the *ryot** of his to resist it. If all simply insist on rights and no duties, there will be utter confusion and chaos.

If instead of insisting on rights everyone does his duty, there will immediately be the rule of order established among mankind. There is no such thing as the divine right of kings to rule and the humble duty of the *ryots* to pay respectful obedience to their masters. Whilst it is true that these hereditary inequalities must go as being injurious to the well-being of society, the unabashed assertion of rights of the hitherto down-trodden millions is equally injurious, if not more so to the same well-being. The latter behaviour is probably calculated to injure the millions rather than the few claimants of divine or other rights. . . . It is, therefore, necessary to understand the correlation of rights and duties.

I venture to suggest that rights that do not flow directly from duty well performed are not worth having.

'Rights or Duties?' *Harijan*, 6 July 1947

100. Non-possession and social relations

26 August 1930

Non-possession is allied to non-stealing. A thing not originally stolen must nevertheless be classified as stolen property if we possess it without needing it. Possession implies provision for the future. A seeker after truth, a follower of the law of love, cannot hold anything against tomorrow. God never stores for the morrow; He never creates more than what is strictly needed for the moment. If, therefore, we repose faith in His providence, we should be assured that He will give us every day our daily bread, meaning everything we require. Saints and men of faith have always found justification for it from their experience. Our ignorance or negligence of the Divine Law, which gives to man from day to day his daily bread and no more, has given rise to inequalities with all the miseries attendant upon them. The rich have a superfluous store of things which they do not need, and which are therefore neglected and wasted; while millions starve to death for want of sustenance. If each retained possession only of what he needed, no one would be in want and all would live in contentment. As it is, the rich are discontented no less than the poor. The poor man would fain become a millionaire, and the millionaire a multi-millionaire. The poor are not content if they get their daily needs. They have a right, however, to get enough for their daily needs and it is the duty of society to help them to satisfy them. The rich should take the initiative in dispossession with a view to universal diffusion of the spirit of contentment. If only they keep their own property within moderate limits, the starving will be easily fed and will learn the lesson of contentment along with the rich.

Perfect fulfilment of the ideal of non-possession requires that man should, like the birds, have no roof over his head, no clothing and no stock of food for the morrow. He will indeed need his daily bread, but it will be God's business, and not his, to provide it. Only very very few, if any at all, can reach this ideal. We ordinary seekers may not be repelled by the seeming impossibility. But we must keep the ideal constantly before us, and in the light thereof critically examine our possessions and try to reduce them. Civilization, in the real sense of the term, consists not in the multiplication, but in the deliberate and voluntary reduction of wants. This alone promotes real happiness and contentment, and increases the capacity for service. Judging by this criterion, we find that in the Ashram we possess many things the necessity for which cannot be proved, and we thus tempt our neighbours to steal. If people try, they can reduce their wants and, as the latter diminish, they become happier, more peaceful and healthier. From the standpoint of pure truth, the body, too, is a possession. It has been truly said that desire for enjoyment creates bodies for the soul and sustains them. When this desire vanishes, there remains no further need for the body and man is free from the vicious cycle of births and deaths. The soul is omnipresent; why should she care to be confined within the cage-like body, or do evil and even kill for the sake of that cage? We thus arrive at the ideal of total renunciation and learn the use of the body for the purposes of service so long as it exists, so much so that service, and not bread, becomes for us the staff of life. We eat and drink, sleep and wake, for service alone. Such an attitude of mind brings us real happiness and the beatific vision in the fulness of time. Let us all examine ourselves from this standpoint.

We should remember that non-possession is a principle applicable to thoughts as well as to things. A man who fills his brain with useless knowledge violates that inestimable principle. Thoughts which turn us away from God or do not turn us towards Him are unnecessary possessions and constitute impediments in our way.

Letter to Narandas Gandhi (G.). *MPWMG*, vol. iii, pp. 473–5

101. Possessions and non-violence

9 February 1942

QUESTION. Why can't you see that whilst there is possession it must be defended against all odds? Therefore your insistence that violence should be eschewed in all circumstances is utterly unworkable and absurd. I think non-violence is possible only for select individuals.

ANSWER. This question has been answered often enough in some form or other in these columns as also in those of *Young India*. But it is an evergreen. I must answer it as often as it is put, especially when it comes from an earnest seeker as this one does. I claim that even now, though the social structure is not based on a conscious acceptance of non-violence, all the world over mankind lives and men retain their possessions on the sufferance of one another. If they had not done so, only the fewest and the most ferocious would have survived. But such is not the case. Families are bound together by ties of love, and so are groups in the so-called civilized society called nations. Only they do not recognize the supremacy of the law of non-violence. It follows, therefore, that they have not investigated its vast possibilities. Hitherto out of sheer inertia, shall I say, we have taken it for granted that complete non-violence is possible only for the few who take the vow of non-possession and the allied abstinences.

Whilst it is true that the votaries alone can carry on research work and declare from time to time the new possibilities of the great eternal law governing man, if it is the law, it must hold good for all. The many failures we see are not of the law but of the followers, many of whom do not even know that they are under that law willy-nilly. When a mother dies for her child she unknowingly obeys the law. I have been pleading for the past fifty years for a conscious acceptance of the law and its zealous practice even in the face of failures. Fifty years' work has shown marvellous results and strengthened my faith. I do claim that by constant practice we shall come to a state of things when lawful possession will command universal and voluntary respect. No doubt such possession will not be tainted. It will not be an insolent demonstration of the inequalities that surround us everywhere. Nor need the problem of unjust and unlawful possessions appal the votary of non-violence. He has at his disposal the non-violent weapon of *satyagraha* and non-co-operation which hitherto has been found to be a complete substitute of violence whenever it has been applied honestly in sufficient measure. I have never claimed to present the complete science of non-violence. It does not lend itself to such treatment. So far as I know no single physical science does, not even the very precise science of mathematics. I am but a seeker, and I have fellow-seekers like the questioner whom I invite to accompany me in the very difficult but equally fascinating search.

'Question Box'. *Harijan*, 22 Feb. 1942

102. Equal distribution of wealth

The real implication of equal distribution is that each man shall have the wherewithal to supply all his natural needs and no more. For example, if one man has a weak digestion and requires only a quarter of a pound of flour for his bread and another needs a pound, both should be in a position to satisfy their wants. To bring this ideal into being the entire social order has got to be reconstructed. A society based on non-violence cannot nurture any other ideal. We may not perhaps be able to realize the goal, but we must bear it in mind and work unceasingly to near it. To the same extent as we progress towards our goal we shall find contentment and happiness, and to that extent too shall we have contributed towards the bringing into being of a non-violent society.

It is perfectly possible for an individual to adopt this way of life without having to wait for others to do so. And if an individual can observe a certain rule of conduct, it follows that a group of individuals can do likewise. It is necessary for me to emphasize the fact that no one need wait for anyone else in order to adopt a right course. Men generally hesitate to make a beginning if they feel that the objective cannot be had in its entirety. Such an attitude of mind is in reality a bar to progress.

Now let us consider how equal distribution can be brought about through non-violence. The first step towards it is for him who has made this ideal part of his being to bring about the necessary changes in his personal life. He would reduce his wants to a minimum, bearing in mind the poverty of India. His earnings would be free of dishonesty. The desire for speculation would be renounced. His habitation would be in keeping with the new mode of life. There would be self-restraint exercised in every sphere of life. When he has done all that is possible in his own life, then only will he be in a position to preach this ideal among his associates and neighbours.

Indeed at the root of this doctrine of equal distribution must lie that of the trusteeship of the wealthy for the superfluous wealth possessed by them. For according to the doctrine they may not possess a rupee more than their neighbours. How is this to be brought about? Non-violently? Or should the wealthy be dispossessed of their possessions? To do this we would naturally have to resort to violence. This violent action cannot benefit society. Society will be the poorer, for it will lose the gifts of a man who knows how to accumulate wealth. Therefore the non-violent way is evidently superior. The rich man will be left in possession of his wealth, of which he will use what he reasonably requires for his personal needs and will act as a trustee for the remainder to be used for the society. In this argument honesty on the part of the trustee is assumed.

As soon as a man looks upon himself as a servant of society, earns for its sake, spends for its benefit, then purity enters into his earnings and there is *ahimsa* in his venture. Moreover, if men's minds turn towards this way of life, there will come about a peaceful revolution in society, and that without any bitterness.

It may be asked whether history at any time records such a change in human nature. Such changes have certainly taken place in individuals. One may not perhaps be able to point to them in a whole society. But this only means that up till now there has never been an experiment on a large scale in non-violence. Somehow or other the wrong belief has taken possession of us that *ahimsa* is pre-eminently a weapon for individuals and its use should therefore be limited to that sphere. In fact this is not the case. *Ahimsa* is definitely an attribute of society. To convince people of this truth is at once my effort and my experiment. In this age of wonders no one will say that a thing or idea is worthless because it is new. To say it is impossible because it is difficult is again not in consonance with the spirit of the age. Things undreamt of are daily being seen, the impossible is ever becoming possible. We are constantly being astonished these days at the amazing discoveries in the field of violence. But I maintain that far more undreamt of and seemingly impossible discoveries will be made in the field of non-violence. The history of religion is full of such examples. To try to root out religion itself from society is a wild goose chase. And were such an attempt to succeed, it would mean the

destruction of society. Superstition, evil customs and other imperfections creep in from age to age and mar religion for the time being.
They come and go. But religion itself remains, because the existence
of the world in a broad sense depends on religion. The ultimate
definition of religion may be said to be obedience to the law of God.
God and His law are synonymous terms. Therefore God signifies an
unchanging and living law. No one has ever really found Him. But
avatars* and prophets have, by means of their *tapasya*,* given to
mankind a faint glimpse of the eternal Law.

If, however, in spite of the utmost effort, the rich do not become
guardians of the poor in the true sense of the term and the latter are
more and more crushed and die of hunger, what is to be done? In
trying to find the solution to this riddle I have lighted on non-violent
non-co-operation and civil disobedience as the right and infallible
means. The rich cannot accumulate wealth without the co-operation
of the poor in society. Man has been conversant with violence from
the beginning, for he has inherited this strength from the animal in
his nature. It was only when he rose from the state of a quadruped
(animal) to that of a biped (man) that the knowledge of the strength
of *ahimsa* entered into his soul. This knowledge has grown within
him slowly but surely. If this knowledge were to penetrate to and
spread amongst the poor, they would become strong and would learn
how to free themselves by means of non-violence from the crushing
inequalities which have brought them to the verge of starvation.

'Equal Distribution'. *Harijanbandhu*, 24 Aug. 1940. *Harijan*, 25 Aug. 1940

103. Bolshevism and the abolition of private property

I must confess that I have not yet been able fully to understand the
meaning of Bolshevism. All that I know is that it aims at the abolition
of the institution of private property. This is only an application of
the ethical ideal of non-possession in the realm of economics and if
the people adopted this ideal of their own accord or could be made to
accept it by means of peaceful persuasion there would be nothing like
it. But from what I know of Bolshevism it not only does not preclude
the use of force but freely sanctions it for the expropriation of private
property and maintaining the collective State ownership of the same.
And if that is so I have no hesitation in saying that the Bolshevik

regime in its present form cannot last for long. For it is my firm conviction that nothing enduring can be built on violence. But be that as it may there is no questioning the fact that the Bolshevik ideal has behind it the purest sacrifice of countless men and women who have given up their all for its sake, and an ideal that is sanctified by the sacrifices of such master spirits as Lenin cannot go in vain: the noble example of their renunciation will be emblazoned for ever and quicken and purify the ideal as time passes.

'My Notes' (G.). *Navajivan*, 21 Oct. 1928. *Young India*, 15 Nov. 1928

104. Avoiding class war

QUESTION. If you will benefit the workers, the peasant and the factory hand, can you avoid class war?

ANSWER. I can, most decidedly, if only the people will follow the non-violent method. The past twelve months* have abundantly shown the possibilities of non-violence adopted even as a policy. When the people adopt it as a principle of conduct, class war becomes an impossibility. The experiment in that direction is being tried in Ahmedabad.* It has yielded most satisfactory results and there is every likelihood of its proving conclusive. By the non-violent method we seek not to destroy the capitalist, we seek to destroy capitalism. We invite the capitalist to regard himself as trustee for those on whom he depends for the making, the retention and the increase of his capital. Nor need the worker wait for his conversion. If capital is power, so is work. Either power can be used destructively or creatively. Either is dependent on the other. Immediately the worker realizes his strength, he is in a position to become a co-sharer with the capitalist instead of remaining his slave. If he aims at becoming the sole owner, he will most likely be killing the hen that lays golden eggs.

Inequalities in intelligence and even opportunity will last till the end of time. A man living on the banks of a river has any day more opportunity of growing crops than one living in an arid desert. But if inequalities stare us in the face the essential equality too is not to be missed. Every man has an equal right to the necessaries of life even as birds and beasts have. And since every right carries with it a corresponding duty and the corresponding remedy for resisting any attack upon it, it is merely a matter of finding out the corresponding duties and remedies to vindicate the elementary fundamental equality. The corresponding duty is to labour with my limbs and the corresponding remedy is to non-co-operate with him who deprives me of the fruit of my labour. And if I would recognize the fundamental equality, as I must, of the capitalist and the labourer, I must not aim at his destruction. I must strive for his conversion.

My non-co-operation with him will open his eyes to the wrong he may be doing. Nor need I be afraid of someone else taking my place when I have non-co-operated. For I expect to influence my co-workers so as not to help the wrongdoing of the employer. This kind of education of the mass of workers is no doubt a slow process, but as it is also the surest, it is necessarily the quickest. It can be easily demonstrated that destruction of the capitalist must mean destruction in the end of the worker and as no human being is so bad as to be beyond redemption, no human being is so perfect as to warrant his destroying him whom he wrongly considers to be wholly evil.

'Questions and Answers'. *Young India*, 26 Mar. 1931

105. Right relations between capital and labour

23 February 1935

There is a conflict of interest between capital and labour, but we have to resolve it by doing our own duty. Just as pure blood is proof against poisonous germs, so will labour, when it is pure, be proof against exploitation. The labourer has but to realize that labour is also capital. As soon as labourers are properly educated and organized and they realize their strength, no amount of capital can subdue them. Organized and enlightened labour can dictate its own terms. It is no use vowing vengeance against a party because we are weak. We have to get strong. Strong hearts, enlightened minds and willing hands can brave all odds and remove all obstacles. No, 'Love thy neighbour as thyself'* is no counsel of perfection. The capitalist is as much a neighbour of the labourer as the latter is a neighbour of the former, and one has to seek and win the willing co-operation of the other. Nor does the principle mean that we should accept exploitation lying down. Our internal strength will render all exploitation impossible.

Speech at a meeting of village workers, Nagpur. *Harijan*, 1 Mar. 1935

106. Trusteeship and society

6 October 1934

You take exception to my wish that the rich should regard themselves as trustees for the whole of society rather than as owners of the wealth they might possess. Of course, it is an uphill task, but by no means impossible. Indeed I see definite signs of that idea spreading and being accepted. You suggest that the poor should be regarded as trustees for the rich. But you forget that it is implied in the proposition I have laid down. Because, have I not said that labour is as much capital as metal? Therefore, workers, instead of regarding themselves as enemies of the rich, or regarding the rich as their natural enemies, should hold their labour in trust for those who are in need of it. This they can do only when, instead of feeling so utterly helpless as they do, they realize their importance in human economy and shed their fear or distrust of the rich. Fear and distrust are twin sisters born of weakness. When labour realizes its strength it won't need to use any force against moneyed people. It will simply command their attention and respect.

Letter to B. Srirangasayi. *The Hindu*, 11 Oct. 1934. *EWMG*, p. 400

107. Theory of trusteeship

6 May 1939

QUESTION. I am either unable to understand your theory of trusteeship or my reason cannot grasp it. Will you kindly explain it?

ANSWER. It is the same thing whether you are unable to understand it or your reason does not accept it. How can I explain such an important principle in a few minutes? Still I shall try to explain it in brief. Just imagine that I have a crore* of rupees in my possession. I can either squander the amount in dissipation or take up the attitude that the money does not belong to me, that I do not own it, that it is a bequest, that it has been put in my possession by God and that only so much of it is mine as is enough for my requirements. My requirements also should be like those of the millions. My requirements cannot be greater because I happen to be the son of a rich man. I cannot spend the money on my pleasures. The man who takes for himself only enough to satisfy the needs customary in his society and spends the rest for social service becomes a trustee.

Ever since the idea of socialism became popular in India, we have been confronted with the question as to what our attitude should be towards the Princes* and millionaires. The socialists say that the Princes and the millionaires should be done away with, that all must become workers. They advocate confiscation of the properties of all these people and say that they should be given the same wages as everyone else—from Rs 5 to eight annas a day or Rs 15 a month. So much for what the socialists say. We too assert that the rich are not the owners of their wealth whereas the labourer is the owner of his labour. He is, therefore, from our point of view, richer than the rich. A zamindar can be recognized as the owner of one, two or ten *bighas** of land. That is to say, of as much as may be necessary for his livelihood. We also want that his wages should not be higher than those of the labourer, that he should maintain himself on eight annas a day and use the rest of his wealth for the welfare of society. But we would not take away his property by force. This is the most important point. We also wish that the Princes and the millionaires too should do manual work and maintain themselves on eight annas a day, considering the rest of their property as national trust.

At this point it may be asked as to how many trustees of this type one can really find. As a matter of fact, such a question should not arise at all. It is not directly related to our theory. There may be just one such trustee or there may be none at all. Why should we worry about it? We should have the faith that we can, without violence or with so little violence that it can hardly be called violence, create such a feeling among the rich. We should act in that faith. That is sufficient for us. We should demonstrate through our endeavour that we can end economic disparity with the help of non-violence. Only those who have no faith in non-violence can ask how many trustees of this kind can be found.

You may say that such a thing can never happen. You may consider it as something not in keeping with human nature. But I cannot believe that you are not able to understand it or that your reason cannot grasp it.

Answers to questions at Gandhi Seva Sangh Meeting, Brindaban—II (H.). *Gandhi Seva Sanghke Panchama Varshik Adhiveshan (Brindaban, Bihar) ka Vivaran*, pp. 50–9. *EWMG*, pp. 403–4

108. The socialist ideal

15 April 1947

Socialism is a term of the modern age but the concept of socialism is not a new discovery. Lord Krishna preaches the same doctrine in the *Gita*. One need have in one's possession only what one requires. It means that all men are created by God and therefore entitled to an equal share of food, clothing and housing. It does not require huge organizations for the realization of this ideal. Any individual can set about to realize it. First of all, in order to translate this ideal into our lives we should minimize our needs, keeping in mind the poorest of the poor in India. One should earn just enough to support oneself and one's family. To have a bank balance would thus be incompatible with this ideal. And whatever is earned should be earned with the utmost honesty. Strict restraint has to be kept over small matters in our lives. Even if a single individual enforces this ideal in his life, he is bound to influence others. Wealthy people should act as trustees of their wealth. But if they are robbed of this wealth through violent means, it would not be in the interest of the country. This is known as communism. Moreover, by adopting violent means we would be depriving society of capable individuals.

Talk with Manu Gandhi (G.). *Biharni Komi Agman*, pp. 201–2.
EWMG, pp. 407–8

109. Gandhi's ideal social order

9/10 November 1934

I believe that every man is born in the world with certain natural tendencies. Every person is born with certain definite limitations which he cannot overcome. From a careful observation of these limitations the law of *varna** was deduced. It established certain spheres of action of certain people with certain tendencies. This avoided all unworthy competition. Whilst, recognizing limitations, the law of *varna* admitted of no distinctions of high and low, on the one hand it guaranteed to each the fruits of his labours and on the other it prevented him from pressing upon his neighbour.

This great law has been degraded and has fallen into disrepute. But my conviction is that an ideal social order will only be evolved when the implications of this law are fully understood and given effect to.

Interview with Nirmal Kumar Bose. Hindustan Times, 17 Oct. 1935

110. Enlightened anarchy

Political power, in my opinion, cannot be our ultimate aim. It is one of the means used by men for their all-round advancement. The power to control national life through national representatives is called political power. Representatives will become unnecessary if the national life becomes so perfect as to be self-controlled. It will then be a state of enlightened anarchy in which each person will become his own ruler. He will conduct himself in such a way that his behaviour will not hamper the well-being of his neighbours. In an ideal State there will be no political institution and therefore no political power. That is why Thoreau has said in his classic statement that that government is the best which governs the least.

'Enlightened Anarchy—A Political Ideal' (H.). *Sarvodaya*, Jan. 1939. *EWMG*, pp. 402–3

111. Village *swaraj*

18 July 1942

My idea of village *swaraj* is that it is a complete republic, independent of its neighbours for its own vital wants, and yet interdependent for many others in which dependence is a necessity. Thus every village's first concern will be to grow its own food crops and cotton for its cloth. It should have a reserve for its cattle, recreation and playground for adults and children. Then if there is more land available, it will grow *useful* money crops, thus excluding *ganja*,* tobacco, opium and the like. The village will maintain a village theatre, school and public hall. It will have its own waterworks, ensuring clean water supply. This can be done through controlled wells or tanks. Education will be compulsory up to the final basic course. As far as possible every activity will be conducted on the co-operative basis. There will be no castes such as we have today with their graded untouchability. Non-violence with its technique of *satyagraha* and non-co-operation will be the sanction of the village community.

There will be a compulsory service of village guards who will be selected by rotation from the register maintained by the village.

The government of the village will be conducted by a Panchayat of five persons annually elected by the adult villagers, male and female, possessing minimum prescribed qualifications. These will have all the authority and jurisdiction required. Since there will be no system of punishments in the accepted sense, this Panchayat will be the legislature, judiciary and executive combined to operate for its year of office. Any village can become such a republic today without much interference even from the present Government whose sole effective connection with the villages is the exaction of the village revenue. I have not examined here the question of relations with the neighbouring villages and the centre if any. My purpose is to present an outline of village government. Here there is perfect democracy based upon individual freedom. The individual is the architect of his own government. The law of non-violence rules him and his government. He and his village are able to defy the might of a world. For the law governing every villager is that he will suffer death in the defence of his and his village's honour.

The reader may well ask me—I am asking myself while penning these lines—as to why I have not been able to model Sevagram* after the picture here drawn. My answer is: I am making the attempt. I can see dim traces of success though I can show nothing visible. But there is nothing inherently impossible in the picture drawn here. To model such a village may be the work of a lifetime. Any lover of true democracy and village life can take up a village, treat it as his world and sole work, and he will find good results. He begins by being the village scavenger, spinner, watchman, medicine man and schoolmaster all at once. If nobody comes near him, he will be satisfied with scavenging and spinning.

'Question Box'. *Harijan*, 26 July 1942. *EWMG*, pp. 358–60

112. Gandhi's vision of an independent India

28 July 1946

In that picture [of Independence], the unit is the village community. The superstructure of Independence is not to be built on the village unit so that the top weighs down and crushes the forty crores of people who constitute the base. The power will vest in the unit itself, which will be economically and politically as autonomous as possible. Today power is perched on Mt. Everest. From there orders are issued and the people have to obey . . .

I have conceived round the village as the centre a series of ever-widening circles, not one on top of the other, but all on the same plane, so that there is none higher or lower than the other. Maine* has said that India was a congeries of village republics. The towns were then subservient to the villages. They were emporia for the surplus village products and beautiful manufactures. That is the skeleton of my picture to serve as a pattern for Independent India. There are many faults in the ancient village system. Unless they are eradicated, there will not only be no hope for the untouchables in a free India but for India in the comity of nations.

Speech at meeting of Deccan princes. *The Hindu*, 1 Aug. 1946.
Harijan, 4 Aug. 1946

113. Building a stateless society

6 September 1946

I am convinced that so long as the army or the police continues to be used for conducting the administration, we shall remain subservient to the British or some other foreign power, irrespective of whether the power is in the hands of the Congress* or others. Let us suppose that Congress ministries do not have faith in *ahimsa*. Let us suppose further that Hindus, Muslims and others seek protection from the army or the police. In that case they will continue to get such protection. Then these Congress Ministers who are votaries of *ahimsa* and do not like to seek help from the army or the police may resign. This means that so long as people have not learnt to settle their quarrels themselves, *goondaism** will continue and we shall never be able to generate the true strength of *ahimsa* in us.

Now the question is how to generate such strength. . . . So long as we do not develop the strength to die bravely, with love in our hearts, we cannot develop in us the non-violence of the brave.

Would there be State power in an ideal society or would such a society be Stateless? I think the question is futile. If we continue to work towards the building of such a society, to some extent it is bound to be realized and to that extent people will benefit by it. Euclid has defined a straight line as having no breadth, but no one has yet succeeded in drawing such a line and no one ever will. Still we can progress in geometry only by postulating such a line. This is true of every ideal.

We might remember though that a Stateless society does not exist anywhere in the world. If such a society is possible it can be established first only in India. For attempts have been made in India towards bringing about such a society. We have not so far shown that supreme heroism. The only way is for those who believe in it to set the example.

'Congress Ministries and *Ahimsa*' (H.). *Harijan*, 15 Sept. 1946. *Harijan Sevak*, 15 Sept. 1946

b. *Ashrams*—centres of personal and social transformation

114. Founding the Satyagraha Ashram

The *Satyagraha* Ashram was founded on the 25th of May 1915. . . .

I had a predilection for Ahmedabad. Being a Gujarati I thought I should be able to render greatest service to the country through the Gujarati language. And then, as Ahmedabad was an ancient centre of handloom weaving, it was likely to be the most favourable field for the revival of the cottage industry of hand-spinning. There was also the hope that, the city being the capital of Gujarat, monetary help from its wealthy citizens would be more available here than elsewhere. . . .

The first thing we had to settle was the name of the Ashram. . . . Our creed was devotion to truth, and our business was the search for and insistence on truth. I wanted to acquaint India with the method* I had tried in South Africa, and I desired to test in India the extent to which its application might be possible. So my companions and I selected the name '*Satyagraha Ashram*', as conveying both our goal and our method of service.

Gandhi, *An Autobiography*, part V, chap. IX

115. Draft Constitution of the Satyagraha Ashram

Before 20 May 1915

OBJECT

The object of the Ashram is to learn how to serve the motherland one's whole life and to serve it.

CLASSES

The Ashram consists of three classes: Controllers, Novitiates and Students.

(1) CONTROLLERS

The Controllers believe that, in order to learn how to serve the country, the following observances should be enforced in their own lives and they have been trying to do so for some time.

1. VOW OF TRUTH

It is not enough for a person under this vow that he does not ordinarily resort to untruth; such a person ought to know that no deception may be practised even for the good of the country. One should consider the example of Prahlad in order to understand how one should behave towards elders such as parents in the interests of Truth.

2. VOW OF NON-VIOLENCE

It is not enough to refrain from taking the life of any living being. He who has pledged himself to this vow may not kill even those whom he believes to be unjust; he may not be angry with them, he must love them; thus, he would oppose the tyranny whether of parents, governments or others, but will never kill or hurt the tyrant. The follower of truth and non-violence will offer *satyagraha* against tyranny and win over the tyrant by love; he will not carry out the tyrant's will but he will suffer punishment even unto death for disobeying his will until the tyrant himself is won over.

3. VOW OF CELIBACY

It is well-nigh impossible to observe these two vows unless celibacy too is observed; and for this vow it is not enough that one does not look upon another woman with a lustful eye, one has so to control the animal passions that they will not be moved even in thought; if one is married, one will not have sexual intercourse even with one's wife, but, regarding her as a friend, will establish with her a relationship of perfect purity.

4. CONTROL OF THE PALATE

Until one has overcome the palate, it is difficult to observe the foregoing vows, more especially that of celibacy. Control of the palate should therefore be treated as a separate observance by one desirous of serving the country and, believing that eating is only for sustaining the body, one should regulate and purify one's diet day by day. Such a person will immediately, or gradually, as he can, leave off such articles of food as may tend to stimulate animal passions.

5. VOW OF NON-STEALING

It is not enough not to steal what is commonly considered as other men's property. One who has pledged himself to this vow should realize that nature provides from day to day just enough and no more for one's daily needs by way of food and so hold it theft to use articles of food, dress, etc., which one does not really need and live accordingly.

6. VOW OF NON-POSSESSION

It is not enough not to possess and keep much, but it is necessary not to keep anything which may not be absolutely necessary for the nourishment and protection of our body: thus, if one can do without chairs, one should do so. He who has taken this vow will always bear this in mind and endeavour to simplify his life more and more.

SUBSIDIARY OBSERVANCES

Two other vows follow from the foregoing.

1. VOW OF *SWADESHI*

The person who has taken the vow of *swadeshi* will never use articles which conceivably involve violation of truth in their manufacture or on the part of their manufacturers. It follows, for instance, that a votary of truth will not use articles manufactured in the mills of Manchester, Germany or India, for he cannot be sure that they involve no such violation of truth. Moreover, labourers suffer much in the mills. The generation of tremendous heat causes enormous destruction of life. Besides, the loss of workers' lives in the manufacture of machines and of other creatures through excessive heat is something impossible to describe. Foreign cloth and cloth made by means of machinery are, therefore, tabooed to a votary of non-violence as they involve triple violence. Further reflection will show that the use of foreign cloth can be held to involve a breach of the vows of non-stealing and non-possession. We follow custom and, for better appearance, wear foreign cloth in preference to the cloth made on our own handlooms with so little effort. Artificial beautifying of the body is a hindrance to a *brahmachari* and so, even from the point of view of that vow, machine-made cloth is taboo. Therefore, the vow of *swadeshi* requires the use of simple clothing made on simple handlooms and stitched in simple style, foreign buttons, cuts, etc., being avoided. The same line of reasoning may be applied to all other articles.

2. VOW OF FEARLESSNESS

He who is acted upon by fear can hardly observe the vows of truth, etc. The Controllers will, therefore, constantly endeavour to be free from the fear of kings or society, one's caste or family, thieves, robbers, ferocious animals such as tigers, and even of death. One who observes the vow of fearlessness will defend himself or others by truth-force or soul-force.

3. VOW AGAINST UNTOUCHABILITY*

According to Hindu religion as traditionally practised, communities such as *Dhed*, *Bhangi*, etc., known by the names of *Antyaj*, *Pancham*, *Achhut* and so on, are looked upon as untouchable. Hindus belonging to other communities believe that they will be defiled if they touch a member of any of the said communities and, if anyone does so accidentally, he thinks that he has committed a sin. The founders of the Ashram believe that this practice is a blot on Hindu religion. Themselves staunch Hindus, they believe that the Hindu race will continue to add to its load of sin so long as it regards a single community as untouchable. Some of the consequences of this practice have been terrible. In order to be free from this sin, the Ashram inmates are under a vow to regard the untouchable communities as touchable; actually one *Dhed* family was staying in the Ashram, and it is still there, when the third edition of these rules was being drawn up. It lives exactly in the same condition as others in the Ashram do. This vow does not extend to association for purpose of eating. All that is desired is the eradication of the evil of untouchability.

VARNASHRAM

The Ashram does not follow the *varnashram dharma*.* Where those in control of the Ashram will take the place of the pupils' parents and where life-long vows of celibacy, non-hoarding, etc., are to be observed, *varnashram dharma* has no scope. The Ashram inmates will be in the stage of *sannyasis* and so it is not necessary for them to follow the rules of this *dharma*. Apart from this, the Ashram has a firm belief in the *varnashram dharma*. The discipline of caste seems to have done no harm to the country; on the contrary, rather. There is no reason to believe that eating in company promotes brotherhood ever so slightly. In order that the *varnashram dharma* and caste discipline might in no way be undermined, the Ashram inmates are under obligation, whenever they stir out, to subsist on fruits if they cannot cook their own food.

MOTHER TONGUE

It is the belief of the Controllers that no nation or any group thereof can make real progress by abandoning its own language; they will, therefore, use their own language. As they desire to be on terms of intimacy with their brethren from all parts of India, they will also learn the chief Indian languages; as Sanskrit is a key to Indian languages, they will learn that too.

MANUAL WORK

The Controllers believe that body labour is a duty imposed by nature upon mankind. Such labour is the only means by which man may sustain himself; his mental and spiritual powers should be used for the common good only. As the vast majority in the world live on agriculture, the Controllers will always devote some part of their time to working on the land; when that is not possible, they will perform some other bodily labour.

WEAVING

The Controllers believe that one of the chief causes of poverty in the land is the virtual disappearance of spinning-wheels and handlooms. They will, therefore, make every effort to revive this industry by themselves weaving cloth on handlooms.

POLITICS

Politics, economic progress, etc., are not unconnected matters; knowing that they are all rooted in religion, the Controllers will make an effort to learn and teach politics, economics, social reform, etc., in a religious spirit and work in these fields with all the zeal that they can command.

(2) NOVITIATES

Those who are desirous of following the foregoing programme but are not able immediately to take the necessary vows may be admitted as Novitiates. It is obligatory upon them to conform to all the observances which are followed by Controllers the while that they are in the Ashram. They will acquire the status of Controllers when they are able to take the necessary vows for life.

(3) STUDENTS

1. Any children, whether boys or girls, from four years and upwards may be admitted with the consent of their parents.*

    2. Parents will have to surrender all control over their children.

    3. Children will not be permitted to visit their parents for any reason until the whole course of study is finished.

    4. Students will be taught to observe all the vows intended for the Controllers.

    5. They will receive instruction in religion, agriculture, hand-loom-weaving and letters.

    6. Instruction in letters will be through the students' own languages and will include History, Geography, Arithmetic, Algebra, Geometry, Economics, etc., the learning of Sanskrit, Hindi and at least one Dravidian language being obligatory.

    7. English will be taught as a second language.

    8. Urdu, Bengali, Tamil, Telugu, Devnagari and Gujarati scripts will be taught to all.

    9. The Controllers believe that the whole course will be completed in ten years.* Upon reaching the age of majority, students will be given the option of taking the vows or retiring from the Ashram. This will make it possible for those to whom the programme has not commended itself to leave the Ashram.

    10. They will exercise this option at an age when they will require no assistance from their parents or guardians.

    11. Every endeavour will be made from the very beginning to see that, when they leave, they will be strong enough to have no fear what they would do for their maintenance.

    12. Grown-up persons also may be admitted as students.

    13. As a rule, everyone will wear the simplest and a uniform style of dress.

14. Food will be simple. Chillies will be excluded altogether and generally no condiments will be used excepting salt, pepper and turmeric. Milk, ghee and other milk products being a hindrance to a celibate life and milk being often a cause of tuberculosis and having the same stimulating qualities as meat, they will be most sparingly used, if at all. Meals will be served thrice a day and will include dried and fresh fruits in liberal quantities. All inmates of the Ashram will be taught the general principles of hygiene.

15. No holidays will be observed in this Ashram but, for one and a half days every week, the ordinary routine will be altered and everyone will have some time to attend to his private work.

16. During three months in the year, those whose health permits it will be taken on a tour, on foot for the most part, of India.

17. Nothing will be charged either from Students or Novitiates towards their monthly expenditure, but parents or the members themselves will be expected to contribute whatever they can towards the expenses of the Ashram.

MISCELLANEOUS

Administration of the Ashram will rest with a body of Controllers. The Chief Controller will have the right to decide whom to admit and to which category.

The expenses of the Ashram are being met from moneys already received by the Chief Controller or to be received from friends who may have some faith in the Ashram.

The Ashram is accommodated in two houses on the banks of the Sabarmati, Ahmedabad, on the road to Sarakhej across the Ellis Bridge.

It is expected that in a few months, about 250 acres of land will be acquired in the vicinity of Ahmedabad and the Ashram located thereon.

A REQUEST

Visitors* are requested to observe all the Ashram rules during their stay there. Every endeavour will be made to make them comfortable; but the management will be thankful to them if they bring with them their bedding and utensils for meals, as the Ashram rules permit the stocking of only a minimum of articles.

Those parents who intend sending their children to the Ashram are advised to pay a visit to the Ashram. No boy or girl will be admitted before he or she has been duly tested.

DAILY ROUTINE*

(1) An effort is being made to see that everyone in the Ashram gets up at 4 o'clock. The first bell rings at 4.

(2) It is obligatory on all, except those who are ill, to get up at 4.30. Everyone finishes bathing by 5.

(3) 5 to 5.30: Prayers and readings from holy books.

(4) 5.30 to 7: Breakfast of fruits, such as bananas.

(5) 7 to 8.30: Manual work. This includes drawing water, grinding, sweeping, weaving, cooking, etc.

(6) 8.30 to 10: School work.

(7) 10 to 12: Meal and cleaning of utensils. The meal consists of dal, rice, vegetables and *rotlis* for five days. On two days, there are *rotlis* and fruits.

(8) 12 to 3: School work.

(9) 3 to 5: Work, as in the morning.

(10) 5 to 6: Meal and cleaning of utensils. The meal mostly follows the same pattern as in the morning.

(11) 6.30 to 7: Prayers, as in the morning.

(12) 7 to 9: Study, receiving visitors, etc.

Before nine, all children go to bed. At ten the lights are put out.

For school work, the subjects of study at present are Sanskrit, Gujarati, Tamil, Hindi and Arithmetic. Study of History and Geography is included in that of languages.

No paid teachers or servants are employed in the Ashram.

In all, the Ashram has at present 35 inmates. Four of them live with their families. There are five teachers to look after teaching. Permanent members of the Ashram include two from North India, nine from Madras Presidency and the rest are from Gujarat and Kathiawar.

Draft Constitution of the Satyagraha Ashram, Ahmedabad (G.). SN 6187 and SN 6189. *MPWMG*, vol. ii, pp. 513–21

116. The work-emphasis of the Satyagraha Ashram

25 March 1924

I do not think you will be satisfied with the Ashram life in Sabarmati. All attention there is today concentrated upon the development of hand-spinning and hand-weaving. The literary side of the Ashram takes the background. Though, therefore, there is a very good library attached to the Ashram, I cannot say that the atmosphere is favourable for philosophical studies. One cannot be reading and thinking whilst all around one are away working for all that they are worth. The Ashram has been given that turn because I am convinced that we have had an overdose of philosophical and political studies. The faculty of working with our hands and feet is all but atrophied. An attempt is being made at the Ashram to revive the taste for hand labour.

Letter to K. G. Rekhade. *CWMG*, vol. xxiii, p. 307

117. Ashrams as centres for social and personal transformation

21 December 1925

Ashrams like this one* are established so that such a way of life in complete harmony with *dharma* may prevail everywhere. I have, therefore, always cherished the hope that these Ashrams will serve as instruments for raising the country and teaching and spreading true *dharma*. I do not worry whether that hope will be fulfilled in the present or after many generations—it is sufficient for us that we go on doing our duty along the path we have chalked out for ourselves. For this, we should strive to cultivate the qualities of both a *Brahmin*—truth and faith—and a *Kshatriya*—strength and non-violence. It is my faith that this Ashram will help its inmates to cultivate both these types of qualities.

Speech at Wardha Ashram (G.). *Navajivan*, 27 Dec. 1925

118. New constitution of the Satyagraha Ashram (1928)

This Ashram was opened on 25th May, 1915. A constitution* was drawn up when it was founded. It underwent a revision during my incarceration.* The copies were exhausted long ago. My colleagues and I found it desirable to recast the constitution in view of the many changes and ups and downs that the Ashram had undergone. Its unexpected expansion too made the old constitution out of date. The burden of preparing the first draft fell on my shoulders.

Though pressure of work was ample excuse for the delay, I know that my subconscious self shirked the task. I was not clear as to the changes that were to be made. But my colleagues would give me no peace and Maganlal's death* hastened the completion. The following constitution is the result of the joint labours of the main workers. It is published purely as a draft, though pending revision it is to be accepted as a binding constitution by the Managing Committee. It is published in order to secure the opinion of friends and critics known and unknown of the Ashram. Any criticism or suggestions that may be sent will be thankfully received. I may be permitted to mention that the Ashram represents a prayerful and scientific experiment. The observances are many but they have been tested for the past 13 years of the existence of the Ashram. Whilst it is impossible to claim their perfect fulfilment by any one of us, the workers have in all humility tried to enforce them in their lives to the best of their ability and with more or less success. The curious will find that the new draft bears very close resemblance to the original constitution as it was drawn up in 1915.

Founded on *Vaishakh Sud 11th, Samvat 1971* — May 25th, 1915 — at Kochrab, and since removed to Sabarmati.

OBJECT

The object of this Ashram is that its members should qualify themselves for, and make a constant endeavour towards, the service of the country, not inconsistent with the universal welfare.

OBSERVANCES

The following observances are essential for the fulfilment of the above object:

1. TRUTH

Truth is not fulfilled by mere abstinence from telling or practising an untruth in ordinary relations with fellow-men. But Truth is God, the one and only Reality. All other observances take their rise from the quest for and the worship of Truth. Worshippers of Truth must not resort to untruth, even for what they may believe to be the good of the country, and they may be required, like Prahlad,* civilly to disobey even the orders of parents and elders in virtue of their paramount loyalty to Truth.

II. NON-VIOLENCE OR LOVE

Mere non-killing is not enough. The active part of Non-violence is love. The law of Love requires equal consideration for all life from the tiniest insect to the highest man. One who follows this law must not be angry even with the perpetrator of the greatest imaginable wrong, but must love him, wish him well and serve him. Although he must thus love the wrongdoer, he must never submit to his wrong or his injustice, but must oppose it with all his might, and must patiently and without resentment suffer all the hardships to which the wrongdoer may subject him in punishment for his opposition.

III. CHASTITY (*BRAHMACHARYA*)

Observance of the foregoing principles is impossible without the observance of celibacy. It is not enough that one should not look upon any woman or man with a lustful eye; animal passion must be so controlled as to be excluded even from the mind. If married, one must not have a carnal mind regarding one's wife or husband, but must consider her or him as one's lifelong friend, and establish relationship of perfect purity. A sinful touch, gesture or word is a direct breach of this principle.

IV. CONTROL OF THE PALATE

The observance of *brahmacharya* has been found, from experience, to be extremely difficult so long as one has not acquired mastery over taste. Control of the palate has, therefore, been placed as a principle by itself. Eating is necessary only for sustaining the body and keeping it a fit instrument for service, and must never be practised for self-indulgence. Food must, therefore, be taken, like medicine, under proper restraint. In pursuance of this principle one must eschew exciting foods, such as spices and condiments. Meat, liquor, tobacco, bhang, etc., are excluded from the Ashram. This principle requires abstinence from feasts or dinners which have pleasure as their object.

V. NON-STEALING

It is not enough not to take another's property without his permission. One becomes guilty of theft even by using differently anything which one has received in trust for use in a particular way, as well as by using a thing longer than the period for which it has been lent. It is also theft if one receives anything which one does not really need.

The fine truth at the bottom of this principle is that Nature provides just enough, and no more, for our daily need.

VI. NON-POSSESSION OR POVERTY

This principle is really a part of No. V. Just as one must not receive, so must one not possess anything which one does not really need. It would be a breach of this principle to possess unnecessary food-stuffs, clothing or furniture. For instance, one must not keep a chair if one can do without it. In observing this principle one is led to a progressive simplification of one's own life.

VII. PHYSICAL LABOUR

Physical labour is essential for the observance of non-stealing and non-possession. Man can be saved from injuring society, as well as himself, only if he sustains his physical existence by physical labour. Able-bodied adults must do all their personal work themselves, and must not be served by others, except for proper reasons. But they must, at the same time, remember that service of children, as well as of the disabled, the old and the sick, is a duty incumbent on every person who has the required strength.

VIII. *SWADESHI*

Man is not omnipotent. He therefore serves the world best by first serving his neighbour. This is *swadeshi*, a principle which is broken when one professes to serve those who are more remote in preference to those who are near. Observance of *swadeshi* makes for order in the world; the breach of it leads to chaos. Following this principle, one must as far as possible purchase one's requirements locally and not buy things imported from foreign lands, which can easily be manufactured in the country. There is no place for self-interest in *swadeshi*, which enjoins the sacrifice of oneself for the family, of the family for the village, of the village for the country, and of the country for humanity.

IX. FEARLESSNESS

One cannot follow Truth or Love so long as one is subject to fear. As there is at present a reign of fear in the country, meditation on and cultivation of fearlessness have a particular importance. Hence its separate mention as an observance. A seeker after Truth must give up the fear of parents, caste, Government, robbers, etc., and he must not be frightened by poverty or death.

X. REMOVAL OF UNTOUCHABILITY

Untouchability, which has taken such deep roots in Hinduism, is altogether irreligious. Its removal has therefore been treated as an independent principle. The so-called untouchables have an equal place in the Ashram with other classes. The Ashram does not believe in caste which, it considers, has injured Hinduism, because its implications of superior and inferior status, and of pollution by contact are contrary to the law of Love. The Ashram however believes in *varnashrama dharma*. The division of *varnas* is based upon occupation, and therefore a person should maintain himself by following the hereditary occupation, not inconsistent with fundamental morals, and should devote all his spare time and energy to the acquisition and advancement of true knowledge. The *ashramas* (the four stages) spoken of in the *smritis** are conducive to the welfare of mankind. Though, therefore, the Ashram believes in *varnashrama dharma*, there is no place in it for distinction of *varnas*, as the Ashram life is conceived in the light of the comprehensive and nonformal *sannyasa* of the *Bhagavad Gita*.

XI. TOLERANCE

The Ashram believes that the principal faiths of the world constitute a revelation of Truth, but as they have all been outlined by imperfect man they have been affected by imperfections and alloyed with untruth. One must therefore entertain the same respect for the religious faiths of others as one accords to one's own. Where such tolerance becomes a law of life, conflict between different faiths becomes impossible, and so does all effort to convert other people to one's own faith. One can only pray that the defects in the various faiths may be overcome, and that they may advance, side by side, towards perfection.

ACTIVITIES

As a result of and in order to help fulfilment of these observances, the following activities are carried on in the Ashram:

I. WORSHIP

The social (as distinguished from the individual) activities of the Ashram commence every day with the congregational morning worship at 4.15 to 4.45 and close with the evening prayer at 7 to 7.30. All inmates are expected to attend the worship. This worship has been conceived as an aid to self-purification and dedication of one's all to God.

II. SANITARY SERVICE

This is an essential and sacred service and yet it is looked down upon in society, with the result that it is generally neglected and affords considerable scope for improvement. The Ashram therefore lays special stress upon engaging no outside labour for this work. The members themselves attend to the whole of the sanitation in turns. New entrants are generally first of all attached to this department. Trenches are sunk to the depth of nine inches and the nightsoil is buried in them and covered with the excavated earth. It thus becomes converted into valuable manure. Calls of nature are attended to only at places assigned for the purpose. Care is taken that the roads and paths should not be spoilt by spitting or otherwise.

III. SACRIFICIAL SPINNING

Today India's most urgent problem is the growing starvation of her millions, which is chiefly due to the deliberate destruction by alien rule of her principal auxiliary industry of hand-spinning. With a view to its rehabilitation in national life, spinning has been made the central activity of the Ashram, and is compulsory for all members, as a national sacrifice. The following are the various branches of work in this department:

1. Cotton cultivation;
2. workshop for making and repairing spinning-wheels, spindles, carding-bows, etc.;
3. ginning;
4. carding;
5. spinning;
6. weaving cloth, carpets, tape, rope, etc.;
7. dyeing and printing.

IV. AGRICULTURE

Cotton for the *khadi* work and fodder crops for the cattle are the chief activities of this department. Vegetables and fruit are also grown in order to make the Ashram as far as possible self-contained.

V. DAIRY

An attempt is being made to convert into a model dairy the Ashram dairy which supplies milk to the inmates. Since last year this dairy is being carried on in consonance with the principles of and with the pecuniary help of the All-India Cow-protection Association, but as an integral part of the Ashram itself. There are at present 27 cows, 47 calves, 10 bullocks, and 4 bulls. The average dairy output of milk is 200 pounds.

VI. TANNERY

At the instance of and with the help of the All-India Cow-protection Association, a tannery has been established for the tanning of dead-cattle hides. There is attached to it a sandal and shoe-making department. The dairy and tannery have been established because the Ashram believes, in spite of the claim Hindus make to the protection of the cow, that Indian cattle will further and further deteriorate and ultimately die out, carrying man along with them, unless vigorous attention is paid to cattle-breeding, cattle-feeding and the utilization in the country of dead-cattle hides.

VII. NATIONAL EDUCATION

An attempt is made in the Ashram to impart such education as is conducive to national welfare. In order that spiritual, intellectual and physical development may proceed side by side, an atmosphere of industry has been created, and letters are not given more than their due importance. Character-building is attended to in the smallest detail. 'Untouchable' children are freely admitted. Women are given special attention with a view to improving their status, and they are accorded the same opportunities for self-culture as the men. The Ashram accepts the following principles of the Gujarat Vidyapith:

1. The principal object of the Vidyapith shall be to prepare workers of character, ability, education and conscientiousness, necessary for the conduct of the movements connected with the attainment of *swaraj*.

2. All the institutions conducted by and affiliated to the Vidyapith shall be fully non-co-operating and shall therefore have nothing to do with any help from Government.

3. Whereas the Vidyapith has come into being in connection with the *swaraj* movement, and Non-violent Non-co-operation as a means thereof, its teachers and trustees shall restrict themselves to those means only which are not inconsistent with truth and non-violence and shall consciously strive to carry them out.

4. The teachers and the trustees of the Vidyapith, as also all the institutions affiliated to it, shall regard untouchability as a blot on Hinduism, shall strive to the best of their power for its removal, and shall not exclude a boy or a girl for reason of his or her untouchability nor shall give him or her differential treatment having once accorded admission to him or her.

5. The teachers and the trustees of and all the institutions affiliated to the Vidyapith shall regard hand-spinning as an essential part of the *swaraj* movement and shall therefore spin regularly, except when disabled, and shall habitually wear *khadi*.

6. The language of the province shall have the principal place in the Vidyapith and shall be the medium of instruction.

EXPLANATION. Languages other than Gujarati may be taught by direct method.

7. The teaching of Hindi-Hindustani shall be compulsory in the curricula of the Vidyapith.

8. Manual training shall receive the same importance as intellectual training and only such occupations as are useful for the life of the nation shall be taught.

9. Whereas the growth of the nation depends not on cities but its villages, the bulk of the funds of the Vidyapith and a majority of the teachers of the Vidyapith shall be employed in the propagation of education conducive to the welfare of the villagers.

10. In laying down the curricula, the needs of village dwellers shall have principal consideration.

11. There shall be complete toleration of all established religions in all institutions conducted by and affiliated to the Vidyapith, and for the spiritual development of the pupils, religious instruction shall be imparted in consonance with truth and non-violence.

12. For the physical development of the nation physical exercise and physical training shall be compulsory in all the institutions conducted by and affiliated to the Vidyapith.

NOTE. Hindi-Hindustani means the language commonly spoken by the masses of the North—both Hindu and Mussalman—and written in the Devanagari or the Arabic script.

The Ashram school has so far sent forth 15 boys and 2 girls.

VIII. KHADI TECHNICAL SCHOOL

A separate technical school is conducted which prepares candidates for the *Khadi* Service on behalf of the All-India Spinners' Association.

There are at present 33 students from various provinces under training. Two hundred and five students have so far availed themselves of this school.

. . . .

MANAGING COMMITTEE

Since *Ashadha Sud* 14th, *Samvat* 1982 (24th July 1926) the Ashram has been managed by a Committee. This Committee is at present constituted as follows:

Sjt. Mahadev Haribhai Desai (Chairman)
    "   Imam Abdul Kadar Bawazir (Vice-Chairman)
    "   Vinoba Bhave
    "   Chhaganlal Khushalchand Gandhi
    "   Narahari Dwarkadas Parikh
    "   Lakshmidas Purushottam Asar
    "   Ramniklal Maganlal Modi
    "   Chimanlal Narsinhdas Shah
    "   Narandas Khushalchand Gandhi
    "   Surendranath
    "   Chhaganlal Nathubhai Joshi (Secretary)

The Committee is empowered to fill up any vacancy caused in it by resignation, death or otherwise.

Election shall be by a majority of at least three-fourths of the existing members.

The Committee shall have the right to elect two more members to it.

The quorum shall be composed of at least three members.

The Committee shall have charge of the entire administration of the Ashram.

NOTE. In accordance with their express wishes Gandhiji and Kakasaheb are not on the Committee.

MEMBERS OF THE ASHRAM

Members of the Ashram shall be such persons as believe in the object and obey the rules and regulations of the Ashram, and who shall be constantly endeavouring to observe its principles, and be faithfully performing the duties assigned to them by the Managing Committee or by the Secretary on its behalf.

MEMBERS OF THE COMMITTEE

Only such persons shall be eligible for membership of the Managing Committee, who are over 21 years of age, who have lived in the Ashram for not less than five years and who have pledged themselves to lifelong service through the activities of the Ashram.

IMPORTANT RESOLUTIONS

The Managing Committee has passed the following important resolutions:

1. Responsible workers of the Ashram, and also residents in the Ashram, whether temporary or permanent, shall all observe *brahmacharya*.

2. Persons desirous of admission to the Ashram shall have observed the rules of the Ashram in their own homes for the period of one year. The Chairman shall have the power of granting exemption from this rule in special cases.

3. It being undesirable that any further kitchens should be started in the Ashram, newcomers, whether single or married, shall dine in the common kitchen.

TO GUESTS

The number of visitors and guests has steadily increased. Such arrangements as are possible are made for showing visitors round the various activities of the Ashram.

Persons wishing to stay in the Ashram are requested to write to the Secretary for permission before coming, and not to arrive without having received an affirmative answer to their enquiries.

The Ashram does not keep a large stock of bedding and eating-utensils. Those intending to stay in the Ashram are therefore requested to bring their own bedding, mosquito net, napkins, plate, bowl and drinking-pot.

No special arrangements are made for visitors from the West. But for those who cannot dine comfortably on the floor, an attempt is made to provide them with a raised seat. A commode is always supplied to them.

Guests are requested to observe the following rules:

1. Attend the worship.
2. Keep the dining hours shown in the daily routine given below.

BRANCH

The Ashram has a branch at Wardha, which observes nearly the same rules, but which is independent of the Ashram in respect of management and finance. Sjt. Vinoba Bhave is the Manager of the branch.

EXPENDITURE

The average monthly expenditure of the Ashram is Rs 3,000 and is met by friends.

PROPERTY

The Ashram possesses land, 132 acres 38 *gunthas* in area, of the value of Rs 26,972-5-6, and buildings worth Rs 2,95,121-15-6, which are held by the following Board of Trustees:

1. Sheth Jamnalal Bajaj
2. Sjt. Revashanker Jagjivan Jhaveri
3. ” Mahadev Haribhai Desai
4. ” Imam Abdul Kadar Bawazir
5. ” Chhaganlal Khushalchand Gandhi

The present population of the Ashram is as follows:

MEN

55 workers in the Ashram.
43 teachers and students of the A.I.S.A. Technical School.
5 professional weavers.
30 agricultural labourers.
------
133 Total

WOMEN

49 sisters in the Ashram.
10 professional labourers.
7 weavers.
------
66 Total

CHILDREN

35 boys.
36 girls.
7 babies.
------
78 Total. Grand Total 277

DAILY ROUTINE

a.m.	4	Rising from bed
"	4.15 to 4.45	Morning prayer
"	5.00 to 6.10	Bath, exercise, study
a.m.	6.10 to 6.30	Breakfast
"	6.30 to 7	Women's prayer class
"	7 to 10.30	Body labour, education and sanitation
"	10.45 to 11.15	Dinner
"	11.15 to 12	Rest
"	12 to 4.30 p.m.	Body labour, including classes
p.m.	4.30 to 5.30	Recreation
"	5.30 to 6	Supper
"	6 to 7	Recreation
"	7 to 7.30	Common Worship
"	7.30 to 9	Recreation
"	9	Retiring bell

NOTE. These hours are subject to change whenever necessary.

'Satyagraha Ashram'. *Young India*, 14 June 1928. *MPWMG*, vol. ii, pp. 535–50

119. Prayer in the life of the ashram*

(i) If insistence on truth constitutes the root of the Ashram, prayer is the principal feeder of that root. The social (as distinguished from the individual) activities of the Ashram commence every day with the congregational morning worship at 4.15 to 4.45 a.m. and close with the evening prayer at 7 to 7.30 p.m. Ever since the Ashram was founded, not a single day has passed to my knowledge without this worship. I know of several occasions when owing to the rains only one responsible person was present on the prayer ground. All inmates are expected to attend the worship except in the case of illness or similar compelling reason for absence. This expectation has been fairly well fulfilled at the evening prayer, but not in the morning.

The time for morning worship was as a matter of experiment fixed at 4, 5, 6 and 7 a.m., one after another. But on account of my persistently strong attitude on the subject, it has been fixed at last at 4.20 a.m. With the first bell at 4 everyone rises from bed and after a wash reaches the prayer ground by 4.20.

I believe that in a country like India the sooner a man rises from bed the better. Indeed millions must necessarily rise early. If the peasant is a late riser, his crops will suffer damage. Cattle are attended to and cows are milked early in the morning. Such being the case, seekers of saving truth, servants of the people or monks may well be up at 2 or 3; it would be surprising if they are not. In all countries of the world devotees of God and tillers of the soil rise early. Devotees take the name of God and peasants work in their fields serving the world as well as themselves. To my mind both are worshippers. Devotees are deliberately such while cultivators by their industry worship God unawares, as it helps to sustain the world. If instead of working in the fields, they took to religious meditation, they would be failing in their duty and involving themselves and the world in ruin.

We may or may not look upon the cultivator as a devotee, but where peasants, labourers and other people have willy-nilly to rise early, how can a worshipper of Truth or servant of the people be a late riser? Again in the Ashram we are trying to co-ordinate work and worship. Therefore I am definitely of opinion that all able-bodied people in the Ashram must rise early even at the cost of inconvenience. Four a.m. is not early but the latest time when we must be up and doing.

Then again we had to take a decision on certain questions. Where should the prayers be offered? Should we erect a temple or meet in the open air? Then again, should we raise a platform or sit in the sands or the dust? Should there be any images? At last we decided to sit on the sands under the canopy of the sky and not to install any image. Poverty is an Ashram observance. The Ashram exists in order to serve the starving millions. The poor have a place in it no less than others. It receives with open arms all who are willing to keep the rules. In such an institution the house of worship cannot be built with bricks and mortar, the sky must suffice for roof and the quarters for walls and pillars. A platform was planned but discarded later on, as its size would depend upon the indeterminate number of worshippers. And a big one would cost a large sum of money. Experience has shown the soundness of the decision not to build a house or even a platform. People from outside also attend the Ashram prayers, so that at times the multitude present cannot be accommodated on the biggest of platforms.

Again as the Ashram prayers are being increasingly imitated elsewhere, the sky-roofed temple has proved its utility. Morning and evening prayers are held wherever I go. Then there is such large attendance, especially in the evening, that prayers are possible only on open grounds. And if I had been in the habit of worshipping in a prayer hall only, I might perhaps never have thought of public prayers during my tours.

Then again all religions are accorded equal respect in the Ashram. Followers of all faiths are welcome there; they may or may not believe in the worship of images. No image is kept at the congregational worship of the Ashram in order to avoid hurting anybody's feelings. But if an Ashramite wishes to keep an image in his room, he is free to do so.

(ii) At the morning prayer we first recite the *shlokas* (verses) printed in *Ashram Bhajanavali* (hymnal), and then sing one *bhajan* (hymn) followed by *Ramdhun* (repetition of *Ramanama*) and *Gitapath* (recitation of the *Gita*). In the evening we have recitation of the last 19 verses of the second chapter of the *Gita*, one *bhajan* and *Ramdhun* and then read some portion of a sacred book.

The *shlokas* were selected by Shri Kaka Kalelkar who has been in the Ashram since its foundation. Shri Maganlal Gandhi met him in Santiniketan, when he and the children of the Phoenix Settlement went there from South Africa while I was still in England. Dinabandhu Andrews and the late Mr Pearson* were then in Santiniketan. I had advised Maganlal to stay at some place selected by Andrews. And Andrews selected Santiniketan for the party. Kaka was a teacher there and came into close contact with Maganlal. Maganlal had been feeling the want of a Sanskrit teacher which was supplied by Kaka. Chintamani Shastri assisted him in the work. Kaka taught the children how to recite the verses repeated in prayer. Some of these verses were omitted in the Ashram prayer in order to save time. Such is the history of the verses recited at the morning prayer all these days.

The recitation of these verses has often been objected to on the ground of saving time or because it appeared to some people that they could not well be recited by a worshipper of truth or by a non-Hindu. There is no doubt that these verses are recited only in Hindu society, but I cannot see why a non-Hindu may not join in or be present at the recitation. Muslim and Christian friends who have heard the verses have not raised any objection. Indeed they need not cause annoyance to anyone who respects other faiths as much as he respects his own. They do not contain any reflection on other people. Hindus being in an overwhelming majority in the Ashram, the verses must be selected from the sacred books of the Hindus. Not that nothing is sung or recited from non-Hindu scriptures. Indeed there were occasions on which Imam Saheb recited verses from the Koran. Muslim and Christian hymns are often sung.

But the verses were strongly attacked from the standpoint of truth. An Ashramite modestly but firmly argued that the worship of Sarasvati, Ganesh and the like was violence done to truth; for no such divinities really existed as Sarasvati seated on a lotus with a *vina* (kind of musical instrument) in her hands, or as Ganesh with a big belly and an elephant's trunk. To this argument I replied as follows:

'I claim to be a votary of truth, and yet I do not mind reciting these verses or teaching them to the children. If we condemn some *shlokas* on the strength of this argument, it would be tantamount to an attack on the very basis of Hinduism. Not that we may not condemn anything in Hinduism which is fit for condemnation, no matter how ancient it is. But I do not believe that this is a weak or vulnerable point of Hinduism. On the other hand I hold that it is perhaps characteristic of our faith. Sarasvati and Ganesh are not independent entities. They are all descriptive names of one God. Devoted poets have given a local habitation and a name to His countless attributes. They have done nothing wrong. Such verses deceive neither the worshippers nor others. When a human being praises God he imagines Him to be such as he thinks fit. The God of his imagination is there for him. Even when we pray to a God devoid of form and attributes we do in fact endow Him with attributes. And attributes too are form. Fundamentally God is indescribable in words. We mortals must of necessity depend upon the imagination which makes and sometimes mars us too. The qualities we attribute to God with the purest of motives are true for us but fundamentally false, because all attempts at describing Him must be unsuccessful. I am intellectually conscious of this and still I cannot help dwelling upon the attributes of God. My intellect can exercise no influence over my heart. I am prepared to admit that my heart in its weakness hankers after a God with attributes. The *shlokas* which I have been reciting every day for the last fifteen years give me peace and hold good for me. In them I find beauty as well as poetry. Learned men tell many stories about Sarasvati, Ganesh and the like, which have their own use. I do not know their deeper meaning, as I have not gone into it, finding it unnecessary for me. It may be that my ignorance is my salvation. I did not see that I needed to go deep into this as a part of my quest of truth. It is enough that I know my God, and although I have still to realize His living presence, I am on the right path to my destination.'

I could hardly expect that the objectors should be satisfied with this reply. An *ad hoc* committee examined the whole question fully and finally recommended that the *shlokas* should remain as they were, for every possible selection would be viewed with disfavour by someone or other.

(iii) A hymn was sung after the *shlokas*. Indeed singing hymns was the only item of the prayers in South Africa. The *shlokas* were added in India. Maganlal Gandhi was our leader in song. But we felt that the arrangement was unsatisfactory. We should have an expert singer for the purpose, and that singer should be one who would observe the Ashram rules. One such was found in Narayan Moreshwar Khare, a pupil of Pandit Vishnu Digambar, whom the master kindly sent to the Ashram. Pandit Khare gave us full satisfaction and is now a full member of the Ashram. He made hymn-singing interesting, and the *Ashram Bhajanavali* (hymnal) which is now read by thousands was in the main compiled by him. He introduced *Ramdhun*, the third item of our prayers.

The fourth item is recitation of verses from the *Gita*. The *Gita* has for years been an authoritative guide to belief and conduct for the Satyagraha Ashram. It has provided us with a test with which to determine the correctness or otherwise of ideas and courses of conduct in question. Therefore we wished that all Ashramites should understand the meaning of the *Gita* and if possible commit it to memory. If this last was not possible, we wished that they should at least read the original Sanskrit with correct pronunciation. With this end in view we began to recite part of the *Gita* every day. We would recite a few verses every day and continue the recitation until we had learnt them by heart. From this we proceeded to the *parayan*.*

And the recitation is now so arranged that the whole of the *Gita* is finished in fourteen days, and everybody knows what verses will be recited on any particular day. The first chapter is recited on every alternate Friday, and we shall come to it on Friday next (June 10, 1932). The seventh and eighth, the twelfth and thirteenth, the fourteenth and fifteenth, and the sixteenth and seventeenth chapters are recited on the same day in order to finish 18 chapters in 14 days.

At the evening prayer we recite the last 19 verses of the second chapter of the *Gita* as well as sing a hymn and repeat *Ramanama*. These verses describe the characteristics of the *sthitaprajna* (the man of stable understanding), which a *satyagrahi* too must acquire, and are recited in order that he may constantly bear them in mind.

Repeating the same thing at prayer from day to day is objected to on the ground that it thus becomes mechanical and tends to be ineffective. It is true that the prayer becomes mechanical. We ourselves are machines, and if we believe God to be our mover, we must behave like machines in His hands. If the sun and other heavenly bodies did not work like machines, the universe would come to a standstill. But in behaving like machines, we must not behave like inert matter. We are intelligent beings and must observe rules as such. The point is not whether the contents of the prayer are always the same or differ from day to day. Even if they are full of variety, it is possible that they will become ineffective. The Gayatri verse among Hindus, the confession of faith (*kalma*) among Mussalmans, the typical Christian prayer in the Sermon on the Mount have been recited by millions for centuries every day; and yet their power has not diminished but is ever on the increase. It all depends upon the spirit behind the recitation. If an unbeliever or a parrot repeats these potent words, they will fall quite flat. On the other hand when a believer utters them always, their influence grows from day to day. Our staple food is the same. The wheat-eater will take other things besides wheat, and these additional things may differ from time to time, but the wheat bread will always be there on the dining table. It is the eater's staff of life, and he will never weary of it. If he conceives a dislike for it, that is a sign of the approaching dissolution of his body. The same is the case with prayer. Its principal contents must be always the same. If the soul hungers after them, she will not quarrel with the monotony of the prayer but will derive nourishment from it. She will have a sense of deprivation on the day that it has not been possible to offer prayer. She will be more downcast than one who observes a physical fast. Giving up food may now and then be beneficial for the body; indigestion of prayer for the soul is something never heard of.

The fact is that many of us offer prayer without our soul being hungry for it. It is a fashion to believe that there is a soul; so we believe that she exists. Such is the sorry plight of many among us. Some are intellectually convinced that there is a soul, but they have not grasped that truth with the heart; therefore they do not feel the need for prayer. Many offer prayer because they live in society and think they must participate in its activities. No wonder they hanker after variety. As a matter of fact however they do not *attend* prayer. They want to enjoy the music or are merely curious or wish to listen to the sermon. They are not there to be one with God.

(iv) *Prarthana* (Gujarati word for prayer) literally means to ask for something, that is, to ask God for something in a spirit of humility. Here it is not used in that sense, but in the sense of praising or worshipping God, meditation and self-purification.

But who is God? God is not some person outside ourselves or away from the universe. He pervades everything, and is omniscient as well as omnipotent. He does not need any praise or petitions. Being immanent in all beings, He hears everything and reads our innermost thoughts. He abides in our hearts and is nearer to us than the nails are to the fingers. What is the use of telling Him anything?

It is in view of this difficulty that *prarthana* is further paraphrased as self-purification. When we speak out aloud at prayer time, our speech is addressed not to God but to ourselves, and is intended to shake off our torpor. Some of us are intellectually aware of God, while others are afflicted by doubt. None has seen Him face to face. We desire to recognize and realize Him, to become one with Him, and seek to gratify that desire through prayer.

This God whom we seek to realize is Truth. Or to put it in another way Truth is God. This Truth is not merely the truth we are expected to speak. It is That which alone is, which constitutes the stuff of which all things are made, which subsists by virtue of its own power, which is not supported by anything else but supports everything that exists. Truth alone is eternal, everything else is momentary. It need not assume shape or form. It is pure intelligence as well as pure bliss. We call It

Ishvara because everything is regulated by Its will. It and the law It promulgates are one. Therefore it is not a blind law. It governs the entire universe. To propitiate this Truth is *prarthana* which in effect means an earnest desire to be filled with the spirit of Truth. This desire should be present all the twenty-four hours. But our souls are too dull to have this awareness day and night. Therefore we offer prayers for a short time in the hope that a time will come when all our conduct will be one continuously sustained prayer.

Such is the ideal of prayer for the Ashram, which at present is far, far away from it. The detailed programme outlined above is something external, but the idea is to make our very hearts prayerful. If the Ashram prayers are not still attractive, if even the inmates of the Ashram attend them under compulsion of a sort, it only means that none of us is still a man of prayer in the real sense of the term.

In heartfelt prayer the worshipper's attention is concentrated on the object of worship so much so that he is not conscious of anything else besides. The worshipper has well been compared to a lover. The lover forgets the whole world and even himself in the presence of the beloved. The identification of the worshipper with God should be closer still. It comes only after much striving, self-suffering (*tapas*) and self-discipline. In a place which such a worshipper sanctifies by his presence, no inducements need be offered to people for attending prayers, as they are drawn to the house of prayer by the force of his devotion.

We have dealt so far with congregational prayer, but great stress is also laid in the Ashram on individual and solitary prayer. One who never prays by himself may attend congregational prayers but will not derive much advantage from them. They are absolutely necessary for a congregation, but as a congregation is made up of individuals, they are fruitless without individual prayers. Every member of the Ashram is therefore reminded now and then that he should of his own accord give himself up to self-introspection at all times of the day. No watch can be kept that he does this, and no account can be maintained of such silent prayer. I cannot say how far it prevails in the Ashram, but I believe that some are making more or less effort in that direction.

'History of the Satyagraha Ashram' (G.). CW 326. *MPWMG*, vol. ii, pp. 569–77

120. Solutions in microcosm

June 1940

Sevagram* is to me a laboratory for ahimsa. If my experiment here were successful and I could find a solution for the little problems that confront me here, I am sure the same formula would provide me a solution for the bigger issues that today face us in the country. That is why I am so reluctant to leave Sevagram. It is my laboratory for satyagraha. It is there that I expect to discover the key to India's independence, not in Simla or New Delhi.

Harijanbandhu, 20 July 1940. *Harijan*, 6 July 1940. *CWMG*, vol. lxxii, p. 211

121. Sevagram—an ideal village

19 January 1945

The thing is that we should bring deliberation into our lives. If we want to work less, we may work less. But what we do should as far as possible be perfect. That is why I have said that if we could mould our lives as we sing in the *bhajan* and make Sevagram an ideal village, we should have done everything.

'Ashram Note' (H.). *Bapuki Chhayamen*, p. 388. *MPWMG*, vol. ii, p. 557

a. Understanding *swaraj*

122. Hind Swaraj

CHAPTER IV: WHAT IS *SWARAJ*?

READER. I have now learnt what the Congress* has done to make India one nation, how the Partition* has caused an awakening, and how discontent and unrest have spread through the land. I would now like to know your views on *swaraj*. I fear that our interpretation is not the same as yours.

EDITOR. It is quite possible that we do not attach the same meaning to the term. You and I and all Indians are impatient to obtain *swaraj*, but we are certainly not decided as to what it is. To drive the English out of India is a thought heard from many mouths, but it does not seem that many have properly considered why it should be so. I must ask you a question. Do you think that it is necessary to drive away the English, if we get all we want?

READER. I should ask of them only one thing, that is: 'Please leave our country.' If, after they have complied with this request, their withdrawal from India means that they are still in India, I should have no objection. Then we would understand that, in their language, the word 'gone' is equivalent to 'remained'.

EDITOR. Well then, let us suppose that the English have retired. What will you do then?

READER. That question cannot be answered at this stage. The state after withdrawal will depend largely upon the manner of it. If, as you assume, they retire, it seems to me we shall still keep their constitution and shall carry on the Government. If they simply retire for the asking, we should have an army, etc., ready at hand. We should, therefore, have no difficulty in carrying on the Government.

EDITOR. You may think so; I do not. But I will not discuss the matter just now. I have to answer your question, and that I can do well by asking you several questions. Why do you want to drive away the English?

READER. Because India has become impoverished by their Government. They take away our money from year to year. The most important posts are reserved for themselves. We are kept in a state of slavery. They behave insolently towards us and disregard our feelings.

EDITOR. If they do not take our money away, become gentle, and give us responsible posts, would you still consider their presence to be harmful?

READER. That question is useless. It is similar to the question whether there is any harm in associating with a tiger if he changes his nature. Such a question is sheer waste of time. When a tiger changes his nature, Englishmen will change theirs. This is not possible, and to believe it to be possible is contrary to human experience.

EDITOR. Supposing we get Self-Government similar to what the Canadians and the South Africans have, will it be good enough?

READER. That question also is useless. We may get it when we have the same powers; we shall then hoist our own flag. As is Japan, so must India be. We must own our navy, our army, and we must have our own splendour, and then will India's voice ring through the world.

EDITOR. You have drawn the picture well. In effect it means this: that we want English rule without the Englishman. You want the tiger's nature, but not the tiger; that is to say, you would make India English. And when it becomes English; it will be called not Hindustan but *Englistan*.* This is not the *swaraj* that I want.

READER. I have placed before you my idea of *swaraj* as I think it should be. If the education we have received be of any use, if the works of Spencer, Mill and others* be of any importance, and if the English Parliament be the Mother of Parliaments, I certainly think that we should copy the English people, and this to such an extent that, just as they do not allow others to obtain a footing in their country, so we should not allow them or others to obtain it in ours. What they have done in their own country has not been done in any other country. It is, therefore, proper for us to import their institutions. But now I want to know your views.

EDITOR. There is need for patience. My views will develop of themselves in the course of this discourse. It is as difficult for me to understand the true nature of *swaraj* as it seems to you to be easy. I shall therefore, for the time being, content myself with endeavouring to show that what you call *swaraj* is not truly *swaraj*.

CHAPTER V: THE CONDITION OF ENGLAND

READER. Then from your statement I deduce that the Government of England is not desirable and not worth copying by us.

EDITOR. Your deduction is justified. The condition of England at present is pitiable. I pray to God that India may never be in that plight. That which you consider to be the Mother of Parliaments is like a sterile woman and a prostitute. Both these are harsh terms, but exactly fit the case. That Parliament has not yet, of its own accord, done a single good thing. Hence I have compared it to a sterile woman. The natural condition of that Parliament is such that, without outside pressure, it can do nothing. It is like a prostitute because it is under the control of ministers who change from time to time. Today it is under Mr Asquith,* tomorrow it may be under Mr Balfour.*

READER. You have said this sarcastically. The term 'sterile woman' is not applicable. The Parliament, being elected by the people, must work under public pressure. This is its quality.

EDITOR. You are mistaken. Let us examine it a little more closely. The best men are supposed to be elected by the people. The members serve without pay* and therefore, it must be assumed, only for the public weal. The electors are considered to be educated and therefore we should assume that they would not generally make mistakes in their choice. Such a Parliament should not need the spur of petitions or any other pressure. Its work should be so smooth that its effects would be more apparent day by day. But, as a matter of fact, it is generally acknowledged that the members are hypocritical and selfish. Each thinks of his own little interest. It is fear that is the guiding motive. What is done today may be undone tomorrow. *It is not possible to recall a single instance in which finality can be predicted for its work*. When the greatest questions are debated, its members have been seen to stretch themselves and to doze. Sometimes the members talk away until the listeners are disgusted. Carlyle* has called it the 'talking shop of the world'. Members vote for their party without a thought. Their so-called discipline binds them to it. If any member, by way of exception, gives an independent vote, he is considered a renegade. If the money and the time wasted by Parliament were entrusted to a few good men, the English nation would be occupying today a much higher platform. Parliament is simply a costly toy of the nation. These views are by no means peculiar to me. Some great English thinkers have expressed them. One of the members of that Parliament recently said that a true Christian could not become a member of it. Another said that it was a baby. And if it has remained a baby after an existence of seven hundred years, when will it outgrow its babyhood?

READER. You have set me thinking; you do not expect me to accept at once all you say. You give me entirely novel views. I shall have to digest them. Will you now explain the epithet 'prostitute'?

EDITOR. That you cannot accept my views at once is only right. If you will read the literature on this subject, you will have some idea of it. Parliament is without a real master. Under the Prime Minister, its movement is not steady but it is buffeted about like a prostitute. The Prime Minister is more concerned about his power than about the welfare of Parliament. His energy is concentrated upon securing the success of his party. His care is not always that Parliament shall do right. Prime Ministers are known to have made Parliament do things merely for party advantage. All this is worth thinking over.

READER. Then you are really attacking the very men whom we have hitherto considered to be patriotic and honest?

EDITOR. Yes, that is true; I can have nothing against Prime Ministers, but what I have seen leads me to think that they cannot be considered really patriotic. If they are to be considered honest because they do not take what are generally known as bribes, let them be so considered, but they are open to subtler influences. In order to gain their ends, they certainly bribe people with honours. I do not hesitate to say that they have neither real honesty nor a living conscience.

READER. As you express these views about Parliament, I would like to hear you on the English people, so that I may have your view of their Government.

EDITOR. To the English voters their newspaper is their Bible. They take their cue from their newspapers which are often dishonest. The same fact is differently interpreted by different newspapers, according to the party in whose interests they are edited. One newspaper would consider a great Englishman to be a paragon of honesty, another would consider him dishonest. What must be the condition of the people whose newspapers are of this type?

READER. You shall describe it.

EDITOR. These people change their views frequently. It is said that they change them every seven years. These views swing like the pendulum of a clock and are never steadfast. The people would follow a powerful orator or a man who gives them parties, receptions, etc. As are the people, so is their Parliament. They have certainly one quality very strongly developed. They will never allow their country to be lost. If any person were to cast an evil eye on it, they would pluck out his eyes. But that does not mean that the nation possesses every other virtue or that it should be imitated. If India copies England, it is my firm conviction that she will be ruined.

READER. To what do you ascribe this state of England?

EDITOR. It is not due to any peculiar fault of the English people, but the condition is due to modern civilization. It is a civilization only in name. Under it the nations of Europe are becoming degraded and ruined day by day.*

.   .   .

CHAPTER VII: WHY WAS INDIA LOST?

READER. You have said much about civilization—enough to make me ponder over it. I do not now know what I should adopt and what I should avoid from the nations of Europe, but one question comes to my lips immediately. If civilization is a disease and if it has attacked England, why has she been able to take India, and why is she able to retain it?

EDITOR. Your question is not very difficult to answer, and we shall presently be able to examine the true nature of *swaraj*; for I am aware that I have still to answer that question. I will, however, take up your previous question. The English have not taken India; we have given it to them. They are not in India because of their strength, but because we keep them. Let us now see whether these propositions can be sustained. They came to our country originally for purposes of trade. Recall the Company Bahadur.* Who made it Bahadur? They had not the slightest intention at the time of establishing a kingdom. Who assisted the Company's officers? Who was tempted at the sight of their silver? Who bought their goods? History testifies that we did all this. In order to become rich all at once we welcomed the Company's officers with open arms. We assisted them. If I am in the habit of drinking *bhang** and a seller thereof sells it to me, am I to blame him or myself? By blaming the seller, shall I be able to avoid the habit? And, if a particular retailer is driven away, will not another take his place? A true servant of India will have to go to the root of the matter. If an excess of food has caused me indigestion, I shall certainly not avoid it by blaming water. He is a true physician who probes the cause of disease, and if you pose as a physician for the disease of India, you will have to find out its true cause.

READER. You are right. Now I think you will not have to argue much with me to drive your conclusions home. I am impatient to know your further views. We are now on a most interesting topic. I shall, therefore, endeavour to follow your thought, and stop you when I am in doubt.

EDITOR. I am afraid that, in spite of your enthusiasm, as we proceed further, we shall have differences of opinion. Nevertheless, I shall argue only when you stop me. We have already seen that the English merchants were able to get a footing in India because we encouraged them. When our Princes fought among themselves, they sought the assistance of Company Bahadur. That corporation was versed alike in commerce and war. It was unhampered by questions of morality. Its object was to increase its commerce and to make money. It accepted our assistance, and increased the number of its warehouses. To protect the latter it employed an army which was utilized by us also. Is it not then useless to blame the English for what we did at that time? The Hindus and the Mahomedans were at daggers drawn. This, too, gave the Company its opportunity and thus we created the circumstances that gave the Company its control over India. Hence it is truer to say that we gave India to the English than that India was lost.

READER. Will you now tell me how they are able to retain India?

EDITOR. The causes that gave them India enable them to retain it. Some Englishmen state that they took and they hold India by the sword. Both these statements are wrong. The sword is entirely useless for holding India. We alone keep them. Napoleon is said to have described the English as a nation of shop-keepers. It is a fitting description. They hold whatever dominions they have for the sake of their commerce. Their army and their navy are intended to protect it. When the Transvaal offered no such attractions, the late Mr Gladstone* discovered that it was not right for the English to hold it. When it became a paying proposition, resistance led to war. Mr Chamberlain* soon discovered that England enjoyed a suzerainty over the Transvaal. It is related that someone asked the late President Kruger* whether there was gold in the moon. He replied that it was highly unlikely because, if there were, the English would have annexed it. Many problems can be solved by remembering that money is their God. Then it follows that we keep the English in India for our base self-interest. We like their commerce; they please us by their subtle methods and get what they want from us. To blame them for this is to perpetuate their power. We further strengthen their hold by quarrelling amongst ourselves. If you accept the above statements, it is proved that the English entered India for the purposes of trade. They remain in it for the same purpose and we help them to do so. Their arms and ammunition are perfectly useless. In this connection I remind you that it is the British flag which is waving in Japan and not the Japanese. The English have a treaty with Japan for the sake of their commerce, and you will see that if they can manage it, their commerce will greatly expand in that country. They wish to convert the whole world into a vast market for their goods. That they cannot do so is true, but the blame will not be theirs. They will leave no stone unturned to reach the goal.

CHAPTER VIII: THE CONDITION OF INDIA

READER. I now understand why the English hold India. I should like to know your views about the condition of our country.

EDITOR. It is a sad condition. In thinking of it my eyes water and my throat gets parched. I have grave doubts whether I shall be able sufficiently to explain what is in my heart. It is my deliberate opinion that India is being ground down, not under the English heel, but under that of modern civilization. It is groaning under the monster's terrible weight. There is yet time to escape it, but every day makes it more and more difficult. Religion is dear to me and my first complaint is that India is becoming irreligious. Here I am not thinking of the Hindu or the Mahomedan or the Zoroastrian religion but of that religion which underlies all religions. We are turning away from God.

READER. How so?

EDITOR. There is a charge laid against us that we are a lazy and that Europeans are industrious and enterprising people. We have accepted the charge and we therefore wish to change our condition.

Hinduism, Islam, Zoroastrianism, Christianity and all other religions teach that we should remain passive about worldly pursuits and active about godly pursuits, that we should set a limit to our worldly ambition and that our religious ambition should be illimitable. Our activity should be directed into the latter channel.

READER. You seem to be encouraging religious charlatanism. Many a cheat has, by talking in a similar strain, led the people astray.

EDITOR. You are bringing an unlawful charge against religion. Humbug there undoubtedly is about all religions. Where there is light, there is also shadow. I am prepared to maintain that humbugs in worldly matters are far worse than the hum-bugs in religion. The humbug of civilization that I am endeavouring to show to you is not to be found in religion.

READER. How can you say that? In the name of religion Hindus and Mahomedans fought against one another. For the same cause Christians fought Christians. Thousands of innocent men have been murdered, thousands have been burned and tortured in its name. Surely, this is much worse than any civilization.

EDITOR. I certainly submit that the above hardships are far more bearable than those of civilization. Everybody understands that the cruelties you have named are not part of religion although they have been practised in its name; therefore there is no aftermath to these cruelties. They will always happen so long as there are to be found ignorant and credulous people. But there is no end to the victims destroyed in the fire of civilization. Its deadly effect is that people come under its scorching flames believing it to be all good. They become utterly irreligious and, in reality, derive little advantage from the world. Civilization is like a mouse gnawing while it is soothing us. When its full effect is realized, we shall see that religious superstition is harmless compared to that of modern civilization. I am not pleading for a continuance of religious superstitions. We shall certainly fight them tooth and nail, but we can never do so by disregarding religion. We can only do so by appreciating and conserving the latter.

READER. Then you will contend that the Pax Britannica is a useless encumbrance?

EDITOR. You may see peace if you like; I see none.

READER. You make light of the terror that the Thugs, the Pindaris and the Bhils* were to the country.

EDITOR. If you give the matter some thought, you will see that the terror was by no means such a mighty thing. If it had been a very substantial thing, the other people would have died away before the English advent. Moreover, the present peace is only nominal, for by it we have become emasculated and cowardly. We are not to assume that the English have changed the nature of the Pindaris and the Bhils. It is, therefore, better to suffer the Pindari peril than that someone else should protect us from it and thus render us effeminate. I should prefer to be killed by the arrow of a Bhil than to seek unmanly protection. India without such protection was an India full of valour. Macaulay* betrayed gross ignorance when he libelled Indians as being practically cowards. They never merited the charge. Cowards living in a country inhabited by hardy mountaineers and infested by wolves and tigers must surely find an early grave. Have you ever visited our fields? I assure you that our agriculturists sleep fearlessly on their farms even today; but the English and you and I would hesitate to sleep where they sleep. Strength lies in absence of fear, not in the quantity of flesh and muscle we may have on our bodies. Moreover, I must remind you who desire Home Rule that, after all, the Bhils, the Pindaris, and the Thugs are our own countrymen. To conquer them is your and my work. So long as we fear our own brethren, we are unfit to reach the goal.

.   .   .

CHAPTER XIV: HOW CAN INDIA BECOME FREE?

READER. I appreciate your views about civilization. I will have to think over them. I cannot take them in all at once. What, then, holding the views you do, would you suggest for freeing India?

EDITOR. I do not expect my views to be accepted all of a sudden. My duty is to place them before readers like yourself. Time can be trusted to do the rest. We have already examined the conditions for freeing India, but we have done so indirectly; we will now do so directly. It is a world-known maxim that the removal of the cause of a disease results in the removal of the disease itself. Similarly if the cause of India's slavery be removed, India can become free.

READER. If Indian civilization is, as you say, the best of all, how do you account for India's slavery?

EDITOR. This civilization is unquestionably the best, but it is to be observed that all civilizations have been on their trial. That civilization which is permanent outlives it. Because the sons of India were found wanting, its civilization has been placed in jeopardy. But its strength is to be seen in its ability to survive the shock. Moreover, the whole of India is not touched. Those alone who have been affected by Western civilization have become enslaved. We measure the universe by our own miserable foot-rule. When we are slaves, we think that the whole universe is enslaved. Because we are in an abject condition, we think that the whole of India is in that condition. As a matter of fact, it is not so, yet it is as well to impute our slavery to the whole of India. But if we bear in mind the above fact, we can see that if we become free, India is free. And in this thought you have a definition of *swaraj*.

It is *swaraj* when we learn to rule ourselves. It is, therefore, in the palm of our hands. Do not consider this *swaraj* to be like a dream. There is no idea of sitting still. The *swaraj* that I wish to picture is such that, after we have once realized it, we shall endeavour to the end of our life-time to persuade others to do likewise. But such *swaraj* has to be experienced, by each one for himself. One drowning man will never save another. Slaves ourselves, it would be a mere pretension to think of freeing others. Now you will have seen that it is not necessary for us to have as our goal the expulsion of the English. If the English become Indianized, we can accommodate them. If they wish to remain in India along with their civilization, there is no room for them. It lies with us to bring about such a state of things.

READER. It is impossible that Englishmen should ever become Indianized.

EDITOR. To say that is equivalent to saying that the English have no humanity in them. And it is really beside the point whether they become so or not. If we keep our own house in order, only those who are fit to live in it will remain. Others will leave of their own accord. Such things occur within the experience of all of us.

READER. But it has not occurred in history.

EDITOR. To believe that what has not occurred in history will not occur at all is to argue disbelief in the dignity of man. At any rate, it behoves us to try what appeals to our reason. All countries are not similarly conditioned. The condition of India is unique. Its strength is immeasurable. We need not, therefore, refer to the history of other countries. I have drawn attention to the fact that, when other civilizations have succumbed, the Indian has survived many a shock.

READER. I cannot follow this. There seems little doubt that we shall have to expel the English by force of arms. So long as they are in the country we cannot rest. One of our poets* says that slaves cannot even dream of happiness. We are day by day becoming weakened owing to the presence of the English. Our greatness is gone; our people look like terrified men. The English are in the country like a blight which we must remove by every means.

EDITOR. In your excitement, you have forgotten all we have been considering. We brought the English, and we keep them. Why do you forget that our adoption of their civilization makes their presence in India at all possible? Your hatred against them ought to be transferred to their civilization. But let us assume that we have to drive away the English by fighting, how is that to be done?

READER. In the same way as Italy did it.

.   .   .

CHAPTER XX: CONCLUSION

READER. From your views I gather that you would form a third party. You are neither an extremist nor a moderate.*

EDITOR. That is a mistake. I do not think of a third party at all. We do not all think alike. We cannot say that all the moderates hold identical views. And how can those who want only to serve have a party? I would serve both the moderates and the extremists. Where I differ from them, I would respectfully place my position before them and continue my service.

READER. What, then, would you say to both the parties?

EDITOR. I would say to the extremists: 'I know that you want Home Rule for India; it is not to be had for your asking. Everyone will have to take it for himself. What others get for me is not Home Rule but foreign rule; therefore, it would not be proper for you to say that you have obtained Home Rule if you have merely expelled the English. I have already described the true nature of Home Rule. This you would never obtain by force of arms. Brute force is not natural to Indian soil. You will have, therefore, to rely wholly on soul-force. You must not consider that violence is necessary at any stage for reaching our goal.'

I would say to the moderates: 'Mere petitioning is derogatory; we thereby confess inferiority. To say that British rule is indispensable is almost a denial of the Godhead. We cannot say that anybody or anything is indispensable except God. Moreover, commonsense should tell us that to state that, for the time being, the presence of the English in India is a necessity, is to make them conceited.

'If the English vacated India, bag and baggage, it must not be supposed that she would be widowed. It is possible that those who are forced to observe peace under their pressure would fight after their withdrawal. There can be no advantage in suppressing an eruption; it must have its vent. If, therefore, before we can remain at peace, we must fight amongst ourselves, it is better that we do so. There is no occasion for a third party to protect the weak. It is this so–called protection which has unnerved us. Such protection can only make the weak weaker. Unless we realize this, we cannot have Home Rule. I would paraphrase the thought of an English divine and say that anarchy under Home Rule were better than orderly foreign rule. Only, the meaning that the learned divine attached to Home Rule is different from Indian Home Rule according to my conception. We have to learn, and to teach others, that we do not want the tyranny of either English rule or Indian rule.'

If this idea were carried out, both the extremists and the moderates could join hands. There is no occasion to fear or distrust one another.

READER. What, then, would you say to the English?

EDITOR. To them I would respectfully say: 'I admit you are my rulers. It is not necessary to debate the question whether you hold India by the sword or by my consent. I have no objection to your remaining in my country, but although you are the rulers, you will have to remain as servants of the people. It is not we who have to do as you wish, but it is you who have to do as we wish. You may keep the riches that you have drained away from this land, but you may not drain riches henceforth. Your function will be, if you so wish, to police India; you must abandon the idea of deriving any commercial benefit from us. We hold the civilization that you support to be the reverse of civilization. We consider our civilization to be far superior to yours. If you realize this truth, it will be to your advantage and, if you do not, according to your own proverb, you should only live in our country in the same manner as we do. You must not do anything that is contrary to our religions. It is your duty as rulers that for the sake of the Hindus you should eschew beef, and for the sake of Mahomedans you should avoid bacon and ham. We have hitherto said nothing because we have been cowed down, but you need not consider that you have not hurt our feelings by your conduct. We are not expressing our sentiments either through base selfishness or fear, but because it is our duty now to speak out boldly. We consider your schools and law courts to be useless. We want our own ancient schools and courts to be restored. The common language of India is not English but Hindi. You should, therefore, learn it. We can hold communication with you only in our national language.

'We cannot tolerate the idea of your spending money on railways and the military. We see no occasion for either. You may fear Russia; we do not. When she comes we shall look after her. If you are with us, we may then receive her jointly. We do not need any European cloth. We shall manage with articles produced and manufactured at home. You may not keep one eye on Manchester and the other on India. We can work together only if our interests are identical.

'This has not been said to you in arrogance. You have great military resources. Your naval power is matchless. If we wanted to fight with you on your own ground, we should be unable to do so, but if the above submissions be not acceptable to you, we cease to play the part of the ruled. You may, if you like, cut us to pieces. You may shatter us at the cannon's mouth. If you act contrary to our will, we shall not help you; and without our help, we know that you cannot move one step forward.

'It is likely that you will laugh at all this in the intoxication of your power. We may not be able to disillusion you at once; but if there be any manliness in us, you will see shortly that your intoxication is suicidal and that your laugh at our expense is an aberration of intellect. We believe that at heart you belong to a religious nation. We are living in a land which is the source of religions. How we came together need not be considered, but we can make mutual good use of our relations.

'You, English, who have come to India are not good specimens of the English nation, nor can we, almost half-Anglicized Indians, be considered good specimens of the real Indian nation. If the English nation were to know all you have done, it would oppose many of your actions. The mass of the Indians have had few dealings with you.

If you will abandon your so-called civilization and search into your own scriptures, you will find that our demands are just. Only on condition of our demands being fully satisfied may you remain in India; and if you remain under those conditions, we shall learn several things from you and you will learn many from us. So doing we shall benefit each other and the world. But that will happen only when the root of our relationship is sunk in a religious soil.'

READER. What will you say to the nation?

EDITOR. Who is the nation?

READER. For our purposes it is the nation that you and I have been thinking of, that is, those of us who are affected by European civilization, and who are eager to have Home Rule.

EDITOR. To these I would say: 'It is only those Indians who are imbued with real love who will be able to speak to the English in the above strain without being frightened, and only those can be said to be so imbued who conscientiously believe that Indian civilization is the best and that the European is a nine days' wonder. Such ephemeral civilizations have often come and gone and will continue to do so. Those only can be considered to be so imbued who, having experienced the force of the soul within themselves, will not cower before brute-force, and will not, on any account, desire to use brute-force. Those only can be considered to have been so imbued who are intensely dissatisfied with the present pitiable condition, having already drunk the cup of poison.

'If there be only one such Indian, he will speak as above to the English and the English will have to listen to him.

'These are not demands, but they show our mental state. We shall get nothing by asking; we shall have to take what we want and we need the requisite strength for the effort and that strength will be available to him only who will act thus:

1. He will only on rare occasions make use of the English language.

2. If a lawyer, he will give up his profession and take up a hand-loom.

3. If a lawyer, he will devote his knowledge to enlightening both his people and the English.

4. If a lawyer, he will not meddle with the quarrels between parties but will give up the courts, and from his experience induce the people to do likewise.

5. If a lawyer, he will refuse to be a judge, as he will give up his profession.

6. If a doctor, he will give up medicine, and understand that rather than mending bodies, he should mend souls.

7. If a doctor, he will understand that no matter to what religion he belongs, it is better that bodies remain diseased rather than that they are cured through the instrumentality of the diabolical vivisection that is practised in European schools of medicine.

8. Although a doctor, he will take up a hand-loom, and if any patients come to him, will tell them the cause of their diseases, and will advise them to remove the cause rather than pamper them by giving useless drugs; he will understand that if by not taking drugs, perchance the patient dies, the world will not come to grief and that he will have been really merciful to him.

9. Although a wealthy man, yet regardless of his wealth, he will speak out his mind and fear no one.

10. If a wealthy man, he will devote his money to establishing hand-looms, and encourage others to use hand-made goods by wearing them himself.

11. Like every other Indian, he will know that this is a time for repentance, expiation and mourning.

12. Like every other Indian, he will know that to blame the English is useless, that they came because of us, and remain also for the same reason, and that they will either go or change their nature only when we reform ourselves.

13. Like others, he will understand that at a time of mourning, there can be no indulgence, and that, whilst we are in a fallen state, to be in gaol or in banishment is much the best.

14. Like others, he will know that it is superstition to imagine it necessary that we should guard against being imprisoned in order that we may deal with the people.

15. Like others, he will know that action is much better than speech; that it is our duty to say exactly what we think and face the consequences and that it will be only then that we shall be able to impress anybody with our speech.

16. Like others, he will understand that we shall become free only through suffering.

17. Like others, he will understand that deportation for life to the Andamans is not enough expiation for the sin of encouraging European civilization.

18. Like others, he will know that no nation has risen without suffering; that, even in physical warfare, the true test is suffering and not the killing of others, much more so in the warfare of passive resistance.

19. Like others, he will know that it is an idle excuse to say that we shall do a thing when the others also do it; that we should do what we know to be right, and that others will do it when they see the way; that when I fancy a particular delicacy, I do not wait till others taste it; that to make a national effort and to suffer are in the nature of delicacies; and that to suffer under pressure is no suffering.'

READER. This is a large order. When will all carry it out?

EDITOR. You make a mistake. You and I have nothing to do with the others. Let each do his duty. If I do my duty, that is, serve myself, I shall be able to serve others. Before I leave you, I will take the liberty of repeating:

1. Real home-rule is self-rule or self-control.

2. The way to it is passive resistance: that is soul-force or love-force.

3. In order to exert this force, *swadeshi* in every sense is necessary.

4. What we want to do should be done, not because we object to the English or because we want to retaliate but because it is our duty to do so. Thus, supposing that the English remove the salt-tax, restore our money, give the highest posts to Indians, withdraw the English troops, we shall certainly not use their machine-made goods, nor use the English language, nor many of their industries. It is worth noting that these things are, in their nature, harmful; hence we do not want them. I bear no enmity towards the English but I do towards their civilization.

In my opinion, we have used the term '*swaraj*' without understanding its real significance. I have endeavoured to explain it as I understand it, and my conscience testifies that my life henceforth is dedicated to its attainment.

Gandhi, *Hind Swaraj*

123. Inward and outward freedom

The outward freedom therefore that we shall attain will only be in exact proportion to the inward freedom to which we may have grown at a given moment. And if this is the correct view of freedom, our chief energy must be concentrated upon achieving reform from within. In this much-needed work all who will can take an equal share. We need neither to be lawyers, nor legislators, to be able to take part in the great effort. When this reform takes place on a national scale no outside power can stop our onward march.

'Notes'. *Young India*, 1 Nov. 1928. *Navajivan*, 4 Nov. 1928

124. Real freedom

19 April 1947

The foreign power will be withdrawn before long,* but for me real freedom will come only when we free ourselves of the domination of Western education, Western culture and Western way[s] of living which have been ingrained in us, because this culture has made our living expensive and artificial, both for men and for women. Emancipation from this culture would mean real freedom for us.

'Talk with Englishwomen' (G.). *Biharni Komi Agman*, pp. 226–7. *MPWMG*, vol. iii, p. 234

125. Parliamentary *swaraj*

But I would warn the reader against thinking that I am today* aiming at the *swaraj* described therein [in *Hind Swaraj*]. I know that India is not ripe for it. It may seem an impertinence to say so. But such is my conviction. I am individually working for the self-rule pictured therein. But today my corporate activity is undoubtedly devoted to the attainment of parliamentary *swaraj* in accordance with the wishes of the people of India.

Young India, 26 Jan. 1921

126. Parliamentary *swaraj*

It must be remembered that it is not Indian Home Rule depicted in that book [in *Hind Swaraj*] that I am placing before India. I am placing before the nation parliamentary, i.e., democratic *swaraj*.

Navajivan, 10 Aug. 1924. *Young India*, 14 Aug. 1924.

127. The practical meaning of *swaraj*

By *swaraj* I mean the Government of India by the consent of the
people ascertained by the vote of the largest number of the adult
population, male or female, native-born or domiciled who have
contributed by manual labour to the service of the State and who
have taken the trouble of having their names registered as voters.
This Government should be quite consistent with the British connection on absolutely honourable and equal terms. Personally I have
not despaired of the substitution for the present servile condition of
equal partnership or association. But I would not for one moment hesitate to countenance or bring about complete severance if it became
necessary, i.e., if the connection impeded India's full growth.

'Interrogatories Answered'. *Young India*, 29 Jan. 1925

128. *Swaraj* and complete independence

28 December 1926*

You are seeking to inculcate a spirit of complete independence
among those who are divided amongst themselves. A wise man does
not attempt to take a bigger bite than he can digest. Supposing complete independence was something infinitely superior to *swaraj*, even
then I suggest to you to be patient and attain what is possible at
the present moment and then mount further steps. One step is now
enough for me, but coming to the rock-bottom, I suggest to you that
swaraj includes complete independence . . . We want to make
it absolutely clear that we want to remain within the Empire if it
may be possible. Why do you lose all faith in human nature and in
yourself? Why do you lose faith in your ability to bend down the
haughtiness of the Englishmen and make them serve you? If you have
repugnance against the white skin, do you want to drive away every
Englishman and not keep any, even for teaching you English? . . . I
shall not be satisfied with any constitution that we may get from the
British Parliament unless it leaves that power with us also. So that if
we choose to declare independence we could do so. Do not impair
the effect that the word carries. Do not limit its interpretation. Who
knows, somebody may give us a still better definition. The potency

of the word increases because it is undefined and is, I would say, undefinable.

Speech at Congress session, Gauhati. *The Searchlight*, 2 Jan. 1927. *EWMG*, p. 350

129. *Swaraj*—concentrating on means rather than definitions

Year after year a resolution is moved in the Congress to amend the Congress creed so as to define *swaraj* as complete independence and year after year happily the Congress throws out the resolution* by an overwhelming majority. The rejection is proof of the sanity of the Congress. The moving of the resolution betrays the impatience . . . of some ardent Congressmen who have lost all faith in the British intentions and who think that the British Government will never render justice to India. The advocates of independence forget that they betray want of faith in human nature and therefore in themselves. Why do they think that there can never be change of heart in those who are guiding the British people? Is it not more correct and more dignified to own that there is no change of heart because we are weak? Nature abhors weakness. We want from the British people and the world at large not mercy but justice that is our due. And justice will come when it is deserved by our being and feeling strong.

I am sure that the staunchest votary of independence does not mean that he will not have any British association on any terms whatsoever. Even when he says so, he means . . . that the British will never accept association on equal terms. That is totally different from rejecting British association on any terms.

Indeed the word *swaraj* is all-embracing. It does include complete independence as it includes many other things. To give it one definite meaning is to narrow the outlook, and to limit what is at present happily limitless. Let the content of *swaraj* grow with the growth of national consciousness and aspirations. We may be satisfied today with dominion status. The future generations may not be, may want something better. *Swaraj* without any qualifying clause includes that which is better than the best one can conceive or have today. *Swaraj* means even under dominion status a capacity to declare independence at will. So long as we have not achieved that capacity, we have no *swaraj* . . . What India will finally have is for her and her alone to determine. This power of determination remains unfettered by the existing creed. What therefore the creed does retain is the possibility of evolution of *swaraj* within the British Empire or call it the British Commonwealth. The cryptic meaning of *swaraj* I have often described to be within the Empire if possible, without if necessary. I venture to think that it is not possible to improve upon that conception. It is totally consistent with national self-respect and it provides for the highest growth of the nation.

After all, the real definition will be determined by our action, the means we adopt to achieve the goal. If we would but concentrate upon the means, *swaraj* will take care of itself.* Our exploration should, therefore, take place in the direction of determining not the definition of an indefinable term like *swaraj* but in discovering the ways and means.

'Independence'. *Young India*, 13 Jan. 1927

130. Condemning the Congress resolution of independence*

I submit that *swaraj* is an all-satisfying goal for all time. We the English-educated Indians often unconsciously make the terrible mistake of thinking that the microscopic minority of English-speaking Indians is the whole of India. I defy anyone to give for independence a common Indian word intelligible to the masses. Our goal at any rate may be known by an indigenous word understood of the three hundred millions. And we have such a word in '*swaraj*' first used in the name of the nation by Dadabhai Naoroji.* It is infinitely greater than and includes independence. It is a vital word. It has been sanctified by the noble sacrifices of thousands of Indians. It is a word which, if it has not penetrated the remotest corner of India, has at least got the largest currency of any similar word. It is a sacrilege to displace that word by a foreign importation of doubtful value. This Independence Resolution is perhaps the final reason for conducting Congress proceedings in Hindustani and that alone. No tragedy like that of the Independence Resolution would then have been possible. The most valiant speakers would then have ornamented the native meaning of the word '*swaraj*' and attempted all kinds of definitions, glorious and inglorious. Would that the independents would profit by their experience and resolve henceforth to work among the masses for whom they desire freedom and taboo English speech in its entirety in so far as mass meetings such as the Congress are concerned.

Personally, I crave not for 'independence', which I do not understand, but I long for freedom from the English yoke. I would pay any price for it. I would accept chaos in exchange for it. For the English peace is the peace of the grave. Anything would be better than this living death of a whole people. This Satanic rule has well-nigh ruined this fair land materially, morally and spiritually. I daily see its law-courts denying justice and murdering truth. I have just come from terrorized Orissa. This rule is using my own countrymen for its sinful sustenance. I have a number of affidavits swearing that, in the district of Khurda, acknowledgments of enhancement of revenue are being forced from the people practically at the point of the bayonet. The unparalleled extravagance of this rule has demented the Rajas and the Maharajas who, unmindful of consequences, ape it and grind their subjects to dust. In order to protect its immoral commerce, this rule regards no means too mean, and in order to keep three hundred millions under the heels of a hundred thousand, it carries a military expenditure which is keeping millions in a state of semi-starvation and polluting thousands of mouths with intoxicating liquor.

But my creed is non-violence under all circumstances. My method is conversion, not coercion; it is self-suffering, not the suffering of the tyrant. I know that method to be infallible. I know that a whole people can adopt it without accepting it as its creed and without understanding its philosophy. People generally do not understand the philosophy of all their acts. My ambition is much higher than independence. Through the deliverance of India, I seek to deliver the so-called weaker races of the earth from the crushing heels of Western exploitation in which England is the greatest partner. If India converts, as it can convert, Englishmen, it can become the predominant partner in a world commonwealth of which England can have the privilege of becoming a partner if she chooses. India has the right, if she only knew, of becoming the predominant partner by reason of her numbers, geographical position and culture inherited for ages. This is big talk, I know. For a fallen India to aspire to move the world and protect weaker races is seemingly an impertinence.

But in explaining my strong opposition to this cry for independence, I can no longer hide the light under a bushel.* Mine is an ambition worth living for and worth dying for. In no case do I want to reconcile myself to a state lower than the best for fear of consequences. It is, therefore, not out of expedience that I oppose independence as my goal. I want India to come to her own and that state cannot be better defined by any single word than '*swaraj*'. Its content will vary with the action that the nation is able to put forth at a given moment. India's coming to her own will mean every nation doing likewise.

'Independence v. *Swaraj*'. *Young India*, 12 Jan. 1928

131. Freedom through non-violence

Oxford*
24 October 1931

You want co-operation between nations for the salvaging of civilization. I want it too, but co-operation presupposes free nations worthy of co-operation. If I am to help in creating or restoring peace and goodwill and resist disturbances thereof I must have ability to do so and I cannot do so unless my country has come to its own. At the present moment, the very movement for freedom in India is India's contribution to peace. For so long as India is a subject nation, not only she is a danger to peace, but also England which exploits India. Other nations may tolerate today England's Imperialist policy and her exploitation of other nations; but they certainly do not appreciate it; and they would gladly help in the prevention of England becoming a greater and greater menace every day. Of course you will say that India free can become a menace herself. But let us assume that she will behave herself with her doctrine of non-violence, if she achieves her freedom through it, and for all her bitter experience of being a victim to exploitation.

The objection about my talking in terms of revolution is largely answered by what I have already said about nationalism. But my movement is conditioned by one great and disturbing factor. You might of course say that there can be no non-violent rebellion and there has been none known to history. Well, it is my ambition to provide an instance, and it is my dream that my country may win its freedom through non-violence. And, I would like to repeat to the whole world times without number that I will not purchase my country's freedom at the cost of non-violence. My marriage with non-violence is such an absolute thing that I would rather commit suicide than be deflected from my position.

Young India, 12 Nov. 1931

132. The mechanism of a Constituent Assembly

19 November 1939

Pandit Jawaharlal Nehru has compelled me to study, among other things, the implications of a Constituent Assembly.* When he first introduced it in the Congress resolutions, I reconciled myself to it because of my belief in his superior knowledge of the technicalities of democracy. But I was not free from scepticism. Hard facts have, however, made me a convert and, for that reason perhaps, more enthusiastic than Jawaharlal himself. For I seem to see in it a remedy, which Jawaharlal may not, for our communal and other distempers, besides being a vehicle for mass political and other education.

. . . It will be the surest index to the popular feeling. It will bring out the best and the worst in us. Illiteracy does not worry me. I would plump for unadulterated adult franchise for both men and women, i.e., I would put them all on the register of voters. It is open to them not to exercise it if they do not wish to. I would give separate vote to the Muslims; but, without giving separate vote, I would, though reluctantly, give reservation, if required, to every real minority according to its numerical strength.

Thus the Constituent Assembly provides the easiest method of arriving at a just solution of the communal problem.* Today we are unable to say with mathematical precision who represents whom. Though the Congress is admittedly the oldest representative organization on the widest scale, it is open to political and semi-political organizations to question, as they do question, its overwhelmingly representative character . . . The Constituent Assembly will represent all communities in their exact proportion. Except it there is no other way of doing full justice to rival claims. Without it there can be no finality to communal and other claims.

Again, the Constituent Assembly alone can produce a constitution indigenous to the country and truly and fully representing the will of the people. Undoubtedly such a constitution will not be ideal, but it will be real, however imperfect it may be in the estimation of the theorists or legal luminaries. Self-government to be self-government has merely to reflect the will of the people who are to govern themselves. If they are not prepared for it, they will make a hash of it. I can conceive the possibility of a people fitting themselves for right government through a series of wrong experiments, but I cannot conceive a people governing themselves rightly through a government imposed from without, even as the fabled jackdaw could not walk like a peacock with feathers borrowed from his elegant companion. A diseased person has a prospect of getting well by personal effort. He cannot borrow health from others.

'The Only Way'. *Harijan*, 25 Nov. 1939

133. Parliamentary work for independence

18 July 1946

My post contains so many letters from persons who want to be in the Constituent Assembly that it frightens me into the suspicion that, if these letters are an indication of the general feeling, the intelligentsia is more anxious about personal aggrandizement than about India's independence . . . These correspondents should know that I take no interest in these elections,* I do not attend meetings at which these applications are considered and that I often only know from newspapers who has been elected. It is on rare occasions that my advice is sought as to the choice to be made. But I write this more to draw attention to the disease of which these applications are a sign than to warn my correspondents against building any expectation of my intervention. It is wrong to think communally in such elections, it is wrong to think that anyone is good enough for the Constituent Assembly, it is altogether wrong to think that the election carries any honour with it, it is a post of service if one is fitted for the labours and, lastly, it is wrong to regard the post as one for making a few rupees while the Assembly lasts.

. . . It is debasing to think that true service consists in getting a seat in the Assembly. True service lies outside. The field of service outside is limitless. In the fight for independence, the Assembly, like the one in course of formation, has a place. Nevertheless it is a very small place and that too if we use it wisely and well; certainly not, if there is a scramble for a seat in it. The scramble warrants the fear that it may become a hunting ground for place-seekers. I am free to confess that a Constituent Assembly is the logical outcome of parliamentary activity. The labour of the late Deshbandhu Chittaranjan Das and Pandit Motilal Nehru* opened my eyes to the fact that the parliamentary programme had a place in the national activity for independence. I strove hard against it. It is certainly inconsistent with pure non-co-operation. But pure non-co-operation never held the field. What came into being also waned. Had there been universal non-co-operation of the non-violent type in the Congress ranks, there would have been no parliamentary programme.

. . . Had there been such complete non-co-operation, there would be *swaraj* today based on non-violence. But this never happened. In the circumstances it would have been vain to struggle against what the nation had been familiar with and from which it could not be completely weaned. The parliamentary step having been taken, it would have been improper to boycott the present effort. But that does not, can never, mean that there should be indecent competition for filling the seats in it. Let us recognize the limitations.

'A Tragic Phenomenon'. *Harijan*, 28 July 1946

134. Possibilities of independence

21 July 1946

QUESTION. You have said in your article in the *Harijan* of July 15, under the caption 'The Real Danger', that Congressmen in general certainly do not know the kind of independence they want. Would you kindly give them a broad but comprehensive picture of the Independent India of your own conception?

ANSWER. I do not know that I have not, from time to time, given my idea of Indian independence. Since, however, this question is part of a series, it is better to answer it even at the risk of repetition.

Independence of India should mean independence of the whole of India, including what is called India of the States and the other foreign powers, French and Portuguese, who are there, I presume, by British sufferance. Independence must mean that of the people of India, not of those who are today ruling over them. The rulers should depend on the will of those who are under their heels. Thus, they have to be servants of the people, ready to do their will.

Independence must begin at the bottom. Thus, every village will be a republic or panchayat having full powers. It follows, therefore, that every village has to be self-sustained and capable of managing its affairs even to the extent of defending itself against the whole world. It will be trained and prepared to perish in the attempt to defend itself against any onslaught from without. Thus, ultimately, it is the individual who is the unit. This does not exclude dependence on and willing help from neighbours or from the world. It will be free and voluntary play of mutual forces. Such a society is necessarily highly cultured in which every man and woman knows what he or she wants and, what is more, knows that no one should want anything that others cannot have with equal labour.

This society must naturally be based on truth and non-violence which, in my opinion, are not possible without a living belief in God, meaning a self-existent, all-knowing living Force which inheres every other force known to the world and which depends on none and which will live when all other forces may conceivably perish or cease to act. I am unable to account for my life without belief in this all-embracing living Light.

In this structure composed of innumerable villages, there will be ever-widening, never-ascending circles. Life will not be a pyramid with the apex sustained by the bottom. But it will be an oceanic circle whose centre will be the individual always ready to perish for the village, the latter ready to perish for the circle of villages, till at last the whole becomes one life composed of individuals, never aggressive in their arrogance but ever humble, sharing the majesty of the oceanic circle of which they are integral units.

Therefore the outermost circumference will not wield power to crush the inner circle but will give strength to all within and derive its own strength from it. I may be taunted with the retort that this is all Utopian and, therefore, not worth a single thought. If Euclid's point, though incapable of being drawn by human agency, has an imperishable value, my picture has its own for mankind to live. Let India live for this true picture, though never realizable in its completeness. We must have a proper picture of what we want, before we can have something approaching it. If there ever is to be a republic of every village in India, then I claim verity for my picture in which the last is equal to the first or, in other words, no one is to be the first and none the last.

In this picture every religion has its full and equal place. We are all leaves of a majestic tree whose trunk cannot be shaken off its roots which are deep down in the bowels of the earth. The mightiest wind cannot move it.

In this there is no room for machines that would displace human labour and that would concentrate power in a few hands. Labour has its unique place in a cultured human family. Every machine that helps every individual has a place. But I must confess that I have never sat down to think out what that machine can be. I have thought of Singer's sewing machine. But even that is perfunctory. I do not need it to fill in my picture.

QUESTION. Do you believe that the proposed Constituent Assembly could be used for the realization of your picture?

ANSWER. The Constituent Assembly has all the possibilities for the realization of my picture. Yet I cannot hope for much, not because the State Paper* holds no such possibilities but because the document, being wholly of a voluntary nature, requires the common consent of the many parties to it. These have no common goal. Congressmen themselves are not of one mind even on the contents of Independence. I do not know how many swear by non-violence or the *charkha* or, believing in decentralization, regard the village as the nucleus. I know on the contrary that many would have India become a first-class military power and wish for India to have a strong centre and build the whole structure round it. In the medley of these conflicts I know that if India is to be leader in clean action based on clean thought, God will confound the wisdom of these big men and will provide the villages with the power to express themselves as they should.

QUESTION. If the Constituent Assembly fizzles out because of the 'danger from within', as you have remarked in the above-mentioned article, would you advise the Congress to accept the alternative of general country-wide strike and capture of power, either non-violently or with the use of necessary force? What is your alternative in that eventuality if the above is not approved by you?

ANSWER. I must not contemplate darkness before it stares me in the face. And in no case can I be party, irrespective of non-violence, to a universal strike and capture of power. Though, therefore, I do not know what I should do in the case of a breakdown, I know that the actuality will find me ready with an alternative. My sole reliance being on the living Power which we call God, He will put the alternative in my hands when the time has come, not a minute sooner.

'Independence'. *Harijan*, 28 July 1946

135. Independence imperilled by the prospect of partition

11 April 1947

India is now on the threshold of independence. But this is not the independence I want. To my mind it will be no independence if India is partitioned* and the minorities do not enjoy security, protection and equal treatment. The country is not yet completely independent. If what is happening today is an earnest of things to come after independence, it bodes no good for the future. We have a proverb saying that the cradle bespeaks the child's future. I, therefore, feel ill at ease. But I am content to leave the future in God's good hands.

Talk with Y. M. Dadoo and O. M. Naicker (G.). *Biharni Komi Agman*, p. 187. *MPWMG*, vol. iii, pp. 268–9

136. Gandhi's agony

1 June 1947

I see clearly that we are setting about this business the wrong way. We may not feel the full effect immediately, but I can see clearly that the future of independence gained at this price* is going to be dark. I pray that God may not keep me alive to witness it . . . But somehow in spite of my being all alone, in my thoughts, I am experiencing an ineffable inner joy and freshness of mind. I feel as if God himself was lighting my path before me. And it is perhaps the reasons why I am able to fight on single-handed. . . .

I shall perhaps not be alive to witness it, but should the evil I apprehend overtake India and her independence be imperilled, let posterity know what agony this old man went through thinking of it. Let not the coming generations curse Gandhi for being a party to India's vivisection. But everyone is today impatient for independence. Therefore there is no alternative.

Talk with Manu Gandhi (G.). *Bihar Pachhi Dilhi*, pp. 50–2. *MPWMG*, vol. iii, pp. 273–4

137. Advice to disband Congress

29 January 1940*

Though split into two, India having attained political Independence through means devised by the Indian National Congress, the Congress in its present shape and form, i.e., as a propaganda vehicle and parliamentary machine, has outlived its use. India has still to attain social, moral and economic independence in terms of its seven hundred thousand villages as distinguished from its cities and towns. The struggle for the ascendancy of civil over military power is bound to take place in India's progress towards its democratic goal. It must be kept out of unhealthy competition with political parties and communal parties. For these and other similar reasons, the A.I.C.C.* [should resolve] to disband the existing Congress organization and flower into a Lok Sevak Sangh [society for the service of the people] under the following rules* . . .

'His Last Will and Testament'. *Harijan*, 15 Feb. 1948

b. Making *swaraj*—the Constructive Programme

138. The implications of the Constructive Programme

A correspondent writes:

What are the qualities that you intend to inculcate in people by laying stress on the constructive programme? What are the qualifications necessary for a constructive worker in order to make his work effective?

The constructive programme is a big undertaking including a number of items: (1) Hindu–Muslim or communal unity; (2) Removal of untouchability; (3) Prohibition; (4) Khadi; (5) Other village industries; (6) Village sanitation; (7) New or basic education; (8) Adult education; (9) Uplift of women; (10) Education in hygiene and health; (11) Propagation of *Rashtrabhasha;** (12) Cultivating love of one's own language; (13) Working for economic equality. This list can be supplemented if necessary, but it is so comprehensive that I think it can be proved to include items appearing to have been omitted.

The reader will see that it is the want of all these things that is responsible for our bondage. He will also see that the constructive programme of the Congress is not supposed to include all the items. That is understood to include only four items, or rather six, now that the Congress has created the All-India Village Industries Association and the Basic Education Board. But we have to go further forward, we have to stabilize and perfect ahimsa, and so we have to make the constructive programme as comprehensive as possible. There should be no room for doubt that, if we can win swaraj purely through non-violence, we can also retain it through the same means. In the fulfilment of the constructive programme lies the non-violent attainment of swaraj.

The items I have mentioned are not in order of importance. I have put them down just as they came to my pen. Generally I talk of khadi only nowadays, because millions of people can take their share in this work, and progress can be arithmetically measured. Communal unity and the removal of untouchability cannot be thus assessed. Once they become part of our daily life, nothing need be done by us as individuals.

Let us now glance at the various items. Without Hindu–Muslim, i.e., communal unity, we shall always remain crippled. And how can a crippled India win swaraj? Communal unity means unity between Hindus, Sikhs, Mussalmans, Christians, Parsis, Jews. All these go to make Hindustan. He who neglects any of these communities does not know constructive work.

As long as the curse of untouchability pollutes the mind of the Hindu, so long is he himself an untouchable in the eyes of the world, and an untouchable cannot win non-violent swaraj. The removal of untouchability means treating the so-called untouchables as one's own kith and kin. He who does treat them so must be free from the sense of high and low, in fact free from all wrong class-sense. He will regard the whole world as one family. Under non-violent swaraj it will be impossible to conceive of any country as an enemy country.

Pure swaraj is impossible of attainment by people who have been or who are slaves of intoxicating drinks and drugs. It must never be forgotten that a man in the grip of intoxicants is generally bereft of the moral sense.

Everyone now may be said to believe that without khadi there is no just and immediate solution of the problem of the starvation of our millions. I need not therefore dilate upon it. I would only add that in the resuscitation of khadi lies the resuscitation of the ruined village artisans. Khadi requisites (wheels, looms, etc.) have to be made by the village carpenter and blacksmith. For unless these requisites are made in the village it cannot be self-contained and prosperous.

The revival of khadi presupposes the revival of all other village industries. Because we have not laid proper stress on this, khadi-wearers see nothing wrong in using other articles which are foreign or mill-made. Such people may be said to have failed to grasp the inner meaning of khadi. They forget that by establishing the Village Industries Association the Congress has placed all other village industries on the same level as khadi. As the solar system will be dark without the sun, even so will the sun be lustreless without the planets. All things in the universe are interdependent. The salvation of India is impossible without the salvation of villages.

If rural reconstruction were not to include rural sanitation, our villages would remain the muck-heaps that they are today. Village sanitation is a vital part of village life and is as difficult as it is important. It needs a heroic effort to eradicate age-long insanitation. The village worker who is ignorant of the science of village sanitation, who is not a successful scavenger, cannot fit himself for village service.

It seems to be generally admitted that without the new or basic education the education of millions of children in India is well-nigh impossible. The village worker has, therefore, to master it, and become a basic education teacher himself.

Adult education will follow in the wake of basic education as a matter of course. Where this new education has taken root, the children themselves become their parents' teachers. Be that as it may, the village worker has to undertake adult education also.

Woman is described as man's better half. As long as she has not the same rights in law as man, as long as the birth of a girl does not receive the same welcome as that of a boy, so long we should know that India is suffering from partial paralysis. Suppression of woman is a denial of ahimsa. Every village worker will, therefore, regard every woman as his mother, sister or daughter as the case may be, and look upon her with respect. Only such a worker will command the confidence of the village people.

It is impossible for an unhealthy people to win swaraj. Therefore we should no longer be guilty of the neglect of the health of our people. Every village worker must have a knowledge of the general principles of health.

Without a common language no nation can come into being. Instead of worrying himself with the controversy about the Hindi-Hindustani and Urdu, the village worker will acquire a knowledge of the *Rashtrabhasha*, which should be such as can be understood by both Hindus and Muslims.

Our infatuation about English has made us unfaithful to provincial languages. If only as penance for this unfaithfulness the village worker should cultivate in the villagers a love of their own speech. He will have equal regard for all the other languages of India, and will learn the language of the part where he may be working, and thus be able to inspire the villagers there with a regard for their speech.

The whole of this programme will, however, be a structure on sand if it is not built on the solid foundation of economic equality. Economic equality must never be supposed to mean possession of an equal amount of worldly goods by everyone. It does mean, however, that everyone will have a proper house to live in, sufficient and balanced food to eat, and sufficient khadi with which to cover himself. It also means that the cruel inequality that obtains today will be removed by purely non-violent means. This question, however, requires to be separately dealt with.

SEVAGRAM, 13 August 1940

Harijan, 18 Aug. 1940. *CWMG*, vol. lxxii, pp. 378–81

139. Constructive Programme: Its Meaning and Place*

13 December 1941

INTRODUCTORY

The constructive programme may otherwise and more fittingly be called construction of *poorna* swaraj or complete independence by truthful and non-violent means.

Effort for construction of independence so called through violent and, therefore, necessarily untruthful means we know only too painfully. Look at the daily destruction of property, life and truth in the present war.

Complete independence through truth and non-violence means the independence of every unit, be it the humblest of the nation, without distinction of race, colour or creed. This independence is never exclusive. It is, therefore, wholly compatible with interdependence within or without. Practice will always fall short of the theory, even as the drawn line falls short of the theoretical line of Euclid. Therefore, complete independence will be complete only to the extent of our approach in practice to truth and non-violence.

Let the reader mentally plan out the whole of the constructive programme, and he will agree with me that, if it could be successfully worked out, the end of it would be the independence we want. . . .

On the other hand there is no such thing as an imaginary or even perfect definition of independence through violence. For it presupposes only ascendancy of that party of the nation which makes the most effective use of violence. In it perfect equality, economic or otherwise, is inconceivable.

But for my purpose, which is to convince the reader of the necessity of following out the constructive programme in the non-violent effort, the acceptance of my argument about the ineffectiveness of violence for the attainment of independence is not required. The reader is welcome to the belief that independence of this humblest unit is possible under a scheme of violence, if this effort enables him also to admit that it is a certainty through the complete execution of the programme by the nation.

Let us now examine the items:

1. COMMUNAL UNITY

Everybody is agreed about the necessity of this unity. But everybody does not know that unity does not mean political unity, which may be imposed. It means an unbreakable heart unity. The first thing essential for achieving such unity is for every Congressman, whatever his religion may be, to represent in his own person Hindu, Muslim, Christian, Zoroastrian, Jew, etc., shortly, every Hindu and non-Hindu. He has to feel his identity with every one of the millions of the inhabitants of Hindustan. In order to realize this, every Congressman will cultivate personal friendship with persons representing faiths other

than his own. He should have the same regard for the other faiths as
he has for his own.

In such a happy state of things there would be no disgraceful cry
at the stations such as 'Hindu water' and 'Muslim water' or 'Hindu
tea' and 'Muslim tea'. There would be no separate rooms or pots
for Hindus and non-Hindus in schools and colleges, no communal
schools, colleges and hospitals. The beginning of such a revolution
has to be made by Congressmen without any political motive behind
the correct conduct. Political unity will be its natural fruit.

We have long been accustomed to think that power comes only
through Legislative Assemblies. I have regarded this belief as a
grave error brought about by inertia or hypnotism. A superficial
study of British history has made us think that all power percolates
to the people from parliaments. The truth is that power resides in
the people and it is entrusted for the time being to those whom they
may choose as their representatives. Parliaments have no power or
even existence independently of the people. It has been my effort
for the last twenty-one years to convince the people of this simple
truth. Civil disobedience is the storehouse of power. Imagine a whole
people unwilling to conform to the laws of the legislature, and prepared to suffer the consequences of non-compliance. They will bring
the whole legislative and executive machinery to a standstill. The
police and the military are of use to coerce minorities however powerful they may be. But no police or military coercion can bend the
resolute will of a people who are out for suffering to the uttermost.

And parliamentary procedure is good only when its members
are willing to conform to the will of the majority. In other words, it
is fairly effective only among compatibles.

Here in India we have been pretending to work the parliamentary
system under separate electorates which have created artificial incom-
patibles. Living unity can never come out of these artificial entities
being brought together on a common platform. Such legislatures
may function. But they can only be a platform for wrangling and
sharing the crumbs of power that may fall from rulers whoever they
may be. These rule with a rod of iron, and prevent the opposing elements from flying at one another's throats. I hold the emergence of
complete independence to be an impossibility out of such a disgrace.

Though I hold such strong views, I have come to the conclusion
that so long as there are undesirable candidates for elective bodies,

Congress should put up candidates in order to prevent reactionaries from entering such bodies.

2. REMOVAL OF UNTOUCHABILITY

At this time of the day it is unnecessary to dilate upon the necessity of the removal of this blot and curse upon Hinduism. Congressmen have certainly done much in this matter. But I am sorry to have to say that many Congressmen have looked upon this item as a mere political necessity and not something indispensable, so far as Hindus are concerned, for the very existence of Hinduism. If Hindu Congressmen take up the cause for its own sake, they will influence the so-called *sanatanis** far more extensively than they have hitherto done. They should approach them not in a militant spirit but, as befits their non-violence, in a spirit of friendliness. And so far as Harijans are concerned, every Hindu should make common cause with them and befriend them in their awful isolation—such isolation as perhaps the world has never seen in the monstrous immensity one witnesses in India. I know from experience how difficult the task is. But it is part of the task of building the edifice of swaraj. And the road to swaraj is steep and narrow. There are many slippery ascents and many deep chasms. They have all to be negotiated with unfaltering step before we can reach the summit and breathe the fresh air of freedom.

3. PROHIBITION

Although like communal unity and removal of untouchability prohibition has been on the Congress programme since 1920, Congressmen have not taken the interest they might have taken in this very vital social and moral reform. If we are to reach our goal through non-violent effort, we may not leave to the future government the fate of lakhs of men and women who are labouring under the curse of intoxicants and narcotics.

Medical men can make a most effective contribution towards the removal of this evil. They have to discover ways of weaning the drunkard and the opium addict from the curse.

Women and students have a special opportunity in advancing this reform. By many acts of loving service they can acquire on addicts a hold which will compel them to listen to the appeal to give up the evil habit.

Congress committees can open recreation booths where the tired labourer will rest his limbs, get healthy and cheap refreshments, and find suitable games. All this work is fascinating and uplifting. The non-violent approach to swaraj is a novel approach. In it old values give place to new. In the violent way such reforms may find no place. Believers in that way, in their impatience and, shall I say, ignorance, put off such things to the day of deliverance. They forget that lasting and healthy deliverance comes from within, i.e., from self-purification. Constructive workers make legal prohibition easy and successful even if they do not pave the way for it.

4. KHADI

Khadi is a controversial subject. Many people think that in advocating khadi I am sailing against a headwind and am sure to sink the ship of swaraj and that I am taking the country to the dark ages. I do not propose to argue the case for khadi in this brief survey. I have argued it sufficiently elsewhere. Here I want to show what every Congressman, and for that matter every Indian, can do to advance the cause of khadi. It connotes the beginning of economic freedom and equality of all in the country. The proof of the pudding is in the eating. Let everyone try, and he or she will find out for himself or herself the truth of what I am saying. Khadi must be taken with all its implications. It means a wholesale swadeshi mentality, a determination to find all the necessaries of life in India and that too through the labour and intellect of the villagers. That means a reversal of the existing process. That is to say that, instead of half a dozen cities of India and Great Britain living on the exploitation and the ruin of the 700,000 villages of India, the latter will be largely self-contained, and will voluntarily serve the cities of India and even the outside world in so far as it benefits both the parties.

This needs a revolutionary change in the mentality and tastes of many. Easy though the non-violent way is in many respects, it is very difficult in many others. It vitally touches the life of every single Indian, makes him feel aglow with the possession of a power that has lain hidden within himself and makes him proud of his identity with every drop of the ocean of Indian humanity. This non-violence is not the inanity for which we have mistaken it through all these long ages; it is the most potent force as yet known to mankind and on which its very existence is dependent. It is that force which I have tried to present to the Congress and through it to the world. Khadi to me is the symbol of unity of Indian humanity, of its economic free-dom and equality and, therefore, ultimately, in the poetic expression of Jawaharlal Nehru,* 'the livery of India's freedom'.

Moreover, khadi mentality means decentralization of the pro-duction and distribution of the necessaries of life. Therefore, the formula so far evolved is, every village to produce all its necessaries and a certain percentage in addition for the requirements of the cities.

Heavy industries will needs be centralized and nationalized. But they will occupy the least part of the vast national activity which will mainly be in the villages.

Having explained the implications of khadi, I must indicate what Congressmen can and should do towards its promotion. Production of khadi includes cotton-growing, picking, ginning, cleaning, card-ing, slivering, spinning, sizing, dyeing, preparing the warp and the woof, weaving, and washing. These, with the exception of dyeing, are essential processes. Every one of them can be effectively handled in the villages and is being so handled in many villages throughout India, which the A.I.S.A.* is covering. According to the latest report the following are the interesting figures: 275,146 villagers, including 19,654 Harijans and 57,378 Muslims, scattered in at least 13,451 villages, received, as spinners, weavers, etc., Rs 3,485,609 in 1940. The spinners were largely women.

Yet the work done is only one-hundredth part of what could be done if Congressmen honestly took up the khadi programme. Since the wanton destruction of this central village industry and the allied handicrafts, intelligence and brightness have fled from the vil-lages, leaving them inane, lustreless, and reduced almost to the state of their ill-kept cattle.

If Congressmen will be true to the Congress call in respect of khadi, they will carry out the instructions of the A.I.S.A. issued from time to time as to the part they can play in khadi planning. Only a few broad rules can be laid down here:

1. Every family with a plot of ground can grow cotton at least for family use. Cotton-growing is an easy process. In Bihar the cultiva-tors were by law compelled to grow indigo on ³⁄₂₀ of their cultivable land. This was in the interest of the foreign indigo planter. Why cannot we grow cotton voluntarily for the nation on a certain portion of our land? The reader will note that decentralization commences

from the beginning of khadi processes. Today cotton crop is central-ized and has to be sent to distant parts of India. Before the war it used to be sent principally to Britain and Japan. It was and still is a money crop and, therefore, subject to the fluctuations of the market. Under the khadi scheme cotton-growing becomes free from this uncertainty and gamble. The grower grows what he needs. The farmer needs to know that his first business is to grow for his own needs. When he does that, he will reduce the chance of a low market ruining him.

2. Every spinner would buy—if he has not his own—enough cotton for ginning, which he can easily do without the hand-ginning roller frame. He can gin his own portion with a board and an iron rolling-pin. Where this is considered impracticable, hand-ginned cotton should be bought and carded. Carding for self can be done well on a tiny bow without much effort. The greater the decentral-ization of labour, the simpler and cheaper the tools. The slivers made, the process of spinning commences. I strongly recommend the *dhanush takli*. I have used it frequently. My speed on it is almost the same as on the wheel. I draw a finer thread and the strength and the evenness of the yarn are greater on the *dhanush takli* than on the wheel. This may not, however, hold good for all. My emphasis on the *dhanush takli* is based on the fact that it is more easily made, is cheaper than and does not require frequent repairs like the wheel. Unless one knows how to make the two *mals** and to adjust them when they slip or to put the wheel right when it refuses to work, the wheel has often to lie idle. Moreover, if the millions take to spinning at once, as they well may have to, the *dhanush takli*, being the instru-ment most easily made and handled, is the only tool that can meet the demand. It is more easily made even than the simple *takli*. The best, easiest and cheapest way is to make it oneself. Indeed one ought to learn how to handle and make simple tools. Imagine the unifying and educative effect of the whole nation simultaneously taking part in the processes up to spinning! Consider the levelling effect of the bond of common labour between the rich and the poor!

Yarn thus produced may be used in three ways: by presenting it to the A.I.S.A. for the sake of the poor, by having it woven for personal use, or by getting as much khadi for it as it can buy. It is clear enough that the finer and better the yarn the greater will be its value. If Congressmen will put their hearts into the work, they will make improvements in the tools and make many discoveries. In our country there has been a divorce between labour and intelligence. The result has been stagnation. If there is an indissoluble marriage between the two, and that in the manner here suggested, the resultant good will be inestimable.

In this scheme of nationwide spinning as a sacrifice, I do not expect the average man or woman to give more than one hour daily to this work.

5. OTHER VILLAGE INDUSTRIES

These stand on a different footing from khadi. There is not much scope for voluntary labour in them. Each industry will take the labour of only a certain number of hands. These industries come in as a handmaid to khadi. They cannot exist without khadi, and khadi will be robbed of its dignity without them. Village economy cannot be complete without the essential village industries such as hand-grinding, hand-pounding, soap-making, paper-making, match-making, tanning, oil-pressing, etc. Congressmen can interest themselves in these and, if they are villagers or will settle down in villages, they will give these industries a new life and a new dress. All should make it a point of honour to use only village articles whenever and wherever available. Given the demand there is no doubt that most of our wants can be supplied from our villages. When we have become village-minded, we will not want imitations of the West or machine-made products, but we will develop a true national taste in keeping with the vision of a new India in which pauperism, starvation and idleness will be unknown.

6. VILLAGE SANITATION

Divorce between intelligence and labour has resulted in criminal negligence of the villages. And so, instead of having graceful hamlets dotting the land, we have dung-heaps. The approach to many villages is not a refreshing experience. Often one would like to shut one's eyes and stuff one's nose; such is the surrounding dirt and offending smell. If the majority of Congressmen were derived from our villages, as they should be, they should be able to make our villages models of cleanliness in every sense of the word. But they have never considered it their duty to identify themselves with the villagers in their daily lives. A sense of national or social sanitation is not a virtue among us. We may take a kind of a bath, but we do not mind dirtying the well or the tank or river by whose side or in which we perform ablutions. I regard this defect as a great vice which is responsible for the disgraceful state of our villages and the sacred banks of the sacred rivers and for diseases that spring from insanitation.

7. NEW OR BASIC EDUCATION

This is a new subject. But the members of the Working Committee felt so much interested in it that they gave a charter to the organizers of the Hindustani Talimi Sangh which has been functioning since the Haripura session.* This is a big field of work for many Congressmen. This education is meant to transform village children into model villagers. It is principally designed for them. The inspiration for it has come from the villages. Congressmen who want to build up the structure of swaraj from its very foundation dare not neglect the children. Foreign rule has unconsciously, though none the less surely, begun with the children in the field of education. Primary education is a farce designed without regard to the wants of the India of the villages and for that matter even of the cities. Basic education links the children, whether of the cities or the villages, to all that is best and lasting in India. It develops both the body and the mind, and keeps the child rooted to the soil with a glorious vision of the future, in the realization of which he or she begins to take his or her share from the very commencement of his or her career in school. Congressmen would find it of absorbing interest benefiting themselves equally with the children with whom they come in contact. Let those who wish put themselves in touch with the Secretary of the Sangh at Sevagram.

8. ADULT EDUCATION

This has been woefully neglected by Congressmen. Where they have not neglected it, they have been satisfied with teaching illiterates to read and write. If I had charge of adult education, I should begin with opening the minds of the adult pupils to the greatness and vastness of their country. The villager's India is contained in his village. If he goes to another village, he talks of his own village as his home. Hindustan is for him a geographical term. We have no notion of the ignorance prevailing in the villages. The villagers know nothing of foreign rule and its evils. What little knowledge they have picked up fills them with the awe the foreigner inspires. The result is the dread and hatred of the foreigner and his rule. They do not know how to get rid of it. They do not know that the foreigner's presence is due to their own weaknesses and their ignorance of the power they possess to rid themselves of the foreign rule. My adult education means, therefore, first, true political education of the adult by word of mouth. Seeing that this will be mapped out, it can be given without fear. I imagine that it is too late in the day for authority to interfere with this type of education; but if there is interference, there must be a fight for this elementary right without which there can be no swaraj. Of course, in all I have written, openness has been assumed. Non-violence abhors fear and, therefore, secrecy. Side by side with the education by the mouth will be the literary education. This is itself a speciality. Many methods are being tried in order to shorten the period of education. A temporary or permanent board of experts may be appointed by the Working Committee to give shape to the idea here adumbrated and guide the workers. I admit that what I have said in this paragraph only points the way but does not tell the average Congressman how to go about it. Nor is every Congressman fitted for this highly special work. But Congressmen who are teachers should find no difficulty in laying down a course in keeping with the suggestions made herein.

9. WOMEN

I have included service of women in the constructive programme, for though satyagraha has automatically brought India's women out from their darkness as nothing else could have in such an incredibly short space of time, Congressmen have not felt the call to see that women become equal partners in the fight for swaraj. They have not realized that woman must be the true helpmate of man in the mission of service. Woman has been suppressed under custom and law for which man was responsible and in the shaping of which she had no hand. In a plan of life based on non-violence, woman has as much right to shape her own destiny as man has to shape his. But as every right in a non-violent society proceeds from the previous performance of a duty, it follows that rules of social conduct must be framed by mutual co-operation and consultation. They can never be imposed from outside. Men have not realized this truth in its fullness in their behaviour towards women. They have considered themselves to be lords and masters of women instead of considering them as their friends and co-workers. It is the privilege of Congressmen to give the women of India a lifting hand. Women are in the position somewhat of the slave of old who did not know that he could or ever had to be free. And when freedom came, for the moment he felt helpless. Women have been taught to regard themselves as slaves of men. It is up to Congressmen to see that they enable them to realize their full status and play their part as equals of men.

This revolution is easy, if the mind is made up. Let Congressmen begin with their own homes. Wives should not be dolls and objects of indulgence, but should be treated as honoured comrades in common service. To this end those who have not received a liberal education should receive such instruction as is possible from their husbands. The same observation applies, with the necessary changes, to mothers and daughters.

It is hardly necessary to point out that I have given a one-sided picture of the helpless state of India's women. I am quite conscious of the fact that in the villages generally they hold their own with their menfolk and in some respects even rule them. But to the impartial outsider the legal and customary status of woman is bad enough throughout and demands radical alteration.

10. EDUCATION IN HEALTH AND HYGIENE

Having given a place to village sanitation, the question may be asked why give a separate place to education in health and hygiene? It might have been bracketed with sanitation, but I did not wish to interfere with the items. Mention of mere sanitation is not enough to include health and hygiene. The art of keeping one's health and the knowledge of hygiene is by itself a separate subject of study and corresponding practice. In a well-ordered society the citizens know and observe the laws of health and hygiene. It is established beyond doubt that ignorance and neglect of the laws of health and hygiene are responsible for the majority of diseases to which mankind is heir. The very high death-rate among us is no doubt due largely to our gnawing poverty, but it could be mitigated if the people were properly educated about health and hygiene.

Mens sana in corpore sano is perhaps the first law for humanity. A healthy mind in a healthy body is a self-evident truth. There is an inevitable connection between mind and body. If we were in possession of healthy minds, we would shed all violence and, naturally obeying the laws of health, we would have healthy bodies without an effort. I hope, therefore, that no Congressman will disregard this item of the constructive programme. The fundamental laws of health and hygiene are simple and easily learnt. The difficulty is about their observance. Here are some:

Think the purest thoughts and banish all idle and impure thoughts.

Breathe the freshest air day and night.

Establish a balance between bodily and mental work.

Stand erect, sit erect, and be neat and clean in every one of your acts, and let these be an expression of your inner condition.

Eat to live for service of fellow-men. Do not live for indulging yourselves. Hence your food must be just enough to keep your mind and body in good order. Man becomes what he eats.

Your water, food and air must be clean, and you will not be satisfied with mere personal cleanliness, but you will infect your surroundings with the same threefold cleanliness that you will desire for yourselves.

11. PROVINCIAL LANGUAGES

Our love of the English language in preference to our own mother tongue has caused a deep chasm between the educated and politically-minded classes and the masses. The languages of India have suffered impoverishment. We flounder when we make the vain attempt to express abstruse thought in the mother tongue. There are no equivalents for scientific terms. The result has been disastrous. The masses remain cut off from the modern mind. We are too near our own times correctly to measure the disservice caused to India by this neglect of its great languages. It is easy enough to understand that unless we undo the mischief the mass mind must remain imprisoned. The masses can make no solid contribution to the construction of swaraj. It is inherent in swaraj based on non-violence that every individual makes his own direct contribution to the Independence movement. The masses cannot do this fully unless they understand every step with all its implications. This is impossible unless every step is explained in their own languages.

12. NATIONAL LANGUAGE

And then for all-India intercourse we need, from among the Indian stock, a language which the largest number of people already know and understand and which the others can easily pick up. This language is indisputably Hindi. It is spoken and understood by both Hindus and Muslims of the North. It is called Urdu when it is

written in the Urdu character. The Congress, in its famous resolution passed at the Cawnpore session in 1925, called this all-
India speech Hindustani. And since that time, in theory at least,
Hindustani has been the *Rashtrabhasha*. I say 'in theory' because even
Congressmen have not practised it as they should have. In 1920 a
deliberate attempt was begun to recognize the importance of Indian
languages for the political education of the masses, as also of an all-
India common speech which politically-minded India could easily
speak and which Congressmen from the different provinces could
understand at all-India gatherings of the Congress. Such national
language should enable one to understand and speak both forms of
speech and write in both the scripts.

I am sorry to have to say that many Congressmen have failed to carry
out that resolution. And so we have, in my opinion, the shameful spectacle of Congressmen insisting on speaking in English and compelling
others to do likewise for their sakes. The spell that English has cast on us
is not yet broken. Being under it, we are impeding the progress of India
towards her goal. Our love of the masses must be skin-deep, if we will
not take the trouble of spending over learning Hindustani as many
months as the years we spend over learning English.

13. ECONOMIC EQUALITY

This last is the master-key to non-violent independence. Working
for economic equality means abolishing the eternal conflict between
capital and labour. It means the levelling down of the few rich in
whose hands is concentrated the bulk of the nation's wealth on the
one hand, and the levelling up of the semi-starved naked millions on
the other. A non-violent system of government is clearly an impossibility so long as the wide gulf between the rich and the hungry
millions persists. The contrast between the palaces of New Delhi and
the miserable hovels of the poor labouring class nearby cannot last
one day in a free India in which the poor will enjoy the same power
as the richest in the land. A violent and bloody revolution is a certainty one day unless there is a voluntary abdication of riches and the
power that riches give and sharing them for the common good.

I adhere to my doctrine of trusteeship in spite of the ridicule that
has been poured upon it. It is true that it is difficult to reach. So is
non-violence. But we made up our minds in 1920 to negotiate that
steep ascent. We have found it worth the effort. It involves a daily
growing appreciation of the working of non-violence. It is expected

that Congressmen will make a diligent search and reason out for themselves the why and the wherefore of non-violence. They should ask themselves how the existing inequalities can be abolished violently or non-violently. I think we know the violent way. It has not succeeded anywhere.

This non-violent experiment is still in the making. We have nothing much yet to show by way of demonstration. It is certain, however, that the method has begun to work though ever so slowly in the direction of equality. And since non-violence is a process of conversion, the conversion, if achieved, must be permanent. A society or a nation constructed non-violently must be able to withstand attack upon its structure from without or within. We have moneyed Congressmen in the organization. They have to lead the way. This fight* provides an opportunity for the closest heart-searching on the part of every individual Congressman. If ever we are to achieve equality, the foundation has to be laid now. Those who think that major reforms will come after the advent of swaraj are deceiving themselves as to the elementary working of non-violent swaraj. It will not drop from heaven all of a sudden one fine morning. But it has to be built up brick by brick by corporate self-effort. We have travelled a fair way in that direction. But a much longer and weary distance has to be covered before we can behold swaraj in its glorious majesty. Every Congressman has to ask himself what he has done towards the attainment of economic equality.

14. KISANS

The programme is not exhaustive. Swaraj is a mighty structure. Eighty crores of hands have to work at building it. Of these *kisans*, i.e., the peasantry, are the largest part. In fact, being the bulk of them (probably over 80%) the *kisans* should be the Congress. But they are not. When they become conscious of their non-violent strength, no power on earth can resist them.

They must not be used for power politics. I consider it to be contrary to the non-violent method. Those who would know my method of organizing *kisans* may profitably study the movement in Champaran* when satyagraha was tried for the first time in India with the result all India knows. It became a mass movement which remained wholly non-violent from start to finish. It affected over twenty lakhs of *kisans*. The struggle centred round one specific grievance which was a century old. There had been several violent revolts to get rid of the grievance. The *kisans* were suppressed. The non-violent remedy succeeded in full in six months. The *kisans* of Champaran became politically conscious without any direct effort. The tangible proof they had of the working of non-violence to remove their grievances drew them to the Congress and led by Babu Brijkishore Prasad and Babu Rajendra Prasad* they gave a good account of themselves during the past civil disobedience campaigns.

The reader may also profitably study the *kisan* movements in Kheda, Bardoli and Borsad. The secret of success lies in a refusal to exploit the *kisans* for political purposes outside their own personal and felt grievances. Organization round a specific wrong they understand. They need no sermons on non-violence. Let them learn to apply non-violence as an effective remedy which they can understand, and later when they are told that the method they were applying was non-violent, they readily recognize it as such.

From these illustrations Congressmen who care could study how work can be done for and among *kisans*. I hold that the method that some Congressmen have followed to organize *kisans* has done them no good and has probably harmed them. Anyway they have not used the non-violent method. Be it said to the credit of some of these workers that they frankly admit that they do not believe in the non-violent method. My advice to such workers would be that they should neither use the Congress name nor work as Congressmen.

The reader will now understand why I have refrained from the competition to organize *kisans* and labour on an all-India basis. How I wish that all hands pulled in the same direction! But perhaps in a huge country like ours it is impossible. Anyway, in non-violence there is no coercion. Cold reason and demonstration of the working of non-violence must be trusted to do the work.

In my opinion, like labour, they should have under the Congress a department working for their specific questions.

15. LABOUR

Ahmedabad Labour Union is a model for all India to copy. Its basis is non-violence, pure and simple. It has never had a set-back in its career. It has gone on from strength to strength without fuss and without show. It has its hospital, its school for the children of the mill-hands, its classes for adults, its own printing press and khadi depot, and its own residential quarters. Almost all the hands are voters and decide the fate of elections. They came on the voters' list at the instance of the Provincial Congress Committee. The organization has never taken part in party politics of the Congress. It influences the municipal policy of the city. It has to its credit very successful strikes which were wholly non-violent. Mill-owners and labour have governed their relations largely through voluntary arbitration. If I had my way, I would regulate all the labour organizations of India, after the Ahmedabad model. It has never sought to intrude itself upon the All-India Trade Union Congress and has been uninfluenced by that Congress. A time, I hope, will come when it will be possible for the Trade Union Congress to accept the Ahmedabad method and have the Ahmedabad organization as part of the All-India Union. But I am in no hurry. It will come in its own time.

16. ADIVASIS

. . . Service of *adivasis** is also a part of the constructive programme. Though they are the sixteenth number in this programme, they are not the least in point of importance. Our country is so vast and the races so varied that the best of us cannot know all there is to know of men and their condition. As one discovers this for oneself, one realizes how difficult it is to make good our claim to be one nation, unless every unit has a living consciousness of being one with every other. . . .

There are several . . . workers in . . . parts of India [serving *adivasis*] and yet [there] are too few. Truly, 'the harvest is rich but the labourers are few'.* Who can deny that all such service is not merely humanitarian but solidly national, and brings us nearer to true independence?

17. LEPERS

Leper is a word of bad odour. India is perhaps a home of lepers next only to Central Africa. Yet they are as much a part of society as the tallest among us. But the tall absorb our attention though they are least in need of it. The lot of the lepers who are much in need of attention is studied neglect. I am tempted to call it heartless, which it certainly is in terms of non-violence. It is largely the missionary who, be it said to his credit, bestows care on him. The only institution run by an Indian, as a pure labour of love, is by Shri Manohar Diwan near Wardha. It is working under the inspiration and guidance of

Shri Vinoba Bhave. If India was pulsating with new life, if we were all in earnest about winning independence in the quickest manner possible by truthful and non-violent means, there would not be a leper or beggar in India uncared for and unaccounted for. In this revised edition I am deliberately introducing the leper as a link in the chain of constructive effort. For what the leper is in India, that we are, if we but look about us, for the modern civilized world. Examine the condition of our brethren across the ocean and the truth of my remark will be borne home to us.

18. STUDENTS

I have reserved students to the last. I have always cultivated close contact with them. They know me and I know them. They have given me service. Many ex-collegians are my esteemed co-workers. I know that they are the hope of the future. In the heyday of non-co-operation they were invited to leave their schools and colleges. Some professors and students who responded to the Congress call have remained steadfast and gained much for the country and themselves. The call has not been repeated for there is not the atmosphere for it. But experience has shown that the lure of the current education, though it is false and unnatural, is too much for the youth of the country. College education provides a career. It is a passport for entrance to the charmed circle. Pardonable hunger for knowledge cannot be satisfied otherwise than by going through the usual rut. They do not mind the waste of precious years in acquiring knowledge of an utterly foreign language which takes the place of the mother tongue. The sin of it is never felt. They and their teachers have made up their minds that the indigenous languages are useless for gaining access to modern thought and the modern sciences. I wonder how the Japanese are faring. For their education, I understand, is all given in Japanese. The Chinese Generalissimo* knows very little, if anything, of English.

But such as the students are, it is from these young men and women that the future leaders of the nation are to rise. Unfortunately they are acted upon by every variety of influences. Non-violence offers them little attraction. A blow for a blow or two for one is an easily understandable proposition. It seems to yield immediate result though momentary. It is a never-ending trial of brute strength as we see in time of war among brutes or among human beings. Appreciation of non-violence means patient research and still more patient and difficult practice. I have not entered the list of competitors for the students' hand, for the reasons that have dictated my course about *kisans* and labour. But I am myself a fellow-student, using the word in its broader sense. My university is different from theirs. They have a standing invitation from me to come to my university and join me in my search. Here are the terms

1. Students must not take part in party politics. They are students, searchers, not politicians.

2. They may not resort to political strikes. They must have their heroes, but their devotion to them is to be shown by copying the best in their heroes, not by going on strikes, if the heroes are imprisoned or die or are even sent to the gallows. If their grief is unbearable and if all the students feel equally, schools or colleges may be closed on such occasions; with the consent of their principals. If the principals will not listen, it is open to the students to leave their institutions in a becoming manner till the managers repent and recall them. On no account may they use coercion against dissentients or against the authorities. They must have the confidence that if they are united and dignified in their conduct, they are sure to win.

3. They must all do sacrificial spinning in a scientific manner. Their tools shall be always neat, clean, and in good order and condition. If possible, they will learn to make them themselves. Their yarn will naturally be of the highest quality. They will study the literature about spinning with all its economic, social, moral and political implications.

4. They will be khadi-users all through and use village products to the exclusion of all analogous things, foreign or machine-made.

5. They may not impose *Vandemataram** or the national flag on others. They may wear national flag buttons on their own persons but not force others to do the same.

6. They can enforce the message of the tricolour flag in their own persons and harbour neither communalism nor untouchability in their hearts. They will cultivate real friendship with students of other faiths and with Harijans as if they were their own kith and kin.

7. They will make it a point to give first aid to their injured neighbours and do scavenging and cleaning in the neighbouring villages and instruct village children and adults.

8. They will learn the national language, Hindustani, in its present double dress, two forms of speech and two scripts, so that they

may feel at home whether Hindi or Urdu is spoken and Nagari or Urdu script is written.

9. They will translate into their own mother tongue everything new they may learn, and transmit it in their weekly rounds to the surrounding villages.

10. They will do nothing in secret, they will be above board in all their dealings, they will lead a pure life of self-restraint, shed all fear and be always ready to protect their weak fellow-students, and be ready to quell riots by non-violent conduct at the risk of their lives. And when the final heat of the struggle comes, they will leave their institutions and, if need be, sacrifice themselves for the freedom of their country.

11. They will be scrupulously correct and chivalrous in their behaviour towards their girl fellow-students.

For working out the programme I have sketched for them, the students must find time. I know that they waste a great deal of time in idleness. By strict economy, they can save many hours. But I do not want to put an undue strain upon any student. I would, therefore, advise patriotic students to lose one year, not at a stretch but spread it over their whole study. They will find that one year so given will not be a waste of time. The effort will add to their equipment, mental, moral and physical, and they will have made even during their studies a substantial contribution to the freedom movement.

PLACE OF CIVIL DISOBEDIENCE

I have said in these pages that civil disobedience is not absolutely necessary to win freedom through purely non-violent effort, if the co-operation of the whole nation is secured in the constructive programme. But such good luck rarely favours nations or individuals. Therefore, it is necessary to know the place of civil disobedience in a nationwide non-violent effort.

It has three definite functions:

1. It can be effectively offered for the redress of a local wrong.

2. It can be offered without regard to effect, though aimed at a particular wrong or evil, by way of self-immolation in order to rouse local consciousness or conscience. Such was the case in Champaran when I offered civil disobedience without any regard to the effect and well knowing that even the people might remain apathetic. That it

proved otherwise may be taken, according to taste, as God's grace or a stroke of good luck.

3. In the place of full response to constructive effort, it can be offered as it was in 1941.* Though it was a contribution to and part of the battle for freedom, it was purposely centred round a particular issue, i.e., free speech. Civil disobedience can never be directed for a general cause such as for independence. The issue must be definite and capable of being clearly understood and within the power of the opponent to yield. This method properly applied must lead to the final goal.

I have not examined here the full scope and possibilities of civil disobedience. I have touched enough of it to enable the reader to understand the connection between the constructive programme and civil disobedience. In the first two cases, no elaborate constructive programme was or could be necessary. But when civil disobedience is itself devised for the attainment of independence, previous preparation is necessary, and it has to be backed by the visible and conscious effort of those who are engaged in the battle. Civil disobedience is thus a stimulation for the fighters and a challenge to the opponent. It should be clear to the reader that civil disobedience in terms of independence without the co-operation of the millions by way of constructive effort is mere bravado and worse than useless.

CONCLUSION

This is not a thesis written on behalf of the Congress or at the instance of the Central Office. It is the outcome of conversations I had with some co-workers in Sevagram. They had felt the want of something from my pen showing the connection between the constructive programme and civil disobedience and how the former might be worked. I have endeavoured to supply the want in this pamphlet. It does not purport to be exhaustive, but, it is sufficiently indicative of the way the programme should be worked.

Let not the reader make the mistake of laughing at any of the items as being part of the movement for independence. Many people do many things, big and small, without connecting them with non-violence or independence. They have then their limited value as expected. The same man appearing as a civilian may be of no consequence, but appearing in his capacity as General he is a big personage, holding the lives of millions at his mercy. Similarly, the charkha in the hands of a poor widow brings a paltry pice* to her, in the hands of a Jawaharlal it is an instrument of India's freedom. It is the office which gives the charkha its dignity. It is the office assigned to the constructive programme which gives it an irresistible prestige and power.

Such at least is my view. It may be that of a mad man. If it makes no appeal to the Congressman, I must be rejected. For my handling of civil disobedience without the constructive programme will be like a paralysed hand attempting to lift a spoon.

Constructive Programme: Its Meaning and Place. CWMG, vol. lxxv, pp. 146–66

140. Independent India needs constructive workers

13 May 1947

Independence is now as good as come. But it is only political independence. Let not anyone think that once the British quit India there will be more comfort and convenience and the Constructive Programme would become superfluous. But from the prevailing atmosphere it seems that for at least a decade after independence our condition would continue to deteriorate. This political freedom no doubt will remove the restraints over us and we shall be able to accomplish our cherished aims. Real hard work will have to be done only after independence. Unless poverty and unemployment are wiped out from India, I would not agree that we have attained freedom. Real wealth does not consist in jewellery and money, but in providing for proper food, clothes, education, and creating healthy conditions of living for every one of us. A country can be called prosperous and free only when its citizens can easily earn enough to meet their needs. But today the situation is so tragic that on the one hand there are people who roll in pomp and luxury and on the other there are people who do not have enough clothes to cover their bodies and who live on the brink of starvation. Today men are sitting idle having no work to do. A man should have full opportunity to develop himself. That will happen only when there is an awakening among the constructive workers.

The country does need politicians. But now when it is necessary to work hard for the prosperity of the country we need devoted constructive workers. I am convinced that people who are wedded to machinery are going to be disillusioned. Everyone, if only after being disillusioned, will have to ply the *charkha*. One has to be self-reliant in everything. If people do not start working of their own free will, time and circumstances will make them do so. But right now I find it suffocating to see the manner in which we are marching towards freedom. I find no light anywhere. Now that the British are contemplating transfer of power every community is keen on grabbing it. But, if we do not do our duty, we will be giving a chance for the people to say that slavery was better than this freedom. To the extent the constructive workers are bold and fearless, these qualities would be reflected in their actions and through their work spread in the atmosphere. If the nation breathes such a healthy air, it would definitely grow healthy. So, the time has come for every constructive worker to gird up his loins and plunge into action. Let him put this moment to good use and justify the life God has granted him.

'Advice to Constructive Workers' (G.). *Biharni Komi Agman*, pp. 346–7. *MPWMG*, vol. iii, pp. 221–2

c. Making *swaraj*—key issues

141. Communal relations*—Muslims and the Indian nation

CHAPTER X: THE CONDITION OF INDIA (CONTINUED): THE HINDUS AND THE MAHOMEDANS

EDITOR. Your last question* is a serious one and yet, on careful consideration, it will be found to be easy of solution. The question arises because of the presence of the railways, of the lawyers and of the doctors. We shall presently examine the last two. We have already considered the railways. I should, however, like to add that man is so made by nature as to require him to restrict his movements as far as his hands and feet will take him. If we did not rush about from place to place by means of railways and such other maddening conveniences, much of the confusion that arises would be obviated. Our difficulties are of our own creation. God set a limit to man's locomotive ambition in the construction of his body. Man immediately proceeded to discover means of overriding the limit. God gifted man with intellect that he might know his Maker. Man abused it so that he might forget his Maker. I am so constructed that I can only serve my immediate neighbours, but in my conceit I pretend to have discovered that I must with my body serve every individual in the Universe. In thus attempting the impossible, man comes in contact with different natures, different religions, and is utterly confounded. According to this reasoning, it must be apparent to you that railways are a most dangerous institution. Owing to them, man has gone further away from his Maker.

READER. But I am impatient to hear your answer to my question. Has the introduction of Mahomedanism not unmade the nation?

EDITOR. India cannot cease to be one nation because people belonging to different religions live in it. The introduction of foreigners does not necessarily destroy the nation; they merge in it. A country is one nation only when such a condition obtains in it. That country must have a faculty for assimilation. India has ever been such a country. In reality, there are as many religions as there are individuals;* but those who are conscious of the spirit of nationality do not interfere with one another's religion. If they do, they are not fit to be considered a nation. If the Hindus believe that India should be peopled only by Hindus, they are living in dreamland. The Hindus, the Mahomedans, the Parsis and the Christians who have made India their country are fellow-countrymen, and they will have to live in unity, if only for their own interest. In no part of the world are one nationality and one religion synonymous terms; nor has it ever been so in India.

READER. But what about the inborn enmity between Hindus and Mahomedans?

EDITOR. That phrase has been invented by our mutual enemy. When the Hindus and Mahomedans fought against one another, they certainly spoke in that strain. They have long since ceased to fight. How, then, can there be any inborn enmity? Pray remember this too, that we did not cease to fight only after British occupation. The Hindus flourished under Moslem sovereigns and Moslems under the Hindu. Each party recognized that mutual fighting was suicidal, and that neither party would abandon its religion by force of arms. Both parties, therefore, decided to live in peace. With the English advent quarrels re-commenced.

The proverbs you have quoted were coined when both were fighting; to quote them now is obviously harmful. Should we not remember that many Hindus and Mahomedans own the same ancestors

and the same blood runs through their veins? Do people become enemies because they change their religion? Is the God of the
Mahomedan different from the God of the Hindu? Religions are
different roads converging to the same point. What does it matter
that we take different roads so long as we reach the same goal?
Wherein is the cause for quarrelling?

Moreover, there are deadly proverbs as between the followers
of Shiva and those of Vishnu, yet nobody suggests that these two
do not belong to the same nation. It is said that the Vedic religion
is different from Jainism, but the followers of the respective faiths
are not different nations. The fact is that we have become enslaved
and, therefore, quarrel and like to have our quarrels decided by
a third party. There are Hindu iconoclasts as there are Mahomedan.
The more we advance in true knowledge, the better we shall understand that we need not be at war with those whose religion we may
not follow.

READER. Now I would like to know your views about cow-
protection.*

EDITOR. I myself respect the cow, that is, I look upon her with
affectionate reverence. The cow is the protector of India because,
being an agricultural country, she is dependent on the cow. The cow
is a most useful animal in hundreds of ways. Our Mahomedan
brethren will admit this.

But, just as I respect the cow, so do I respect my fellow-men. A man
is just as useful as a cow no matter whether he be a Mahomedan or
a Hindu. Am I, then, to fight with or kill a Mahomedan in order to
save a cow? In doing so, I would become an enemy of the Mahomedan
as well as of the cow. Therefore, the only method I know of protecting the cow is that I should approach my Mahomedan brother
and urge him for the sake of the country to join me in protecting
her. If he would not listen to me I should let the cow go for the
simple reason that the matter is beyond my ability. If I were overfull
of pity for the cow, I should sacrifice my life to save her but not
take my brother's. This, I hold, is the law of our religion.

When men become obstinate, it is a difficult thing. If I pull one
way, my Moslem brother will pull another. If I put on superior airs,
he will return the compliment. If I bow to him gently, he will do it
much more so; and if he does not, I shall not be considered to have
done wrong in having bowed. When the Hindus became insistent,

the killing of cows increased. In my opinion, cow-protection societies may be considered cow-killing societies. It is a disgrace to us that we should need such societies. When we forgot how to protect cows, I suppose we needed such societies.

What am I to do when a blood-brother is on the point of killing a cow? Am I to kill him, or to fall down at his feet and implore him? If you admit that I should adopt the latter course, I must do the same to my Moslem brother.

Who protects the cow from destruction by Hindus when they cruelly ill-treat her? Whoever reasons with the Hindus when they mercilessly belabour the progeny of the cow with their sticks? But this has not prevented us from remaining one nation.

Lastly, if it be true that the Hindus believe in the doctrine of non-killing and the Mahomedans do not, what, pray, is the duty of the former? It is not written that a follower of the religion of ahimsa (non-killing) may kill a fellow-man. For him the way is straight. In order to save one being, he may not kill another. He can only plead—therein lies his sole duty.

But does every Hindu believe in *ahimsa*? Going to the root of the matter, not one man really practises such a religion because we do destroy life. We are said to follow that religion because we want to obtain freedom from liability to kill any kind of life. Generally speaking, we may observe that many Hindus partake of meat and are not, therefore, followers of *ahimsa*. It is, therefore, preposterous to suggest that the two cannot live together amicably because the Hindus believe in *ahimsa* and the Mahomedans do not.

These thoughts are put into our minds by selfish and false religious teachers. The English put the finishing touch. They have a habit of writing history; they pretend to study the manners and customs of all peoples.* God has given us a limited mental capacity, but they usurp the function of the Godhead and indulge in novel experiments. They write about their own researches in most laudatory terms and hypnotize us into believing them. We in our ignorance then fall at their feet.

Those who do not wish to misunderstand things may read up the Koran, and they will find therein hundreds of passages acceptable to the Hindus; and the *Bhagavad-gita* contains passages to which not a Mahomedan can take exception. Am I to dislike a Mahomedan because there are passages in the Koran I do not understand or like? It takes two to make a quarrel. If I do not want to quarrel with a Mahomedan, the latter will be powerless to foist a quarrel on me; and, similarly, I should be powerless if a Mahomedan refuses his assistance to quarrel with me. An arm striking the air will become disjointed. If everyone will try to understand the core of his own religion and adhere to it, and will not allow false teachers to dictate to him, there will be no room left for quarrelling.

READER. But will the English ever allow the two bodies to join hands?

EDITOR. This question arises out of your timidity. It betrays our shallowness. If two brothers want to live in peace, is it possible for a third party to separate them? If they were to listen to evil counsels we would consider them to be foolish. Similarly, we Hindus and Mahomedans would have to blame our folly rather than the English, if we allowed them to put us asunder. A clay pot would break through impact, if not with one stone, then with another. The way to save the pot is not to keep it away from the danger point but to bake it so that no stone would break it. We have then to make our hearts of perfectly baked clay. Then we shall be steeled against all danger. This can be easily done by the Hindus. They are superior in numbers; they pretend that they are more educated; they are, therefore, better able to shield themselves from attack on their amicable relations with the Mahomedans.

There is mutual distrust between the two communities. The Mahomedans, therefore, ask for certain concessions from Lord Morley.* Why should the Hindus oppose this? If the Hindus desisted, the English would notice it, the Mahomedans would gradually begin to trust the Hindus, and brotherliness would be the outcome. We should be ashamed to take our quarrels to the English. Everyone can find out for himself that the Hindus can lose nothing by desisting. That man who has inspired confidence in another has never lost anything in this world

I do not suggest that the Hindus and the Mahomedans will never fight. Two brothers living together often do so. We shall sometimes have our heads broken. Such a thing ought not to be necessary, but all men are not equitable. When people are in a rage, they do many foolish things. These we have to put up with. But when we do quarrel, we certainly do not want to engage counsel and resort to English or any law-courts. Two men fight; both have their heads broken, or one only. How shall a third party distribute justice amongst them? Those who fight may expect to be injured.

Gandhi, *Hind Swaraj*, chap. X

142. Supporting the Khilafat campaign

In response to the invitation [to attend a war conference] I went to Delhi. I had, however, objections to taking part in the conference, the principal one being the exclusion from it of leaders like the Ali Brothers.* They were then in jail. I had met them only once or twice, though I had heard much about them. . . . I was seeking the friend-ship of good Musalmans, and was eager to understand the Musalman mind through contact with their purest and most patriotic repre-sentatives . . .

I had realized early enough in South Africa that there was no genuine friendship between the Hindus and the Musalmans. I never missed a single opportunity to remove obstacles in the way of unity. It was not in my nature to placate anyone by adulation, or at the cost of self-respect. But my South African experiences had convinced me that it would be on the question of Hindu–Muslim unity that my *Ahimsa* would be put to its severest test, and that the question pre-sented the widest field for my experiments in *Ahimsa*. The con-viction is still there. Every moment of my life I realize that God is putting me on trial.

Having such strong conviction on the question when I returned from South Africa, I prized the contact with the Brothers. But before closer touch could be established they were isolated . . .

. . . I opened correspondence with the government for the release of the Brothers. In that connection I studied the Brothers' views and activities about the Khilafat.* I had discussions with Musalman friends. I felt that, if I would become a true friend of the Muslims, I must render all possible help in securing the release of the Brothers, and a just settlement of the Khilafat question . . .

Friends and critics have criticized my attitude regarding the Khilafat question. In spite of the criticism I feel that I have no reason to revise it or to regret my co-operation with the Muslims. I should adopt the same attitude, should a similar occasion arise.

Gandhi, *An Autobiography*, part V, chap. XXVI

143. A duty to associate with Muslim concern for the Khilafat

It goes without saying that it is the bounden duty of the Hindus and other religious denominations to associate themselves with their Mohammedan brethren. It is the surest and the simplest method of bringing about the Hindu–Mohammedan unity. It is the privilege of friendship to extend the hand of friendship, and adversity is the crucible in which friendship is tested. Let millions of Hindus show to the Mohammedans that they are one with them in sorrow.

Young India, 4 Oct. 1919. *CWMG*, vol. xvi, p. 207

144. Khilafat—the chance of a life-time for unity

That unity is strength is not merely a copy-book maxim but a rule of life, is in no case so clearly illustrated as in the problem of Hindu–Muslim unity. Divided we must fall. Any third power may easily enslave India so long as we Hindus and Mussalmans are ready to cut each other's throats. Hindu–Muslim unity means not unity only between Hindus and Mussalmans, but between all those who believe India to be their home, no matter to what faith they belong.

I am fully aware that we have not yet attained that unity to such an extent as to bear any strain. It is a daily growing plant, as yet in delicate infancy, requiring special care and attention . . . I hold that we may not dignify every trifle into a matter of deep religious importance. Therefore, a Hindu may not insist on playing music whilst passing a mosque. He may not even quote precedents in his own or any other place for the sake of playing music. It is not a matter of vital importance for him to play music whilst passing a mosque. One can easily appreciate the Mussalman sentiment of having solemn silence near a mosque . . . What is non-essential to a Hindu may be an essential to a Mussalman. And in all non-essential matters, a Hindu must yield for the asking. It is criminal folly to quarrel over trivialities. The unity we desire will last only if we cultivate a yielding and a charitable disposition towards one another. The cow is as dear as life to a Hindu; the Mussalman should, therefore, voluntarily accommodate his Hindu brother. Silence at his prayer is a precious thing for a Mussalman. Every Hindu should voluntarily respect his brother's sentiment. This, however, is a counsel of perfection. There are nasty

Hindus as there are nasty Mussalmans who would pick a quarrel for nothing. For these, we must provide Panchayats of unimpeachable probity and imperturbability whose decisions must be binding on both parties. Public opinion should be cultivated in favour of the decisions of such Panchayats so that no one would question them.

I know that there is much, too much, distrust of one another as yet. Many Hindus distrust Mussalmans' honesty. They believe that Swaraj means Mussalman Raj, for they argue that without the British, Mussalmans of India will aid Mussalman powers to build up a Mussalman empire in India. Mussalmans, on the other hand, fear that the Hindus being in an overwhelming majority will smother them. Such an attitude of mind betokens impotence on either's part. If not their nobility, their desire to live in peace would dictate a policy of mutual trust and mutual forbearance. There is nothing in either religion to keep the two apart . . . The fact is, we have never before now endeavoured to come together, to adjust our differences and to live as friends bound to one another as children of the same sacred soil. We have both now an opportunity of a life-time. The Khilafat question will not recur for another hundred years. If the Hindus wish to cultivate eternal friendship with the Mussalmans, they must perish with them in the attempt to vindicate the hour of Islam.

Young India, 11 May 1921. *CWMG*, vol. xx, pp. 89–90

145. Learning unity

Everybody knows that without unity between Hindus and Mussulmans, no certain progress can be made by the nation. There is no doubt that the cement binding the two is yet loose and wet. There is still mutual distrust. The leaders have come to recognize that India can make no advance without both feeling the need of trust and common action. But though there is a vast change among the masses, it is still not a permanent quantity. The Mussulman masses do not still recognize the same necessity for swaraj as the Hindus do. The Mussulmans do not flock to public meetings in the same numbers as the Hindus. This process cannot be forced. Sufficient time has not passed for the national interest to be awakened among the Mussulmans. Indeed it is a marvel that whereas but a year ago the Mussulmans as a body hardly took any interest in Congress affairs, all over India thousands have registered themselves as members.* This in itself is an immense gain.

But much more yet remains to be done. It is essentially the work of the Hindus. Wherever the Mussulmans are still found to be apathetic, they should be invited to come in. One often hears from Hindu quarters the complaint that Mussulmans do not join the Congress organizations or do not pay to the Swaraj Fund. The natural question is, have they been invited? In every district Hindus must make special efforts to draw out their Mussulman neighbours. There will never be real equality so long as one feels inferior or superior to the other. There is no room for patronage among equals. Mussulmans must not feel the lack of education or numbers where they are in a minority. Deficiency in education must be corrected by taking education. To be in a minority is often a blessing. Superiority in numbers has frequently proved a hindrance. It is character that counts in the end. But I have not commenced this article to lay down counsels of perfection or to state the course of conduct in the distant future.

My main purpose is to think of the immediate task lying before us. *Bakr-i-Id** will be soon upon us. What are we to do to frustrate the attempts that will then be made to foment quarrels between us— Hindus and Mussulmans? Though the situation has improved considerably in Bihar, it is not yet free from anxiety. Over-zealous and impatient Hindus are trying to force matters. They lend themselves an easy prey to the machinations of mischief-makers not always prompted by the Government side. Protection of the cow is the nearest to the Hindu heart. We are therefore apt to lose our heads over it, and thus be unconsciously fundamental in doing an injury to the very cause we seek to espouse. Let us recognize that our Mussulman brethren have made great efforts to save the cow for the sake of their Hindu brethren. It would be a grave mistake to underrate them. But immediately we become assertive, we make all effort on their part nugatory. We have throughout all these many years put up with cow-slaughter either without a murmur or under ineffective and violent protest. We have never tried to deserve self-imposed restraint on the part of our Mussulman countrymen by going out of our way to cultivate friendly relations with them. We have more or less gratuitously assumed the impossibility of the task.

But we are now making a deliberate and conscious attempt in standing by their side in the hour of their need. Let us not spoil the good effect by making our free offering a matter of bargain. Friendship can never be a contract. It is a status carrying no consideration with it. Service is a duty, and duty is a debt which it is a sin not to discharge. If we would prove our friendship, we must help our brethren whether they save the cow or not. We throw the responsibility for their conduct towards us on their own shoulders. We dare not dictate it to them as consideration for our help. Such help will be hired service, which the Mussulmans cannot be blamed if they summarily reject. I hope, therefore, that the Hindus of Bihar and indeed all the parts of India will realize the importance of observing the strictest forbearance, no matter what the Mussulmans do on *Bakr-i-Id*. We must leave them to take what course they choose. . . . The greater the pressure put upon the Mussulmans the greater must be the slaughter of the cow. We must leave them to their own sense of honour and duty. And we shall have done the greatest service to the cow.

The way to save the cow is not to kill or quarrel with the Mussulmans. The way to save the cow is to die in the act of saving the Khilafat without mentioning the cow. Cow-protection is a process of purification. It is *tapasya*, i.e., self-suffering. When we suffer voluntarily and, therefore, without expectation of reward, the cry of suffering (one might say) literally ascends to heaven and God above hears it and responds. That is the path of religion, and it has answered even if one man has adopted it *in its entirety*. I make bold to assert without fear of contradiction that it is not Hinduism to kill a fellow-man even to save the cow. Hinduism requires its votaries to immolate themselves for the sake of their religion, i.e., for the sake of saving the cow. The question is how many Hindus are ready without bargaining with the Mussulmans to die for them and for their religion? If the Hindus can answer it in the religious spirit, they will not only have secured Mussulman friendship for eternity, but they will have saved the cow for all time from the Mussulmans. Let us not swear even by the greatest among them. They can but help. They cannot undertake to change the hearts of millions of men who have hitherto given no thought to the feelings of their Hindu neighbours when they slaughter the cow. But God Almighty can in a moment change them and move them to pity. Prayer accompanied by adequate suffering is a prayer of the heart. That alone counts with God. To my Mussulman friends I would but say one word. They must not be irritated by the acts of irresponsible or ignorant but fanatical Hindus. He who exercises restraint under provocation wins the battle. Let them know and *feel* sure that responsible Hindus are not on their side in their trial in any bargaining spirit. They are helping because they know that the Khilafat is a just cause and that to help them in a good cause is to serve India, for they are even as blood-brothers, born of the same mother—*Bharata Mata.**

Young India, 28 July 1921. *CWMG*, vol. xx, pp. 436–9

146. No *swaraj* without unity

7 February 1924

It is clear that, without unity between Hindus, Mahomedans, Sikhs, Parsis and Christians and other Indians, all talk of swaraj is idle. The unity which I had fondly believed, in 1922, had been nearly achieved has, so far as Hindus and Mussalmans are concerned, I observe, suffered a severe check. Mutual trust has given place to distrust. An indissoluble bond between the various communities must be established if we are to win freedom. Will the thanksgiving of the nation over my release* be turned into a solid unity between the communities? That will restore me to health far quicker that any medical treatments or rest-cure. When I heard in the jail of the tension between Hindus and Mussalmans in certain places, my heart sank within me. The rest I am advised to have will be no rest with the burden of disunion preying upon me.

Letter to M. Ali. *Young India*, 14 Feb. 1924. *CWMG*, vol. xxiii, pp. 200–1

147. *Hindu–Muslim Tension: Its Cause and its Cure**

Had I been a prophet and foreseen all that has happened, I should have still thrown myself into the Khilafat agitation. In spite of the present strained relations between the two communities, both have gained. The awakening among the masses was a necessary part of the training. It is itself a tremendous gain. I would do nothing to put the people to sleep again. Our wisdom consists now in directing the awakening in the proper channel. What we see before us is sad but not disheartening, if we have faith in ourselves. The storm is but the forerunner of the coming calm that comes from a consciousness of strength, not from the stupor of exhaustion and disappointment.

The public will not expect me to give judgement upon the riots in the different places. I have no desire for giving judgement. And even if I had, I have not the facts before me.

.   .   .

TIRED OF NON-VIOLENCE

The immediate cause is the most dangerous. The thinking portion seems to be tired of non-violence. It has not as yet understood my suspension of satyagraha after Ahmedabad and Viramgam tragedies, then after the Bombay rowdyism, and, lastly, after the Chauri Chaura outrage.* The last was the last straw. The thinking men imagined that all hope of satyagraha, and therefore of swaraj too in the near future, was at an end. Their faith in non-violence was skin-deep. Two years ago, a Mussalman friend said to me in all sincerity, 'I do not believe [in] your non-violence. At least, I would not have my Mussalmans to learn it. Violence is the law of life. I would not have swaraj by non-violence as you define the latter. I must hate my enemy.' This friend is an honest man. I entertain great regard for him. Much the same has been reported of another very great Mussalman friend of mine. The report may be untrue, but the reporter himself is not an untrue man.

HINDU REPUGNANCE

Nor is this repugnance to non-violence confined to Mussalmans. Hindu friends have said the same thing, if possible, with greater vehemence. My claim to Hinduism has been rejected by some, because I believe [in] and advocate non-violence in its extreme form. They say that I am a Christian in disguise. I have been even seriously told that I am distorting the meaning of the *Gita* when I ascribe to that great poem the teaching of unadulterated non-violence. Some of my Hindu friends tell me that killing is a duty enjoined by the *Gita* under certain circumstances. A very learned Shastri only the other day scornfully rejected my interpretation of the *Gita* and said that there was no warrant for the opinion held by some commentators that the *Gita* represented the eternal duel between forces of evil and good, and inculcated the duty of eradicating evil within us without hesitation, without tenderness.

I state these opinions against non-violence in detail, because it is necessary to understand them if we would understand the solution I have to offer. What I see around me today is, therefore, a reaction against the spread of non-violence. I feel the wave of violence coming. The Hindu–Muslim tension is an acute phase of this tiredness.

I must be dismissed out of consideration. My religion is a matter solely between my Maker and myself. If I am a Hindu, I cannot cease to be one even though I may be disowned by the whole of the Hindu population. I do, however, suggest that non-violence is the end of all religions.

LIMITED NON-VIOLENCE

But I have never presented to India that extreme form of non-violence, if only because I do not regard myself fit enough to re-deliver that ancient message. Though my intellect has fully understood and grasped it, it has not as yet become part of my whole being. My strength lies in my asking people to do nothing that I have not tried repeatedly in my own life. I am then asking my countrymen today to adopt non-violence as their final creed, only for the purpose of regulating the relations between the different races, and for the purpose of attaining swaraj. Hindus and Mussalmans, Christians, Sikhs and Parsis must not settle their differences by resort to violence, and the means for the attainment of swaraj must be non-violent. This I venture to place before India, not as a weapon of the weak, but of the strong. Hindus and Mussalmans prate about no compulsion in religion. What is it but compulsion if Hindus will kill a Mussalman for saving a cow? It is like wanting to convert a Mussalman to Hinduism by force. And similarly, what is it but compulsion if Mussalmans seek to prevent by force Hindus from playing music before mosques? Virtue lies in being absorbed in one's prayers in the presence of din and noise. We shall both be voted irreligious savages by posterity if we continue to make a futile attempt to compel one another to respect our religious wishes. Again, a nation of three hundred million people should be ashamed to have to resort to force to bring to book one hundred thousand Englishmen. To convert them or, if you will, even to drive them out of the country, we need, not force of arms, but force of will. If we have not the latter, we shall never get the former. If we develop the force of will, we shall find that we do not need the force of arms.

Acceptance of non-violence, therefore, for the purposes mentioned by me, is the most natural and the most necessary condition of our national existence. It will teach us to husband our corporate physical strength for a better purpose, instead of dissipating it, as now, in a useless fratricidal strife, in which each party is exhausted after the effort. And every armed rebellion must be an insane act unless it is backed by the nation. But almost any item of non-co-operation fully backed by the nation can achieve the aim without shedding a single drop of blood.

I do not say 'eschew violence in your dealing with robbers or thieves or with nations that may invade India.' But in order that we are better able to do so, we must learn to restrain ourselves. It is a sign not of strength but of weakness to take up the pistol on the slightest pretext. Mutual fisticuffs are a training, not in violence, but in emasculation. My method of non-violence can never lead to loss of strength, but it alone will make it possible if the nation wills it, to offer disciplined and concerted violence in time of danger.

NOT TRULY NON-VIOLENT

If those who believe that we were becoming supine and inert because of the training in non-violence, will but reflect a little, they will discover that we have never been non-violent in the only sense in which the word must be understood. Whilst we have refrained from causing actual physical hurt, we have harboured violence in our breast. If we had honestly regulated our thought and speech in the strictest harmony with our outward act, we would never have experienced the fatigue we are doing. Had we been true to ourselves, we would have by this time evolved matchless strength of purpose and will.

I have dwelt at length upon the mistaken view of non-violence, because I am sure that, if we can but revert to our faith, if we ever had any, in non-violence limited only to the two purposes above referred to, the present tension between the two communities will largely subside. For, in my opinion, an attitude of non-violence in our mutual relations is an indispensable condition prior to a discussion of the remedies for the removal of the tension. It must be common cause between the two communities that neither party shall take the law into its own hands, but that all points in dispute, where ever and whenever they arise, shall be decided by reference either to private arbitration, or to the law-courts if they wish. This is the

whole meaning of non-violence, so far as communal matters are concerned. To put it another way, just as we do not break one another's
heads in respect of civil matters, so may we not do even in respect of
religious matters. This is the only pact that is immediately necessary
between the parties, and I am sure that everything else will follow.

THE BULLY AND THE COWARD

Unless this elementary condition is recognized, we have no atmosphere for considering the ways and means of removing misunderstanding and arriving at an honourable, lasting settlement. But
assuming that the acceptance of the elementary condition will be
common cause between the two communities, let us consider the
constant disturbing factors. There is no doubt in my mind that in
the majority of quarrels the Hindus come out second best. My own
experience but confirms the opinion that the Mussalman as a rule is
a bully, and the Hindu as a rule is a coward. I have noticed this in
railway trains, on public roads, and in the quarrels which I had the
privilege of settling. Need the Hindu blame the Mussalman for his
cowardice? Where there are cowards, there will always be bullies.
They say that in Saharanpur* the Mussalmans looted houses, broke
open safes and, in one case, a Hindu woman's modesty was outraged.
Whose fault was this? Mussalmans can offer no defence for the exe-
crable conduct, it is true. But I as a Hindu am more ashamed of
Hindu cowardice than I am angry at the Mussalman bullying. Why
did not the owners of the houses looted die in the attempt to defend
their possessions? Where were the relatives of the outraged sister
at the time of the outrage? Have they no account to render of
themselves? My non-violence does not admit of running away from
danger and leaving dear ones unprotected. Between violence and
cowardly flight, I can only prefer violence to cowardice. I can no
more preach non-violence to a coward than I can tempt a blind man
to enjoy healthy scenes. Non-violence is the summit of bravery. And
in my own experience, I have had no difficulty in demonstrating to
men trained in the school of violence the superiority of non-violence.
As a coward, which I was for years, I harboured violence. I began to
prize non-violence only when I began to shed cowardice. Those
Hindus who ran away from the post of duty when it was attended
with danger did so not because they were non-violent, or because
they were afraid to strike, but because they were unwilling to die or

even suffer any injury. A rabbit that runs away from the bull-terrier is not particularly non-violent. The poor thing trembles at the sight of the terrier and runs for very life. Those Hindus who ran away to save their lives would have been truly non-violent and would have covered themselves with glory and added lustre to their faith and won the friendship of their Mussalman assailants, if they had stood bare breast with smiles on their lips, and died at their post. They would have done less well, though still well, if they had stood at their post and returned blow for blow. If the Hindus wish to convert the Mussalman bully into a respecting friend, they have to learn to die in the face of the heaviest odds.

THE WAY

The way however does not lie through *akhadas**—not that I mind them. On the contrary, I want them for physical culture. Then they should be for all. But, if they are meant as a preparation for self-defence in the Hindu–Mussalman conflicts, they are foredoomed to failure. Mussalmans can play the same game and such preparations secret or open do but cause suspicion and irritation. They can provide no present remedy. It is for the thoughtful few to make quarrels impossible by making arbitration popular and obligatory.

The remedy against cowardice is not physical culture but the braving of dangers. So long as parents of the middle-class Hindus, themselves timid, continue to transmit their timidity by keeping their grown-up children in cotton wool, so long will there be the desire to shun danger and run no risks. They will have to dare to leave their children alone, let them run risks and even, at times, get killed in so doing. The puniest individual may have a stout heart. The most muscular Zulus cower before English lads. Each village has to find out its stout hearts.

THE 'GOONDAS'

It is a mistake to blame the *goondas*. They never do mischief unless we create an atmosphere for them. I was eyewitness to what happened in Bombay on the Prince's day in 1921.* We sowed the seed and the *goondas* reaped the harvest. Our men were at their back. . . . We must resolutely discountenance the practice of absolving the respectable class from blame.

Therefore, I hold that Hindus will commit a grave blunder if they organize Hindu *goondas* for defence. From the frying pan they will jump into the fire. The Bania and the Brahmin must learn to defend himself even violently, if not non-violently, or surrender his women-folk and possessions to the *goondas*. They are a class apart, whether they are labelled Mussalman or Hindu. It was said with gusto that, protected by untouchables (for they feared not death) a Hindu pro-cession (playing triumphant music) quite recently passed a mosque unhurt.

It is a very mundane use to make of a sacred cause. Such exploita-tion of our untouchable brothers can serve neither Hinduism in gen-eral nor the suppressed classes in particular. A few processions so doubtfully protected may pass a few mosques safely. But it can only aggravate the growing tension, and degrade Hinduism. The middle-class people must be prepared for a beating if they wish to play music in the teeth of opposition, or they must befriend Mussalmans in a self-respecting manner.

The Hindus have to do penance for the past and still continu-ing disabilities imposed by them upon the suppressed brothers. There can be no question of expecting any return from them for a debt we owe them. If we use them to cover our cowardice, we shall raise in them false hopes we shall never be able to fulfil, and if the retribution comes, it will be a just punishment for our inhuman treat-ment of them. If I have any influence with Hindus, I would beseech them not to use them as a shield against anticipated Mussalman attack.

GROWING DISTRUST

Another potent cause of the tension is the growing distrust even among the best of us.

.   .   .

PACT

In view of what I have said above, it is clear that we have not even arrived at the stage when a pact is even a possibility. There can be, it is clear to me, no question of bargain about cow-slaughter and music. On either side it must be a voluntary effort and, therefore, can never be the basis of a pact.

For political matters, a pact or an understanding is certainly necessary. But, in my opinion, the restoration of friendly feeling is a condition precedent to any effectual pact. Are both parties sin-cerely willing to accept the proposition that no disputes, religious or otherwise, between the communities should ever be decided by an appeal to force, i.e., violence? I am convinced that the masses do not want to fight, if the leaders do not. If, therefore, the leaders agree that mutual rows should be as in all advanced countries, erased out of our public life as being barbarous and irreligious, I have no doubt that the masses will quickly follow them.

So far as the political matters are concerned, as a non-co-operator I am quite uninterested in them; but, for the future understanding, I hold that it is up to the Hindus as the major party not to bargain, but leave the pen in the hands of, say, Hakim Saheb Ajmal Khan* and abide by his decision. I would similarly deal with the Sikhs, the Christians and the Parsis and be satisfied with the residue. It is, in my opinion, the only just, equitable, honourable and dignified solution. Hindus, if they want unity among different races, must have the courage to trust the minorities. Any other adjustment must have a nasty taste in the mouth. Surely the millions do not want to become legislators and municipal councillors. And if we have understood the proper use of satyagraha, we should know that it can be and should be used against an unjust administrator whether he be a Hindu, Mussalman or of any other race or denomination, whereas a just administrator or representative is always and equally good, whether he be a Hindu or a Mussalman. We want to do away with the communal spirit. The majority must, therefore, make the beginning and thus inspire the minorities with confidence in their *bona fides*. Adjustment is possible only when the more powerful take the initiative without waiting for response from the weaker.

So far as employment in the Government departments is concerned, I think it will be fatal to good government, if we introduce there the communal spirit. For administration to be efficient, it must always be in the hands of the fittest. There should be certainly no favouritism. But, if we want five engineers, we must not take one from each community, but we must take the fittest five even if they were all Mussalmans or all Parsis. The lowest posts must, if need be, be filled by examination by an impartial board consisting of men belonging to different communities. But, distribution of posts should never be according to the proportion of the numbers of each community. The educationally backward communities will have a right to receive favoured treatment in the matter of education at the hands of the national government. This can be secured in an effective manner. But those who aspire to occupy responsible posts in the Government of the country can only do so if they pass the required test.

TRUST BEGETS TRUST

For me the only question for immediate solution before the country is the Hindu–Mussalman question. I agree with Mr Jinnah* that Hindu–Muslim unity means swaraj. I see no way of achieving anything in this afflicted country without a lasting heart unity between Hindus and Mussalmans of India. I believe in the immediate possibility of achieving it, because it is so natural, so necessary for both, and because I believe in human nature. Mussalmans may have much to answer for. I have come in closest touch with even what may be considered a 'bad lot'. I cannot recall a single occasion when I had to regret it. The Mussalmans are brave, they are generous and trusting the moment their suspicion is disarmed. Hindus, living as they do in glass houses, have no right to throw stones at their Mussalman neighbours. See what we have done, are still doing, to the suppressed classes! . . . God does not punish directly; His ways are inscrutable. Who knows that all our woes are not due to that one black sin?* The history of Islam, if it betrays aberrations from the moral height, has many a brilliant page. In its glorious days it was not intolerant. It commanded the admiration of the world. When the West was sunk in darkness, a bright star rose in the Eastern firmament and gave light and comfort to a groaning world. Islam is not a false religion. Let Hindus study it reverently and they will love it even as I do. If it has become gross and fanatical here, let us admit that we have had no small share in making it so. If Hindus set their house in order, I have not a shadow of doubt that Islam will respond in a manner worthy of its liberal traditions. The key to the situation lies with the Hindus. We must shed timidity or cowardice. We must be brave enough to trust, all will be well.

The reader of *Young India* will pardon me for devoting practically the whole of *Young India* to the question of Hindu–Muslim unity. He will readily do so if he holds with me that there is no question more important and more pressing than this. In my opinion, it blocks all progress. I therefore invite the reader to peruse the statement most carefully and favour me with views or information (not necessarily for publication) that may throw additional light on the question or correct any errors of fact or opinion.

Young India, 29 May 1924. *CWMG*, vol xxiv, pp. 136–54

148. Solving communal tension

Let me summarize the long statement* issued last week on this the greatest of all questions for the Indian patriot. The posterity will judge both the faiths by the manner in which the followers of each acquit themselves in the matter. However good Hinduism or Islam may be in the abstract, the only way each can be judged is by the effect produced by each on its votaries considered as a whole.

The following then is the summary of the statement.

CAUSES

1. The remote cause of the tension is the Moplah rebellion.*

2. The attempt of Mr Fazl Hussain* to rearrange the distribution of posts in the education department consistently with the number of Mussalmans in the Punjab and consequent Hindu opposition.

3. The *shuddhi** movement.

4. The most potent being tiredness of non-violence and the fear that the communities might, by a long course of training in non-violence, forget the law of retaliation and self-defence.

5. Mussalman cow-slaughter and Hindu music.

6. Hindu cowardice and consequent Hindu distrust of Mussalmans.

7. Mussalman bullying.

8. Mussalman distrust of Hindu fair play.

CURE

1. The master-key to the solution is the replacement of the rule of the sword by that of arbitration.

Honest public opinion should make it impossible for aggrieved parties to take the law into their own hands and every case must be referred to private arbitration or to law-courts if the parties do not believe in non-co-operation.

2. Ignorant fear of cowardly non-violence, falsely so called, taking the place of violence should be dispelled.

3. Growing mutual distrust among the leaders must, if they believe in unity, give place to trust.

4. Hindus must cease to fear the Mussalman bully and the Mussalmans should consider it beneath their dignity to bully their Hindu brothers.

5. Hindus must not imagine they can force Mussalmans to give up cow-sacrifice. They must trust, by befriending Mussalmans, that the latter will, of their own accord, give up cow-sacrifice out of regard for their Hindu neighbours.

6. Nor must Mussalmans imagine they can force Hindus to stop music or *arati** before mosques. They must befriend the Hindus and trust them to pay heed to reasonable Mussalman sentiment.

7. Hindus must leave to the Mussalmans and the other minorities the question of representation on elected bodies, and gracefully and whole-heartedly give effect to the findings of such referee. If I had my way I should appoint Hakim Saheb Ajmal Khan* as the sole referee, leaving him free to consult Mussalmans, Sikhs, Christians, Parsis, etc., as he considers best.

8. Employment under national government must be according to merit to be decided by a board of examiners representing different communities.

9. *Shuddhi* or *tabligh** as such cannot be disturbed, but either must be conducted honestly and by men of proved character. It should avoid all attack on other religions. There should be no secret propaganda and no offer of material rewards.

10. Public opinion should be so cultivated as to put under the ban all the scurrilous writings, principally in a section of the Punjab Press.

11. Nothing is possible without the Hindus shedding their timidity. Theirs is the largest stake and they must be prepared to sacrifice the most.

But how is the cure to be effected? Who will convince the Hindu maniac that the best way to save the cow is for him to do his duty by her and not goad his Mussalman brother? Who will convince the Mussalman fanatic that it is not religion but irreligion to break the head of his Hindu brother when he plays music in front of his mosque? Or, again, who will make the Hindu see that he will lose nothing by the minorities being even over-represented on the elective public secular bodies? These are fair questions and show the difficulty of working out the solution.

But if the solution is the only true solution, all difficulties must be overcome. In reality the difficulty is only apparent. If there are even a few Hindus and a few Mussalmans who have a living faith in the solution, the rest is easy. Indeed, even if there are a few Hindus only, or a few Mussalmans only with that faith, the solution would be still easy. They have but to work away single-heartedly and the others will follow them. And the conversion of only one party is enough because the solution requires no bargains. For instance, Hindus should cease to worry Mussalmans about the cow without expecting any consideration from the latter. They should yield to the Mussalman demand, whatever it may be, regarding representation, again without requiring any return. And if the Mussalmans insist on stopping Hindu music or *arati* by force, the Hindus will continue playing it although every single Hindu should die at his post, but without retaliation. The Mussalmans will then be shamed into doing the right thing in an incredibly short space of time. Mussalmans can do likewise, if they choose, and shame the Hindus into doing the right thing. One has to dare to believe.

But in practice it will not be thus; on the contrary, both will act simultaneously as soon as the workers become true to themselves. Unfortunately they are not. They are mostly ruled by passion and prejudice. Each tries to hide the shortcomings of his co-religionists and so the circle of distrust and suspicion ever widens.

I hope that, at the forthcoming meeting of the All-India Congress Committee, it will be possible to find out a method of work which will bring a speedy end to the tension.

It has been suggested to me that the Government are fomenting these dissensions. I should hope not. But assuming that they are, surely it is up to us to neutralize such efforts by ourselves acting truly and faithfully.

Young India, 5 June 1924. *CWMG*, vol. xxiv, pp. 188–90

149. Fast for communal unity

18 September 1924

The recent events* have proved unbearable for me. My helplessness is still more unbearable. My religion teaches me that whenever there is distress which one cannot remove, one must fast and pray. I have done so in connection with my own dearest ones. Nothing evidently that I say or write can bring the two communities together. I am therefore imposing on myself a fast of 21 days commencing from today and ending on Wednesday, October 8. I reserve the liberty to drink water with or without salt. It is both a penance and a prayer.

As penance I need not have taken the public into my confidence, but I publish the fast as (let me hope) an effective prayer both to Hindus and Mussalmans, who have hitherto worked in unison, not to commit suicide. I respectfully invite the heads of all the communities, including Englishmen, to meet and end this quarrel which is a disgrace to religion and to humanity. It seems as if God has been dethroned. Let us reinstate Him in our hearts.

Statement announcing fast. *Young India*, 26 Sept. 1924. *CWMG*, vol. xxv, pp. 171–2

150. A hopeless tangle

7 March 1925

Those of you who know how to spin will understand the simile I am about to give you. Indifferent spinners amongst you know how sometimes when you are unwinding your yarn from the spindle it becomes sometimes a tangle. You know the more you try to undo the tangle the more knotty it becomes, and a wise spinner leaves his tangle aside for a moment when he has lost his temper and approaches it after he has cooled down. So it is with the Hindu–Muslim question. It has become a hopeless tangle at the present moment. I thought I was an expert in solving that tangle as I think I am an expert in spinning. But for the time being I have put away in my cupboard this Hindu–Muslim tangle. That does not mean that I have despaired of a solution. My mind will eternally work at it till I find out a solution. But I must confess to you today that I cannot present a workable solution that you will accept. In the atmosphere surcharged as it is with mutual distrust I cannot persuade either the Hindus or the Mussalmans to accept my solution.

Speech in Madras. *The Hindu*, 9 Mar. 1925. *CWMG*, vol. xxvi, p. 244

151. Helpless in the face of disunity

16 January 1927

I said at Comilla that the problem had passed out of human hands, and that God had taken it into His own. Maybe the statement springs from my egotism. But I do not think so. I have ample reason for it. With my hand on my breast, I can say that not a minute in my life am I forgetful of God. For over twenty years I have been doing everything that I have done as in the presence of God. Hindu–Muslim unity I had made a mission of my life. I worked for it in South Africa, I toiled for it here, I did penance for it, but God was not satisfied, God did not want me to take any credit for the work. And so I have now washed my hands, I am helpless. I have exhausted all my effort. But as a believer in God, as I never for a moment lose faith in Him, as I content myself with the joy and sorrow that He wills for me, I may feel helpless, but I never lose hope. Something within me tells me that Hindu–Muslim unity must come and will sooner than we might dare to hope, that God will one day force it on us, in spite of ourselves. That is why I say that it has passed into hands of God.

Speech at Sewan. *Young India*, 27 Jan. 1927. *CWMG*, vol. xxxii, p. 572

152. A new method of approach

My interest and faith in Hindu–Muslim unity and unity among all the communities remain as strong as ever. My method of approach has changed. Whereas formerly I tried to achieve it by addressing meetings, joining in promoting and passing resolutions, now I have no faith in these devices. We have no atmosphere for them. In an atmosphere which is surcharged with distrust, fear and hopelessness, in my opinion these devices rather hinder than help heart-unity. I, therefore, rely upon prayer and such individual acts of friendship as are possible. Hence, I have lost all desire to attend meetings held for achieving unity. This, however, does not mean that I disapprove of such attempts. On the contrary, those who have faith in such meetings must hold them. I should wish them all success.

I am out of tune with the present temper of both the communities, From their own standpoint, they are perhaps entitled to say that my method has failed. I recognize that among those whose opinions count, I am in a hopeless minority. But by taking part in meetings and the like, I could not render any useful service. And as I have no other interest but to see real unity established, where I cannot serve by my presence I regard it as some service if I abstain.

Young India, 1 Dec. 1927. *CWMG*, vol. xxxv, p. 353

153. Apparent inaction

I have more than once heard the complaint that the establishment of Hindu–Muslim unity is being delayed owing to lack of sufficient effort in its behalf on my part; that if only I would concentrate myself on it exclusively, it could be realized today. May I assure you that if I do not *seem* to be doing that today, it is not because my passion for Hindu–Muslim unity has grown less. But I have realized, as I had never done before, my own imperfections as an instrument for this high mission and the inadequacy of mere external means for the attainment of big objects. I have learnt more and more to resign myself utterly to His grace.

If you could dissect my heart, you would find that the prayer and spiritual striving for the attainment of Hindu–Muslim unity goes on there unceasingly all the twenty-four hours without even a moment's interruption, whether I am awake or asleep. I want Hindu–Muslim unity if only because I know that without it there can be no Swaraj . . . I must be impatient for Hindu–Muslim unity because I am impatient for Swaraj. And I have full faith that true and lasting heart-unity between the Hindus and Mussalmans, not a merely patched-up political compromise, will come sooner or later, sooner perhaps than later. I have the vividest recollection of my father's days, how the Hindus and Mussalmans of Rajkot used to mix together and participate in one another's domestic functions and ceremonies like blood-brothers. I believe that those days will dawn once again over the country. The present bickerings and petty recriminations between the communities are an unnatural aberration. They cannot last for ever.

The greatest of things in this world are accomplished not through unaided human effort. They come in their own good time. God has His own way of choosing His instruments. Who knows, in spite of my incessant heart prayer, I may not be found worthy for this great work. We must all keep our loins girt and our lamps well trimmed;* we do not know when or on whom His choice may fall. You may not shirk your responsibility by shoving it all on me. Pray for me that my dream may be fulfilled in my life-time. We must never give way to despair or pessimism. God's ways are more than man's arithmetic.

Speech at Abbotabad, late July 1939. *Harijan*, 5 Aug. 1939. *CWMG*, vol. lxx, pp. 22–3

154. Rebels at the idea of partitioning India

9 April 1940

As a man of non-violence, I cannot forcibly resist the proposed partition* if the Muslims of India really insist upon it. But I can never be a willing party to the vivisection. I would employ every non-violent means to prevent it. For, it means the undoing of centuries of work done by numberless Hindus and Muslims to live together as one nation. Partition means a patent untruth. My whole soul rebels against the idea that Hinduism and Islam represent two antagonistic cultures and doctrines. To assent to such a doctrine is for me denial of God. For, I believe with my whole soul that the God of the Quran is also the God of the *Gita*, and that we are all, no matter by what name designated, children of the same God. I must rebel against the idea that millions of Indians, who were Hindus the other day,* changed their nationality on adopting Islam as their religion.

But that is my belief. I cannot thrust it down the throats of the Muslims who think that they are a different nation. I refuse, however, to believe that eight crores of Muslims will say that they have nothing in common with their Hindu and other brethren.

Harijan, 13 Apr. 1940. *CWMG*, vol. lxxi, p. 412

155. The source of Gandhi's horror at untouchability

I regard untouchability* as the greatest blot on Hinduism. This idea was not brought home to me by my bitter experiences during the South African struggle. It is not due to the fact that I was once an agnostic. It is equally wrong to think—as some people do—that I have taken my views from my study of Christian religious literature. These views date as far back as the time when I was neither enamoured of, nor was acquainted with, the Bible or the followers of the Bible.

I was hardly yet twelve when this idea had dawned on me. A scavenger named Uka, an 'untouchable', used to attend our house for cleaning latrines. Often I would ask my mother why it was wrong to touch him, why I was forbidden to touch him. If I accidentally touched Uka, I was asked to perform ablutions, and though I naturally obeyed, it was not without smilingly protesting that untouchability was not sanctioned by religion, that it was impossible that it should be so. I was a very dutiful and obedient child, and so far as it was consistent with respect for parents, I often had tussles with them on this matter. I told my mother that she was entirely wrong in considering physical contact with Uka as sinful.

While at school I would often happen to touch the 'untouchables', and as I never would conceal the fact from my parents, my mother would tell me that the shortest cut to purification after the unholy touch was to cancel the touch by touching a Musalman passing by. And simply out of reverence and regard for my mother I often did so, but never did so believing it to be a religious obligation. After some time we shifted to Porbandar, where I made my first acquaintance with Sanskrit. I was not yet put to an English school, and my brother and I were placed in the charge of a Brahmana who taught us Ramaraksha and Vishnu Puja.* The texts *jale Vishnuh, sthale Vishnuh* (the Lord is present in water, the Lord is present on land) have never gone out of my memory. A motherly old dame* used to live close by. Now it happened that I was very timid then, and would conjure up ghosts and goblins whenever the lights went out, and it was dark. The old mother, to disabuse me of fears, suggested that I should mutter the Ramaraksha texts whenever I was afraid, and all evil spirits would fly away. This I did and, as I thought, with good effect. I could never believe then that there was any text in the Ramaraksha pointing to the contact of the 'untouchables' as a sin. I did not understand its meaning then, or understood it very imperfectly. But I was confident that Ramaraksha, which would destroy all fear of ghosts, could not countenance any such thing as fear of contact with the 'untouchables'.

The Ramayana used to be regularly read in our family. A Brahmana called Ladha Maharaj used to read it. He was stricken with leprosy, and he was confident that a regular reading of the Ramayana would cure him of leprosy, and indeed, he was cured of it. 'How can the Ramayana,' I thought to myself, 'in which one who is regarded nowadays as an "untouchable" took Rama across the Ganga in his boat, countenance the idea of any human beings being "untouchables" on the ground that they were polluted souls?' The fact that we addressed God as the 'purifier of the polluted' and by similar appellations, shows that it is a sin to regard any one born in Hinduism as polluted or 'untouchable'—that it is Satanic to do so. I have hence been never tired of repeating that it is a great sin. I do not pretend that this thing had crystallized as a conviction in me at the age of twelve, but I do say that I did then regard untouchability as a sin. I narrate this story for the information of the Vaishnavas and orthodox Hindus.

Speech in Ahmedabad. *Young India*, 27 Apr. 1921. *RU*, pp. 3–5

156. The Ahmedabad *ashram* admits untouchables

The Ashram had been in existence only a few months when we were put to a test such as I had scarcely expected [the request to admit an untouchable family]. . . .

The family consisted of Dudabhai, his wife Danibehn and their daughter, Lakshmi, then a mere toddling babe. Dudabhai had been a teacher in Bombay. They all agreed to abide by the rules and were accepted.

But their admission created a flutter amongst the friends who had been helping the Ashram. The very first difficulty was found with regard to the use of the well, which was partly controlled by the owner of the bungalow. The man in charge of the water-lift objected that drops of water from our bucket would pollute him. So he took to swearing at us and molesting Dudabhai. I told everyone to put up with the abuse and continue drawing water at any cost. When he saw that we did not return his abuse, the man became ashamed and ceased to bother us.

All monetary help, however, was stopped. . . .

With the stopping of monetary help came rumours of proposed social boycott. We were prepared for all this. I had told my companions that, if we were boycotted and denied the usual facilities, we would not leave Ahmedabad. We would rather go and stay in the untouchables' quarter and live on whatever we could get by manual labour.

[Gandhi then recounts how an Ahmedabad business man offered him help and gave him Rs 13,000 in notes and just drove away in his car.]

I had never expected this help, and what a novel way of rendering it! The gentleman had never before visited the Ashram. So far as I can remember, I had met him only once. No visit, no enquiries, simply rendering help and going away! This was a unique experience for me. The help deferred the exodus to the untouchables' quarter. We now felt quite safe for a year.

Just as there was a storm outside, so there was a storm in the Ashram itself. Though in South Africa untouchable friends used to come to my place and live and feed with me, my wife and other women did not seem quite to relish the admission into the Ashram of the untouchable friends. My eyes and ears easily detected their indifference, if not their dislike towards Danibehn. The monetary difficulty had caused me no anxiety, but this internal storm was more than I could bear. Danibehn was an ordinary woman. Dudabhai was a man with slight education but of good understanding. I liked his patience. Sometimes he did flare up, but on the whole I was well impressed with his forbearance. I pleaded with him to swallow minor insults. He not only agreed, but prevailed upon his wife to do likewise.

The admission of this family proved a valuable lesson to the Ashram. In the very beginning we proclaimed to the world that the Ashram would not countenance untouchability.* Those who wanted to help the Ashram were thus put on their guard, and the work of the Ashram in this direction was considerably simplified. The fact that it is mostly the real orthodox Hindus who have met the daily growing expenses of the Ashram is perhaps a clear indication that untouchability is shaken to its foundation. There are indeed many other proofs of this, but the fact that good Hindus do not scruple to help an Ashram where we go to the length of dining with the untouchables is no small proof.

Gandhi, *An Autobiography*, part V, chap. X

157. Untouchability is no part of Hinduism

Untouchability in its extreme form has always caused me so much pain, because I consider myself to be a Hindu of Hindus saturated with the spirit of Hinduism. I have failed to find a single warrant for the existence of untouchability as we believe and practise it today in all those books which we call as Hindu Shastras. But as I have repeatedly said in other places, if I found that Hinduism really countenanced untouchability I should have no hesitation in renouncing Hinduism itself. For I hold that religion, to be worthy of the name, must not be inconsistent with the fundamental truths of ethics and morality. But as I believe that untouchability is no part of Hinduism, I cling to Hinduism, but daily become more and more impatient of this hideous wrong.

Speech in Trivandrum. *Young India*, 20 Oct. 1927. *RU*, p. 16

158. No sanction for untouchability in Hinduism

I assure you that in Hinduism there is no sanction for treating a single human being as untouchable. In the estimation of a Brahmana knowing and living his religion, a Shudra is as good as himself. The Bhagavad gita has nowhere taught that a Chandala is in any way inferior to a Brahmana. A Brahmana ceases to be a Brahmana, immediately he becomes insolent and considers himself a superior being. India owes a deep debt to the Brahmanas who voluntarily sacrificed themselves for the betterment of all. It was Brahmanas who have called God Servant of servants, the Purifier of the fallen. It was Brahmanas who taught that the prostitute and the Chandala could attain Moksha if she or he only purified her or his heart.

But unfortunately for the human race the Brahmana shares with mankind the frailties of all. In common with others he has neglected his duty of giving knowledge to mankind, of guiding them in the right and truest path. We glibly charge Englishmen with insolence and haughtiness. Let us, before we cast the stone at them, free ourselves from liability to reproach. Let us put our own house in order.

Speech in Ellore. *Young India*, 11 May 1921. *RU*, p. 18

159. Hinduism does not sanction the contemporary practice of untouchability

I do not believe that all class distinctions can be obliterated. I believe in the doctrine of equality as taught by Lord Krishna in the Gita. The Gita teaches us that members of all the four castes should be treated on an equal basis. It does not prescribe the same *dharma* for the Brahmana as for the Bhangi. But it insists that the latter shall be entitled to the same measure of consideration and esteem as the former with all his superior learning. It is therefore our duty to see that the 'untouchables' do not feel that they are despised or looked down upon. Let them not be offered leavings from our plates for their subsistence. How can I accord differential treatment to any person, be he a Brahmana or Bhangi, who worships the same God and keeps his body and soul pure and clean? I for one would regard myself as having sinned if I gave to a Bhangi unclean food from the leavings from the kitchen or failed to render him personal assistance when he was in need.

Let me make my position absolutely clear. While I do hold that the institution of untouchability as it stands today has no sanction in Hinduism, Hinduism does recognize 'untouchability' in a limited sense and under certain circumstances. For instance, every time that my mother handed unclean things she became untouchable for the time being and had to cleanse herself by bathing. As a Vaishnava I refuse to believe that anyone can be regarded untouchable by reason of his or her birth, and such untouchability as is recognized by religion is by its very nature transitory—easily removable and referable to the deed, not the doer. Not only that. Just as we revere our mother for the sanitary service that she renders us when we are infants, and the greater her service the greater is our reverence for her, similarly, the Bhangis are entitled to our highest reverence for the sanitary service they perform for society.

Young India, 22 Jan. 1925. *RU*, pp. 22–3

160. Untouchability corrodes Hinduism

Untouchability is the product, not of the caste system but of the distinction of high and low that has crept into Hinduism and is corroding it. The attack on untouchability is thus an attack upon this 'high-and-low'ness. The moment untouchability goes, the caste system itself will be purified, that is to say according to my dream, it will resolve itself into the true Varnadharma, the four divisions of society, each complementary of the other and none inferior or superior to any other, each as necessary for the whole body of Hinduism as any other.

Harijan, 11 Feb. 1933. *RU*, p. 51

161. *Swaraj* impossible if untouchability persists

So long as the Hindus wilfully regard untouchability as part of their religion, so long as the mass of Hindus consider it a sin to touch a section of their brethren, Swaraj is impossible of attainment. Yudhishthira* would not enter heaven without his dog. How can, then, the descendants of that Yudhishthira expect to obtain Swaraj without the 'untouchables'?

We are guilty of having suppressed our brethren; we make them crawl on their bellies; we have made them rub their noses on the ground; with eyes red with rage, we push them out of railway compartments—what more than this has British rule done? What charge, that we bring against Dyer and O'Dwyer,* may not other and even our own people, lay at our doors? We ought to purge ourselves of this pollution. It is idle to talk of Swaraj so long as we do not protect the weak and helpless, or so long as it is possible for a single Swarajist to injure the feelings of any individual. Swaraj means that not a single Hindu or Muslim shall for a moment arrogantly think that he can crush with impunity meek Hindus or Muslims. Unless this condition is fulfilled we will gain Swaraj only to lose it the next moment. We are no better than the brutes until we have purged ourselves of the sins we have committed against our weaker brethren.

But I have faith in me still. In the course of my peregrinations in India I have realized that the spirit of kindness of which the Poet Tulsidas sings so eloquently, which forms the corner-stone of the Jain and Vaishnava religions, which is the quintessence of the Bhagawat and with which every verse of the Gita is saturated—this kindness, this love, this charity, is slowly but steadily gaining ground in the hearts of the masses of this country.

Speech in Ahmedabad. *Young India*, 4 May 1921. *RU*, p. 9

162. Untouchability—barrier to *swaraj*

The existence of untouchability must remain an impassable barrier in the path of our progress, which we must break down with supreme effort. There seems to be a lurking thought with many of us, that we can gain Swaraj and keep untouchability. They do not even see the contradiction inherent in the thought. Swaraj is as much for the 'untouchable' as for the 'touchable'. A correspondent from Narayanavaram writes: 'In our parts Panchamas are very badly treated by the Hindus, especially the Brahmanas. In the villages they are not allowed to go about the streets inhabited by Brahmanas. They must stand at a considerable distance when speaking to Brahmanas.' Read Sahebs* for Brahmanas and Indians for Panchamas, and see how you feel. And yet I have no doubt, that some Sahebs are infinitely better than some Brahmanas. God will not let us have Swaraj so long as we treat a brother as an outcaste by reason of his birth.

Young India, 22 Sept. 1921. *RU*, p. 10

163. Foreign rule—just retribution

The curse of foreign domination and the attendant exploitation is the justest retribution meted out by God to us for our exploitation of a sixth of our own race and their studied degradation in the sacred name of religion. Hence is it that I have put the removal of untouchability as an indispensable condition of attainment of Swaraj. Slave-holders ourselves, we have no business to quarrel with our own slavery if we are not prepared unconditionally to enfranchise our own slaves. We must first cast out the beam of untouchability from our own eyes before we attempt to remove the mote from that of our masters.*

Young India, 13 Oct. 1921. *RU*, p. 11

164. Removing untouchability

Has not a just nemesis overtaken us for the crime of untouchability? Have we not reaped as we have sown? Have we not practised Dyerism and O'Dwyerism* on our own kith and kin? We have segregated the 'pariah' and we are in turn segregated in the British Colonies.

We deny him the use of public wells; we throw the leavings of our plates at him. His very shadow pollutes us. Indeed there is no charge that the 'pariah' cannot fling in our faces and which we do not fling in the faces of Englishmen.

How is this blot on Hinduism to be removed? 'Do unto others as you would that others should do unto you.'* I have often told English officials that, if they are friends and servants of India, they should come down from their pedestal, cease to be patrons, demonstrate by their loving deeds that they are in every respect our friends, and believe us to be equals in the same sense they believe fellow Englishmen to be their equals. After the experiences of the Punjab and Khilafat,* I have gone a step further and ask them to repent and change their hearts. Even so is it necessary for us Hindus to repent of the wrong we have done, to alter our behaviour towards those whom we have 'suppressed' by a system as devilish as we believe the English system of the Government of India to be. We must not throw a few miserable schools at them: we must not adopt the air of superiority towards them. We must treat them as our blood-brothers as they are in fact. We must return to them the inheritance of which we have robbed them. And this must not be the act of a few English-knowing reformers merely, but it must be a conscious voluntary effort on the part of the masses. We may not wait till eternity for this much belated reformation. We must aim at bringing it about within this year of grace, probation, preparation and *tapasya*.

Young India, 19 Jan. 1921. *RU*, pp. 5–6

165. The role of law

Untouchability will not be removed by the force even of law. It can only be removed when the majority of Hindus realize that it is a crime against God and man and are ashamed of it. In other words, it is a process of conversion, i.e., purification, of the Hindu heart. The aid of law has to be invoked when it hinders or interferes with the progress of the reform as when, in spite of the willingness of the trustees and the temple-going public, the law prohibits the opening of a particular temple.*

Harijan, 23 Sept. 1939. *RU*, p. 57

166. Befriending Harijans

The only way in which we can expiate this sin of centuries is to befriend the Harijans by going to their quarters, by hugging their children as you do your own, by interesting yourselves in their welfare, by finding out whether they get enough to eat, whether they get pure water to drink, whether they have the fresh light and air that you enjoy as of right. The other way is for each of you to start the spinning sacrifice and to pledge yourselves to wear Khadi, which supports millions of these submerged human beings. The spinning sacrifice will help you in some slight measure to identify yourselves with them, and every yard of Khadi you wear will mean some coppers going into the pockets of the Harijans and the poor. The last thing is to contribute your mite to the Harijan Fund, which has no other end but the amelioration of the lot of the Harijans.

'A Talk with Women'. *Harijan*, 13 Aug. 1934. *RU*, p. 62

167. The character required for Harijan service

The one thing needful for effective Harijan service, and for that matter all service of the poor, the forlorn, the helpless, is purity of personal character in the servant. Without it possession of even the highest intellectual ability and administrative capacity is of no account. It may even prove a hindrance, whereas possession of a pure character combined with love of such service will assuredly develop or provide the requisite intellectual and administrative capacity.

There is in modern public life a tendency to ignore altogether the character of a public worker so long as he works efficiently as a unit in an administrative machinery. It is said that everybody's character is his own private concern. Though I have known this view to have been often taken I have never been able to appreciate, much less to adopt, it. I have known the serious consequences overtaking organizations that have counted private character as a matter of no consequence. Nevertheless the reader will have observed that for my immediate purpose I have restricted the application of my proposition only to organizations like the Harijan Sevak Sangh* which make themselves trustees for the welfare of dumb millions. I have no manner of doubt that possession of a spotless character is the indispensable requisite of such service. Workers in the Harijan cause or for Khadi or for village industries must come in closest touch with utterly unsophisticated, innocent, ignorant men and women who might be likened to children in intelligence. If they have not character, they must fail in the end and for ever damn the cause they espouse in the surroundings in which they are known. I write from experience of such cases. Happily they are rare enough for the numbers engaged in such services, but frequent enough to call for public warning and caution on the part of organizations and workers who are engaged in such services. These last cannot be too watchful or too exacting of themselves.

Harijan, 7 Nov. 1936. *RU*, pp. 215–16

168. Unapproachability

Vykom of which till lately no one outside Travancore, at most the Madras Presidency, knew anything has suddenly leapt to fame because it has become the seat of Satyagraha.* The Press contains daily bulletins of the progress of the movement. It has been undertaken on behalf of the 'untouchables' of Travancore. The movement has given us another word to describe the condition of the suppressed classes. It is unapproachability. These poor countrymen of ours may not only not touch any other Caste Hindus but they may not even approach them within a stated distance. The leaders of the movement with a view to remedying the evil have taken up only a fragment of the evil, hoping no doubt that if they deal with it successfully, they will have dealt it a death-blow at least in that part of India in which direct action is now going on. In the prosecution of the campaign some of the staunchest workers of Malabar have been imprisoned. There can now be no receding. The struggle may last long if orthodox Hindu opinion is actively hostile to the movement. The Satyagrahis are certain to break down the wall of prejudice, no matter how strong and solid it may be if they continue firm, but humble, truthful and non-violent. They must have faith enough in these qualities to know that they will melt the stoniest hearts.

Young India, 17 Apr. 1924. *RU*, p. 105

169. Fast against separate electorates

16 September 1932

The fast* which I am approaching was resolved upon in the name of God for His work and, as I believe in all humility, at His call. Friends have urged me to postpone the date for the sake of giving the public a chance to organize itself. I am sorry it is not open to me to change even the hour . . .

The impending fast is against those who have faith in me, whether Indians or foreigners, and for those who have it not. Therefore it is not against the English official world, but it is against those Englishmen and women who, in spite of the contrary teaching of the official world, believe in me and the justice of the cause I represent. Nor is it against those of my countrymen who have no faith in me, whether they be Hindus or others; but it is against those countless Indians (no matter to what persuasion they belong) who believe that I represent a just cause. Above all, it is intended to sting the Hindu conscience into right religious action.

The contemplated fast is no appeal to mere emotion. By the fast I want to throw the whole of my weight (such as it is) in the scales of justice pure and simple. Therefore, there need be no undue haste or feverish anxiety to save my life. I implicitly believe in the truth of the saying that not a blade of grass moves but by His will. He will save it if He needs it for further service in this body. None can save it against His will. Humanly speaking, I believe it will stand the strain for some time.

The separate electorate is merely the last straw. No patched-up agreement between caste Hindu leaders and rival 'depressed' class leaders will answer the purpose. The agreement to be valid has to be real. If the Hindu mass mind is not yet prepared to banish untouchability root and branch, it must sacrifice me without the slightest hesitation.

There should be no coercion of those who are opposed to joint electorates I have no difficulty in understanding their bitter opposition. They have every right to distrust me. Do I not belong to that Hindu section miscalled a superior class, or caste Hindus, who have ground down to powder the so-called untouchables? The marvel is that the latter have remained nevertheless in the Hindu fold.

But whilst I can justify this opposition, I believe that they are in error. They will, if they can, separate the 'depressed' class entirely from the Hindu society and form them into a separate class—a standing and living reproach to Hinduism. I should not mind if thereby their interest could be really served.

But my intimate acquaintance with every shade of untouchability convinces me that their lives, such as they are, are so intimately mixed with those of the caste Hindus in whose midst and for whom they live, that it is impossible to separate them. They are part of an indivisible family.

Their revolt against the Hindus with whom they live and their apostasy from Hinduism I should understand. But this so far as I can see they will not do. There is a subtle something—quite indefinable—in Hinduism which keeps them in it even in spite of themselves.

And this fact makes it imperative for a man like me, with a living experience of it, to resist the contemplated separation even though the effort should cost life itself.

The implications of this resistance are tremendous. No compromise which does not ensure the fullest freedom for the 'depressed classes' inside the Hindu fold can be an adequate substitute for the contemplated separation. Any betrayal of the trust can merely postpone the day of immolation for me and henceforth for those who think with me. The problem before responsible Hindus is to consider whether in the event of social, civic or political persecution of the 'depressed' classes they are prepared to face satyagraha in the shape of perpetual fast, not of one reformer like me but an increasing army of reformers whom I believe to exist today in India and who will count their lives of no cost to achieve the liberation of these classes and therethrough [rid] Hinduism of an age-long superstition.

Let fellow-reformers who have worked with me also appreciate the implications of the fast.

It is either a hallucination of mine or an illumination. If it is the former, I must be allowed to do my penance in peace. It will be the lifting of a dead weight on Hinduism. If it is an illumination, may my agony purify Hinduism and even melt the hearts of those who are at present disposed to distrust me.

Since there appears to be a misunderstanding as to the application of my fast, I may repeat that it is aimed at a statutory separate electorate, in any shape or form, for the 'depressed' classes. Immediately that threat is removed once for all, my fast will end. I hold strong views about reservation of seats, as also about the most proper method of dealing with the whole question. But I consider myself unfit as a prisoner to set forth my proposals. I should however abide by an agreement on the basis of joint electorate that may be arrived at between the responsible leaders of caste Hindus and the 'depressed' classes and which has been accepted by mass meetings of all Hindus.

One thing I must make clear. The satisfactory ending to the 'depressed' classes question, if it is to come, should in no way mean that I would be committed to the acceptance of His Majesty's Government's decision on the other parts of the communal question. I am personally opposed to many other parts of it, which to my mind make the working of any free and democratic constitution well-nigh impossible, nor would a satisfactory solution of this question in any way bind me to accept the constitution that may be framed. These are political questions for the National Congress to consider and determine. They are utterly outside my province in my individual capacity. Nor may I as a prisoner air my individual views on these questions. My fast has a narrow application. The 'depressed' classes question being predominantly a religious matter, I regard it as specially my own by reason of my lifelong concentration on it. It is a sacred personal trust which I may not shirk.

The fasting for light and penance is a hoary institution. I have observed it in Christianity and Islam. Hinduism is replete with instances of fasting for purification and penance. But it is a privilege, if it is also a duty. Moreover, to the best of my light, I have reduced it to a science. As an expert, therefore, I would warn friends and sympathizers against copying me blindly or out of false or hysterical sympathy. Let all such qualify themselves by hard work and selfless service of the 'untouchables' and they would have independent light if their time for fasting has come.

Lastly, in so far as I know myself this fast is being undertaken with the purest of motives and without malice or anger to any single soul. For me it is an expression of, and the last seal on, non-violence. Those, therefore, who would use violence in this controversy against those whom they may consider to be inimical to me or the cause I represent will simply hasten my end. Perfect courtesy and consideration towards opponents is an absolute essential of success in this case at least if not in all cases.

GN 3857. *CWMG*, vol. li, pp. 62–5

170. Fasting for an end to untouchability

4 November 1932

With rare exceptions, at hundreds of these mass meetings or at private meetings in all parts of India, there has been no protest against my presentation of the case against untouchability. Crowds have passed resolutions denouncing untouchability and pledging themselves to remove it from their midst, and they have on innumerable occasions called God as witness to their pledge and asked for His blessings that He may give them strength to carry out their pledge.

It was against these millions that my fast was undertaken, and it was their spontaneous love that brought about a transformation inside of five days and brought into being the Yeravda Pact.* And it will be against them that the fast will be resumed if that Pact is not carried out by them in its fulness. The Government are now practically out of it. Their part of the obligation they fulfilled promptly. The major part of the resolutions of the Yeravda Pact has to be fulfilled by these millions, the so-called Caste Hindus, who have flocked to the meetings I have described. It is they who have to embrace the suppressed brethren and sisters as their own, whom they have to invite to their temples, to their homes, to their schools. The 'untouchables' in the villages should be made to feel that their shackles have been broken, that they are in no way inferior to their fellow-villagers, that they are worshippers of the same God as other villagers, and are entitled to the same rights and privileges that the latter enjoy. But if these vital conditions of the Pact are not carried out by Caste Hindus, could I possibly live to face God and man? I ventured even to tell Dr Ambedkar, Rao Bahadur Raja* and other friends belonging to the suppressed group that they should regard me as a hostage for the due fulfilment by Caste Hindus of the conditions of the Pact.

The (impending) fast,* if it has to come, will not be for the coercion of those who are opponents of the reform, but it will be intended to sting into action those who have been my comrades or who have taken pledges for the removal of untouchability. If they belie their pledges, or if they never meant to abide by them and their Hinduism was a mere camouflage, I should have no interest left in life. My fast, therefore, ought not to affect the opponents of the reform, nor even fellow-workers and the millions who have led me to believe that they were with me and the Congress in the campaign against untouchability, if the latter have on second thoughts come to the conclusion that untouchability is not after all a crime against God and humanity. In my opinion, fasting for purification of self and others is an age-long institution and it will subsist so long as man believes in God. It is the prayer to the Almighty from an anguished heart. But whether my argument is wise or foolish, I cannot be dislodged from my position so long as I do not see the folly or the error of it. The fast will be resumed only in obedience to the inner voice, and only if there is a manifest breakdown of the Yeravda Pact, owing to the criminal neglect of Caste Hindus to implement its conditions. Such neglect would mean a betrayal of Hinduism. I should not care to remain its living witness.

My Soul's Agony (1933), pp. 2–4. *RU*, pp. 58–9

171. Need to open temples to untouchables

This movement against untouchability has been daily gathering strength. It was in last September* that leading Hindus, claiming to represent the whole of Hindu India, met together and unanimously passed a resolution, condemning untouchability and pledging themselves to abolish it by law, if possible even during the existing regime, and, failing that, when India had a Parliament of her own.

Among the marks of untouchability to be removed was the prohibition against temple-entry by Harijans. In the course of the struggle, it was discovered that the British Courts in India had recognized this evil custom, so much so that certain acts done by 'untouchables' as such came to be offences under the British India Penal Code. Thus, the entry by an 'untouchable' into a Hindu temple would be punishable as a crime under the I.P.C.*

Before, therefore, the movement of temple-entry can make headway, it has become imperative to have this anomaly removed. It is for this purpose that Shri Ranga Iyer has given notice of two bills to be introduced in the Central Legislature.

With due regard to the Sanatanists, it is difficult to understand the cry of 'religion in danger'. Under neither bill will a single temple be opened against the will of the majority of temple-goers in question. The second bill expressly says so. The first bill takes up a neutral attitude.

It does not help a Harijan to force his way into a temple. The reform-ers do not seek to compel the opponents to their will. They desire, by the fairest means possible, to convert the majority or the minority, as the case may be, to their view of untouchability.

It is said that the Harijans themselves do not want temple-entry and that they want only betterment of their economic and political condition. The reformer, too, wants the latter, but he believes that this betterment will be much quicker brought about, if religious equality is attained. The reformer denies that the Harijans do not want temple-entry. But it may be that they are so disgusted with Caste Hindus and Hindu religion itself as to want nothing from them. They may in sullen discontent choose to remain outside the religious pale. Any penance on the part of Caste Hindus may be too late.

Nevertheless, the Caste Hindus who recognize that untouchabil-ity is a blot on Hinduism have to atone for the sin of untouchability. Whether, therefore, Harijans desire temple-entry or not, Caste Hindus have to open their temples to Harijans, precisely on the same terms as to other Hindus. For a Caste Hindu with any sense of honour, temple prohibition is a continuous breach of the pledge taken at the Bombay meeting of September last. These, who gave their word to the world and to God that they would have the temples opened for the Harijans, have to sacrifice their all, if need be, for redeeming the pledge. Temple-entry is the one spiritual act that would constitute the message of freedom to the 'untouchables' and assure them that they are not outcastes before God.

Harijan, 11 Feb. 1933. *RU*, pp. 83–4

172. Harijans' own work

Just one word at this great meeting to Harijan brothers and sisters who may be present. You cannot be free from this self-purification. You, too, have to bring your own sacrifice to this altar and that consists in the strict observance of the laws of sanitation—internal and exter-nal, and secondly, in the giving up of carrion- and beef-eating, wher-ever that habit still persists. In every part of the civilized world carrion is abhorred. It is considered unfit for human consumption. And no one can call himself a Hindu and partake of beef. Sacredness of the cow and her worship are an integral part of Hinduism. Thirdly, I would ask every Harijan, man and woman present here, to give up the habit of drinking. Let no Harijan say to himself or herself or to me that many Savarna Hindus also drink. I would beseech you as a fellow-Harijan by choice to shun all vices of Savarna Hindus. In spite of all the reparation that Hindus may make to you, in spite of all the repentance they may show in the presence of God, after all, in the ultimate resort, your salvation will rest with yourselves.

Speech in Bangalore. *Harijan*, 19 Jan. 1934. *RU*, p. 182

173. The roles of Harijans and caste Hindus in reform

I do preach to the Harijans cleanliness, abstention from carrion-eating and intoxicating drinks and drugs, necessity of taking education themselves and giving it to their children, also abstention from eating the leavings from Caste Hindus' plates, etc. Only, I do not put these before Harijans as conditions precedent to the removal of untouchability. On the contrary, I suggest to Caste Hindus that the shortcomings are not inherent to Harijans but that they are due to our criminal neglect of—even deliberate suppression of—these brethren of ours. Therefore, the disappearance of these shortcomings will take place sooner for our fraternizing with Harijans even as they are, and then helping them to become better men and women. That is the least penance Caste Hindus can do for the past wrongs. We must approach Harijans as penitents or debtors, not as their patrons or creditors extending generosity to the undeserving.

Harijan, 28 Sept. 1934. *RU*, p. 183

174. The name, 'Harijan'

Harijan* means 'a man of God'. All the religions of the world describe God pre-eminently as the Friend of the friendless, Help of the helpless and Protector of the weak. The rest of the world apart, in India who can be more friendless, helpless or weaker than the forty million or more Hindus of India who are classified as 'untouchables'? If, therefore, any body of people can be fitly described as men of God, they are surely these helpless, friendless and despised people. Hence, in the pages of *Navajivan*, I have always adopted Harijan as the name signifying 'untouchables'. Not that the change of name brings about any change of status, but one may at least be spared the use of a term which is itself one of reproach. When Caste Hindus have of their own inner conviction and, therefore, voluntarily, got rid of the present-day untouchability, we shall all be called Harijans; for, according to my humble opinion, Caste Hindus will then have found favour with God and may therefore be fitly described as His men.

Harijan, 11 Feb. 1933. *RU*, p. 15

175. A woman's status in marriage

Husbands are always eager to read sermons to their wives. Wives are even told to consider themselves the husband's property. The husband feels that he has the same proprietary rights over his wife as he has over his goods and chattels and livestock . . . There is no doubt that a man who treats his wife like an animal, who considers her as his property, cuts himself from his better half.

It is the duty of the husband to consider his wife a true companion,* helper and his better half. He should share her joys and sorrows. A wife is never to be considered her husband's slave, nor merely meant to be the object of his lust. She has a right to the same freedoms which the husband wants for himself.

The culture in which women are not honoured is doomed. The world cannot go on without either the men or the women, it can go on only by their mutual co-operation . . .

Hindu culture has always respected women. They have always been given pride of place . . . A civilization so noble cannot bring the status of women down to the level of goods and chattels.

. . . It is my firm belief that a wife has full right to her husband's earnings. She has an inalienable right to his property. It is the husband's duty to protect his wife and do what he can to provide her food and clothing.

Hindi Navajivan, 8 Aug. 1929 (H.). *CWMG*, vol. xli, pp. 268–9

176. Women's rights

I do not need to be a girl to be wild over man's atrocities towards woman. I count the law of inheritance among the least in the list. The Sarda Bill* deals with an evil far greater than the one which the law of inheritance connotes. But I am uncompromising in the matter of woman's rights. In my opinion she should labour under no legal disability not suffered by man. I should treat the daughters and sons on a footing of perfect equality. As women begin to realize their strength, as they must in proportion to the education they receive, they will naturally resent the glaring inequalities to which they are subjected.

But to remove legal inequalities will be a mere palliative. The root of the evil lies much deeper than most people realize. It lies in man's greed of power and fame, and deeper still in mutual lust . . .

Whilst therefore I would always advocate the repeal of all legal disqualifications, I should have the enlightened women of India to deal with the root cause. Woman is the embodiment of sacrifice and suffering, and her advent to public life should therefore result in purifying it, in restraining unbridled ambition and accumulation of property . . .

. . . Thus viewed, it is a serious problem the enlightened daughters of Bharat Mata are called upon to solve. They may not ape the manner of the West which may be suited to its environment. They must apply methods suited to the Indian genius and Indian environment. Theirs must be the strong, controlling, purifying, steadying hand, conserving what is best in our culture and unhesitatingly rejecting what is base and degrading.

Young India, 17 Oct. 1929. *CWMG*, vol. xlii, pp. 4–6

177. Family life first

What I want to see is the opening of all offices, professions and employments to women; otherwise there can be no real equality. But I most sincerely hope that woman will retain and exercise her ancient prerogative as queen of the household.

From this position she must never be dethroned. It would indeed be a dreary home of which a woman was not the centre. I cannot, for instance, imagine a really happy home in which the wife is a typist and scarcely ever in it. Who would look after the children? What, after all, is a home without children, the brightest jewels in the poorest household? . . .

It is a woman's work to bring up her little ones and mould their character. A precious work, too. Equality in status with men, I desire for women, but if the mother fails in her sacred trust towards her children, then nothing can atone for the loss.

Whatever the race, family life is the first and greatest thing. Its sanctity must remain. Upon it rests the welfare of the nation. For good or for ill home influence persists. Of that there can be no possible doubt, and no State can survive unless the sacred security of its home life is preserved. Individuals there may be who in pursuit of some great principle of ideal, forgo, like myself, the solace of family life, choosing instead one of self-sacrifice and celibacy; but for the mass of the people the preservation of home life is essential.

Daily Herald, 28 Sept. 1931. *CWMG*, vol. xlviii, pp. 80–1

178. Women become public activists in South Africa

CHAPTER XXXIX: WHEN MARRIAGE IS NOT A MARRIAGE

As if unseen by anyone God was preparing the ingredients for the Indians' victory and demonstrating still more clearly the injustice of the Europeans in South Africa, an event happened which none had expected. Many married men came to South Africa from India, while some Indians contracted a marriage in South Africa itself. There is no law for the registration of ordinary marriages in India, and the religious ceremony suffices to confer validity upon them. The same custom ought to apply to Indians in South Africa as well and although Indians had settled in South Africa for the last forty years, the validity of marriages solemnized according to the rites of the various religions of India had never been called in question. But at this time there was a case in which Mr Justice Searle of the Cape Supreme Court gave judgment on March 14, 1913 to the effect that all marriages were outside the pale of legal marriages in South Africa with the exception of such as were celebrated according to Christian rites and registered by the Registrar of Marriages. This terrible judgment thus nullified in South Africa at a stroke of the pen all marriages celebrated according to the Hindu, Musalman and Zoroastrian rites. The many married Indian women in South Africa in terms of this judgment ceased to rank as the wives of their husbands and were degraded to the rank of concubines, while their progeny were deprived of their right to inherit the parents' property. This was an insufferable situation for women no less than men, and the Indians in South Africa were deeply agitated.

According to my usual practice I wrote to the Government, asking them whether they agreed to the Searle judgment and whether, if the judge was right in interpreting it, they would amend the law so as to recognize the validity of Indian marriages consecrated according to the religious customs of the parties and recognized as legal in India. The Government were not then in a mood to listen and could not see their way to comply with my request.

The Satyagraha Association held a meeting to consider whether they should appeal against the Searle judgment, and came to the conclusion that no appeal was possible on a question of this nature. If there was to be an appeal, it must be preferred by Government, or if they so desired, by the Indians provided that the Government openly sided with them through their Attorney General. To appeal when these conditions were not satisfied would be in a way tantamount to tolerating the invalidation of Indian marriages. Satyagraha would have to be resorted to, even if such an appeal was made and if it was rejected. In these circumstances therefore it seemed best not to prefer any appeal against this unspeakable insult.

A crisis now arrived, when there could not be any waiting for an auspicious day or hour. Patience was impossible in the face of this insult offered to our womanhood. We decided to offer stubborn Satyagraha irrespective of the number of fighters. Not only could the women now be not prevented from joining the struggle, but we decided even to invite them to come into line along with the men. We first invited the sisters who had lived on Tolstoy Farm. I found that they were only too glad to enter the struggle. I gave them an idea of the risks incidental to such participation. I explained to them that they would have to put up with restraints in the matter of food, dress and personal movements. I warned them that they might be given hard work in jail, made to wash clothes and even subjected to insult by the warders. But these sisters were all brave and feared none of these things. One of them was pregnant while six of them had young babies in arms. But one and all were eager to join and I simply could not come in their way. These sisters were with one exception all Tamilians. Here are their names:

1. Mrs Thambi Naidoo, 2. Mrs N. Pillay, 3. Mrs K. Murugasa Pillay, 4. Mrs A. Perumal Naidoo, 5. Mrs P. K. Naidoo, 6. Mrs K. Chinnaswami Pillay, 7. Mrs N. S. Pillay, 8. Mrs R. A. Mudalingam,

9. Mrs Bhavani Dayal, 10. Miss Minachi Pillay, 11. Miss Baikum Murugasa Pillay.

It is easy to get into prison by committing a crime but it is difficult to get in by being innocent. As the criminal seeks to escape arrest, the police pursue and arrest him. But they lay their hands upon the innocent man who courts arrest of his own free will only when they cannot help it. The first attempts of these sisters were not crowned with success. They entered the Transvaal at Vereeniging without permits, but they were not arrested. They took to hawking without a licence, but still the police ignored them. It now became a problem with the women how they should get arrested. There were not many men ready to go to jail and those who were ready could not easily have their wish.

We now decided to take a step which we had reserved till the last, and which in the event fully answered our expectations. I had contemplated sacrificing all the settlers in Phoenix at a critical period. That was to be my final offering to the God of Truth. The settlers at Phoenix were mostly my close co-workers and relations. The idea was to send all of them to jail with the exception of a few who would be required for the conduct of *Indian Opinion* and of children below sixteen. This was the maximum of sacrifice open to me in the circumstances. The sixteen stalwarts to whom I had referred in writing to Gokhale were among the pioneers of the Phoenix settlement. It was proposed that these friends should cross over into the Transvaal and as they crossed over, get arrested for entering the country without permits. We were afraid that Government would not arrest them if we made a previous announcement of our intention, and therefore we guarded it as a secret except from a couple of friends. When the pioneers entered the Transvaal, the police officer would ask them their names and addresses, and it was part of the programme not to supply this information as there was an apprehension that if their identity was disclosed, the police would come to know that they were my relations and therefore would not arrest them. Refusal to give name and address to an officer was also held to be a separate offence. While the Phoenix group entered the Transvaal, the sisters who had courted arrest in the Transvaal in vain were to enter Natal. As it was an offence to enter the Transvaal from Natal without a permit it was equally an offence to enter Natal from the Transvaal. If the sisters were arrested upon entering Natal, well and good. But if they were not arrested, it was arranged that they should proceed to and post themselves at Newcastle, the great coal-mining centre in Natal, and advise the indentured Indian labourers there to go on strike. The mother tongue of the sisters was Tamil, and they could speak a little Hindustani besides. The majority of labourers on the coal mines hailed from Madras State and spoke Tamil or Telugu, though there were many from North India as well. If the labourers struck in response to the sisters' appeal, Government was bound to arrest them along with the labourers, who would thereby probably be fired with still greater enthusiasm. This was the strategy I thought out and unfolded before the Transvaal sisters.

I went to Phoenix, and talked to the settlers about my plans. First of all I held a consultation with the sisters living there. I knew that the step of sending women to jail was fraught with serious risk. Most of the sisters in Phoenix spoke Gujarati. They had not had the training or experience of the Transvaal sisters. Moreover, most of them were related to me, and might think of going to jail only on account of my influence with them. If afterwards they flinched at the time of actual trial or could not stand the jail, they might be led to apologize, thus not only giving me a deep shock but also causing serious damage to the movement. I decided not to broach the subject to my wife, as she could not say no to any proposal I made, and if she said yes, I would not know what value to attach to her assent, and as I knew that in a serious matter like this the husband should leave the wife to take what step she liked on her own initiative, and should not be offended at all even if she did not take any step whatever. I talked to the other sisters who readily fell in with my proposal and expressed their readiness to go to jail. They assured me that they would complete their term in jail, come what might. My wife overheard my conversation with the sisters, and addressing me, said, 'I am sorry that you are not telling me about this. What defect is there in me which disqualifies me for jail? I also wish to take the path to which you are inviting the others.' 'You know I am the last person to cause you pain,' I replied. 'There is no question of my distrust in you. I would be only too glad if you went to jail, but it should not appear at all as if you went at my instance. In matters like this everyone should act relying solely upon one's own strength and courage. If I asked you, you might be inclined to go just for the sake of complying with my request. And then if you began to tremble in the law court or were terrified by hardships in jail, I could not find fault with you, but how would it stand with me? How could I then harbour you or look the world in the face? It is fears like these which have prevented me from asking you too to court jail.' 'You may have nothing to do with me,' she said, 'if being unable to stand jail I secure my release by an apology. If you can endure hardships and so can my boys, why cannot I? I am bound to join the struggle.' 'Then I am bound to admit you to it,' said I. 'You know my conditions and you know my temperament. Even now reconsider the matter if you like, and if after mature thought you deliberately come to the conclusion not to join the movement, you are free to withdraw. And you must understand that there is nothing to be ashamed of in changing your decision even now.'

'I have nothing to think about, I am fully determined,' she said.

I suggested to the other settlers also that each should take his or her decision independently of all others. Again and again, and in a variety of ways I pressed this condition on their attention that none should fall away whether the struggle was short or long, whether the Phoenix settlement flourished or faded, and whether he or she kept good health or fell ill in jail. All were ready. The only member of the party from outside Phoenix was Rustomji Jivanji Ghorkhodu, from whom these conferences could not be concealed, and Kakaji, as he was affectionately called, was not the man to lag behind on an occasion like the present. He had already been to jail, but he insisted upon paying it another visit. The 'invading' party was composed of the following members:

1. Mrs Kasturbai Gandhi, 2. Mrs Jayakunvar Manilal Doctor, 3. Mrs Kashi Chhaganlal Gandhi, 4. Mrs Santok Maganlal Gandhi, 5. Parsi Rustomji Jivanji Ghorkhodu, 6. Chhaganlal Khushalchand Gandhi, 7. Ravjibhai Manibhai Patel, 8. Maganbhai Haribhai Patel, 9. Solomon Royeppen, 10. Raju Govindu, 11. Ramdas Mohandas Gandhi, 12. Shivpujan Badari, 13. V. Govindarajulu, 14. Kuppuswami Moonlight Mudaliar, 15. Gokuldas Hansraj, and 16. Revashankar Ratansi Sodha.

The sequel must be taken up in a fresh chapter.

CHAPTER XL: WOMEN IN JAIL

These 'invaders' were to go to jail for crossing the border and entering the Transvaal without permits. The reader who has seen the list of their names will have observed, that if some of them were disclosed beforehand, the police might not perhaps arrest the persons bearing them. Such in fact had been the case with me. I was arrested twice or thrice but after this the police ceased to meddle with me at the border. No one was informed of this party having started and the news was of course withheld from the papers. Moreover the party had been instructed not to give their names even to the police and to state that they would disclose their identity in court.

The police were familiar with cases of this nature. After the Indians got into the habit of courting arrest, they would often not give their names just for the fun of the thing, and the police therefore did not notice anything strange about the behaviour of the Phoenix party, which was arrested accordingly. They were then tried and sentenced to three months' imprisonment with hard labour (September 23, 1913).

The sisters who had been disappointed in the Transvaal now entered Natal but were not arrested for entering the country without permits. They therefore proceeded to Newcastle and set about their work according to the plans previously settled. Their influence spread like wildfire. The pathetic story of the wrongs heaped up by the £3 tax touched the labourers to the quick, and they went on strike. I received the news by wire and was as much perplexed as I was pleased. What was I to do? I was not prepared for this marvellous awakening. I had neither men nor the money which would enable me to cope with the work before me. But I visualized my duty very clearly. I must go to Newcastle and do what I could. I left at once to go there.

Government could not now any longer leave the brave Transvaal sisters free to pursue their activities. They too were sentenced to imprisonment for the same term—three months—and were kept in the same prison as the Phoenix party (October 21, 1913).

These events stirred the heart of the Indians not only in South Africa but also in the motherland to its very depths. Sir Pherozeshah* had been so far indifferent. In 1901 he had strongly advised me not to go to South Africa. He held that nothing could be done for Indian emigrants beyond the seas so long as India had not achieved her own freedom, and he was little impressed with the Satyagraha movement in its initial stages. But women in jail pleaded with him as nothing else could. As he himself put it in his Bombay Town Hall speech, his blood boiled at the thought of these women lying in jails herded with ordinary criminals and India could not sleep over the matter any longer.

The women's bravery was beyond words. They were all kept in Maritzburg* jail, where they were considerably harassed. Their food was of the worst quality and they were given laundry work as their task. No food was permitted to be given them from outside nearly till the end of their term. One sister was under a religious vow to restrict herself to a particular diet. After great difficulty the jail authorities allowed her that diet, but the food supplied was unfit for human consumption. The sister badly needed olive oil. She did not get it at first, and when she got it, it was old and rancid. She offered to get it at her own expense but was told that jail was no hotel, and she must take what food was given her. When this sister was released she was a mere skeleton and her life was saved only by a great effort.

Another returned from jail with a fatal fever to which she succumbed within a few days of her release (February 22, 1914). How can I forget her? Valliamma R. Munuswami Mudaliar was a young girl of Johannesburg only sixteen years of age. She was confined to bed when I saw her. As she was a tall girl, her emaciated body was a terrible thing to behold.

'Valliamma, you do not repent of your having gone to jail?' I asked.

'Repent? I am even now ready to go to jail again if I am arrested,' said Valliamma.

'But what if it results in your death?' I pursued.

'I do not mind it. Who would not love to die for one's motherland?' was the reply.

Within a few days after this conversation Valliamma was no more with us in the flesh, but she left us the heritage of an immortal name. Condolence meetings were held at various places, and the Indians resolved to erect 'Valliamma Hall', to commemorate the supreme sacrifice of this daughter of India. Unfortunately the resolution has not still been translated into action. There were many difficulties. The community was torn by internal dissensions; the principal workers left one after another. But whether or not a hall is built in stone and mortar, Valliamma's service is imperishable. She built her temple of service with her own hands, and her glorious image has a niche even now reserved for it in many a heart. And the name of Valliamma will live in the history of South African Satyagraha as long as India lives.

It was an absolutely pure sacrifice that was offered by these sisters, who were innocent of legal technicalities, and many of whom had no idea of country, their patriotism being based only upon faith. Some of them were illiterate and could not read the papers. But they knew that a mortal blow was being aimed at the Indians' honour, and their going to jail was a cry of agony and prayer offered from the bottom of their heart, was in fact the purest of all sacrifices. Such heart prayer is always acceptable to God. Sacrifice is fruitful only to the extent that it is pure. God hungers after devotion in man. . . . The imprisonment of many might have been fruitless but the devoted sacrifice of a single pure soul could never go in vain. None can tell whose sacrifice in South Africa was acceptable to God, and hence bore fruit. But we do know that Valliamma's sacrifice bore fruit and so did the sacrifice of the other sisters.

Souls without number spent themselves in the past, are spending themselves in the present and will spend themselves in the future in the service of country and humanity, and that is in the fitness of things as no one knows who is pure. But Satyagrahis may rest assured, that even if there is only one among them who is pure as crystal, his sacrifice suffices to achieve the end in view. The world rests upon the bedrock of *satya* or truth. *Asatya* meaning untruth also means non-existent, and *satya* or truth also means that which *is*. If untruth does not so much as exist, its victory is out of the question. And truth being that which *is* can never be destroyed. This is the doctrine of Satyagraha in a nutshell.

Gandhi, *Satyagraha in South Africa* (G.)

179. Women's public participation vital for *swaraj*

16 January 1925

To women I talk about *Ramarajya*.* *Ramarajya* is more than swar-ajya. Let me therefore talk about what *Ramarajya* will be like—not about swaraj. *Ramarajya* can come about only when there is likelihood of a Sita* arising. Among the many *shlokas* recited by Hindus, one is on women. It enumerates women who are worthy of being remembered prayerfully early in the morning. Who are these women by taking whose names men and women become sanctified? Among such virtuous women Sita's name is bound to figure. We never say Rama-Sita but Sita-Rama, not Krishna-Radha, but Radha-Krishna.

It is thus that we tutor even the parrot. The reason why we think of Sita's name first is that, without virtuous women, there can be no virtuous men. A child will take after the mother, not the father. It is the mother who holds its reins. The father's concerns lie outside the home and that is why I keep saying that, as long as the women of India do not take part in public life, there can be no salvation for the country. Only those can take part in public life who are pure in body and mind. As long as women whose body and mind tend in one direction—i.e., towards the path of virtue—do not come into public life and purify it, we are not likely to attain *Ramarajya* or swaraj. Even if we did, I would have no use for that kind of swaraj to which such women have not made their full contribution. One could well stretch oneself on the ground in obeisance to a woman of purity of mind and heart. I should like such women to take part in public life.

Who shall we say is a woman of this kind? It is said that a virtuous woman can be recognized by the grace of her face. Must we then accept all the prostitutes in India as virtuous? For it is their trade to deck themselves up. Not at all. The thing needed for grace is not beauty of face but purity of heart. A woman who is pure of heart and mind is ever fit to be worshipped. It is a law of nature that our outward appearance reflects what we really are within. If inwardly we are sullied, so shall we appear without. The eyes and the voice are external signs. The discerning can recognize virtue by voice.

Then what does it mean to be virtuous? What is the sign of virtue? I accept khadi as the symbol of virtue. I do not suggest that anyone who wears khadi has become sanctified for that reason alone.

I ask you to participate in public life. What does it mean to participate in public life? Public work does not mean attendance at meetings, but wearing khadi—the symbol of purity—and serving the men and women of India. After all, what service can we render to the Rajas and Maharajas? If we try to approach the Maharajas, the sentry at the gate may not even let us in. Likewise, we do not have to wait on millionaires: To serve India therefore is to serve its poor. God we cannot see with our eyes; it would do if we serve those whom we can see. The object of our public life is to serve the visible God, that is the poor. If you want to serve them, take the name of God, go amidst them and ply the spinning-wheel.

To take part in public life is to serve your poor sisters. Their lot is wretched. I met them on the banks of the Ganga . . . They were in a pitiful state. They had scanty clothes, but I could not give them saris because I had not found the charkha then. Indian women remain naked even if they have clothes, because as long as one Indian woman has to go naked it must be said that all are naked. Or even if a woman is adorned in a variety of ways but is of unworthy soul, she would still be naked. We have to think of ways of making them spin, weave and thus covering themselves truly.

At present when people go to the villages to render service, the villagers imagine that they have come to exact *chauth*.* Why do they imagine this? You must realize that you go to the villages to give and not to take.

Were our mothers mad that they used to spin? Now when I ask you to spin, I must appear mad to you. But it is not Gandhi who is mad; it is yourself who are so. You do not have any compassion for the poor. Even so you try to convince yourself that India has become prosperous and sing of that prosperity. If you want to enter public life, render public service, then spin on the charkha, wear khadi. If your body and mind are pure you will become truly swadeshi. Spin in the name of God. To spin for your poor sisters is to worship God. Giving in charity to the poor means an offering to God. That alone is charity by which the poor become happy. If you give in charity to whomsoever you please, it would be said that you indulge your whims. If you give in charity to those who have a pair of hands, a pair of legs and good health, it would be said that you were out to impoverish them. Do not give alms to a Brahmin because he is a Brahmin. Make him spin and give him a handful of jowar or rice. The finest sign of purity of mind is to go and work for khadi amidst such people.

The second sign of virtue is service to *Antyajas*.* Brahmins and gurus of today regard touching an *Antyaja* as sinful. I say that it is a meritorious act, not a sin. I do not ask you to eat and drink with them, but to mix with them in order to render service. It is meritorious to serve sick *Antyaja* boys who are worthy of service. *Antyajas* eat, drink, stand and sit, and so do we all. It is not that doing this is either sinful or meritorious. My mother used to become *Antyaja* for some time* and then she would not allow anyone to touch her. My wife similarly used to become an *Antyaja*. At this time she became an untouchable. Our *Bhangis*.* also become untouchable when they do their work. As long as they do not bathe, one can understand not touching them. But if you would not touch them even when they have bathed and tidied up, for whose sake do they bathe then? They have no God even. . . .

The third sign of virtue is furtherance of friendship with the Muslims. If someone tells you that 'they are Mias' or 'Mia and Mahadev cannot get on', then tell him that you cannot harbour enmity towards the Muslims.

If you do these three things, you will be said to have taken full part in public life. By doing so you will become worthy of being prayerfully remembered early in the morning; and it would be said that you have worked for India's salvation. I beseech you to become thus worthy.

Speech at women's conference in Gujarat (G.). *Mahadevbhaini Diary*, vol. vii, pp. 87–90. *CWMG*, vol. xxvi, pp. 2–5

180. The purity of women in public life

A long letter lies before me. It contains a well-deserved but gentle criticism of our present movement and of the workers engaged in it . . .

I have not understood what the correspondent has in mind in the veiled reference he has made to the subject of association with women. The point did not become clear to me even after I had read the whole letter. But one can guess a little from the analogy the writer has used. I have no doubt that seeking women's company for its own sake is sinful and reprehensible. Workers who are guilty of this can render little service to the people. But association with women in the ordinary course of public work is unavoidable and, therefore, to be accepted. We have kept women very much suppressed. They have lost their womanhood. A woman has a right to go out of her home in order to serve, it is her duty to do so. As day by day women come to take greater part in our movement, we shall see more and more men and women coming together in meetings. This seems to me quite a normal situation.

That *brahmacharya* which can be observed only by living in a forest is neither *brahmacharya* nor self-control. Many would like to live in a forest. Everyone will find such solitude beneficial in some measure. But it is to be sought in order that it may help one in reflection and in striving for self-realization, and not for one's safety.

He alone who, though living in the midst of the busy world, is unaffected by its concerns is a man of self-control and lives in safety.

The walls which were erected in the old days may have been necessary in those times. But we see in Europe in these days that, though large numbers of men and women mix with great freedom, they are able to preserve their moral character and purity. If anyone believes that it is impossible to preserve one's purity in Europe, he betrays his utter ignorance. It is true, certainly, that it is difficult for us to preserve our purity in Europe. But the reason is not that women enjoy great freedom in Europe, but that people there look upon enjoyment as the only good in life. Moreover we are not accustomed to the freedom that obtains in Europe in these matters.

The example of Europe is useful to us only to a certain extent. To follow it in every respect would be dangerous. My aim in referring to it is merely to show that the idea of association with women being reprehensible in all circumstances, or its being sinful for a man of self-control, is not true at all times and in all places.

In introducing whatever reforms are necessary in our culture, we should take into account the general atmosphere in our country. On the one hand, we have to introduce reforms in the conditions of women's life and, on the other, we have to guard against any harmful consequence during the transitional stage. We shall also have to take some risks. I have received complaints from one or two places to the effect that all is not well there. I have been inquiring into the matter to the extent that it lies in my power to do so.

According to me, it is desirable for a man and a woman to avoid being alone together at all times and in all places, in order to safeguard their purity. If the relationship is pure, there is no need for privacy. There is need for reform in our education, our speech, our diet and our habits. The very thought of our obeying in modern times some of the injunctions of the Shastras which were laid down for their times makes me shudder. As it was thought to be a sin even to look at a woman, the fear has taken possession of us that we cannot look at a woman without evil thoughts. A son feels purified by the sight of his mother. There can be no sin in a brother's innocent look at his sister. Sin depends on the state of one's mind. A man who can never look at a woman without an evil thought had better put out his eyes, or live in a forest till he was pure enough. Anyone who keeps looking at a woman without reason and yet protests that he has no evil thought in his mind is a hypocrite. But the man who is afraid to look at a woman when he happens to meet one should overcome his timidity. It is definitely sinful to stare at a woman who is not known to us, but there can be no inflexible rule in this matter. No matter how many screens you erect, a polluted mind will look for opportunities for sin and, not getting them, will at any rate go on sinning mentally. A pure mind will survive temptations which assail unexpectedly and preserve unsullied purity.

Finally, the man of self-control should, without resentment, keep in mind the suggestions made by the correspondent, be vigilant and go on with his work of service.

Navajivan, 24 May 1925 (G.). *CWMG*, vol. xxvii, pp. 151–3

181. Memories of child marriage

About the time of my marriage,* little pamphlets costing a pice, or a pie (I now forget how much), used to be issued, in which conjugal love, thrift, child marriages, and other such subjects were discussed. Whenever I came across any of these, I used to go through them cover to cover, and it was a habit with me to forget what I did not like, and to carry out in practice whatever I liked. Lifelong faithfulness to the wife, inculcated in these booklets as the duty of the husband, remained permanently imprinted on my heart. Furthermore, the passion for truth was innate in me, and to be false to her was therefore out of the question. And then there was very little chance of my being faithless at that tender age.

But the lesson of faithfulness had also an untoward effect. 'If I should be pledged to be faithful to my wife, she also should be pledged to be faithful to me,' I said to myself. The thought made me a jealous husband. Her duty was easily converted into my right to exact faithfulness from her, and if it had to be exacted, I should be watchfully tenacious of the right. I had absolutely no reason to suspect my wife's fidelity, but jealousy does not wait for reasons. I must needs be forever on the look-out regarding her movements, and therefore she could not go anywhere without my permission. This sowed the seeds of a bitter quarrel between us. The restraint was virtually a sort of imprisonment. And Kasturbai was not the girl to brook any such thing. She made it a point to go out whenever and wherever she liked. More restraint on my part resulted in more liberty being taken by her, and in my getting more and more cross. Refusal to speak to one another thus became the order of the day with us, married children. I think it was quite innocent of Kasturbai to have taken those liberties with my restrictions. How could a guileless girl brook any restraint on going to the temple or on going on visits to friends? If I had the right to impose restrictions on her, had not she also a similar right? All this is clear to me today. But at that time I had to make good my authority as a husband!

Let not the reader think, however, that ours was a life of unrelieved bitterness. For my severities were all based on love. I wanted to *make* my wife an ideal wife. My ambition was to *make* her live a pure life, learn what I learnt, and identify her life and thought with mine.

I do not know whether Kasturbai had any such ambition. She was illiterate. By nature she was simple, independent, persevering and, with me at least, reticent. She was not impatient of her ignorance and I do not recollect my studies having ever spurred her to go in for a similar adventure. I fancy, therefore, that my ambition was all one-sided. My passion was entirely centred on one woman, and I wanted it to be reciprocated. But even if there were no reciprocity, it could not be all unrelieved misery because there was active love on one side at least.

I must say I was passionately fond of her. Even at school I used to think of her, and the thought of nightfall and our subsequent meeting was ever haunting me. Separation was unbearable. I used to keep her awake till late in the night with my idle talk. If with this devouring passion there had not been in me a burning attachment to duty, I should either have fallen a prey to disease and premature death, or have sunk into a burdensome existence. But the appointed tasks had to be gone through every morning, and lying to anyone was out of the question. It was this last thing that saved me from many a pitfall.

I have already said that Kasturbai was illiterate. I was very anxious to teach her, but lustful love left me no time. For one thing the teaching had to be done against her will, and that too at night. I dared not meet her in the presence of the elders, much less talk to her. Kathiawad* had then, and to a certain extent has even today, its own peculiar, useless and barbarous *Purdah*. Circumstances were thus unfavourable. I must therefore confess that most of my efforts to instruct Kasturbai in our youth were unsuccessful. And when I awoke from the sleep of lust, I had already launched forth into public life, which did not leave me much spare time. I failed likewise to instruct her through private tutors. As a result Kasturbai can now with difficulty write simple letters and understand simple Gujarati. I am sure that, had my love for her been absolutely untainted with lust, she would be a learned lady today; for I could then have conquered her dislike for studies. I know that nothing is impossible for pure love.

I have mentioned one circumstance that more or less saved me from the disasters of lustful love. There is another worth noting. Numerous examples have convinced me that God ultimately saves him whose motive is pure. Along with the cruel custom of child marriages, Hindu society has another custom which to a certain extent diminishes the evils of the former. Parents do not allow young couples to stay together long. The child-wife spends more than half her time at her father's place. Such was the case with us. That is to say, during the first five years of our married life (from the age of 13 to 18), we could not have lived together longer than an aggregate period of three years. We would hardly have spent six months together, when there would be a call to my wife from her parents. Such calls were very unwelcome in those days, but they saved us both. At the age of eighteen I went to England, and this meant a long and healthy spell of separation. Even after my return from England we hardly stayed together longer than six months. For I had run up and down between Rajkot and Bombay. Then came the call from South Africa and that found me already fairly free from the carnal appetite.

Gandhi, *An Autobiography*, part I, chap. IV

182. Child marriage—'a brutal custom'

Mrs Margaret E. Cousins* has sent me notes of a tragic case that appears to have just occurred in Madras and has arisen out of a child marriage, the girl being 13 years and the 'husband' 26. Hardly had the pair lived together for 13 days when the girl died of burning. The jury have found that she committed suicide owing to the unbearable and inhuman solicitations of the so-called husband. The dying deposition of the girl would go to show that the 'husband' had set fire to her clothes. Passion knows no prudence, no pity.

But how the girl died is beside the point. The indisputable facts are:

(1) that the girl was married when she was only 13;

(2) that she had no sexual desire inasmuch as she resisted the advances of the 'husband';

(3) that the 'husband' did make cruel advances;

(4) and that she is now no more.

It is irreligion, not religion, to give religious sanction to a brutal custom. The *smritis* bristle with contradictions. The only reasonable deduction to be drawn from the contradictions is that the texts that may be contrary to known and accepted morality, more especially, to the moral precepts enjoined in the *smritis* themselves, must be rejected as interpolations. Inspiring verses on self-restraint could not be written at the same time and by the same pen that wrote the verses encouraging the brute in man. Only a man innocent of self-restraint and steeped in vice could call it a sin not to marry a girl before she reached the age of monthly periods. It should be held sinful to marry a girl for several years after the periods begin. There cannot be even the thought of marriage before the periods begin. A girl is no more fit to bear children on beginning the periods than a lad is to procreate as soon as he grows the first hair on his upper lip.

The custom of child marriage is a moral as well as a physical evil. For it undermines our morals and induces physical degeneration. By countenancing such customs we recede from God as well as swaraj. A man who has no thought of the tender age of a girl has none of God. And undergrown men have no capacity for fighting battles of freedom or, having gained it, of retaining it. Fight for swaraj means not mere political awakening but an all-round awakening—social, educational, moral, economic and political.

Legislation* is being promoted to raise the age of consent. It may be good for bringing a minority to book. But it is not legislation that will cure a popular evil, it is enlightened public opinion that can do it. I am not opposed to legislation in such matters but I do lay greater stress on cultivation of public opinion. The Madras case would have been impossible if there had been a living public opinion against child marriages. The young man in question is not an illiterate labourer but an intelligent educated typist. It would have been impossible for him to marry or touch the girl if public opinion had been against the marriage or the consummation of the marriage of girls of tender age. Ordinarily, a girl under 18 years should never be given in marriage.

Young India, 26 Aug. 1926. *CWMG*, vol. xxxi, pp. 329–30

183. Appropriate and inappropriate widowhood

I have known Basanti Devi* since the year 1919. I came closer to her in 1921. I had heard a great deal about her goodness, her intelligence and her hospitality, and also had some experience of them. As I drew closer to Deshbandhu in Darjeeling, so did I to Basanti Devi. In her widowhood, I have come much closer to her. I have been practically by her side from the day they came from Darjeeling to Calcutta with Deshbandhu's body. My first meeting with her as a widow was in her son-in-law's house. She sat surrounded by a number of women. In the old days, as soon as I entered the house she herself would come out to receive and welcome me. Now that she was a widow, who would talk to me? I had to recognize her in the midst of all those women sitting as still as statues. For a minute, my eyes searched for her. Vermilion at the parting of the hair, *tika* on the forehead, betel-leaf in the mouth, bangles on the wrists, a bordered sari and a smiling face—without any of these signs how could I recognize Basanti Devi? I went and sat where I thought she should be and scanned the face. The sight was too much. Yes, I recognized the face. I found it difficult to keep back my tears, let alone hardening my heart and offering consolation.

Where was today the usual smile on her face? I tried in many ways to console her, to cheer her up and make her speak. After a long time I succeeded a little.

Devi smiled faintly.

That gave me courage and I said, 'You cannot weep. If you do, others also will weep. We have quietened Mona (elder daughter) with the utmost difficulty. As for Baby (younger daughter) you know her condition. Sujata (daughter-in-law) has been crying uncontrollably and has barely stopped. You should have compassion on these. We want you to do many things yet.'

The brave woman replied with great firmness of mind: 'I will not weep. How can I, when tears don't come?' I understood what this meant and was satisfied. Crying lightens the heart. But this bereaved sister did not want to lighten her grief. She wanted to bear the burden. So, why should she weep? How could I say, now: 'Come, let us brother and sister weep and pour out our grief to each other'?

A Hindu widow is an image of suffering. She has taken upon herself the misery of the world. She has learnt to find happiness in suffering, has accepted suffering as sacred.

Basanti Devi had no objection to eating any type of food. In the period of her life up to 1920, all manner of delicacies were cooked in her kitchen and hundreds of people feasted in her house. She could not go without *pan* even for an hour. A box containing betel-leaves was always to be found with her.

And, now, she has given up all adornment, given up betel-leaves, sweet dishes and meat and fish too. All the time, her thoughts are fixed on her husband and on God.

I plead with many women to pay less attention to adorning their person, ask many of them to give up addictions. Rarely does any give up these things. But think what a widow does? The moment a Hindu woman becomes a widow, she gives up addictions and lays aside jewellery and other adornments as the snake casts off its slough. She needs neither persuasion nor help from anyone for doing that. Is there anything which custom does not make easy?

Is it a virtue or a sin to suffer in this way? We do not find this practice among the followers of any other religion. Could the authors of the Hindu Shastras have made a mistake? When I see Basanti Devi, I do not think they have; I see in the practice the purest spirit of dharma. The widow's manner of life is the glory of Hinduism. Let the world say what it will, the life of dharma has its glory in renunciation, not in enjoyment.

But what is that widow's life which the Hindu Shastras admire and praise? Certainly not that of the fifteen-year-old girl who does not know even the meaning of marriage. For a girl married and widowed in childhood, a widow's life means not virtue, but sin. . . . But what does a fifteen-year-old girl know about the beauty of widowhood? For her, such a life is cruelty. In the increasing number of such widows, I see the destruction of Hinduism. In women like Basanti Devi leading the customary life of widows, I see a source of strength for dharma. There is no inviolable law that in all circumstances, in all places and at all times a widow must remain a widow and lead a widow's life. This is a dharma only for a woman who can follow it.

It is good to swim in the waters of tradition, but to sink in them is suicide.

There should be the same rule for men as for women. Rama acted in this manner. He could not bear separation from Sita, whom he had sent away. He himself sent her away and yet suffered for what he had done. After she had left, he gradually lost the light and power which were his. He abandoned Sita physically, but installed her as the queen of his heart. From that time onwards, he felt no interest in dressing himself well or in other kingly pleasures. He attended, disinterestedly, to the affairs of his kingdom as a matter of duty and lived a peaceful life.

Hinduism will remain imperfect as long as men do not accept suffering as Basanti Devi did and, like her, withdraw their interest from the pleasures of this life. Sweets to the one and thorns to the other—such perverted justice can never be, and is not, acceptable in God's court. But among the Hindus at present, disregarding the divine law, men have ordained perpetual widowhood for women and conferred on themselves the right to fix marriage with another partner, on the cremation-ground itself.

Basanti Devi has not till now shed a drop of tear in anyone's presence. Even then, the light on her face has not returned. It seems as dull as if she had recovered from a long illness. Seeing her in this condition, I requested her to go out with me for a little fresh air. She did come along with me and sat in the car but did not speak a word. I talked about many things. She listened, but hardly said anything in reply. She had a drive, but felt miserable afterwards. She could not sleep the whole night. 'Cursed that I am, I enjoyed today what was so dear to me. Is this all that my grief comes to?' She spent the whole night in such thoughts. Bhombal (her son) came and told me about this. Today is my silence day. I simply wrote on a piece of paper: 'We must cure mother of this madness. There are many things which our beloved one may have loved and which we have no choice but to do. Mother did not have a drive for enjoyment, she had it for the sake of her health. She was in great need of fresh air. We must strengthen her and take care of her health. We must keep her alive so that we may be worthy of the legacy of Father's work and carry it forward. Convey this to Mother.'

He said: 'Mother had asked me not to tell you this. But I could not help telling you; so I have come. It would be better if, for some time, you did not ask her to go out in a car.'

Poor Bhombal! He who would not be controlled by anyone, God bless him, has become today as meek as a lamb.

But what should we think about this good widow? Widowhood may be cherished but it appears unbearable. . . . May chaste and virtuous women ever cling to their suffering. Their suffering is not suffering, but happiness. Thinking of them, many have found deliverance and many more will find it in the future.

Navajivan, 28 June 1925 (G.). *CWMG*, vol. xxvii, pp. 306–10

184. The evil of child widowhood.

1 April 1926

I have your letter regarding 'widow marriage' . . . Could you consider that to be marriage where the girl knows nothing about what a husband can be, where, perhaps, she has not even seen the man who is to be her partner for life and where they have not even lived together for one single night? I know nothing in Hinduism to warrant such a connection being accepted as marriage. Then again, what is the use of defending widowhood of girls of tender age under plea of advocating purity on the part of men? The latter should certainly be advocated but it cannot be used in order to cover the wrong heaped upon the fair sex. The sanctity of widowhood must be felt by the widow, cannot be imposed upon her. Divorce and other irregularities going on in the West have surely nothing to do with the very simple question of doing elementary justice to the thousands of our own sisters. Hinduism is in grave danger of being undermined by our own fanaticism and the habit of defending every practice of Hinduism no matter how repugnant it may be to the normal moral sense of the world.

Letter to K. Chakravarti. SN 19408. *CWMG*, vol. xxx, pp. 216–17

185. Widows' work

In this case* teaching means imparting a knowledge of letters. This knowledge is necessary to some extent; in my opinion, however, the more important teaching is how to stave off starvation. And every day, I am more firmly convinced that this lies in the spinning-wheel. If we of the middle class who are educated, and who look upon ourselves as belonging to the higher castes give a thought to the condition of the poorer classes, nothing else but the spinning-wheel will occur to us. The spinning-wheel will be plied mainly by women as it is primarily they who have time to spare. Hence I have been crying from the house-tops at various places, day and night, that it is through them that we would prevent crores of rupees from being drained out of the country and secure true swaraj—*Ramarajya*.

It is women who can readily approach others of their sex. Here in the Province of Orissa where I happen to write this, and where even the poorer women observe *purdah*, who can set aside *purdah* and approach them? I sent Mirabehn* who has accompanied me to the women of a certain village. About fifty women surrounded her and became crazy with joy; they started asking her about many things and the spinning-wheel came up for discussion. These women were absolutely naive, simple and ignorant. It is innumerable women of this type who should really be educated. Widows with pure character can readily impart such education, serve their own interest and, at the same time, help India solve its problems. Widows who are benevolently inclined can easily learn this work and do justice to it. However, an important prior condition for this is that they should be keen on going to villages and, while living there, should not get impatient. A widow who takes the vow of celibacy is not a helpless, crippled individual. If she is fit for self-realization, she is a strong independent woman capable of protecting herself. Compared with this, the education given to girls today is, I think, of little consequence. If however a widow refuses to go to the villages, idles away her time or, year after year, runs from one place of supposed pilgrimage to another, mistaking this for dharma, it is obviously better if she stayed even in the city and engaged herself in teaching children. She has before her the vast field of nursing the sick. Very few Hindu women take up the profession of nursing.* Widows in Maharashtra are found undergoing this training. Outside Maharashtra, very few widows are prepared to undergo this training. However, the jobs that I have suggested should also be regarded only as examples. Every sensible widow who wishes to practise celibacy should seek out some useful activity for herself and devote her whole life to it.

Navajivan, 25 Dec. 1927 (G.). *CWMG*, vol. xxxv, pp. 419–20

186. Opposition to artificial birth-control

It is not without the greatest hesitation and reluctance that I approach the subject. The question of using artificial methods for birth-control has been referred to me by correspondents ever since my return to India. Though I have answered them personally, I have never hitherto dealt with the subject publicly. My attention was drawn to the subject, now thirty-five years ago, when I was a student in England. There was then a hot controversy raging between a purist who would not countenance anything but natural means and a doctor who advocated artificial means. It was at that early time in my life that I became, after leanings for a brief period towards artificial means, a convinced opponent of them. I now observe that in some Hindi papers the methods are described in a revoltingly open manner which shocks one's sense of decency. I observe, too, that one writer does not hesitate to cite my name as among the supporters of artificial methods of birth-control. I cannot recall a single occasion when I spoke or wrote in favour of such methods. I have seen also two distinguished names having been used in support. I hesitate to publish them without reference to their owners.

There can be no two opinions about the necessity of birth-control. But the only method handed down from ages past is self-control or *brahmacharya*. It is an infallible sovereign remedy doing good to those who practise it. And medical men will earn the gratitude of mankind, if instead of devising artificial means of birth-control they will find out the means of self-control. The union is meant not for pleasure but for bringing forth progeny. And union is a crime when the desire for progeny is absent.

Artificial methods are like putting a premium upon vice. They make men and women reckless. And respectability that is being given to the methods must hasten the dissolution of the restraints that public opinion puts upon one. Adoption of artificial methods must result in imbecility and nervous prostration. The remedy will be found to be worse than the disease. It is wrong and immoral to seek to escape the consequences of one's acts. It is good for a person who overeats to have an ache and a fast. It is bad for him to indulge his appetite and then escape the consequence by taking tonics or other medicine. It is still worse for a person to indulge in his animal passions and escape the consequences of his acts. Nature is relentless and will have full revenge for any such violation of her laws. Moral results can only be produced by moral restraints. All other restraints defeat the very purpose for which they are intended. The reasoning underlying the use of artificial methods is that indulgence is a necessity of life. Nothing can be more fallacious. Let those who are eager to see the births regulated explore the lawful means devised by the ancients and try to find out how they can be revived. An enormous amount of spade-work lies in front of them. Early marriages are a fruitful source of adding to the population. The present mode of life has also a great deal to do with the evil of unchecked procreation. If these causes are investigated and dealt with, society will be morally elevated. If they are ignored by impatient zealots and if artificial methods become the order of the day, nothing but moral degradation can be the result. A society that has already become enervated through a variety of causes will become still further enervated by the adoption of artificial methods. Those men therefore who are light-heartedly advocating artificial methods cannot do better than study the subject afresh, stay their injurious activity and popularize *brahmacharya* both for the married and the unmarried. That is the only noble and straight method of birth-control.

Young India, 12 Mar. 1925. *CWMG*, vol. xxvi, pp. 279–80

187. Contraception—'most pernicious education'

From a serious discussion I had with a sister* I fear that my position on the use of contraceptives has not yet been sufficiently understood. My opposition is not due to their having come to us from the West. I thankfully use some Western things when I know that they benefit us as they benefit those in the West. My opposition to contraceptives is based on merits.

I take it that the wisest among the protagonists of contraception restrict their use to married women who desire to satisfy their and their husbands' sexual appetite without wanting children. I hold this desire as unnatural in the human species and its satisfaction detrimental to the spiritual progress of the human family . . .

But I object to contraceptives also on special grounds in India. Young men in India do not know what sexual restraint is. It is not their fault. They are married early. It is the custom. Nobody tells them to exercise restraint in married life. Parents are impatient to see grandchildren. The poor girl-wives are expected by their surroundings to bear children as fast as they can. In such surroundings, the use of contraceptives can only further aggravate the mischief. The poor girls who are expected to submit to their husbands' desires are now to be taught that it is a good thing to desire sexual satisfaction without the desire to have children. And in order to fulfil the double purpose they are to have recourse to contraceptives!!!

I regard this to be most pernicious education for married women. I do not believe that woman is prey to sexual desire to the same extent as man. It is easier for her than for man to exercise self-restraint. I hold that the right education in this country is to teach woman the art of saying no even to her husband, to teach her it is no part of her duty to become a mere tool or a doll in her husband's hands. She has rights as well as duties. Those who see in Sita* a willing slave under Rama do not realize the loftiness of either her independence or Rama's consideration for her in everything. Sita was no helpless weak woman incapable of protecting herself or her honour. To ask India's women to take to contraceptives is, to say the least, putting the cart before the horse. The first thing is to free her from mental slavery, to teach her the sacredness of her body and to teach her the dignity of national service and the service of humanity. It is not fair to assume that India's women are beyond redemption and that they have therefore to be simply taught the use of contraceptives for the sake of preventing births and preserving such health as they may be in possession of.

Let not sisters who are rightly indignant over the miseries of women who are called upon to bear children whether they will or no, be impatient. Not even the propaganda in favour of contraceptives is going to promote the desired end overnight. Every method is a matter of education. My plea is for the right type.

Harijan, 2 May 1936. *CWMG*, vol. lxii, pp. 361–3

188. The evil of *purdah*

A visitor at the Conference* informs me that there was unbounded enthusiasm there. About fifteen thousand Rajputs must have gathered on the occasion. Even the number of women present exceeded anyone's expectations. There must have been a thousand of them. The number was indeed very large. But the curtains were so effectively disposed that a stranger could not know that somewhere in the Conference *pandal** there were women too present. Even the arrangements for carrying them from where they were lodged to the

Conference site were so skilful that no one could judge that women were passing along.

The organizers of the Conference certainly deserve congratulations on making such perfect arrangements. But one can only express sorrow for the fact of curtains having been put up. The time, one may say, when curtains were necessary is past. There seem to have been no curtains during Rama's rule. It is of course true that we still do not have *Ramarajya*, but, if we so desire, we may act right from now as if we had it. We have yet to show that, even in the absence of curtains, we can conduct ourselves with decorum. None can say that the communities which do not observe *purdah** show any the less decorum. When women were regarded as chattels and were often kidnapped, the *purdah* might well have been necessary. If men were kidnapped, they too might have to remain under *purdah*. In places where a man, when seen, is made to do forced labour, the men observe purdah even today, that is, they hide themselves. The *purdah*, however, is not the means of saving women from men's evil eye; the only means is men's own purity of character.

A woman can take a big hand in teaching men such purity. But how can a woman who remains in *purdah*, suppressed, teach a man purity? If she is taught to live in fear of men right from the beginning, how can she reform them? Moreover, the very fact of keeping a woman behind *purdah* has the effect of creating moral weakness in her. I believe that *purdah* helps not the maintenance but the destruction of morality. What is necessary for promoting it is education in morality, a moral environment and moral conduct among the elders. I do not write at this length about *purdah* with a view to finding fault with the Conference. It would have been difficult to abolish *purdah* right at the start. But a few Rajputs must start working for the future.

Navajivan, 22 June 1924 (G.). *CWMG*, vol. xxvi, pp. 277–8

189. *Purdah*—a cruel impediment to *swaraj*

The appeal [by some prominent Biharis to abolish *purdah*] fixes the 8th of July next as the date on which to inaugurate an intensive campaign against the system which puts a cruel ban on social service by one half of Bihar humanity and which denies it freedom in many cases and even the use of light and fresh air. The sooner it is recognized that many of our social evils impede our march towards swaraj, the greater will be our progress towards our cherished goal. To postpone social reform till after the attainment of swaraj is not to know the meaning of swaraj. Surely we must be incapable of defending our-selves or healthily competing with the other nations, if we allow the better half of ourselves to become paralysed.

Young India, 28 June 1928. *CWMG*, vol. xxxvi, p. 470

190. Jewellery—symbols of slavery

But what about women? The uplift of women is one of the principal aims of running *Navajivan*. During my tour of the U.P., I was very much irritated at the sight of the ornaments worn by rich and poor women alike. At that very time, I read Mr Brayne's book.* I was largely convinced by his criticism of ornaments. He has held the men-folk too responsible for this fondness for ornaments. I believe that men are or were responsible for this; their responsibility may now have decreased, but the women's responsibility for this fondness is no less. I was unable to convince women to give up their ornaments.

How and whence did women develop this fondness? I do not know its history, hence I have only made some conjectures. The ornaments which women wear on their hands and feet are a sign of their bondage. Some of the ornaments worn on the feet are so heavy that a woman cannot walk fast, let alone run. Some women wear such heavy orna-ments on their arms that they prevent them from fully utilizing the latter. Hence I regard these ornaments as fetters on the hands and feet. I have found that by means of the ornaments which are worn by piercing the nose and ears, the men lead the women as they wish. Even a child, by firmly taking hold of a nose or ear ornament of a woman, can render the latter helpless. Hence I have looked upon these principal ornaments as mere symbols of slavery.

I have found even the designs of these ancient ornaments ugly. I have beheld no true art in them. I have seen and known them as objects which harbour dirt. A woman who is loaded with ancient ornaments on her hands, feet, ears, nose and hair cannot even keep these parts of her body clean. I have seen layers of dirt collected on those parts. Many of these ornaments are not even removable every day. When some women gave me their heavy anklets and bangles, they had to call in a goldsmith to have these removed from their hands and feet. When these were taken out, they left a good band of dirt on the hands and ankles, and the designs carved on the ornaments were full of layers of dirt. These women too felt as if they were rid of an age–old burden.

The modern woman is oblivious of this origin of ornaments and, regarding them as objects which beautify her gets delicate ones made for her. She has them made in such a way that they can be readily worn and removed and if she happens to be very wealthy, she has them made of diamonds and pearls instead of gold and silver. They may gather less dirt, it may well be the case that they are regarded [as] artistic, but they have no utilitarian value and their capacity to beautify is also imaginary. Women of other countries would not wear the ornaments worn by our women. Their idea of adorning them-selves is different. Ideas of adornment and artistic beauty vary from one country to another; hence we know that in such matters we have no absolute standards of beauty or art.

Why is it then that many reasonable, educated women still con-tinue to be fond of ornaments? On considering the matter, it seems that as in other matters, here too tradition reigns supreme. We do not find reasons for all our actions and do not even stop to consider whether they are proper or otherwise. We do them because it is cus-tomary to do so and later we like them independently. This is called thoughtless life.

However, why should all those women who are awakened, who have started thinking for themselves, who wish to serve the country, who are taking or wish to take part in the *yajna* of swaraj, not exer-cise their discretion with regard to ornaments, etc.?

If the origin of ornaments is what I have imagined it to be, they are fit to be renounced, however light or beautiful they may be. Fetters, though made of gold, diamonds or pearls, are fetters only. Whether in a small dark room or in a palace, men and women imprisoned in either will be regarded as prisoners only.

Moreover, wherein lies the beauty of a woman? Does it lie in her ornaments, her mannerisms, her new clothes which she changes daily, or in her heart, thought and action? The cobra which has a pre-cious stone on its hood has poison in its fangs. Hence, despite the fact that it wears a crown of precious stone, it is not considered worthy of *darshan** or of being embraced. If a woman realizes that this 'artistic device' leads to the downfall of countless men, why should she garner these ornaments although they may possess any amount of artistic value? This is not a matter of individual freedom, nor is it a question of the rights of an individual; it is merely a wilful act and hence fit to be renounced, because it involves cruelty. It is the dharma of every thoughtful and compassionate man and woman to see what effect his or her actions have on others and to desist from them if they are not otherwise proved to be useful and produce a harmful effect.

Finally, in this poverty-stricken land, where the average daily income of a person is seven pice or at the most eight pice, who has the right to wear even the lightest of rings? A thoughtful woman who moreover wishes to serve her country, cannot ever touch ornaments. Looking at it from the economic standpoint, the gold and silver that we lock up in making ornaments causes threefold harm to the country. The first harm is that where there is a shortage of food, we increase it by wearing ornaments. It should be borne in mind that our average daily income is seven or eight pice. As those whose daily income is a thousand rupees are also included in these calculations, even if we leave the destitutes aside and take into account only the poorer classes, their income would amount to one or two pice. Hence the amount spent on jewellery is something that we have taken away from the poor. The second is that these ornaments do not yield any interest, hence we prevent an increase in the national wealth to that extent. The third is that a large portion of these ornaments finally wears off or, in other words, that amount of wealth is lost for ever. Just as if an individual throws away some of the gold bars in his possession into the ocean, his wealth will decrease to that extent, almost the same can be said of a woman who invests her money in ornaments. I use the word 'almost', as some ornaments are sold in straitened circumstances and hence they may be regarded as having been put to some use. The loss that they have suffered through wear and tear before their sale is of course there; moreover, anyone who buys them can never recover their original value when reselling them, and the loss suffered thereby is also there. Therefore, any woman who wishes to keep aside ornaments as her own property or as property which may be useful in times of distress should put their equivalent in cash in her name; either her parents or her parents-in-law should open an account in a bank and give her the pass-book. Such times may well be far off. However, if thoughtful women, who wish to render service, give up their love of ornaments, I would regard this article as having fully served its purpose at least for the time being.

Navajivan, 22 Dec. 1929. *CWMG*, vol. xlii, pp. 304–7

191. The meaning of *swadeshi*

We examined the balance-sheet of the last year. We were unhappy at the thought that we had to follow an alien calendar in making our calculations. No cause for unhappiness would remain if *swadeshi** were to replace everything foreign. We can easily attain happiness if we exert ourselves to that end during the year that has just commenced. *Swadeshi* carries a great and profound meaning. It does not mean merely the use of what is produced in one's own country. That meaning is certainly there in *swadeshi*. But there is another meaning implied in it which is far greater and much more important. *Swadeshi* means reliance on our own strength. We should also know what we mean by 'reliance on our own strength'. 'Our strength' means the strength of our body, our mind and our soul. From among these, on which should we depend? The answer is brief. The soul is supreme, and therefore soul-force is the foundation on which man must build. Passive resistance or *satyagraha* is a mode of fighting which depends on such force. That, then, is the only real key to success for the Indians.

'New Year' (G.). *Indian Opinion*, 2 Jan. 1909

192. A *swadeshi* vow

8 April 1919

Although the desire for *swadeshi* animating a large number of people at the present moment* is worthy of all praise, it seems to me that they have not fully realized the difficulty in the way of its observance. Vows are always taken only in respect of matters otherwise difficult of accomplishment. When after a series of efforts we fail in doing certain things, by taking a vow to do them we draw a cordon round ourselves, from which we may never be free and thus we avoid failures. Anything less than such inflexible determination cannot be called a vow. It is not a pledge or vow when we say we shall so far as possible do certain acts. If by saying that we shall so far as we can only use *swadeshi* articles, we can be deemed to have taken the *swadeshi* vow, then from the Viceroy down to the labouring man very few people would be found who could not be considered to have taken the pledge, but we want to go outside this circle and aim at a much higher goal. And there is as much difference between the act contemplated by us and the acts above described as there is between a right angle and all other angles. And if we decide to take the *swadeshi* vow in this spirit, it is clear that it is well nigh impossible to take an all-comprehensive vow.

After having given deep consideration to the matter for a number of years, it is sufficiently demonstrated to me that we can take the full *swadeshi* vow only in respect of our clothing, whether made of cotton, silk or wool. Even in observing this vow, we shall have to face many difficulties in the initial stages and that is only proper. By patronizing foreign cloth we have committed a deep sin. We have condoned an occupation which in point of importance is second only to agriculture, and we are face to face with a total disruption of a calling to which Kabir* was born and which he adorned. One meaning of the *swadeshi* vow suggested by me is that in taking it we desire to do penance for our sins, that we desire to resuscitate the almost lost art of hand-weaving, and that we are determined to save our Hindustan crores of rupees which go out of it annually in exchange for the cloth we receive. Such high results cannot be attained without difficulties; there must be obstacles in the way. Things easily obtained are practically of no value, but however difficult of observance that pledge may be, some day or other there is no escape from it if we want our country to rise to its full height. And we shall then accomplish the vow when we shall deem it a religious duty to use only that cloth which is entirely produced in the country and refrain from using any other.

Friends tell me that at the present moment we have not enough *swadeshi* cloth to supply our wants and that the existing mills are too few for the purpose. This appears to me to be a hasty generalization. We can hardly expect such good fortune as to have thirty crores of covenanters for *swadeshi*. A hardened optimist dare not expect more than a few *lakhs* and I anticipate no difficulty in providing them with *swadeshi* cloth, but where there is a question of religion there is no room for thoughts of difficulties. The general climate of India is such that we require very little clothing. It is an exaggeration to say that three-fourths of the middle class population use much unnecessary clothing. Moreover, when many men take the vow, there would be set up many spinning-wheels and hand-looms. India can produce innumerable weavers. They are merely awaiting encouragement. Mainly two things are needful, viz., self-denial and honesty. It is self-evident that the covenanter must possess these two qualities, but in order to enable people to observe such a great vow comparatively easily, our merchants also will need to be blessed with these qualities. An honest and self-denying merchant will spin his yarn only from Indian cotton and confine weaving only to such cotton. He will only use those dyes which are made in India. When a man desires to do a thing he cultivates the necessary ability to remove difficulties in his path.

It is not enough that we manage if necessary with as little clothing as possible, but for a full observance it is further necessary to destroy all foreign clothing in our possession. If we are satisfied that we erred in making use of foreign cloth, that we have done an immense injury to India, that we have all but destroyed the race of weavers, cloth stained with such sin is only fit to be destroyed. In this connection, it is necessary to understand the distinction between *swadeshi* and boycott. *Swadeshi* is a religious conception. It is the natural duty imposed upon every man. The well-being of people depends upon it and the *swadeshi* vow cannot be taken in a punitive or revengeful spirit. The *swadeshi* vow is not derived from any extraneous happening, whereas boycott is a purely worldly and political weapon. It is rooted in ill-will and a desire for punishment, and I can see nothing but harm in the end for a nation that resorts to boycott. One who wishes to be a *satyagrahi* for ever cannot participate in any boycott movement and a perpetual *satyagraha* is impossible without *swadeshi*. This is the meaning I have understood to be given to boycott. It has been suggested that we should boycott British goods till the Rowlatt legislation is withdrawn and that the boycott should terminate with the removal of that legislation. In such a scheme of boycott, it is open to us to take Japanese or other foreign goods even though they may be rotten. If I must use foreign goods, having political relations with England, I would only take English goods and consider such conduct to be proper.

In proclaiming a boycott of British goods, we expose ourselves to the charge of desiring to punish the English but we have no quarrel with them; our quarrel is with the governors. And, according to the law of *satyagraha*, we may not harbour any ill will even against the rulers, and as we may harbour no ill will, I cannot see the propriety of resorting to boycott.

For a complete observance of the restricted *swadeshi* vow suggested above, I would advise the following text: 'With God as my witness, I solemnly declare that from today I shall confine myself, for my personal requirements, to the use of cloth, manufactured in India from Indian cotton, silk and wool; and I shall altogether abstain from using foreign cloth, and I shall destroy all foreign cloth in my possession.'

I hope that many men and women will be ready to take this vow, and the public taking of the pledge will be desirable only if many men and women are ready for it. Even a few men and women may publicly take the pledge, but in order to make *swadeshi* a national movement, it is necessary that many should join it. Those who approve of the proposed movement should, in my opinion, lose no time in taking effective steps to begin it. It is necessary to interview merchants. At the same time, there need be no undue haste. The foundation of *swadeshi* should be well and truly laid. This is the right time for it as I have found that when a purifying movement like *satyagraha* is going on allied activities have an easy chance of success.

'The *Swadeshi* Vow—I'. *Bombay Chronicle*, 17 Apr. 1919. *New India*, 19 Apr. 1919. *MPWMG*, vol. iii, pp. 338–41

193. Observance of the *swadeshi* vow

8 April 1919

The following is the text of the *swadeshi* vow:

With God as my witness, I solemnly declare that from today I shall confine myself, for my personal requirements, to the use of cloth manufactured in India from Indian cotton, silk or wool and I shall altogether abstain from using foreign cloth; and I shall destroy all foreign cloth in my possession.

For a proper observance of the pledge, it is really necessary to use only hand-woven cloth made out of hand-spun yarn. Imported yarn, even though spun out of Indian cotton and woven in India, is not *swadeshi* cloth. We shall reach perfection only when our cotton is spun in India on indigenous spinning-wheels and yarn so spun is woven on similarly made handlooms. But requirements of the foregoing pledge are met, if we all only use cloth woven by means of imported machinery from yarn spun from Indian cotton by means of similar machinery.

I may add that covenanters to the restricted *swadeshi* referred to here will not rest satisfied with *swadeshi* clothing only. They will extend the vow to all other things as far as possible.

I am told that there are in India English-owned mills which do not admit Indian share-holders. If this information be true, I would consider cloth manufactured in such mills to be foreign cloth. Moreover, such cloth bears the taint of ill-will. However well made such cloth may be, it should be avoided. The majority do not give thought to such matters. All cannot be expected to consider whether their actions promote or retard the welfare of their country, but it behoves those who are learned, those who are thoughtful, whose intellects are trained or who are desirous of serving their country, to test every action of theirs, whether public or private, in the manner aforesaid, and when ideals which appear to be of national importance and which have been tested by practical experience should be placed before the people as has been said in the Divine Song, 'the multitude will copy the actions of the enlightened'. Even thoughtful men and women have not hitherto generally carried on the above-mentioned self-examination. The nation has therefore suffered by reason of this neglect. In my opinion, such self-examination is only possible where there is religious perception.

Thousands of men believe that by using cloth woven in Indian mills, they comply with the requirements of the *swadeshi* vow. The fact is that most fine cloth is made of foreign cotton spun outside. Therefore the only satisfaction to be derived from the use of such cloth is that it is woven in India. Even on hand-looms for very fine cloth only foreign yarn is used. The use of such cloth does not amount to an observance of *swadeshi*. To say so is simple self-deception. *Satyagraha*, i.e., insistence on truth, is necessary even in *swadeshi*. When men will say, 'we shall confine ourselves to pure *swadeshi* cloth, even though we may have to remain satisfied with a mere loin cloth', and when women will resolutely say, 'we shall observe pure *swadeshi* even though we may have to restrict ourselves to clothing just enough to satisfy the sense of modesty', then shall we be successful in the observance of the great *swadeshi* vow. If a few thousand men and women were to take the *swadeshi* vow in this spirit, others will try to imitate them so far as possible. They will then begin to examine their wardrobes in the light of *swadeshi*. Those who are not attached to pleasures and personal adornment, I venture to say, can give a great impetus to *swadeshi*.

Generally speaking, there are very few villages in India without weavers. From time immemorial, we have had village farmers and village weavers, as we have village carpenters, shoemakers, blacksmiths, etc., but our farmers have become poverty-stricken and our weavers have patronage only from the poor classes. By supplying them with Indian cloth spun in India, we can obtain the cloth we may need. For the time being it may be coarse, but by constant endeavours, we can get our weavers to weave out of fine yarn and so doing we shall raise our weavers to a better status, and if we would go a step still further, we can easily cross the sea of difficulties lying in our path. We can easily teach our women and our children to spin and weave cotton, and what can be purer than cloth woven in our own home? I tell it from my experience that acting in this way we shall be saved from many a hardship, we shall be ridding ourselves of many an unnecessary need, and our life will be one song of joy and beauty. I always hear divine voices telling me in my ears that such life was a matter of fact once in India, but even if such an India be the idle dream of the poet, it does not matter. Is it not necessary to create such an India now . . .?

I have been travelling throughout India. I cannot bear the heart-rending cry of the poor. The young and old tell me, 'We cannot get cheap cloth, we have not the means wherewith to purchase dear cloth. Everything is dear—provisions, cloth and all. What are we to do?' And they heave a sigh of despair. It is my duty to give these men a satisfactory reply. It is the duty of every servant of the country, but I am unable to give a satisfactory reply. It should be intolerable for all thinking Indians that our raw materials should be exported to Europe and that we have to pay heavy prices therefor. The first and the last remedy for this is *swadeshi*. We are not bound to sell our cotton to anybody and when Hindustan rings with the echoes of *swadeshi*, no producer of cotton will sell it for its being manufactured in foreign countries. When *swadeshi* pervades the country, everyone will be set a-thinking why cotton should not be refined and spun and woven in the place where it is produced, and when the *swadeshi mantra* resounds in every ear, millions of men will have in their hands the key to the economic salvation of India. Training for this does not require hundreds of years. When the religious sense is awakened, people's thoughts undergo a revolution in a single moment. Only selfless sacrifice is the *sine qua non*.

The spirit of sacrifice pervades the Indian atmosphere at the present moment. If we fail to preach *swadeshi* at this supreme moment, we shall have to wring our hands in despair. I beseech every Hindu, Mussulman, Sikh, Parsi, Christian and Jew, who believes that he belongs to this country, to take the *swadeshi* vow and to ask others also to do likewise. It is my humble belief that if we cannot do even this little for our country, we are born in it in vain. Those who think deep will see that such *swadeshi* contains pure economics. I hope that every man and woman will give serious thought to my humble suggestion. Imitation of English economics will spell our ruin.

'The *Swadeshi* Vow—II'. *Bombay Chronicle*, 18 Apr. 1919. *New India*, 22 Apr. 1919. *EWMG*, pp. 363–6

194. The long-term results of *swadeshi*

8 August 1919

These days the theme of my addresses is *swadeshi*. I save time from other activities and give all of it to *swadeshi*. It is through *swadeshi* that we shall get *swaraj*. When I spoke on '*Swadeshi* and *Swaraj*' at Surat, it occurred to me that I should explain to the people, how *swadeshi* would cover all that I had at heart. At the present time, I want to propagate this idea and it is my hope that, in a few days or maybe months, everyone in India, from the Viceroy down to the sweeper, will realize that *swadeshi* can bring *swaraj*.

To this end, it is imperative that the ideal of *swadeshi* should be kept pure; it is so great a thing that it should not be debased.

India is suffering at present from afflictions of three kinds:

1. DISEASE: At no time in the past were the people of India afflicted with so many diseases as at present. The number of people rotting with disease in this country is greater than that in all the rest of the world.

2. HUNGER: The simple fact borne out by experience during the past few years is that a large section of the Indian people do not have

enough to eat. Sir William Wilson Hunter* said categorically forty years ago that three crores in India got only one meal a day, and that too consisting of no more than plain bread and salt. More than this, they got no ghee, oil or chillies. This was our misfortune forty years ago. Every official has been obliged to admit in the blue books that India's poverty is increasing day by day, and the cultivator's lot, especially, is the worst, as they alone know who move in villages. If you inquire of the people in Gujarat, you will know what great difficulty they experience in getting milk. They are hard put to it to get milk even for an infant six months old. Whenever I questioned the people in the villages around Ahmedabad, I was told that, let alone themselves, even their children could get no milk. You will see from this that our present plight is much worse than it was forty years ago.

3. INSUFFICIENT COVERING FOR THE BODY: At present India is also afflicted with a cloth famine. According to Sir Dinshaw Wacha's* estimate, four years ago people in India got 13 yards of cloth per head, whereas now they get only 9. That is, there has been a reduction of four yards per head and to that extent our poverty has increased.

When I was working in Champaran two years ago, I had personal experience of women protesting to me, without mincing words, that they did not have even a piece of cloth with which to cover their bare limbs; how, then, they asked, could they bathe and wash to keep themselves clean? My heart bled to see our pure-hearted sisters in such a pitiable condition.

A land afflicted with this triple disease loses the qualities of courage, fortitude and truthfulness. The people of such a country have no *dharma* in them and I would even employ the term 'unmanly' to describe them. Here in India, too, we have been using this term these days.

When, with this idea in mind, I questioned people, one reply I got was that *dharma* should be restored. No doubt we have lost our *dharma*, but, in the present circumstances, restoring it is quite a difficult job, for it is extraordinarily difficult for a man in utter misery to follow *dharma*. Only a rare soul can do so. I call such persons *yogis.** Not all people, however, can become *yogis*. And thus, for the purity of the *atman*, purity of the body is also essential. 'A pure *atman* can dwell only in a pure body.' In order to revive the qualities of courage, and so on, this triple affliction should be got rid of. A man who follows *dharma* in the midst of such suffering I would call a *yogi*.

For curing the disease, a bold effort, requiring knowledge, is called for. We shall have to sacrifice our time to save people afflicted with such diseases. We should first ascertain whether people go hungry because of their lethargy or because of want. Of food, there is plenty in India; the hungry should have it. But they need money with which to buy it, and it is for want of money that India is poor.

Swadeshi is needed to fight this state of affairs. By *swadeshi* we mean protecting our cotton and silk. This is my restricted definition of *swadeshi* in the circumstances which obtain today. Last year, we paid to foreign countries 56 crores of rupees for cotton goods and four for silk goods. The revered Dadabhai Naoroji* used to say that India was being drained of her funds. It is true that a good deal of this money is spent on the military department and in paying pensions; personally, however, I would say that in no other way is so much money drained as on account of the absence of *swadeshi*. Eighteen crores were paid last year for sugar. There is much drain in other ways which I do not care to mention at the moment. I want to get hold of the trunk and once that is done the drain in other ways will stop by itself. Our first duty then, in the present circumstances, is to follow *swadeshi* in its restricted meaning; to this end, the three vows which I have given should be kept. Get control of the trade in yarn and you will get the rest easily enough.

We are unable today to produce sufficient cloth to meet our needs. Our mills cannot supply as much. We should take steps so that India is enabled to produce things which she does not do at present; this is one problem. I am at present discussing this problem with mill-owners and, in the course of our conversation, Sir Fazalbhai Karimbhai told me that it would take fifty years still before the mills could supply cloth in the required quantity. Should we then wait for fifty years? We see from the report of the Industrial Commission that in the country one-third the quantity of cloth can be produced through hand-weaving and that, if this industry is developed, things will become easier for us. Mills require machinery and for this we are dependent on others. Foreign countries do not have all that machinery to spare. Some say that it takes a mill one year to obtain one machine and installing it presents much difficulty. Having regard to all these obstacles, hand-weaving seems very easy, for it does not require all this effort. A man of average ability can learn the work in six months' time and one with some intelligence can pick it up in three months. The method of making yarn is altogether simple. I took no more than 15 days to learn it.

A hundred and fifty years ago, we ourselves produced our cloth. Every mother in India did the work for the love of God. Traces of this age-old desire of the Indian woman for spinning are still visible. . . .

If we refuse to take up this work, we shall lose this inheritance. I appeal to you not to give up faith. If we but try, a favourable environment will be created and we shall get back the inheritance we have disowned. Principal Paranjapye* said that we would fail in the competition with the rest of the world. But there is no question of competition in this. This is a question, rather, of the economic freedom of peasants and of the poor. The farmer is the father of the world. Take the example of America or Japan. They help the cultivator there. Our Governor, too, is anxious to know how the cultivator may be helped. The problem can be solved in accordance with the principles of economics.

It is my advice to young people to take up this work. It is easy enough and requires no special effort, nor does it require much intelligence. All that is necessary is some experience. One enjoys greater freedom through this work. The man who spins earns three annas daily, but the man who weaves earns eight annas. Talking to the weavers of Madanwadi in Bombay, I came to know that many of them earned as much as one rupee, even two rupees, daily. This industry is useful to us. It should be widely popularized. Even the educated class should learn a little of the craft. In the same way as every boy in England knows some naval work, we should all learn this work.

If, thus, India understands this *mantra* and starts working as a matter of religious duty, the country's economic condition will improve and hunger and disease will disappear from our midst. Since you understand the idea, it is my prayer that you will put it into practice.

Speech at Gujarati Bandhu Sabha, Poona (G.). *Indian Opinion*, 10 Oct. 1919

195. *Swadeshi* v. machinery?

14 September 1919

I have observed that this doubt is felt by many people, and accordingly I have given the reply too. Pure *swadeshi* is not at all opposed to machinery. The *swadeshi* movement is meant only against the use of foreign cloth. There is no objection to weaving mill-made cloth. But I do not myself wear mill-made cloth and in the explanations to the *swadeshi* vow I have certainly suggested that it should be the ideal of every Indian to wear hand-spun and hand-woven cloth. If, fortunately for India, crores of people happen to translate this ideal into practice, the mills may perhaps have to suffer some loss. But if the whole of India makes that pure resolve, I am sure that even our mill-owners would welcome that resolve, respect its purity and associate themselves with it. But it takes long to outgrow inveterate habits. There is thus room in the country for both the mill industry and the handloom weaving. So let mills increase as also spinning-wheels and handlooms. And I should think that these latter are no doubt machines. The handloom is a miniature weaving mill. The spinning-wheel is a miniature spinning-mill. I would wish to see such beautiful little mills in every home. But the country is fully in need of the hand-spinning and hand-weaving industry.

Agriculturists in no country can live without some industry to supplement agriculture. And in India, which is entirely dependent on favourable monsoons, the spinning-wheel and the handloom are like Kamadhenus.* This movement is thus intended in the interests of 21 crore peasants of India. Even if we have sufficient mills in the country to produce cloth enough for the whole country, we are bound to provide our peasantry, daily being more and more impoverished, with some supplementary industry, and that which can be suitable to crores of people is hand-spinning and hand-weaving. Opposition to mills or machinery is not the point. What suits our country most is the point. I am not opposed to the movement of manufacturing machines in the country, nor to making improvements in machinery. I am only concerned with what these machines are meant for. I may ask, in the words of Ruskin,* whether these machines will be such as would blow off a million men in a minute or they will be such as would turn waste lands into arable and fertile land. And if legislation were in my hands, I would penalize the manufacture of labour-saving machines and protect the industry which manufactures nice ploughs which can be handled by every man.

'*Swadeshi* v. Machinery?' *Young India*, 17 Sept. 1919

196. Genuine *swadeshi*

At this juncture, it is very necessary to understand thoroughly some fundamental principles of *swadeshi*. Will it advance the cause of *swadeshi* if Muslims take the *swadeshi* vow in their hundreds of thousands? I think it will, provided that either there is an increase in the production of *swadeshi* goods to meet their needs or they and others reduce their requirements of cloth.

The cloth which our cotton mills produce is not enough for India's needs and the mills are not in a position to increase the production of cloth in the immediate future. Their weaving capacity is greater than their spinning capacity. If, therefore, we use mill-yarn for handloom cloth, it will mean that the mills will produce less correspondingly and not that there will be an increase in the total production of cloth. The result will be large imports, not of cloth, but of yarn. That will leave us just where we are. We need not believe that we shall be saving on weaving, for yarn will cost more. This is not *swadeshi*.

The *swadeshi* of our conception safeguards both *dharma* and *artha*.* Not to be able to serve our own neighbours, our own kith and kin— to wrest a morsel from their mouths and put it into those of strangers, surely this would not be serving the higher end of life, this would not be compassion. That would only mean our deserting our own field of duty. We are, therefore, morally bound to encourage our sisters who spin and our weavers. In the process, we shall be sending 60 crores of rupees to the homes of our starving millions and this will safe-guard *artha*. The *swadeshi dharma* is thus the royal road for safe-guarding both our *dharma* and *artha*.

We can follow this only if we take to hand-spinning and hand-weaving. The true and genuine *swadeshi* movement, therefore, con-sists in increasing the production of yarn, getting the yarn woven and then marketing the cloth thus produced. It is, therefore, my sugges-tion to all lovers of *swadeshi* and to all owners of *swadeshi* stores that they should get women to spin and should popularize the cloth woven out of the yarn they produce. I know that this work is difficult and heart-breaking. But no progress is ever possible without our venturing on a path beset with difficulties. The way to the Dhaulagiri peak* is strewn with the bones of countless travellers. The weak of heart lose their enthusiasm right at the foot; there is no way, though, except through hills and valleys. If, therefore, those who take up the *swadeshi* cause do so after fully understanding the basic principle of *swadeshi*, they will save themselves from disappointment. It does not matter if every worker does no more than spin and infects a few with his zeal; but there will be great harm, if the *swadeshi* movement does not make headway, in being satisfied with what goes under the name of *swadeshi*. No piece of brass, however shining, can serve for gold; nor a bit of glass for a diamond. Just as mistakenly accepting glass as diamond will only delay our getting the latter, in the same way we shall only retard the progress of *swadeshi* if we accept spurious *swadeshi* as genuine *swadeshi*.

Some people may wonder why, if the idea is to produce yarn, some 10 or 20 new mills should not be set up instead of trying to persuade millions of women to spin. I have already answered this question in *Navajivan*. New mills are not easily set up. Nor does anyone need especially to make the effort. The rich make the attempt on their own and keep adding to the number. But the setting up of new mills will mean being permanently dependent on foreigners for machinery. It is, besides, no remedy for the hunger of the millions, nor does it enable us to put 60 crores of rupees in circulation among them every year. India's population numbering millions and spread over a length of 1900 miles will never be saved from starvation till we introduce a subsidiary occupation into the homes of the millions living on agriculture. Such an occupation can only be hand-spinning and, to some extent, hand-weaving. This industry flourished in India a hundred and fifty years ago and at that time we were not as miserably poor as we are today.

'Pure *Swadeshi*' (G.). *Navajivan*, 11 July 1920

197. *Swadeshi* and *swaraj*

The Congress resolution* has rightly emphasized the importance of *swadeshi* and thereanent of greater sacrifice by merchants.

India cannot be free so long as India voluntarily encourages or tolerates the economic drain which has been going on for the past century and a half. Boycott of foreign goods means no more and no less than boycott of foreign cloth. Foreign cloth constitutes the largest drain voluntarily permitted by us. It means sixty crores of rupees annually paid by us for piece-goods. If India could make a successful effort to stop that drain, she can gain *swaraj* by that one act.

India was enslaved for satisfying the greed of the foreign cloth manufacturer. When the East India Company came in, we were able to manufacture all the cloth we needed, and more for export. By processes that need not be described here, India has become practically wholly dependent upon foreign manufacture for her clothing.

But we ought not to be dependent. India has the ability to manufacture all her cloth if her children will work for it. Fortunately India has yet enough weavers to supplement the out-turn of her mills. The mills do not and cannot immediately manufacture all the cloth we want. The reader may not know that, even at the present moment, the weavers weave more cloth than the mills. But the latter weave five crore yards of fine foreign counts, equal to forty crore yards of coarser counts. The way to carry out a successful boycott of foreign cloth is to increase the output of yarn. And this can only be done by hand-spinning.

To bring about such a boycott, it is necessary for our merchants to stop all foreign importation, and to sell out, even at a loss, all foreign cloth already stocked in India, preferably to foreign buyers. They must cease to speculate in cotton, and keep all the cotton required for home use. They must stop purchasing all foreign cotton.

The mill-owners should work their mills not for their profits but as a national trust and therefore cease to spin finer counts, and weave only for the home market.

The householder has to revise his or her ideas of fashion and, at least for the time being, suspend the use of fine garments which are not always worn to cover the body. He should train himself to see art and beauty in the spotlessly white *khaddar* and to appreciate its soft unevenness. The householder must learn to use cloth as a miser uses his hoard.

And even when the householders have revised their tastes about dress, somebody will have to spin yarn for the weavers. This can only be done by everyone spinning during spare hours either for love or money.

We are engaged in a spiritual war. We are not living in normal times. Normal activities are always suspended in abnormal times. And if we are out to gain *swaraj* in a year's time, it means that we must concentrate upon our goal to the exclusion of everything else. I therefore venture to suggest to the students all over India to suspend their normal studies for one year and devote their time to the manufacture of yarn by hand-spinning. It will be their greatest act of service to the motherland, and their most natural contribution to the attainment of *swaraj*. During the late War our rulers attempted to turn every factory into an arsenal for turning out bullets of lead. During this war of ours, I suggest every national school and college being turned into a factory for preparing cones of yarns for the nation. The students will lose nothing by the occupation: they will gain a kingdom here and hereafter. There is a famine of cloth in India. To assist in removing this dearth is surely an act of merit. If it is sinful to use foreign yarn, it is a virtue to manufacture more *swadeshi* yarn in order to enable us to cope with the want that would be created by the disuse of foreign yarn.

The obvious question asked would be, 'If it is so necessary to manufacture yarn, why not pay every poor person to do so?' The answer is that hand-spinning is not, and never was, a calling like weaving, carpentry, etc. Under the pre-British economy of India, spinning was an honourable and leisurely occupation for the women of India. It is difficult to revive the art among the women in the time at our disposal. But it is incredibly simple and easy for the school-goers to respond to the nation's call. Let no one decry the work as being derogatory to the dignity of man or of students. It was an art confined to the women of India because the latter had more leisure. And being graceful, musical, and as it did not involve any great exertion, it had become the monopoly of women. But it is certainly as graceful for either sex as is music, for instance. In hand-spinning is hidden the protection of women's virtue, the insurance against famine, and the cheapening of prices. In it is hidden the secret of *swaraj*. The revival of hand-spinning is the least penance we must do for the sin of our forefathers in having succumbed to Satanic influences of the foreign manufacturer.

The school-goers will restore hand-spinning to its respectable status. They will hasten the process of making *khaddar* fashionable. For no mother, or father, worth the name will refuse to wear cloth made out of yarn spun by their children. And the scholars' practical recognition of art will compel the attention of the weavers of India. If we are to wean the Punjabi from the calling* not of a soldier but of the murderer of innocent and free people of other lands, we must give back to him the occupation of weaving. The race of the peaceful *julahis** of the Punjab is all but extinct. It is for the scholars of the Punjab to make it possible for the Punjabi weaver to return to his innocent calling.

I hope to show in a future issue how easy it is to introduce this change in the schools and how quickly, on these terms, we can nationalize our schools and colleges. Everywhere the students have asked me what new things I would introduce into our nationalized schools. I have invariably told them I would certainly introduce spinning. I feel, so much more clearly than ever before, that, during the transition period, we must devote exclusive attention to spinning and certain other things of immediate national use, so as to make up for past neglect. And the students will be better able and equipped to enter upon the new course of studies.

Do I want to put back the hand of the clock of progress? Do I want to replace the mills by hand-spinning and hand-weaving? Do I want to replace the railway by the country cart? Do I want to destroy machinery altogether? These questions have been asked by some journalists and public men. My answer is: I would not weep over the disappearance of machinery or consider it a calamity. But I have no design upon machinery as such. What I want to do at the present moment is to supplement the production of yarn and cloth through our mills, save the millions we send out of India, and distribute them in our cottages. This I cannot do unless and until the nation is prepared to devote its leisure hours to hand-spinning. To that end we must adopt the methods I have ventured to suggest for popularizing spinning as a duty rather than as a means of livelihood.

'The Secret of *Swaraj*'. *Young India*, 19 Jan. 1921

198. Hand-spinning and cooperation

Probably very few workers have noticed that progress of hand-spinning means the greatest voluntary co-operation the world has ever seen. It means co-operation among millions of human beings scattered over a very wide area and working for their daily bread. No doubt agriculture has required much co-operative effort, but hand-spinning requires still greater and more honest co-operation. Wheat grows more by nature's honesty than by man's. Manufacture of yarn in our cottages is dependent solely on human honesty. Hand-spinning is impossible without the willing and intelligent co-operation of millions of human beings. We have to arrive at a stage when the spinner like the grain-seller is assured of a steady market for his yarn as well as the supply of cotton slivers if he or she does not know the process of carding. Is it any wonder if I claim that hand-spinning can drive away as if by magic the growing pauperism of the masses? An English friend sends me a newspaper cutting showing the progress of machinery in China. He has evidently imagined that in advocating hand-spinning I am propagating my ideas about machinery. I am doing nothing of the kind.

I would favour the use of the most elaborate machinery if thereby India's pauperism and resulting idleness be avoided. I have suggested hand-spinning as the only ready means of driving away penury and making famine of work and wealth impossible. The spinning-wheel itself is a piece of valuable machinery, and in my own humble way I have tried to secure improvements in it in keeping with the special conditions of India. The only question therefore that a lover of India and humanity has to address himself to is how best to devise practical means of alleviating India's wretchedness and misery. No scheme of irrigation or other agricultural improvement that human ingenuity can conceive can deal with the vastly scattered population of India or provide work for masses of mankind who are constantly thrown out of employment. Imagine a nation working only five hours per day on an average, and this not by choice but by force of circumstances, and you have a realistic picture of India.

If the reader would visualize the picture, he must dismiss from his mind the busy fuss of the city life or the grinding fatigue of the factory life or the slavery of the plantations. These are but drops in the ocean of Indian humanity. If he would visualize the picture of the Indian skeleton, he must think of the eighty per cent of the population which is working its own fields and which has practically no occupation for at least four months in the year and which therefore lives on the borderland of starvation. This is the normal condition. The ever-recurring famines make a large addition to this enforced idleness. What is the work that these men and women can easily do in their own cottages so as to supplement their very slender resources? Does anyone still doubt that it is only hand-spinning and nothing else? And I repeat that this can be made universal in a few months' time, if only the workers will. Indeed it is on a fair way to becoming universal. Experts only are needed to organize it.

People are ready, and what is most in favour of hand-spinning is that it is not a new and untried method but people have up to recently been using it. Its successful reintroduction does need skilful endeavour, honesty and co-operation on the largest scale known to the world. And if India can achieve this co-operation, who shall deny that India has by that one act achieved *swaraj*?

'Co-operation'. *Young India*, 3 Nov. 1921

199. *Swadeshi*—a religious duty

Swadeshi is an eternal religious duty. The manner of following it may, and ought to, change from age to age. The principle of *swadeshi* is the soul and *khadi* is its body in this age and in this country. If in the course of time this body perishes, *swadeshi* will assume a new body but the soul dwelling in it will be the same. *Swadeshi* is service, and if we understand its nature we shall simultaneously benefit ourselves, our families, our country and the world. *Swadeshi* is not intended to serve self-interest but is pure altruism, and hence I call it a form of *yajna*. It certainly benefits ourselves, but there is no room in it for hatred of others. There can be no absolute duty of not importing anything at any time; only, we may not import anything which may harm the country. Nor can it be accepted as an absolute principle that everything that belongs to or is produced by one's own country is good. Anything, whether indigenous or foreign, which is good and serves our interest should be readily accepted, and likewise anything, indigenous or foreign, which is bad and harmful should be rejected. The country produces a huge quantity of liquor, but all of it deserves to be shunned. There is no reason to believe that, if the whole country gives up drinking, those engaged in the liquor trade will be ruined. Their present business harms themselves and the country and they will not starve if they lose it; there will be other, better occupations which they can follow.

'Swadeshi v. Foreign' (G.). *Navajivan*, 19 June 1927

200. The spinning-wheel and real *swaraj*

27 December 1936

This speech was scheduled for 8.30. I am sorry that it is being delivered so late at 9.15. But there was no alternative. People have turned up here in such large numbers and as our exhibition has only screens of unseasoned bamboo for walls, if everyone makes a rush for it they would collapse. Hence, arrangements had to be made to protect things and the organizers took some time in doing this. They were not prepared for such an onrush. You will feel that there has been a trick in putting my speech on the programme. This was deliberate. If for no other reason, people would come to hear me and give two annas for the exhibition. While doing so if they by accident or mistake purchase some *khadi* and have a glimpse of rural art, they will earn some merit without any particular effort and so will I.

You must have seen that the whole of Tilaknagar is like an exhibition. The credit for this goes to Shri Nandalal Bose. It was he who decided that the plan for both the exhibition and the Congress should be the same. Only a paltry sum has been spent in doing so. I do not know of any Congress session which has been organized at such a low cost. Of course, in my opinion, some expenses have been unnecessarily incurred, but, then, is this not the first Congress to be held in a village? A fair amount had to be spent in obtaining land. But we have done something which will encourage us to hold the future sessions of the Congress in villages. You can see the crowd is increasing. There are many volunteers, but they seem to get lost in the crowd. There are so many persons who have to be fed that it has become difficult to make arrangements for them.

I am going to say nothing new today. The cult of the spinning-wheel is 18 years old. I said in 1918 that we could win *swaraj* through the spinning-wheel. My faith in the ability of the spinning-wheel is as bright today as when I first declared it in 1918. It has become richer for the experience and experiment of all these years.

But you should know the implications of the wheel or *khadi*, its product. It is not enough that one wears *khadi* on ceremonial occasions or even wears it to the exclusion of all other cloth if he surrounds himself with *videshi* in everything else. *Khadi* means the truest *swadeshi* spirit, identification with the starving millions.

Let there be no mistake about my conception of *swaraj*. It is complete independence of alien control and complete economic independence. So at one end you have political independence, at the other the economic. It has two other ends. One of them is moral and social, the corresponding end is *dharma*, i.e., religion in the highest sense of the term. It includes Hinduism, Islam, Christianity, etc., but is superior to them all. You may recognize it by the name of Truth, not the honesty of expedience but the living Truth that pervades everything and will survive all destruction and all transformation. Moral and social uplift may be recognized by the term we are used to, i.e., non-violence. Let us call this the square of *swaraj*, which will be out of shape if any of its angles is untrue. In the language of the Congress we cannot achieve this political and economic freedom without truth and non-violence, in concrete terms without a living faith in God and hence moral and social elevation.

By political independence I do not mean an imitation of the British House of Commons, or the Soviet rule of Russia or the Fascist rule of Italy or the Nazi rule of Germany. They have systems suited to their genius. We must have ours suited to ours. What that can be is more than I can tell. I have described it as *Ramarajya*, i.e., sovereignty of the people based on pure moral authority. The Congress constitutions of Nagpur and Bombay for which I am mainly responsible are an attempt to achieve this type of *swaraj*.

Then take economic independence. It is not a product of industrialization of the modern or the Western type. Indian economic independence means to me the economic uplift of every individual, male and female, by his or her own conscious effort. Under that system all men and women will have enough clothing—not the mere loincloth, but what we understand by the term necessary articles of clothing and enough food including milk and butter which are today denied to millions.

This brings me to socialism. Real socialism has been handed down to us by our ancestors who taught: 'All land belongs to Gopal, where then is the boundary line? Man is the maker of the line and he can therefore unmake it.' Gopal literally means shepherd; it also means God. In modern language it means the State, i.e., the people. That the land today does not belong to the people is too true. But the fault is not in the teaching. It is in us who have not lived up to it.

I have no doubt that we can make as good an approach to it as is possible for any nation, not excluding Russia, and that without violence. The most effective substitute for violent dispossession is the wheel with all its implications. Land and all property is his who will work it. Unfortunately the workers are or have been kept ignorant of this simple fact.

Let us now see how India came to be utterly impoverished. History tells us that the East India Company ruined the cotton manufacture and by all kinds of means made her dependent upon Lancashire for her cloth, the next great necessity of man. It is still the largest item of import. It thus created a huge army of partially unemployed men and women counted in millions and gave them no other employment in return. With the destruction of hand-ginning, carding, spinning and weaving to a certain extent, perished the other industries of India's villages. Continuous unemployment has induced in the people a kind of laziness which is most depressing. Thus whilst the alien rule is undoubtedly responsible for the growing pauperism of the people, we are more responsible for it. If the middle-class people, who betrayed their trust and bartered away the economic independence of India for a mess of pottage, would now realize their error and take the message of the wheel to the villagers and induce them to shed their laziness and work at the wheel, we can ameliorate the condition of the people to a great extent. It would be a terrible thing if laziness replaces industry and despair triumphs over hope.

The parliamentary programme* is in the air. It has come to stay and rightly. But it cannot bring us independence. Its function is strictly limited though quite necessary. Its success will prevent the Government from claiming that Ordinance rule or any measure restricting our progress to the goal was sanctioned by popular representatives. Hence the necessity for voters voting for the Congress candidates who dare not vote for unpopular measures without being liable to Congress discipline. The success of that programme may also bring some relief in individual cases such as the release of Shri Subhas Bose or the détenus. But that is not independence, political or economic.

Then look at it in another way. Only a limited number of men and women can become members of legislatures, say 1,500. How many from this audience can become legislators? And just now no more than 3½ crores can vote for these 1,500 members. What about the remaining 31½ crores? In our conception of *swaraj* they are the real masters and the 3½ crores are the former's servants who in their turn are masters of the 1,500. Thus the latter are doubly servants, if they will be true to their trust.

But the 31½ crores have also a trust to discharge towards themselves and the nation of which they as individuals are but tiny parts. And if they remain lazy, know nothing of *swaraj* and how to win it, they will themselves become slaves of the 1,500 legislators. For my argument the 3½ crores of voters here belong to the same category as the 31½ crores. For if they do not become industrious and wise, they will be so many pawns in the hands of 1,500 players, it is of little consequence whether they are Congressmen or otherwise. If the voters wake up only to register their votes every three years or more and then go off to sleep, their servants will become their masters.

The only way I know to prevent such a catastrophe is for the 35 crores to be industrious and wise. This they can only be if they will take up the spinning-wheel and the other village industries. They will not take to them unintelligently. I can tell you from experience that the effort means adult education of the correct type and requires possession of patience, moral fibre and a scientific and practical knowledge of the industry the worker seeks to introduce in the village of his choice.

In such a scheme the spinning-wheel becomes its centre. If you call it the solar system, the wheel becomes the golden disc and the industries the planets revolving round it in obedience to the inviolable law of the system. When the sun lost its illuminating power by the action of the East India Company, the planets lost their power and became invisible or almost so. The sun is being reinstated in his past status now and the planets are regaining their motion in exact proportion to the strength of the sun.

Now perhaps you will understand the meaning and the message of the *charkha*. I said in 1920 that if the Congress truly and successfully worked the programme laid down in 1920 including the fourfold Constructive Programme of *khadi*, communal unity, prohibition of intoxicants and removal by Hindus of untouchability, the attainment of *swaraj* within a year was a certainty. I am neither sorry for nor ashamed of having made that declaration. I would like to repeat that declaration before you today. Whenever the fourfold programme is achieved in its fulness, you can have *swaraj* for the asking. For you will then have attained the power to take it. . . .

This is the non-violent way in action. If we could fulfil this programme, there would be no need to offer civil disobedience, there would certainly be no need to do violence. Thirty-five crores of people conscious of their numerical strength as one man would be ashamed of doing violence to 70,000 white men in India, no matter how capable they are of dealing destruction and administering poison gas to millions in a moment. The *charkha* understood intelligently can spin not only economic salvation but can also revolutionize our minds and hearts and demonstrate to us that the non-violent approach to *swaraj* is the safest and the easiest. Though the progress may seem slow, it will prove quickest in the long run.

Believe me if Jawaharlal* is not in jail today, it is not because he is afraid of it. He is quite capable of walking into prison doors as of mounting the gallows with a smile on his lips. I do not think I have lost the power or faith in the efficacy of such suffering. But there is no issue for it today as far as I can see. But what I feel is that all that suffering can be avoided if by united faith and will we achieve the Constructive Programme. If we can, I promise that we won't need to struggle with or against the British nation, but Lord Linlithgow* will come to us and own that he was mistaken in his disbelief of our non-violence and truth and will undertake on behalf of his nation to abide by our decisions. Whether he does or not, I am working towards that and no other. 'All belong to God.'

Speech at Exhibition Ground, Faizpur. *Harijan*, 2 Jan. 1937.
Harijanbandhu, 3 Jan. 1937. *MPWMG*, vol. iii, pp. 369–74

201. *Charkha* and equality

28 April 1947

How can we afford to forget the *charkha*? The spirit behind spinning implies equality of all. The *charkha* teaches us the unique lesson of identifying ourselves with the forty crores and be in perfect harmony with them. It will not admit of any distinction of high and low, master and servant, which is the cause of conflict in the world today, isn't it? The *charkha* warns us against it. How can we, therefore, fail to worship God in the form of the *charkha*?

'Remark to Manu Gandhi' (G.). *Biharni Komi Agman*, p. 273. *MPWMG*, vol. iii, p. 375

202. The importance of the mother tongue

London, 5 October 1909

These days a new idea is in the air in India. Hindus, Muslims, Parsis—all are filled with the spirit of 'my country' and 'our country'. We shall not on this occasion go into the political aspects of the matter. Thinking of it from the point of view of language, it requires little effort to see that we must cultivate pride in our language before we can speak of 'our country' with genuine feeling . . .

Personally . . . I think it is a welcome development that everyone in India, young or old, is beginning to turn his attention to his own language . . . If only we make on Indian languages half the effort we waste on English, thanks to certain notions of ours, the situation will change altogether. India's uplift is, to a very considerable extent, bound up with this. I had been under the sway of Macaulay's ideas on Indian education.* Others, too, are. I have now been disillusioned. I wish that others should be . . .

To the Indians in England I say that—while here, we must not show indifference to this language which is our heritage, but cultivate greater love for it, taking a lesson from the British. If they make it a point to use their own ancestral language in writing or speaking to one another, that will ensure its quicker development. India will make progress, in consequence, and they will be deemed to have discharged their duty . . .

Speech at meeting of Gujaratis in London. *Indian Opinion*, 20 Nov. 1909 (G.). *CWMG*, vol. ix, pp. 457–60

203. English education has enslaved the nation

CHAPTER XVIII: EDUCATION*

READER. In the whole of our discussion, you have not demonstrated the necessity for education; we always complain of its absence among us. We notice a movement for compulsory education in our country . . . Is all this effort then of no use?

EDITOR. If we consider our civilization to be the highest, I have regretfully to say that much of the effort you have described is of no use. The motive of [those] who have been working in this direction is perfectly pure. They, therefore, undoubtedly deserve great praise. But we cannot conceal from ourselves the result that is likely to flow from their effort.

What is the meaning of education? It simply means a knowledge of letters. It is merely an instrument, and an instrument may be well used or abused. The same instrument that may be used to cure a patient may be used to take his life, and so may a knowledge of letters. We daily observe that many men abuse it and very few make good use of it; and if this is a correct statement, we have proved that more harm has been done by it than good.

The ordinary meaning of education is a knowledge of letters. To teach boys reading, writing and arithmetic is called primary education. A peasant earns his bread honestly. He has ordinary knowledge of the world. He knows fairly well how he should behave towards his parents, his wife, his children and his fellow-villagers. He understands and observes the rules of morality. But he cannot write his own name. What do you propose to do by giving him a knowledge of letters? Will you add an inch to his happiness? Do you wish to make him discontented with his cottage or his lot? And even if you want to do that, he will not need such an education. Carried away by the flood of Western thought we came to the conclusion, without weighing pros and cons, that we should give this kind of education to the people.

Now let us take higher education. I have learnt Geography, Astronomy, Algebra, Geometry, etc. What of that? In what way have I benefited myself or those around me? Why have I learnt these things? Professor Huxley* has thus defined education:

That man I think has had a liberal education who has been so trained in youth that his body is the ready servant of his will and does with ease and pleasure all the work that as a mechanism it is capable of; whose intellect is a clear, cold logic[al] engine . . . whose mind is stored with a knowledge of the fundamental truths of nature whose passions are trained to come to heel by a vigorous will, the servant of a tender conscience . . . who has learnt to hate all vileness and to respect others as himself. Such a one and no other, I conceive, has had a liberal education, for he is in harmony with nature. He will make the best of her and she of him.

If this is true education, I must emphatically say that the sciences I have enumerated above I have never been able to use for controlling my senses. Therefore, whether you take elementary education or higher education, it is not required for the main thing. It does not make men of us. It does not enable us to do our duty.

READER. If that is so, I shall have to ask you another question. What enables you to tell all these things to me? If you had not received higher education, how would you have been able to explain to me the things that you have?

EDITOR. You have spoken well. But my answer is simple: I do not for one moment believe that my life would have been wasted, had I not received higher or lower education. Nor do I consider that I necessarily serve because I speak. But I do desire to serve and in endeavouring to fulfil that desire, I make use of the education I have received. And, if I am making good use of it, even then it is not for the millions, but I can use it only for such as you, and this supports my contention. Both you and I have come under the bane of what is mainly false education. I claim to have become free from its ill effect, and I am trying to give you the benefit of my experience and in doing so, I am demonstrating the rottenness of this education.

Moreover, I have not run down a knowledge of letters in all circumstances. All I have now shown is that we must not make of it a fetish. It is not our Kamadhuk.* In its place it can be of use and it has its place when we have brought our senses under subjection and put our ethics on a firm foundation. And then, if we feel inclined to receive that education, we may make good use of it. As an ornament it is likely to sit well on us. It now follows that it is not necessary to make this education compulsory. Our ancient school system is enough. Character-building has the first place in it and that is primary education. A building erected on that foundation will last.

READER. Do I then understand that you do not consider English education necessary for obtaining Home Rule?

EDITOR. My answer is yes and no. To give millions a knowledge of English is to enslave them. The foundation that Macaulay laid of education has enslaved us. I do not suggest that he had any such intention, but that has been the result. Is it not a sad commentary that we should have to speak of Home Rule in a foreign tongue?

And it is worthy of note that the systems which the Europeans have discarded are the systems in vogue among us. Their learned men continually make changes. We ignorantly adhere to their cast-off systems. They are trying each division to improve its own status. Wales is a small portion of England. Great efforts are being made to revive a knowledge of Welsh among Welshmen. The English Chancellor, Mr Lloyd George,* is taking a leading part in the movement to make Welsh children speak Welsh. And what is our condition? We write to each other in faulty English, and from this even our M.A.s are not free; our best thoughts are expressed in English; the proceedings of our Congress are conducted in English; our best newspapers are printed in English. If this state of things continues for a long time, posterity will—it is my firm opinion—condemn and curse us.

It is worth noting that, by receiving English education, we have enslaved the nation. Hypocrisy, tyranny, etc., have increased; English-knowing Indians have not hesitated to cheat and strike terror into the people. Now, if we are doing anything for the people at all, we are paying only a portion of the debt due to them.

Is it not a painful thing that, if I want to go to a court of justice, I must employ the English language as a medium, that when I become a barrister, I may not speak my mother tongue and that someone else should have to translate to me from my own language? Is not this absolutely absurd? Is it not a sign of slavery? Am I to blame the English for it or myself? It is we, the English-knowing Indians, that have enslaved India. The curse of the nation will rest not upon the English but upon us.

I have told you that my answer to your last question is both yes and no. I have explained to you why it is yes. I shall now explain why it is no.

We are so much beset by the disease of civilization, that we cannot altogether do without English education. Those who have already received it may make good use of it wherever necessary. In our dealings with the English people, in our dealings with our own people, when we can only correspond with them through that language, and for the purpose of knowing how disgusted they have themselves become with their civilization, we may use or learn English, as the case may be. Those who have studied English will have to teach morality to their progeny through their mother tongue and to teach them another Indian language; but when they have grown up, they may learn English, the ultimate aim being that we should not need it. The object of making money thereby should be eschewed. Even in learning English to such a limited extent we shall have to consider what we should learn through it and what we should not. It will be necessary to know what sciences we should learn. A little thought should show you that immediately we cease to care for English degrees, the rulers will prick up their ears.

READER. Then what education shall we give?

EDITOR. This has been somewhat considered above, but we will consider it a little more. I think that we have to improve all our languages. What subjects we should learn through them need not be elaborated here. Those English books which are valuable, we should translate into the various Indian languages. We should abandon the pretension of learning many sciences. Religious, that is ethical, education will occupy the first place. Every cultured Indian will know in addition to his own provincial language, if a Hindu, Sanskrit; if a Mahomedan, Arabic; if a Parsee, Persian; and all, Hindi. Some Hindus should know Arabic and Persian; some Mahomedans and Parsees, Sanskrit. Several Northerners and Westerners should learn Tamil. A universal language for India should be Hindi, with the option of writing it in Persian or Nagari characters. In order that the Hindus and the Mahomedans may have closer relations, it is necessary to know both the characters. And, if we can do this, we can drive the English language out of the field in a short time. All this is necessary for us, slaves. Through our slavery the nation has been enslaved, and it will be free with our freedom.

READER. The question of religious education is very difficult.

EDITOR. Yet we cannot do without it. India will never be godless. Rank atheism cannot flourish in this land. The task is indeed difficult. My head begins to turn as I think of religious education. Our religious teachers are hypocritical and selfish; they will have to be approached. The *Mullas*, the *Dasturs* and the *Brahmins** hold the key in their hands, but if they will not have the good sense, the energy that we have derived from English education will have to be devoted to religious education. This is not very difficult. Only the fringe of the ocean has been polluted and it is those who are within the fringe who alone need cleansing. We who come under this category can even cleanse ourselves because my remarks do not apply to the millions. In order to restore India to its pristine condition, we have to return to it. In our own civilization there will naturally be progress, retrogression, reforms and reactions; but one effort is required, and that is to drive out Western civilization. All else will follow.

Gandhi, *Hind Swaraj*

204. Plan for a National School

January 1917

PROSPECTUS

For many years past, several friends and I have felt that our present education is not national and that in consequence people do not get from it the benefit they ought to. Our children languish as a result of this education. They become incapable of any great achievement and the knowledge they acquire does not spread among the masses—not even in their families. Nor do the young people have any aim in mind in taking this modern education except to get a job and make money. It is one of the fundamental principles of education that it should be planned with a view to the needs of the people. This idea finds no place at all in our schools.

Wherever I have travelled in India, I have discussed this question with the leaders and, without exception, almost *everyone has admitted that our educational system must change*.

To look to the Government for this will be sheer waste of time. The Government will wait on public opinion and, being foreign, move very timidly; it cannot understand our needs, its advisers may be ill-informed or they may have interests of their own to serve. For a variety of such reasons, it will probably be quite long before there is any serious change in the present system; the time that passes meanwhile is so much loss to the people.

It is, however, not intended to suggest here that we should not try to get the Government to move. Let petitions be made to it and let public opinion be ascertained. But the best petition to the Government will be an actual demonstration by us and this will also be the easiest way of cultivating public opinion. It has accordingly been decided, in consultation with some educated gentlemen, to start a *national school*.*

EDUCATION IN THE SCHOOL

Basic principle: The education will be physical, intellectual and religious.

For physical education, there will be training in agriculture and hand-weaving and in the use of carpenter's and blacksmith's tools incidental to these. That will provide sufficient exercise for the pupils. In addition, they will be given drill, which is both an entertainment and a practical utility and, as part of this, they will be taught how to march in squads and how each one may work with quiet efficiency in case of accidents such as fire.

They will have instruction on how to preserve health and on home remedies for ordinary ailments, with as much of physiology and botany as may be necessary for the purpose.

For intellectual training, they will study Gujarati, Marathi, Hindi and Sanskrit as compulsory subjects. Urdu, Tamil and Bengali will also be taught.

There will be no teaching of English during the first three years.

In addition, the pupils will be taught Mathematics (Arithmetic, Algebra and Geometry). Instruction in multiplication tables, Indian book-keeping and the measures, weights, etc., currently in use will begin at once and the rest of the curriculum will be covered progressively.

There will be instruction in History, Geography, Elements of Astronomy and Elements of Chemistry.

By way of instruction in religion, pupils will be taught general ethical principles and we are hopeful that the teachers will demonstrate by their conduct that the essence of religion is good character.

All teaching will be through Gujarati, right up to the highest stage, and most of it will be oral during the first few years. The intention is to put across to the children, before they learn to read and write, quite a few things orally by way of stories, as was the practice in old days, and so help their minds to grow, and to give them some general knowledge as they play about, rather than repress them by doing nothing more than remarking, 'Oh dear, dear! How dirty', and so on.

EXPLANATION

The aim at present is that after a few years of such education, the student's equipment will approximate to that of a well-informed graduate. That is, he will have a reduced load by way of learning English and, during the time so saved, he will be given all the useful knowledge a graduate acquires. He will be freed from the fear of examinations. All the students will be tested from time to time, but that will be by the teachers of the school itself. The use to which the student puts his abilities after leaving school will be the true measure of the worth of his education. Every opportunity will be taken to rid his mind of the fallacious notion that the aim of education is to get employment. And, finally, every pupil joining this school is likely to develop such self-confidence in a few years that he will not be troubled with doubts or fears about how he will make a living. A pupil who has been in the school for five years will be fixed up, if he so desires, in some work in the school itself and be paid for it. The school will make arrangements with some factories, etc., so that they provide training in vocations and give a start to those who wish to set themselves up independently. If, after ten years of study, anyone wants to pursue a subject further, necessary arrangements for the purpose are left to the future.

FREE EDUCATION

No fees will be charged in this school, the expenses being met from donations received.

TEACHERS

Paid teachers will be engaged and will be, all of them, grown-up men who have reached the college level or possess equivalent attainments. The idea is that children should have the best teachers in the early stages.

SN 6195a (G.). *CWMG*, vol. xiii, pp. 332–4

205. Educational experiment in the Ahmedabad *ashram*

July 1917

. . . The system of education at present in vogue is, it is held, wholly unsuited to India's needs, is a bad copy of the Western model and it has by reason of the medium of instruction being a foreign language sapped the energy of the youths who have passed through our schools and colleges and has produced an army of clerks and office-seekers. It has dried up all originality, impoverished the vernaculars and has deprived the masses of the benefit of higher knowledge which would otherwise have percolated to them through the intercourse of the educated classes with them. The system has resulted in creating a gulf between educated India and the masses. It has stimulated the brain but starved the spirit for want of a religious basis for education and emaciated the body for want of training in handicrafts. It has criminally neglected the greatest need of India in that there is no agricultural training worth the name provided in the course. The experiment now being carried on at the Ashram* seeks to avoid all the defects above noted. The medium of instruction is the provincial vernacular. Hindi is taught as a common medium and handloom-weaving and agriculture are taught from the very commencement. Pupils are taught to look up to these as a means of livelihood and the knowledge of letters as a training for the head and the heart and as a means of national service.

Circular letter requesting funds for *ashram*, July 1917. GN 6297.
SN 6378. *CWMG*, vol. xiii, p. 462

206. The defects of the current educational system

20 October 1917

It should be obvious to everyone that the first thing to do in this connection is to come to a definite decision about the medium of instruction. Unless that is done, all other efforts, I fear, are likely to prove fruitless. To impart education without first considering the question of the medium of instruction will be like raising a building without a foundation.

On this point, two views prevail among educationists. Some hold that education should be imparted through the mother tongue; that is, through Gujarati. Others contend that it should be imparted through English. Both parties are honest in their views, for both have the welfare of the country at heart. But mere good intentions are not enough to gain the end we desire. It is the experience of the world that good intentions do occasionally take us to unworthy places. We must, therefore, critically examine both these views and, if possible, come to a unanimous decision on this great and important question. There is no doubt whatsoever that the issue is of the utmost importance and we cannot consider it too carefully.

This question concerns the whole of India. But each Presidency or Province may decide this matter for itself. It is erroneous to think that, until unanimity has been reached about it, Gujarat cannot go ahead by itself. . . .

It requires a minimum of 16 years to complete one's education through the medium of English. If the same subjects were taught through the mother tongue, it would take ten years at the most. This is the opinion expressed by many experienced teachers. A saving of six years for each of the thousands of students means a saving of thousands of years for the nation.

Education through a foreign language entails an excessive strain which only our boys could bear; they must needs pay dearly for it, though. To a large extent, they lose the capacity of shouldering any other burden afterwards. Our graduates, therefore, are a useless lot, weak of body, without any zest for work, and mere imitators. They suffer an atrophy of the creative faculty and of the capacity for original thinking, and grow up without the spirit of enterprise and the qualities of perseverance, courage and fearlessness. That is why we are unable to make new plans or carry out those we make. A few who do show promise of these qualities usually die young. An Englishman has said that there is the same difference between Europeans and the people of other countries as between an original piece of writing and its impression on a piece of blotting paper. The element of truth in this statement is not to be attributed to any natural or innate incapacity on the part of the Asians. The reason lies, in a large measure, in the unsuitable medium of instruction. The natives of South Africa are enterprising, strongly built and endowed with character. They do not have such evils as child marriage, etc., which we have, and yet their condition is similar to ours. Why? Because the medium of their education is Dutch. They are able to acquire mastery over the language within a short period as we do [over English], and like us they, too, become weak of body and mind at the end of their education and often turn out to be mere imitators. From them, too, originality disappears along with the mother tongue. It is only we, the English-educated people, who are unable to assess the great loss that results. Some idea of it may be had if we estimate how little has been our influence on the general mass of our people. The occasional remarks which our parents are led to make about the worthlessness of our education have some point. . . .

. . . The system under which we are educated through a foreign language results in incalculable harm.

The continuity that should exist, on the one hand, between the culture the child imbibes along with the mother's milk and the sweet words it receives and, on the other, the training school, is broken when education is imparted through a foreign tongue. Those who are responsible for this are enemies of the people, howsoever honest their motives. To be a voluntary victim of this system of education is to betray one's duty to one's mother. The harm done by this education received through a foreign tongue does not stop here but goes much further. It has created a gulf between the educated classes and the masses. We do not know them and they do not know us. They regard us as sahibs to be feared and may distrust us. If this state of affairs continues very long, the time may come when Lord Curzon's* charge that the educated classes do not represent the common people would be true.

Fortunately, our educated classes appear to be awakening from their slumber. Now that they are beginning to come in contact with the people, they themselves realize the handicaps described above. How may they infect the people with their own enthusiasm? English certainly will not avail us, whereas we have little or no aptitude to do the thing through Gujarati. I always hear people say that they experience great difficulty in expressing themselves in the mother tongue. This barrier dams up the current of popular life. Macaulay's* motive in introducing English education was sincere. He despised our literature. His contempt infected us, too, and we also lost our balance. Indeed, we have left our masters, the English, far behind us in this matter. Macaulay wanted us to become propagandists of Western civilization among our masses. His idea was that English education would help us to develop strength of character and then some of us would disseminate new ideas among the people. It would be irrelevant here to consider whether or not those ideas were good enough to be spread among the people. We have only to consider the question of the medium of instruction. We saw in English education an opportunity to earn money and, therefore, gave importance to the use of English. Some learned patriotism from it. Thus the original idea became secondary and we suffered much harm from the use of English which extended beyond Macaulay's original intention.

If we had political power in our hands, we would have discovered the error soon enough and would have found it impossible to give up the mother tongue. The officials did not give it up. Many perhaps do not know that our court language is supposed to be Gujarati. The Government gets the laws translated into Gujarati as well. Speeches read at durbars are translated into Gujarati simultaneously. We know that in currency notes Gujarati is used alongside with English. Mathematical calculations which land-surveyors have to learn are difficult. If they had to do so through English, the work of the Revenue Department would have become very expensive. So they evolved Gujarati terminology for the use of the surveyors. These terms will give us a pleasant surprise. If we have a sincere love for our language, we can this very moment put to use the resources at our disposal. If lawyers start using Gujarati for their work, much of the clients' money would be saved. Clients would also get the requisite knowledge of law and come to know their rights. The expenses on the services of interpreters would also be saved. Legal terms would pass into current use. Of course, lawyers would have to put themselves to some trouble to do all this. I believe, and the belief is supported by experience, that this will not harm the interests of the client. There is no reason to fear that arguments in Gujarati would carry less weight with the Court than in English. It is compulsory for Collectors and other Government officials to know Gujarati. But, because of our unreasoning craze for English, we allow their knowledge to rust.

It has been contended that there was nothing wrong in our people learning English and using it for earning money and cultivating a sense of patriotism through it. But the contention has no bearing on the use of English as the medium of instruction. We shall respect a person who learns English for acquiring wealth or for doing good to the country. But we cannot, on this account, assert that English should be used as the medium of instruction. All that is intended here is to bring out the harmful consequences of English having established itself as the medium of education . . .

. . . The truth is that, when English comes to occupy its own place and the mother tongue has gained its rightful status, our minds which are imprisoned at present will be set free from the prison-house and, for brains which are well cultivated, well exercised and yet fresh, learning English will not be too much of a strain. I even believe that the English we learn under such conditions will be more of a credit to us than it is at present. What is more, with our intelligence vigorous and fresh, we shall be able to use it to better advantage. From the practical point of view of gain and loss, the course proposed will be found effective in promoting all our interests.

When we start receiving education through our own language, our relations in the home will take on a different character. Today, we cannot make our wives real life-companions. They have very little idea of what we do outside. Our parents know nothing about what we learn at school. If, however, we were to receive education through our mother tongue, we would find it easy to educate the washerman, the barber, the *Bhangi* and others who serve us. In England, they discuss politics with the hair-dresser while having a hair-cut. Here, we cannot do so even with the members of our own families. The reason is not that they are ignorant. They, too, know as much as the English barber. We talk with them on the *Mahabharata*, the *Ramayana* and of holy places, because it is these things which our people hear and learn about. But, the knowledge we get at school does not seep down to others, not even to the members of our families, because we cannot impart to them what we learn in English.

At present the proceedings of our Legislative Assemblies are in English. It is the same story with other bodies. Consequently, the riches of our knowledge lie buried in the ground, much like the wealth of the miser. The same thing happens in our courts of law. The judges offer useful counsel. Litigants are eager enough to know what they say, but they get to know nothing except the dry judgment at the end. They cannot even follow the arguments of their lawyers. It is the same with doctors, educated in schools through English. They cannot educate the patients as may be required. They do not even know the Gujarati names for the various parts of the body. In consequence, most of them show no interest in their patients except to write out prescriptions for them. It is said that, in our thoughtlessness, we allow huge masses of water flowing down the hills to go waste. In the same way, we produce precious manure worth millions, but, in the result, we get only diseases. Similarly, crushed under the weight of English and wanting in foresight, we fail to give our people what they are entitled to get. This is no exaggeration. It only expresses the intensity of my feeling on this point. We shall have to pay heavily for our disregard of the mother tongue. This has already done us great harm. I consider it the first duty of the educated to save our masses from any further harm on this account. . . .

Since education is not exactly my sphere of work, I feel diffident in saying anything on this subject. When I see a person talk about a thing of which he has no practical experience and which is, therefore, outside his range, I want to tell him off and grow impatient with him. It would be natural for a lawyer to feel impatient and angry with a physician talking of law. In the same way, I hold that those who have no experience in the field of education have no right to offer criticism on matters connected with it. I should, therefore, like to say a few words about my qualifications to speak on this subject.

I started thinking about modern education twenty-five years ago. I had my children and the children of my brothers and sisters to look after. I was aware of the defects in our schools. I therefore carried out experiments on my children. No doubt, I tossed them about a good deal in the process. Some I sent to one place and some to others. A few I taught myself. My dissatisfaction with the prevailing system remained the same as ever even after I had left for South Africa, and I had to apply my mind further to the subject. . . . During the satya-graha struggle in South Africa, there were fifty boys studying under my supervision. The general line of work in the school was laid down by me. It had nothing in common with the system in vogue in Government or other schools. A similar effort is now being made here and a National School* has been started in Ahmedabad with the blessings of Acharya Dhruva and other scholars. It is now five months old. Prof. Sankalchand Shah, formerly of the Gujarat College, is its Principal. He received his education under Prof. Gajjar and there are many other lovers of the language associated with him. In the main, the responsibility for the scheme is mine, but it has the active approval of all the teachers connected with it. They have dedicated themselves to the work, content to receive a salary just enough to meet their needs. Though circumstances do not permit me to under-take actual teaching work in this school, its affairs constantly engage my attention. Thus, my contribution is more like an amateur's but, I believe, not altogether devoid of thought. I would request you to keep this in mind in considering my criticism of the prevailing system of education.

It has always appeared to me that the present system of education pays no attention to the general pattern of life in our families. Naturally enough, our needs were not taken into account when the scheme was drawn up.

Macaulay despised our literature. He thought we were over-much given to superstitions. Most of those who drew up this scheme were utterly ignorant of our religion. Some of them thought that it was a false religion. Our scriptures were regarded as mere collections of superstitions. Our civilization seemed full of defects to them. Because we had fallen on evil times, it was thought that our institutions must be defective. With the best of motives, therefore, they raised a faulty structure. Since a fresh start was being made, the planners could only think of the immediate needs of the situation. The whole thing was devised with this idea in mind, that the rulers would need lawyers, doctors, and clerks to help them and that the people should have the new knowledge. Consequently, books were written without any regard for our way of living. Thus, to use an English proverb, 'The cart was placed before the horse'.

Shri Malabari* said that, if History and Geography were to be taught to children, a beginning should be made with the history and geography of the home. I remember, however, that I was made to memorize the counties of England, with the result that an interesting subject like geography became poison to me. I found nothing in History to enthuse me. History is a good means of inculcating patriotism. But the way it was taught in the school gave me no reason to take pride in this country. To learn that, I have had to read other books.

In teaching Arithmetic and other allied subjects, too, the traditional method hardly finds any place. It is almost completely abandoned. With the disappearance of the indigenous method of learning tables, we have lost the capacity for making speedy calculations which our elders possessed.

Science tends to be dry and dull. Our children cannot make much use of what they are taught in this field. A science like astronomy which should be taught to the boys in the open by actually showing them the stars in the sky is taught through books. I do not think many boys remember how to decompose water into its constituent elements once they leave school.

As to Hygiene, it is no exaggeration to say that it is not taught at all. We do not know, after 60 years of education, how to protect ourselves against epidemics like cholera and plague. I consider it a very serious blot on the state of our education that our doctors have not found it possible to eradicate these diseases. I have seen hundreds of homes. I cannot say that I have found any evidence in them of a knowledge of hygiene. I have the greatest doubt whether our graduates know what one should do in case one is bitten by a snake. If our doctors could have started learning medicine at an earlier age, they would not make such a poor show as they do. This is the disastrous result of the system under which we are educated. People in almost all the parts of the world have managed to eradicate the plague. Here it seems to have made a home and thousands of Indians die untimely deaths. If this is to be attributed to poverty, it would still be up to the Education Department to answer why, even after 60 years of education, there is poverty in India.

Let us now turn our attention to the subjects which are not taught at all. All education must aim at building character. I cannot see how this can be done except through religion. We are yet to realize that gradually we are being reduced to a state in which we shall have lost our own without having acquired the new. I cannot go more into this, but I have met hundreds of teachers and they sighed in pain as they told me of their experiences. This is an aspect which the Conference cannot but deeply ponder over. If pupils in schools lose their character, everything will have been lost.

In our country, 85 to 90 per cent of people are engaged in agriculture. Needless to say that no knowledge of this particular field of work can be too much. And yet it has no place at all in the school syllabus up to the end of the high school education. It is only in India that such an anomalous position can exist.

The weaving industry is also falling into ruin. It provided work to farmers during their free hours. The craft finds no place in the curriculum. Our education can only produce clerks and, its general tendency being what it is, even goldsmiths, blacksmiths and cobblers, once they are caught up in its meshes, become clerks. We desire that everyone should have a good education. But how will it profit us if our education makes us all clerks?

Military science finds no place in our education. Personally, I am not unhappy over this. I even regard it as an accidental gain. But the people want to learn the use of arms. Those who do so should not be denied the opportunity of learning it. But this science seems to have been completely lost sight of, as it were in our scheme of education.

Nowhere do I find a place given to music. It exercises a powerful influence over us. We do not realize this vividly enough, otherwise we would have done everything possible to teach music to our boys and girls. The Vedic hymns seem to follow musical tunes in their composition. Harmonious music has the power to soothe the anguish of the soul. At times, we find restlessness in a large gathering. This can be arrested and calmed if a national song is sung by all. That hundreds of boys may sing a poem full of courage and the spirit of adventure and bravery and be inspired with the spirit of heroism is no commonplace fact. We have an example of the power of music in the fact that boatmen and other labourers raise, in unison, the cry of *Harahar* and *Allabeli* and this helps them in their work. I have seen English friends trying to fight cold by singing songs. Our boys learn to sing songs from popular plays in all manner of tunes and without regard to time and place, and try their hands on noisy harmoniums and other instruments, and this does them harm. If, instead, they were to be correctly trained in music, they would not waste their time singing, or attempting to sing, music-hall songs. Just as a trained singer never sings out of tune or at the wrong time, even so one who has learnt classical music will not go in for street music. Music must get a place in our efforts at popular awakening. . . .

I include in the term 'physical training' sports, games, etc. These, too, have been little thought of. Indigenous games have been given up and tennis, cricket and football hold sway. Admittedly, these games are enjoyable. If, however, we had not been carried away by enthusiasm for all things Western, we would not have given up our inexpensive but equally interesting games like *gedi-dado*, *gilli-danda*, *kho-kho*, *mag-matali*, *kabaddi*, *kharo pat*, *nava nagelio*, *sat tali*, etc. Exercises which provided the completest training for every bodily organ and the old style gymnasium where they taught wrestling have almost totally disappeared. I think if anything from the West deserves copying, it is drill. A friend once remarked that we did not know how to walk, particularly when we had to walk in squads and keep step. Silently to walk in step, by hundreds and thousands of us in twos and fours, shifting the directions from time to time is something we can never do. It is not that such drill is useful only in actual battle. It can be of great use in many other activities in the sphere of public service. For example, in extinguishing fire, in rescuing people from drowning, in carrying the sick and disabled in a *doli*,* etc., [previous practice in] drill is a valuable aid. Thus, it is necessary to introduce in our schools indigenous games, exercises and the Western type of drill.

The education of women is as faulty as that of men. No thought has been given to the relations of men and women or to the place of woman in Indian society.

Primary education for the two sexes can have much in common. There are important differences at all other levels. As Nature has made men and women different, it is necessary to maintain a difference between the education of the two. True, they are equals in life, but their functions differ. It is woman's right to rule the home, Man is master outside it. Man is the earner, woman saves and spends. Woman looks after the feeding of the child. She shapes its future. She is responsible for building its character. She is her children's education, and hence, mother to the Nation. Man is not father [in that sense]. After a certain period, a father ceases to influence his son; the mother never abdicates her place. The son, even after attaining manhood, will play with the mother even as the child does. He cannot do that with his father.

If this is the scheme of Nature, and it is just as it should be, woman should not have to earn her living. A state of affairs in which women have to work as telegraph clerks, typists or compositors can be, I think, no good, such a people must be bankrupt and living on their capital.

Hence, just as, on the one hand, it is wrong to keep women in ignorance and under suppression, so, on the other, it is a sign of decadence and it is tyrannical to burden them with work which is ordinarily done by men.

There must be provision, therefore, for separate arrangements for the education of women after their attaining a certain age. They should be taught the management of the home, the things they should or should not do during pregnancy, and the nursing and care of children. Drawing up such a scheme presents difficulties. The idea is new. The right course would be to constitute a committee of men and women, of good character and well-informed, who would think further and arrive at conclusions, and ask them to produce a suitable plan for the purpose. . . .

I am convinced that petitioning the Government is not the royal road for correcting all the foregoing deficiencies. The Government cannot change things radically in a day. It is for leaders of the people to take the initiative in such ventures. The British Constitution leaves particular scope for such initiative. If we think that anything can be done only if the Government moves, we are not likely to realize our aims for ages. As they do in England, we must first make experiments and show results before asking the Government to adopt new measures. Whoever finds a deficiency in any field can try to correct it by his own efforts and, after he has succeeded, can move the Government for the desired improvement. For such pioneering ventures, it is necessary to establish a number of special educational bodies.

There is one great obstacle in the way—the lure of degrees. We think our entire life depends on success at examinations. This results in great harm to the people. We forget that a degree is useful only for those who want to go in for Government service. But the edifice of national life is not to be raised on the salaried class. We also see that people are able to earn money quite well even without taking up any service. When those who are almost illiterate can become millionaires by their intelligence and shrewdness, there is no reason why the educated cannot do the same. If the educated would only give up their fear, they could be as capable as the unlettered.

If this lure of degrees could be shaken off, any number of private schools could flourish. No government can provide fully for all the education which the people need. In America, education is mostly a private enterprise. In England, too, private enterprise runs a number of institutions. They give their own certificates.

It will require Herculean efforts to put our education on a sound foundation. We shall have to make sacrifices and dedicate ourselves body, mind and soul to the task.

Speech by Gandhi at Gujarat Educational Conference. *CWMG*, vol. xiv, pp. 8–36.

207. What is education?

The English word 'education' etymologically means 'drawing out'. That means an endeavour to develop our latent talents. The same is the meaning of *kelavani*, the Gujarati word for education. When we say that we develop a certain thing, it does not mean that we change its kind or quality, but that we bring out the qualities latent in it. Hence 'education' can also mean 'unfoldment'.

In this sense, we cannot look upon knowledge of the alphabet as education. This is true even if that knowledge gains us the M.A. degree or enables us to adorn the place of a *shastri* in some *pathshala*** with the requisite knowledge of Sanskrit. It may well be that the highest literary knowledge is a fine instrument for education or unfoldment, but it certainly does not itself constitute education.

True education is something different. Man is made of three constituents, the body, mind and spirit. Of them, spirit is the one permanent element in man. The body and the mind function on account of it. Hence we can call that education which reveals the qualities of spirit. That is why the seal of the Vidyapith carries the dictum 'Education is that which leads to *moksha*.'

Education can also be understood in another sense; that is, whatever leads to a full or maximum development of all the three, the body, mind and spirit, may also be called education. The knowledge that is being imparted today may possibly develop the mind a little, but certainly it does not develop the body and spirit. I have a doubt about the development of the mind too, because it does not mean that the mind has developed if we have filled it with a lot of information. We cannot therefore say that we have educated our mind. A well-educated mind serves man in the desired manner. Our literate mind of today pulls us hither and thither. That is what a wild horse does. Only when a wild horse is broken in can we call it a trained horse. How many 'educated' young men of today are so trained?

Now let us examine our body. Are we supposed to cultivate the body by playing tennis, football or cricket for an hour every day? It does, certainly, build up the body. Like a wild horse, however, the body will be strong but not trained. A trained body is healthy, vigorous and sinewy. The hands and feet can do any desired work. A pick-axe, a shovel, a hammer, etc., are like ornaments to a trained hand and it can wield them. That hand can ply the spinning-wheel well as also the ring and the comb while the feet work a loom. A well-trained body does not get tired in trudging 30 miles. It can scale mountains without getting breathless. Does the student acquire such physical culture? We can assert that modern curricula do not impart physical education in this sense.

The less said about the spirit the better. Only a seer or a seeker can enlighten the soul. Who will awaken that dormant spiritual energy in us all? Teachers can be had through an advertisement. Is there a column for spiritual quest in the testimonials which they have to produce? Even if there is one, what is its value? How can we get through advertisements teachers who are seekers after self-realization? And education without such enlightenment is like a wall without a foundation or, to employ an English saying, like a whited sepulchre. Inside it there is only a corpse eaten up or being eaten by insects.

It is and should be the ideal of the Gujarat Vidyapith* to impart this three-fold education. Even if one young man or woman is brought up in conformity with this ideal, I shall regard the Vidyapith's existence as worth while.

'What is Education?' (G.). *Navajivan*, 28 Feb. 1926

208. Planning a new scheme of education

The propositions I shall submit to the conference* for consideration will be, so far as they occur to me at present, as follows:

1. The present system of education does not meet the requirements of the country in any shape or form. English, having been made the medium of instruction in all the higher branches of learning, hascreated a permanent bar between the highly educated few and the uneducated many. It has prevented knowledge from percolating to the masses. This excessive importance given to English has cast upon the educated class a burden which has maimed them mentally for life and made them strangers in their own land. Absence of vocational training has made the educated class almost unfit for productive work and harmed them physically. Money spent on primary education* is a waste of expenditure inasmuch as what little is taught is soon forgotten and has little or no value in terms of the villages or cities. Such advantage as is gained by the existing system of education is not gained by the chief taxpayer, his children getting the least.

2. The course of primary education should be extended at least to seven years and should include the general knowledge gained up

to the matriculation standard less English and plus a substantial vocation.

3. For the all-round development of boys and girls all training should so far as possible be given through a profit-yielding vocation. In other words vocations should serve a double purpose—to enable the pupil to pay for his tuition through the products of his labour and at the same time to develop the whole man or woman in him or her through the vocation learnt at school.

Land, buildings and equipment are not intended to be covered by the proceeds of the pupil's labour.

All the processes of cotton, wool and silk, commencing from gathering, cleaning, ginning (in the case of cotton), carding, spinning, dyeing, sizing, warp-making, double-twisting, designing and weaving, embroidery, tailoring, paper-making, cutting, book-binding, cabinet-making, toy-making, *gur*-making* are undoubtedly occupations that can easily be learnt and handled without much capital outlay.

This primary education should equip boys and girls to earn their bread, by the State guaranteeing employment in the vocations learnt or by buying their manufactures at prices fixed by the State.

4. Higher education should be left to private enterprise and for meeting national requirements whether in the various industries, technical arts, belles-lettres or fine arts.

The State Universities should be purely examining bodies, self-supporting through the fees charged for examinations.

Universities will look after the whole of the field of education and will prepare and approve courses of studies in the various departments of education. No private school should be run without the previous sanction of the respective Universities. University charters should be given liberally to any body of persons of proved worth and integrity, it being always understood that the Universities will not cost the State anything except that it will bear the cost of running a Central Education Department.

The foregoing scheme does not absolve the State from running such seminaries as may be required for supplying State needs.

It is claimed that if the whole scheme is accepted, it will solve the question of the greatest concern to the State—training of its youth, its future makers.

209. The need for a new scheme of education

22 October 1937

Gandhiji, after thanking all those who had come in response to the invitations, said whether he was there as Chairman or member, he had invited them in order to listen to their opinion and advice on the propositions* he had formulated, especially of those who were opposed to them. He asked for a free, frank and full discussion, as he regretted his inability to meet the friends outside of the pandal for reasons of health.

The propositions, he said, referred both to primary education and college education, but they would largely have to address themselves to a consideration of primary education. He had included secondary in primary education because primary education was the only education so called that was available to a very small fraction of the people in our villages, many of which he had seen during his peregrinations since 1915. He was speaking exclusively about the needs of these rural boys and girls, the bulk of whom were illiterate. He had no experience of college education, though he had come in contact with hundreds of college boys, had heart-to-heart chats and correspondence with them, knew their needs, failings and the disease they suffered from. But they might restrict themselves to a consideration of primary education. For, the moment that primary question was solved the secondary one of college education would also be solved.

He was deliberately of opinion that the present system of primary education was not only wasteful but harmful. Most of the boys were lost to the parents and to the occupation to which they were born. They picked up evil habits, affected urban ways, and got a smattering of something which may be anything else but not education. The remedy, he thought, lay in educating them by means of vocational or manual training. He had some experience of it having trained his own sons and the children on the Tolstoy Farm in South Africa, belonging to all castes and creeds, who were good, bad and indifferent, through some manual training, e.g., carpentry or shoe-making which he had learnt from Kallenbach* who had training in a Trappist monastery. His sons and all these children, he was confident, had lost nothing, though he could not give them an education that either satisfied himself or them, as the time at his disposal was limited and his preoccupations numerous.

The core of his emphasis was not the occupations but education through manual training—all education, of letters, history, geography, mathematics, science, etc., through manual training. It might be objected that in the Middle Ages nothing else was taught. But the occupational training then was far from serving an educational purpose. In this age those born to certain professions had forgotten them, taken to clerical careers, and were lost to the countryside. As a result, go wherever we might, it was impossible to find an efficient carpenter or a smith in an average village. The handicrafts were nearly lost, and the spinning-wheel being neglected was taken to Lancashire where it was developed, thanks to the English genius for developing crafts, to an extent that was to be seen today. This he said irrespective of his views on industrialism.

The remedy lay in imparting the whole art and science of a craft through practical training and therethrough imparting education. Teaching of *takli*-spinning,* for instance, presupposed imparting of knowledge of various varieties of cotton, different soils in different provinces of India, the history of the ruin of the handicraft, its political reasons which would include the history of the British rule in India, knowledge of arithmetic, and so on. He was trying the experiment on his little grandson who scarcely felt that he was being taught, for he all the while played and laughed and sang.

He was specially mentioning the *takli* in order that they might put to him questions about it, and as he had much to do with it, and had seen its power and its romance; also because the handicraft of making cloth was the only one which could be universally taught and because the *takli* required no expense. It had more than proved its worth. The constructive programme, to the extent it had been carried out, had led to the formation of the Congress Ministries* in seven provinces, and their success also would depend on the extent to which we carried it out.

He had contemplated a seven years' course which so far as the *takli* was concerned would culminate in practical knowledge of weaving (including dyeing, designing, etc.). The custom for all the cloth we could produce was there ready.

He was very keen on finding the expenses of the teacher through the product of the manual work of his pupils, as he was convinced that there was no other way to carry education to crores of our children. We could not wait until we had the necessary revenue, until the

Viceroy reduced the military expenditure, and so on. He asked them to remember that this primary education would include the elementary principles of sanitation, hygiene, nutrition, of doing their own work, helping parents at home, etc. The present generation of boys knew no cleanliness, no self-help, and physically were C 3. He would therefore give compulsory physical training through musical drill, etc.

The speaker had been accused of being opposed to literary training. Far from it. He simply wanted to show the *way* in which it should be given. The self-supporting aspect had also been attacked. Whereas, it was said, we should be expending millions on primary education, we were going to exploit the children. It was also feared that there would be enormous waste. This fear was falsified by experience. As for exploiting or burdening the children, he would ask whether it was burdening the child to save him from a disaster. *Takli* was a good enough toy to play with. It was no less a toy because it was a productive toy. Even today children helped their parents to a certain extent. The Segaon children knew the details of agriculture better than he, having worked with their parents on the fields. Whilst the child would be encouraged to spin and help his parents with agricultural jobs, he would also be made to feel that he did not belong only to his parents, but to the village and to the country and that he must make some return to them. That was the only way. He would tell the Ministers that they would make children helpless by doling out education to them. They would make them self-confident and brave by their paying for their own education by their own labour.

This system was to be common to all—Hindus, Mussalmans, Parsis, Christians. Why did he not lay any stress on religious instruction, he was asked. Because he was teaching them practical religion, the religion of self-help.

The State, continued Gandhiji, was bound to find employment, if they needed it, for all the pupils thus trained. As for teachers, Prof. Shah had suggested the method of conscription. He had demonstrated its value by citing instances from Italy and other lands. If Mussolini could impress the youth of Italy for the service of his country, why should not we? Was it fair to label as slavery the compulsory enlistment of service of our youth for a year or longer before they began their career? The youths had contributed a lot to the success of the movement for freedom during the past 17 years, and the speaker would call upon them to freely give a year of their lives to the service of the nation. Legislation, if it was necessary in this respect, would not be compulsion, as it could not be passed without the consent of the majority of our representatives.

Gandhiji would therefore ask them to say whether this imparting of education through manual training appealed to them. For him to make it self-supporting would be a test of its efficiency. The children ought at the end of seven years to be able to pay for their instruction and be earning units.

College education was largely an urban proposition. He would not say that it was an unmitigated failure, as primary education was, but the results were fairly disappointing. Why should any one of the graduates have to be unemployed?

Takli he had proposed as a concrete instance because Vinoba had the largest amount of practical experience in it, and he was there to answer their objections, if any. Kakasaheb would also be able to tell them something, though his experience was more theoretical than practical. He had especially drawn Gandhiji's attention to Armstrong's *Education for Life*, especially the chapter on 'Education of the Hand'. The late Madhusudan Das was a lawyer, but he was convinced that without the use of our hands and feet our brain would be atrophied, and even if it worked it would be the home of Satan. Tolstoy had taught the same lesson through many of his tales.

Gandhiji concluded by inviting the attention of the audience to the very fundamentals of his plan of self-supporting primary education:

We have communal quarrels—not that they are peculiar to us. England had also its Wars of the Roses, and today British Imperialism is the enemy of the world. If we want to eliminate communal strife and international strife, we must start with foundations pure and strong by rearing our younger generation on the education I have adumbrated. That plan springs out of non-violence. I suggested it in connection with the nation's resolve to effect complete prohibition, but I may tell you that even if there was to be no loss of revenue, and our exchequer was full, this education would be a *sine qua non* if we did not want to urbanize our boys. We have to make them true representatives of our culture, our civilization, of the true genius of our nation. We cannot do so otherwise than by giving them a course of self-supporting primary education. Europe is no example for us. It plans its programmes in terms of violence because it believes in violence. I would be the last to minimize the achievement of Russia, but the whole structure is based on force and violence. If India has resolved to eschew violence, this system of education becomes an integral part of the discipline she has to go through. We are told that England expends millions on education, America also does so, but we forget that all that wealth is obtained through exploitation. They have reduced the art of exploitation to a science and might well give their boys the costly education they do. We cannot, will not, think in terms of exploitation, and we have no alternative but this plan of education* which is based on non-violence.

Report on a speech by Gandhi at educational conference, Wardha. *Harijan*, 30 Oct. 1937. *CWMG*, vol. lxvi, pp. 263–6

V · NON-VIOLENCE
AS POLITICAL ACTION

a. The birth of non-violent action*

210. Looking back on the Indian struggle in South Africa

This richly illustrated and important special issue of *Indian Opinion* . . .
has, for the last eleven years, in an unpretentious and humble manner,
endeavoured to serve my countrymen and South Africa, a period
covering the most critical stage that they will, perhaps, ever have to
pass through. It marks the rise and growth of Passive Resistance,
which has attracted world-wide attention. The term does not fit the
activity of the Indian community during the past eight years. Its
equivalent in the vernacular [*Satyagraha*], rendered into English,
means Truth-Force. I think Tolstoy called it also Soul-Force or
Love-Force, and so it is. Carried out to its utmost limit, this force
is independent of pecuniary or other material assistance; certainly,
even in its elementary form, of physical force or violence. Indeed,
violence is the negation of this great spiritual force, which can only
be cultivated or wielded by those who will entirely eschew violence.
It is a force that may be used by individuals as well as by communities.
It may be used as well in political as in domestic affairs. Its universal
applicability is a demonstration of its permanence and invincibility.
It can be used alike by men, women and children.

   It is totally untrue to say that it is a force to be used only by the
weak so long as they are not capable of meeting violence by violence.
This superstition arises from the incompleteness of the English
expression. It is impossible for those who consider themselves to be
weak to apply this force. Only those who realize that there is something in man which is superior to the brute nature in him, and that
the latter always yields to it, can effectively be Passive Resisters. This
force is to violence and, therefore, to all tyranny, all injustice, what
light is to darkness. In politics, its use is based upon the immutable
maxim that government of the people is possible only so long as they
consent either consciously or unconsciously to be governed. We did not

want to be governed by the Asiatic Act of 1907* of the Transvaal, and it had to go before this mighty force. Two courses were open to us—to use violence when we were called upon to submit to the Act, or to suffer the penalties prescribed under the Act, and thus to draw out and exhibit the force of the soul within us for a period long enough to appeal to the sympathetic chord in the governors or the law-makers. We have taken long to achieve what we set about striving for. That was because our Passive Resistance was not of the most complete type.

All Passive Resisters do not understand the full value of the force, nor have we men who always from conviction refrain from violence. The use of this force requires the adoption of poverty, in the sense that we must be indifferent whether we have the wherewithal to feed or clothe ourselves. During the past struggle, all Passive Resisters, if any at all, were not prepared to go to that length. Some again were only Passive Resisters so-called. They came without any conviction, often with mixed motives, less often with impure motives. Some even, whilst engaged in the struggle, would gladly have resorted to violence but for most vigilant supervision. Thus it was that the struggle became prolonged; for the exercise of the purest soul-force, in its perfect form, brings about instantaneous relief. For this exercise, prolonged training of the individual soul is an absolute necessity, so that a perfect Passive Resister has to be almost, if not entirely, a perfect man. We cannot all suddenly become such men, but, if my proposition is correct—as I know it to be correct—the greater the spirit of Passive Resistance in us, the better men we will become. Its use, therefore, is, I think, indisputable, and it is a force which, if it became universal, would revolutionize social ideals and do away with despotisms and the ever-growing militarism under which the nations of the West are groaning and are being almost crushed to death, and which fairly promises to overwhelm even the nations of the East.

If the past struggle has produced even a few Indians who would dedicate themselves to the task of becoming Passive Resisters as nearly perfect as possible, they would not only have served themselves in the truest sense of the term, they would also have served humanity at large. Thus viewed, Passive Resistance is the noblest and the best education. It should come, not after the ordinary education in letters of children, but it should precede it. It will not be denied that a child, before it begins to write its alphabet and to gain worldly knowledge, should know what the soul is, what truth is, what love is, what powers are latent in the soul. It should be an essential of real education that a child should learn that, in the struggle of life, it can easily conquer hate by love, untruth by truth, violence by self-suffering. It was because I felt the force of this truth, that, during the latter part of the struggle, I endeavoured, as much as I could, to train the children at Tolstoy Farm and then at Phoenix along these lines, and one of the reasons for my departure to India* is still further to realize, as I already do in part, my own imperfection as a Passive Resister, and then to try to perfect myself, for I believe that it is in India that the nearest approach to perfection is most possible.

'The Theory and Practice of Passive Resistance'. *Indian Opinion, Golden Number*, 1 Dec. 1914

211. The significance of the South African non-violent struggle

27 July 1916

In brief, the significance of *satyagraha* consists in the quest for a principle of life. We did not say to anyone in so many words that our fight was in pursuance of this quest. If we had said so, the people there would only have laughed at us. We only made known the secondary aim of our movement, which was that the Government there, thinking us lowly and mean, was making laws to oust us from the country, and that it was right for us to defy these laws and show that we were brave. Suppose the Government passes a law saying that coloured persons shall wear yellow caps; in fact, a law of this kind was made in Rome for the Jews. If the Government intended to treat us in a similar fashion and made a law that appeared to humiliate us, it was for us to make it clear to the Government that we would not obey such a law. If a child says to his father: 'Please put on your turban the wrong side up for me', the father understands that the child wants to have a laugh at his expense and at once obeys the command. But when someone else, with uncharitable motives, says the same thing, he clearly answers, 'Look, brother, so long as my head is on my shoulders, you cannot humiliate me in this manner. You conquer my head first and then make me wear my turban in any fashion you please.'

The Government there in a similar way, thinking the Indians lowly, wanted to treat them as slaves and as far as possible to prevent their coming into the country. And with this end in view, it began inventing ever new laws, such as putting names of Indians in a separate register, making them give finger-prints in the manner of thieves and bandits, forcing them to live in particular areas, forbidding their movement beyond a specified boundary, making rules for them to walk on particular foot-paths and board specified carriages in trains, treating their wives as concubines if they could not produce marriage certificates, levying from them an annual tax of forty-five rupees per capita, etc., etc. Often a disease manifests itself in the body in various forms. The disease in this case, as has been explained, was the evil purpose of the Government of South Africa, and all the rules and regulations mentioned above were the various forms that it took. We, therefore, had to prepare ourselves to fight against these.

There are two ways of countering injustice. One way is to smash the head of the man who perpetrates injustice and to get your own head smashed in the process. All strong people in the world adopt this course. Everywhere wars are fought and millions of people are killed. The consequence is not the progress of a nation but its decline. Soldiers returning from the front have become so bereft of reason that they indulge in various anti-social activities. One does not have to go far for examples. In the Boer War, when the British won a victory at Mafeking,* the whole of England, and London in particular, went so mad with joy that for days on end everyone did nothing but dance night and day! They freely indulged in wickednesses and rowdyism and did not leave a single bar with a drop of liquor in it. *The Times*, commenting, said that no words could describe the way those few days were spent, that all that could be said was that 'the English nation went amafficking . . . '. Pride makes a victorious nation bad-tempered. It falls into luxurious ways of living. Then for a time, it may be conceded, peace prevails. But after a short while, it comes more and more to be realized that the seeds of war have not been destroyed but have become a thousand times more nourished and mighty. No country has ever become, or will ever become, happy through victory in war. A nation does not rise that way, it only falls further. In fact, what comes to it is defeat, not victory. And if, perchance, either our act or our purpose was ill-conceived, it brings disaster to both belligerents.

But through the other method of combating injustice, we alone suffer the consequences of our mistakes, and the other side is wholly spared. This other method is *satyagraha*. One who resorts to it does not have to break another's head; he may merely have his own head broken. He has to be prepared to die himself suffering all the pain. In opposing the atrocious laws of the Government of South Africa, it was this method that we adopted. We made it clear to the said Government that we would never bow to its outrageous laws. No clapping is possible without two hands to do it, and no quarrel without two persons to make it. Similarly, no State is possible without two entities, the rulers and the ruled. You are our sovereign, our Government, only so long as we consider ourselves your subjects. When we are not subjects, you are not the sovereign either. So long as it is your endeavour to control us with justice and love, we will let you do so. But if you wish to strike at us from behind, we cannot permit it. Whatever you do in other matters, you will have to ask our opinion about the laws that concern us. If you make laws to keep us suppressed in a wrongful manner and without taking us into confidence, these laws will merely adorn the statute-books. We will never obey them. Award us for it what punishment you like, we will put up with it. Send us to prison and we will live there as in a paradise. Ask us to mount the scaffold and we will do so laughing. Shower what sufferings you like upon us, we will calmly endure all and not hurt a hair of your body. We will gladly die and will not so much as touch you. But so long as there is yet life in these our bones, we will never comply with your arbitrary laws.

It all began on a Sunday evening in Johannesburg when I sat on a hillock with another gentleman called Hemchandra. The memory of that day is so vivid that it might have been yesterday. At my side lay a Government *Gazette*. It contained the several clauses of the law concerning Indians. As I read it, I shook with rage. What did the Government take us for? Then and there I produced a translation of that portion of the *Gazette* which contained the said laws and wrote under it: 'I will never let these laws govern me.' This was at once sent for publication to *Indian Opinion* at Phoenix. I did not dream at the time that even a single Indian would be capable of the unprecedented heroism the Indians revealed or that the *satyagraha* movement would gain the momentum it did.

Immediately, I made my view known to fellow-Indians and many of them declared their readiness for *satyagraha*. In the first conflict, people took part under the impression that our aim would be gained after only a few days of suffering. In the second conflict, there were only a very few people to begin with but later many more came along. Afterwards when, on the visit of Mr Gokhale,* the Government of South Africa pledged itself to a settlement, the fight ceased. Later, the Government treacherously refused to honour its pledge; on which a third *satyagraha* battle became necessary. Gokhale at that time asked me how many people I thought would take part in the *satyagraha*. I wrote saying they would be between 30 and 60. But I could not find even that number. Only 16 of us took up the challenge. We were firmly decided that so long as the Government did not repeal its atrocious laws or make some settlement, we would accept every penalty but would not submit. We had never hoped that we should find many fellow-fighters. But the readiness of one person without self-interest to offer himself for the cause of truth and country always has its effect. Soon there were twenty thousand people in the movement. There was no room for them in the prisons, and the blood of India boiled. Many people say that if Lord Hardinge* had not intervened, a compromise would have been impossible. But these people forget to ask themselves why it was that Lord Hardinge intervened. The sufferings of the Canadian Indians were far greater than those of the South African Indians. Why did he not use his good offices there? Where the spiritual might of thousands of men and women has been mustered, where innumerable men and women are eager to lay down their lives, what indeed is impossible? There was no other course open for Lord Hardinge than to offer mediation and he only showed his wisdom in adopting it.

What transpired later is well known to you: the Government of South Africa was compelled to come to terms with us. All of which goes to show that we can gain everything without hurting anybody and through soul-force or *satyagraha* alone. He who fights with arms has to depend on arms and on support from others. He has to turn from the straight path and seek tortuous tracks. The course that a *satyagrahi* adopts in his fight is straight and he need look to no one for help. He can, if necessary, fight by himself alone. In that case, it is true, the outcome will be somewhat delayed. If I had not found as many comrades in the South African fight as I did, all that would have happened is that you would not have seen me here in your midst today. Perhaps all my life would have had to be spent in the struggle there. But what of that? The gain that has been secured would only have been a little late in coming. For the battle of *satyagraha* one only needs to prepare oneself. We have to have strict self-control. If it is necessary for this preparation to live in forests and caves, we should do so.

The time that may be taken up in this preparation should not be considered wasted. Christ, before he went out to serve the world, spent forty days in the wilderness, preparing himself for his mission. Buddha too spent many years in such preparation. Had Christ and Buddha not undergone this preparation, they would not have been what they were. Similarly, if we want to put this body in the service of truth and humanity, we must first raise our soul by developing virtues like celibacy, non-violence and truth. Then alone may we say that we are fit to render real service to the country.

In brief, the aim of the *satyagraha* struggle was to infuse manliness in cowards and to develop the really human virtues, and its field was the passive resistance against the Government of South Africa.

Speech on 'The Secret of *Satyagraha* in South Africa', Satyagraha Ashram, Ahmedabad (H.). Ramchandra Varma, *Mahatma Gandhi*. *EWMG*, pp. 303–8

212. *Satyagraha*—not 'passive resistance'

*c.*2 September 1917

The force denoted by the term 'passive resistance' and translated into Hindi as *nishkriya pratirodha* is not very accurately described either by the original English phrase or by its Hindi rendering. Its correct description is '*satyagraha*'. *Satyagraha* was born in South Africa in 1908. There was no word in any Indian language denoting the power which our countrymen in South Africa invoked for the redress of their grievances. There was an English equivalent, namely, 'passive resistance', and we carried on with it. However, the need for a word to describe this unique power came to be increasingly felt, and it was decided to award a prize to anyone who could think of an appropriate term. A Gujarati-speaking gentleman* submitted the word '*satyagraha*', and it was adjudged the best.

'Passive resistance' conveyed the idea of the Suffragette Movement in England. Burning of houses by these women was called 'passive resistance' and so also their fasting in prison. All such acts might very well be 'passive resistance' but they were not '*satyagraha*'. It is said of 'passive resistance' that it is the weapon of the weak, but the power which is the subject of this article can be used only by the strong. This power is not 'passive' resistance; indeed it calls for intense activity. The movement in South Africa was not passive but active. The Indians of South Africa believed that Truth was their object, that Truth ever triumphs, and with this definiteness of purpose they persistently held on to Truth. They put up with all the suffering that this persistence implied. With the conviction that Truth is not to be renounced even unto death, they shed the fear of death. In the cause of Truth, the prison was a palace to them and its doors the gateway to freedom.

Satyagraha is not physical force. A *satyagrahi* does not inflict pain on the adversary; he does not seek his destruction. A *satyagrahi* never resorts to firearms. In the use of *satyagraha*, there is no ill-will whatever.

Satyagraha is pure soul-force. Truth is the very substance of the soul. That is why this force is called *satyagraha*. The soul is informed with knowledge. In it burns the flame of love. If someone gives us pain through ignorance, we shall win him through love. . . . Non-violence is a dormant state. In the waking state, it is love. Ruled by love, the world goes on. In English there is a saying, 'Might is Right'. Then there is the doctrine of the survival of the fittest. Both these ideas are contradictory to the above principle. Neither is wholly true. If ill-will were the chief motive-force, the world would have been destroyed long ago; and neither would I have had the opportunity to write this article nor would the hopes of the readers be fulfilled. We are alive solely because of love. We are all ourselves the proof of this. Deluded by modern Western civilization, we have forgotten our ancient civilization and worship the might of arms.

We forget the principle of non-violence, which is the essence of all religions. The doctrine of arms stands for irreligion. It is due to the sway of that doctrine that a sanguinary war* is raging in Europe.

'*Satyagraha*—not Passive Resistance' (H.). Ramchandra Varma, *Mahatma Gandhi. EWMG*, pp. 308–9

213. A competition to find the name

Events were so shaping themselves in Johannesburg as to make this self-purification* on my part a preliminary as it were to *Satyagraha*.

I can now see that all the principal events of my life, culminating in the vow of *brahmacharya*, were secretly preparing me for it. The principle called *Satyagraha* came into being before the name was invented. Indeed when it was born, I myself could not say what it was. In Gujarati also we used the English phrase 'passive resistance' to describe it. When in a meeting of Europeans I found that the term 'passive resistance' was too narrowly construed, that it was supposed to be a weapon of the weak, that it could be characterized by hatred, and that it could finally manifest itself as violence, I had to demur to all these statements and explain the real nature of the Indian movement. It was clear that a new word must be coined by the Indians to designate their struggle.

But I could not for the life of me find out a new name, and therefore offered a nominal prize through *Indian Opinion* to the reader who made the best suggestion on the subject. As a result Maganlal Gandhi* coined the word Sadagraha (*Sat*: truth, *Agraha*: firmness) and won the prize. But in order to make it clearer I changed the word to *Satyagraha* which has since become current in Gujarati as a designation for the struggle.

Gandhi, *An Autobiography*, part IV, chap. XXVI

b. The essence of *satyagraha*

214. *Satyagraha* and Indian self-rule

CHAPTER XVII. *SATYAGRAHA* — SOUL-FORCE

READER. Is there any historical evidence as to the success of what you have called soul-force or truth-force? No instance seems to have happened of any nation having risen through soul-force. I still think that evil-doers will not cease doing evil without physical punishment.

EDITOR. The poet Tulsidas* has said: 'Of religion, pity, or love, is the root, as egotism of the body. Therefore, we should not abandon pity so long as we are alive.' This appears to me to be a scientific truth. I believe in it as much as I believe in two and two being four. The force of love is the same as the force of the soul or truth. We have evidence of its working at every step. The universe would disappear without the existence of that force. But you ask for historical evidence.

It is, therefore, necessary to know what history means. The Gujarati equivalent means: 'It so happened.'* If that is the meaning of history, it is possible to give copious evidence. But, if it means the doings of kings and emperors, there can be no evidence of soul-force or passive resistance in such history. You cannot expect silver ore in a tin mine.

History, as we know it, is a record of the wars of the world, and so there is a proverb among Englishmen that a nation which has no history, that is, no wars, is a happy nation. How kings played, how they became enemies of one another, how they murdered one another, is found accurately recorded in history, and if this were all that had happened in the world, it would have been ended long ago. If the story of the universe had commenced with wars, not a man would have been found alive today. Those people who have been warred against have disappeared as, for instance, the natives of Australia of whom hardly a man was left alive by the intruders. Mark, please, that these natives did not use soul-force in self-defence, and it does not require much foresight to know that the Australians will share the same fate as their victims. 'Those that take the sword shall perish by the sword.'* With us the proverb is that professional swimmers will find a watery grave.

The fact that there are so many men still alive in the world shows that it is based not on the force of arms but on the force of truth or love. Therefore, the greatest and most unimpeachable evidence of the success of this force is to be found in the fact that, in spite of the wars of the world, it still lives on. Thousands, indeed tens of thousands, depend for their existence on a very active working of this force. Little quarrels of millions of families in their daily lives disappear before the exercise of this force. Hundreds of nations live in peace. History does not and cannot take note of this fact. History is really a record of every interruption of the even working of the force of love or of the soul. Two brothers quarrel; one of them repents and re-awakens the love that was lying dormant in him; the two again begin to live in peace; nobody takes note of this. But if the two brothers, through the intervention of solicitors or some other reason take up arms or go to law—which is another form of the exhibition of brute force—their doings would be immediately noticed in the Press, they would be the talk of their neighbours and would probably go down to history. And what is true of families and communities is true of nations. There is no reason to believe that there is one law for families and another for nations. History, then, is a record of an interruption of the course of nature. Soul-force, being natural, is not noted in history.

READER. According to what you say, it is plain that instances of this kind of passive resistance are not to be found in history. It is necessary to understand this passive resistance more fully. It will be better, therefore, if you enlarge upon it.

EDITOR. *Satyagraha* is referred to in English as passive resistance. Passive resistance is a method of securing rights by personal suffering; it is the reverse of resistance by arms. When I refuse to do a thing that is repugnant to my conscience, I use soul-force. For instance, the Government of the day has passed a law which is applicable to me. I do not like it. If by using violence I force the Government to repeal the law, I am employing what may be termed body-force. If I do not obey the law and accept the penalty for its breach, I use soul-force. It involves sacrifice of self.

Everybody admits that sacrifice of self is infinitely superior to sacrifice of others. Moreover, if this kind of force is used in a cause that is unjust, only the person using it suffers. He does not make others suffer for his mistakes. Men have before now done many things which were subsequently found to have been wrong. No man can claim that he is absolutely in the right or that a particular thing is wrong because he thinks so, but it is wrong for him so long as that is his deliberate judgement. It is therefore meet that he should not do that which he knows to be wrong, and suffer the consequence whatever it may be. This is the key to the use of soul-force.

READER. You would then disregard laws—this is rank disloyalty. We have always been considered a law-abiding nation. You seem to be going even beyond the extremists. They say that we must obey the laws that have been passed, but that if the laws be bad, we must drive out the law-givers even by force.

EDITOR. Whether I go beyond them or whether I do not is a matter of no consequence to either of us. We simply want to find out what is right and to act accordingly. The real meaning of the statement that we are a law-abiding nation is that we are passive resisters. When we do not like certain laws, we do not break the heads of law-givers but we suffer and do not submit to the laws. That we should obey laws whether good or bad is a new-fangled notion.* There was no such thing in former days. The people disregarded those laws they did not like and suffered the penalties for their breach. It is contrary to our manhood if we obey laws repugnant to our conscience. Such teaching is opposed to religion and means slavery. If the Government were to ask us to go about without any clothing, should we do so? If I were a passive resister, I would say to them that I would have nothing to do with their law. But we have so forgotten ourselves and become so compliant that we do not mind any degrading law.

A man who has realized his manhood, who fears only God, will fear no one else. Man-made laws are not necessarily binding on him. Even the Government does not expect any such thing from us. They do not say: 'You must do such and such a thing', but they say: 'If you do not do it, we will punish you.' We are sunk so low that we fancy that it is our duty and our religion to do what the law lays down. If man will only realize that it is unmanly to obey laws that are unjust, no man's tyranny will enslave him. This is the key to self-rule or home rule.

It is a superstition and ungodly thing to believe that an act of a majority binds a minority. Many examples can be given in which acts of majorities will be found to have been wrong and those of minorities to have been right. All reforms owe their origin to the initiation of minorities in opposition to majorities. If among a band of robbers a knowledge of robbing is obligatory, is a pious man to accept the obligation? So long as the superstition that men should obey unjust laws exists, so long will their slavery exist. And a passive resister alone can remove such a superstition.

To use brute-force, to use gunpowder, is contrary to passive resistance, for it means that we want our opponent to do by force that which we desire but he does not. And if such a use of force is justifiable, surely he is entitled to do likewise by us. And so we should never come to an agreement. We may simply fancy, like the blind horse moving in a circle round a mill, that we are making progress. Those who believe that they are not bound to obey laws which are repugnant to their conscience have only the remedy of passive resistance open to them. Any other must lead to disaster.

READER. From what you say I deduce that passive resistance is a splendid weapon of the weak, but that when they are strong they may take up arms.

EDITOR. This is gross ignorance. Passive resistance, that is, soul-force, is matchless. It is superior to the force of arms. How, then, can it be considered only a weapon of the weak? Physical-force men are strangers to the courage that is requisite in a passive resister. Do you believe that a coward can ever disobey a law that he dislikes? Extremists are considered to be advocates of brute force. Why do they, then, talk about obeying laws? I do not blame them. They can say nothing else. When they succeed in driving out the English and they themselves become governors, they will want you and me to obey their laws. And that is a fitting thing for their constitution. But a passive resister will say he will not obey a law that is against his conscience, even though he may be blown to pieces at the mouth of a cannon.

What do you think? Wherein is courage required—in blowing others to pieces from behind a cannon, or with a smiling face to approach a cannon and be blown to pieces? Who is the true warrior—he who keeps death always as a bosom-friend, or he who controls the death of others? Believe me that a man devoid of courage and manhood can never be a passive resister.

This, however, I will admit: that even a man weak in body is capable of offering this resistance. One man can offer it just as well as millions. Both men and women can indulge in it. It does not require the training of an army; it needs no jiu-jitsu. Control over the mind is alone necessary, and when that is attained, man is free like the king of the forest and his very glance withers the enemy.

Passive resistance is an all-sided sword, it can be used anyhow; it blesses him who uses it and him against whom it is used. Without drawing a drop of blood it produces far-reaching results. It never rusts and cannot be stolen. Competition between passive resisters does not exhaust. The sword of passive resistance does not require a scabbard. It is strange indeed that you should consider such a weapon to be a weapon merely of the weak.

READER. You have said that passive resistance is a speciality of India. Have cannons never been used in India?

EDITOR. Evidently, in your opinion, India means its few princes. To me it means its teeming millions on whom depends the existence of its princes and our own.

Kings will always use their kingly weapons. To use force is bred in them. They want to command, but those who have to obey commands do not want guns: and these are in a majority throughout the world. They have to learn either body-force or soul-force. Where they learn the former, both the rulers and the ruled become like so many madmen; but where they learn soul-force, the commands of the rulers do not go beyond the point of their swords, for true men disregard unjust commands. Peasants have never been subdued by the sword, and never will be. They do not know the use of the sword, and they are not frightened by the use of it by others. That nation is great which rests its head upon death as its pillow. Those who defy death are free from all fear. For those who are labouring under the delusive charms of brute-force, this picture is not overdrawn. The fact is that, in India, the nation at large has generally used passive resistance in all departments of life. We cease to co-operate with our rulers when they displease us. This is passive resistance.

I remember an instance when, in a small principality, the villagers were offended by some command issued by the prince. The former immediately began vacating the village. The prince became nervous, apologized to his subjects and withdrew his command. Many such instances can be found in India. Real Home Rule is possible only where passive resistance is the guiding force of the people. Any other rule is foreign rule.

READER. Then you will say that it is not at all necessary for us to train the body?

EDITOR. I will certainly not say any such thing. It is difficult to become a passive resister unless the body is trained. As a rule, the mind, residing in a body that has become weakened by pampering, is also weak, and where there is no strength of mind there can be no strength of soul. We shall have to improve our physique by getting rid of infant marriages and luxurious living. If I were to ask a man with a shattered body to face a cannon's mouth, I should make a laughing-stock of myself.

READER. From what you say, then, it would appear that it is not a small thing to become a passive resister, and, if that is so, I should like you to explain how a man may become one.

EDITOR. To become a passive resister is easy enough but it is also equally difficult. I have known a lad of fourteen years become a passive resister; I have known also sick people do likewise; and I have also known physically strong and otherwise happy people unable to take up passive resistance. After a great deal of experience it seems to me that those who want to become passive resisters for the service of the country have to observe perfect chastity, adopt poverty, follow truth, and cultivate fearlessness.

Chastity is one of the greatest disciplines without which the mind cannot attain requisite firmness. A man who is unchaste loses stamina, becomes emasculated and cowardly. He whose mind is given over to animal passions is not capable of any great effort. This can be proved by innumerable instances. What, then, is a married person to do is the question that arises naturally; and yet it need not. When a husband and wife gratify the passions, it is no less an animal indulgence on that account. Such an indulgence, except for perpetuating the race, is strictly prohibited. But a passive resister has to avoid even that very limited indulgence because he can have no desire for progeny. A married man, therefore, can observe perfect chastity. This subject is not capable of being treated at greater length. Several questions arise: How is one to carry one's wife with one, what are her rights, and other similar questions. Yet those who wish to take part in a great work are bound to solve these puzzles.

Just as there is necessity for chastity, so is there for poverty. Pecuniary ambition and passive resistance cannot well go together. Those who have money are not expected to throw it away, but they *are* expected to be indifferent about it. They must be prepared to lose every penny rather than give up passive resistance.

Passive resistance has been described in the course of our discussion as truth-force. Truth, therefore, has necessarily to be followed and that at any cost. In this connection, academic questions such as whether a man may not lie in order to save a life, etc., arise, but these questions occur only to those who wish to justify lying. Those who want to follow truth every time are not placed in such a quandary; and if they are, they are still saved from a false position.

Passive resistance cannot proceed a step without fearlessness. Those alone can follow the path of passive resistance who are free from fear, whether as to their possessions, false honour, their relatives, the government, bodily injuries or death.

These observances are not to be abandoned in the belief that they are difficult. Nature has implanted in the human breast ability to cope with any difficulty or suffering that may come to man unprovoked. These qualities are worth having, even for those who do not wish to serve the country. Let there be no mistake, as those who want to train themselves in the use of arms are also obliged to have these qualities more or less. Everybody does not become a warrior for the wish. A would-be warrior will have to observe chastity and to be satisfied with poverty as his lot. A warrior without fearlessness cannot be conceived of. It may be thought that he would not need to be exactly truthful, but that quality follows real fearlessness. When a man abandons truth, he does so owing to fear in some shape or form. The above four attributes, then, need not frighten anyone. It may be as well here to note that a physical-force man has to have many other useless qualities which a passive resister never needs. And you will find that whatever extra effort a swordsman needs is due to lack of fearlessness. If he is an embodiment of the latter, the sword will drop from his hand that very moment. He does not need its support. One who is free from hatred requires no sword. A man with a stick suddenly came face to face with a lion and instinctively raised his weapon in self-defence. The man saw that he had only prated about fearlessness when there was none in him. That moment he dropped the stick and found himself free from all fear.

Gandhi, *Hind Swaraj*

215. The essential law of *satyagraha*

25 April 1919

I feel that the time has now arrived to examine the meaning of *satyagraha*. The word was newly coined some years ago, but the principle which it denotes is as ancient as time. This is the literal meaning of *satyagraha*—insistence on truth, and force derivable from such insistence. In the present movement,* we are making use of *satyagraha* as a force: that is to say, in order to cure the evil in the shape of the Rowlatt legislation, we have been making use of the force generated by *satyagraha*, that is, insistence on truth. One of the axioms of religion is, there is no religion other than truth. Another is, religion is love. And as there can be only one religion, it follows that truth is love and love is truth. We shall find too, on further reflection, that conduct based on truth is impossible without love. Truth-force then is love-force. We cannot remedy evil by harbouring ill-will against the evil-doer. This is not difficult of comprehension. It is easy enough to understand. In thousands of our acts, the propelling power is truth or love. The relations between father and son, husband and wife, indeed our family relations are largely guided by truth or love. And we therefore consciously or unconsciously apply *satyagraha* in regulating these relations.

If we were to cast a retrospective glance over our past life, we would find that out of a thousand of our acts affecting our families, in nine hundred and ninety-nine we were dominated by truth, that in our deeds, it is not right to say we generally resort to untruth or ill-will. It is only where a conflict of interests arises, then arise the progeny of untruth, viz., anger, ill-will, etc., and then we see nothing but poison in our midst. A little hard thinking will show us that the standard that we apply to the regulation of domestic relations is the standard that should be applied to regulate the relations between rulers and the ruled, and between man and man. Those men and women who do not recognize the domestic tie are considered to be very like brutes or barbarous, even though they in form have the human body. They have never known the law of *satyagraha*. Those who recognize the domestic tie and its obligations have to a certain extent gone beyond that brute stage. But if challenged, they would say 'what do we care though the whole universe may perish so long as we guard the family interest?' The measure of their *satyagraha*, therefore, is less than that of a drop in the ocean.

When men and women have gone a stage further, they would extend the law of love, i.e., *satyagraha*, from the family to the village. A still further stage away from the brute life is reached when the law of *satyagraha* is applied to provincial life, and the people inhabiting a province regulate their relations by love rather than by hatred. And when as in Hindustan we recognize the law of *satyagraha* as a binding force even between province and province and the millions of Hindustan treat one another as brothers and sisters, we have advanced a stage further still from the brute nature.

In modern times, in no part of the earth have the people gone beyond the nation stage in the application of *satyagraha*. In reality, however, there need be no reason for the clashing of interest between nation and nation, thus arresting the operation of the great law. If we were not in the habit generally of giving no thought to our daily conduct, if we did not accept local custom and habit as matters of course, as we accept the current coin, we would immediately perceive that to the extent that we bear ill-will towards other nations or show disregard at all for life, to that extent we disregard the law of *satyagraha* or love, and to that extent we are still not free from the brute nature. But there is no religion apart from that which enables us entirely to rid ourselves of the brute nature. All religious sects and divisions, all churches and temples, are useful only so long as they serve as a means towards enabling us to recognize the universality of *satyagraha*. In India we have been trained from ages past in this teaching and hence it is that we are taught to consider the whole universe as one family. I do wish to submit as a matter of experience that it is not only possible to live the full national life, by rendering obedience to the law of *satyagraha*, but that the fullness of national life is impossible without *satyagraha*, i.e., without a life of true religion. That nation which wars against another has to an extent disregarded the great law of life. I shall never abandon the faith I have that India is capable of delivering this truth to the whole world, and I wish that all Indians, men and women, whether they are Hindus or Mahomedans, Parsis, Christians or Jews, will share with me this unquenchable faith.

'*Satyagraha*: Its Significance'. *Satyagraha* Leaflet Series, No. 6. *EWMG*, pp. 315–17

216. Essentials of *satyagraha*

25 January 1920

I have drawn the distinction between passive resistance as understood and practised in the West and *satyagraha* before I had evolved the doctrine of the latter to its full logical and spiritual extent. I often used 'passive resistance' and '*satyagraha*' as synonymous terms: but as the doctrine of *satyagraha* developed, the expression 'passive resistance' ceases even to be synonymous, as passive resistance has admitted of violence as in the case of suffragettes and has been universally acknowledged to be a weapon of the weak. Moreover passive resistance does not necessarily involve complete adherence to truth under every circumstance. Therefore it is different from *satyagraha* in three essentials: *Satyagraha* is a weapon of the strong; it admits of no violence under any circumstance whatever; and it ever insists upon truth. I think I have now made the distinction perfectly clear.

Letter to an unknown correspondent. SN 7071. *EWMG*, p. 318

c. Appropriate behaviour for *satyagrahis*

217. Conditions for becoming a *satyagrahi*

The *satyagraha* campaign in the Transvaal* has lasted so long and has been so conducted that we have been able to see—learn—a great many things from it. Many have had personal experience of it. This much at least has been realized by everyone—that, in a struggle of this kind, there is no room for defeat. If, on any occasion, we fail, we shall discover that the failure was due to some deficiency in the *satyagrahi* and did not argue the inefficacy of *satyagraha* as such. The point needs to be carefully grasped. No such rule can be applied to physical fighting. When two armies engage in such fighting, the defeat of either will not necessarily be the result of the inferior fighting quality of the troops. The combatants may have a high morale, and yet, insufficiency in other matters may lead to defeat. For instance, one side may have better arms than the other, or may be favourably placed in the battle-field, or may command superior technical skill. There are many such extraneous factors which account for the victory or defeat of the parties to a physical fight. But such factors offer no difficulties to those fighting the battle of *satyagraha*. Their deficiency alone can come in their way. Moreover, in the usual kind of fighting, all the members of the losing side should be deemed to have been defeated, and in fact they do think that way. In *satyagraha*, the victory of a single member may be taken to mean the victory of all, but the defeat of the side as a whole does not spell defeat for the person who has not himself yielded. For instance, in the Transvaal fight, even if a majority of Indians were to submit to the obnoxious Act, he who remains unyielding will be victorious indeed, for the fact remains that he has not yielded.

That being so, it is necessary to inquire as to who can offer so admirable a battle—one which admits of no defeat—which can have only one result. The inquiry will enable us to understand some of the results of the Transvaal campaign, and to decide how and by whom a campaign of this kind can be fought elsewhere or on some other occasion.

If we inquire into the meaning of *satyagraha*, we find that the first condition is that anyone who wants to engage in this kind of fighting should show a special regard for truth—should have the strength that flows from truthfulness. That is to say, such a man should depend on truth alone. . . . It is absurd to suggest that *satyagraha* is being resorted to only by those who are deficient in physical strength or who, finding physical strength unavailing, can think of no alternative but *satyagraha*. Those who hold such a view, it may be said, do not know what this fight means. *Satyagraha* is more potent than physical strength, which is as worthless as straw when compared with the former. Essentially, physical strength means that a man of such strength fights on the battle-field with little regard for his body, that is to say, he knows no fear. A *satyagrahi*, on his part, gives no thought whatever to his body. Fear cannot touch him at all. That is why he does not arm himself with any material weapons, but continues resistance till the end without fear of death. This means that the *satyagrahi* should have more courage than the man who relies on physical strength. Thus, the first thing necessary for a *satyagrahi* is pursuit of truth, faith in truth.

He must be indifferent to wealth. Wealth and truth have always been in conflict with each other, and will remain so till the end of time. We have found from many examples of Indians in the Transvaal that he who clings to wealth cannot be loyal to truth. This does not mean that a *satyagrahi* can have no wealth. He can, but he cannot make his wealth his God. Money is welcome if one can have it consistently with one's pursuit of truth; otherwise one must not hesitate even for a moment to sacrifice it as if it were no more than dirt on one's hand. No one who has not cultivated such an attitude can practise *satyagraha*. Moreover, in a land where one is obliged to offer *satyagraha* against the rulers, it is not likely that the *satyagrahi* will be able to own wealth. The power of a king may be unavailing against an individual. But it can touch his property, or play on his fear of losing it. The king bends the subjects to his will by threatening them with loss of property or physical harm. Therefore, under the rule of a tyrannical king, for the most part, it is only those who make themselves accomplices in his tyranny who can retain or amass wealth. Since a *satyagrahi* cannot allow himself to be an accomplice in tyranny, he must, in such circumstances, be content to think himself rich in his poverty. If he owns any wealth, he must hold it in some other country.

A *satyagrahi* is obliged to break away from family attachments. This is very difficult to do. But the practice of *satyagraha*, if *satyagraha* is to be worthy of its name, is like walking on the edge of a sword. In the long run, even the breaking away from family attachments will prove beneficial to the family. For, the members of the family will come to feel the call for *satyagraha*, and those who have felt such a call will have no other desire left. When faced with suffering of any kind—loss of wealth or imprisonment—one need not be concerned about the future of one's family. He who has given us teeth will provide us with food to eat. If He provides for such dangerous creatures as the snake, the scorpion, the tiger and the wolf, He is not likely to be unmindful of mankind. It is not a pound of millets or a handful of corn that we hanker after, but the delights of the palate; not just the clothes that we need to enable us to bear cold, but garments of brocaded silk. If we abandon all this restless craving, there will hardly be any need for anxiety as to the means for maintaining one's family.

In this connection, it is worth while to bear in mind that many of these things have to be sacrificed even if physical force is resorted to. One is obliged to suffer hunger and thirst, to bear heat and cold, to sacrifice family bonds, to put up with pecuniary loss. The Boers went through all this when they resorted to physical force. The one great difference between the physical resistance that they offered and our resistance based on truth is that the game they played was in the nature of a gamble. Physical strength, moreover, has made them proud. Their partial success made them forgetful of their former condition. Having fought with deadly arms against a deadly enemy, they are bearing hard upon us as deadly tyrants. When a *satyagrahi* wins in battle, his success cannot but be beneficial to him and to others. A *satyagrahi*, if he is to remain loyal to truth, can never be a tyrant.

. This inquiry, then, leads at last to the conclusion that he alone can offer *satyagraha* who has true faith in religion. 'The name of Rama on the lips, and a dagger under the arm'*—that is no faith. It is no religion to speak in its name and to do exactly the opposite of what it teaches. But anyone who has true religion and faith in him can offer *satyagraha*. In other words, he who leaves everything to God can never know defeat in this world. Such men are not defeated in fact simply because people say that they are defeated. So also one cannot claim success simply because people believe that one has succeeded. There can be no arguing about this; if you know the difference, you know it, else you don't.

This is the real nature of *satyagraha*. The Transvaal Indians have partially understood it. Having done so, they have been faithful to it in practice, again partially. Even so, we have been able to taste its priceless sweetness. He who has sacrificed everything for *satyagraha* has gained everything, for he lives in contentment. Contentment is happiness. Who has ever known any happiness other than this? Every other kind of happiness is but a mirage. The nearer we approach it, the farther it recedes.

We hope that every Indian will think of the matter this way and make himself a *satyagrahi*. If we learn the use of the weapon of *satyagraha*, we can employ it to overcome all hardships originating from injustice. It is not here in South Africa alone that the weapon is useful; it will be more so in our home-country. Only we must know its true nature, which is easy to do, and yet difficult. Men of great physical strength are rare. Rarer still must be those who derive their strength from truth.

'Who Can Offer *Satyagraha*?' (G.). *Indian Opinion*, 29 May 1909

218. Instructions for *satyagrahis*

17 April 1918

1. The volunteers must remember that, as this is a *satyagraha* campaign,* they must abide by truth under all circumstances.

2. In *satyagraha*, there can be no room for rancour; which means that a *satyagrahi* should utter no harsh word about anyone, from a *ravania* to the Governor himself; if someone does so, it is the volunteer's duty to stop him.

3. Rudeness has no place in *satyagraha*. Perfect courtesy must be shown even to those who may look upon us as their enemies and the villagers must be taught to do the same. Rudeness may harm our cause and the struggle may be unduly prolonged. The volunteers should give the most serious attention to this matter and think out in their minds as many examples as possible of the advantages accruing from courtesy and the disadvantages resulting from rudeness and explain them to the people.

4. The volunteers must remember that this is a holy war. We embarked upon it because, had we not, we would have failed in

our *dharma*. And so all the rules which are essential for living a religious life must be observed here too.

5. We are opposing the intoxication of power, that is, the blind application of law, and not authority as such. The difference must never be lost sight of. It is, therefore, our duty to help the officers in their other work.

6. We are to apply here the same principle that we follow in a domestic quarrel. We should think of the Government and the people as constituting a large family and act accordingly.

7. We are not to boycott or treat with scorn those who hold different views from ours. It must be our resolve to win them over by courteous behaviour.

8. We must not try to be clever. We must always be frank and straightforward.

9. When they stay in villages, the volunteers should demand the fewest services from the village-folk. Wherever it is possible to reach a place on foot, they should avoid using a vehicle. We must insist on being served the simplest food. Restraining them from preparing dainties will add grace to the service we render.

10. As they move about in villages, the volunteers should observe the economic condition of the people and the deficiencies in their education and try, in their spare time, to make them good.

11. If they can, they should create opportunities when they may teach the village children.

12. If they notice any violation of the rules of good health, they should draw the villagers' attention to the fact.

13. If, at any place, they find people engaged in quarrelling among themselves, the volunteers should try to save them from their quarrels.

14. They should read out to the people, when the latter are free, books which promote *satyagraha*. They may read out stories of Prahlad, Harishchandra and others. The people should also be made familiar with instances of pure *satyagraha* to be found in the West and in Islamic literature.

15. At no time and under no circumstances is the use of arms permitted in *satyagraha*. It should never be forgotten that in this struggle the highest type of non-violence is to be maintained. *Satyagraha* means fighting oppression through voluntary suffering. There can be no question here of making anyone else suffer. *Satyagraha* is always

successful; it can never meet with defeat: let every volunteer understand this himself and then explain it to the people.

'Instructions to Volunteers' (G.). *Kheda Satyagraha. EWMG*,
pp. 314–15

219. Rules for *satyagrahis*

Satyagraha literally means insistence on truth. This insistence arms
the votary with matchless power. This power or force is connoted by
the word *satyagraha*. *Satyagraha*, to be genuine, may be offered
against parents, against one's wife or one's children, against rulers,
against fellow-citizens, even against the whole world.

Such a universal force necessarily makes no distinction between
kinsmen and strangers, young and old, man and woman, friend and
foe. The force to be so applied can never be physical. There is in it
no room for violence. The only force of universal application can,
therefore, be that of *ahimsa* or love. In other words, it is soul-force.

Love does not burn others, it burns itself. Therefore, a *satyagrahi*,
i.e., a civil resister, will joyfully suffer even unto death.

It follows, therefore, that a civil resister, whilst he will strain every
nerve to compass the end of the existing rule, will do no intentional
injury in thought, word or deed to the person of a single Englishman.
This necessarily brief explanation of *satyagraha* will perhaps enable
the reader to understand and appreciate the following rules:

AS AN INDIVIDUAL

1. A *satyagrahi*, i.e., a civil resister, will harbour no anger.

2. He will suffer the anger of the opponent.

3. In so doing he will put up with assaults from the opponent,
never retaliate; but he will not submit, out of fear of punishment or
the like, to any order given in anger.

4. When any person in authority seeks to arrest a civil resister, he
will voluntarily submit to the arrest, and he will not resist the attachment or removal of his own property, if any, when it is sought to be
confiscated by authorities.

5. If a civil resister has any property in his possession as a trustee,
he will refuse to surrender it, even though in defending it he might
lose his life. He will, however, never retaliate.

6. Non-retaliation excludes swearing and cursing.

7. Therefore a civil resister will never insult his opponent, and therefore also not take part in many of the newly coined cries which are contrary to the spirit of *ahimsa*.

8. A civil resister will not salute the Union Jack, nor will he insult it or officials, English or Indian.

9. In the course of the struggle if anyone insults an official or commits an assault upon him, a civil resister will protect such official or officials from the insult or attack even at the risk of his life.

AS A PRISONER

10. As a prisoner, a civil resister will behave courteously towards prison officials, and will observe all such discipline of the prison as is not contrary to self-respect; as for instance, whilst he will *salaam** officials in the usual manner, he will not perform any humiliating gyrations and refuse to shout 'Victory to *Sarkar'** or the like. He will take cleanly cooked and cleanly served food, which is not contrary to his religion, and will refuse to take food insultingly served or served in unclean vessels.

11. A civil resister will make no distinction between an ordinary prisoner and himself, will in no way regard himself as superior to the rest, nor will he ask for any conveniences that may not be necessary for keeping his body in good health and condition. He is entitled to ask for such conveniences as may be required for his physical or spiritual well-being.

12. A civil resister may not fast for want of conveniences whose deprivation does not involve any injury to one's self-respect.

AS A UNIT

13. A civil resister will joyfully obey all the orders issued by the leader of the corps, whether they please him or not.

14. He will carry out orders in the first instance even though they appear to him insulting, inimical or foolish, and then appeal to higher authority. He is free before joining to determine the fitness of the corps to satisfy him, but after he has joined it, it becomes a duty to submit to its discipline, irksome or otherwise. If the sum total of the energy of the corps appears to a member to be improper or immoral, he has a right to sever his connection, but being within it, he has no right to commit a breach of its discipline.

15. No civil resister is to expect maintenance for his dependents. It would be an accident if any such provision is made. A civil resister entrusts his dependants to the care of God. Even in ordinary warfare wherein hundreds of thousands give themselves up to it, they are able to make no previous provision. How much more, then, should such be the case in *satyagraha*? It is the universal experience that in such times hardly anybody is left to starve.

IN COMMUNAL FIGHTS

16. No civil resister will intentionally become a cause of communal quarrels.

17. In the event of any such outbreak, he will not take sides, but he will assist only that party which is demonstrably in the right. Being a Hindu he will be generous towards Mussalmans and others, and will sacrifice himself in the attempt to save non-Hindus from a Hindu attack. And if the attack is from the other side, he will not participate in any retaliation but will give his life in protecting Hindus.

18. He will, to the best of his ability, avoid every occasion that may give rise to communal quarrels.

19. If there is a procession of *satyagrahis* they will do nothing that would wound the religious susceptibilities of any community, and they will not take part in any other processions that are likely to wound such susceptibilities.

'Some Rules of *Satyagraha*' (G.). *Navajivan*, 23 Feb. 1930. *Young India*, 27 Feb. 1930

220. Basic attitudes needed

14 October 1938

Now I am in a position to state what, in my opinion, are basic assumptions underlying the doctrine of *satyagraha*:

1. There must be common honesty among *satyagrahis*.

2. They must render heart discipline to their commander. There should be no mental reservation.

3. They must be prepared to lose all, not merely their personal liberty, not merely their possessions, land, cash, etc., but also the liberty and possessions of their families, and they must be ready cheerfully to face bullets, bayonets, or even slow death by torture.

4. They must not be violent in thought, word or deed towards the 'enemy' or among themselves.

Harijan, 22 Oct. 1938

221. Behaviour of *satyagrahis* as prisoners

The argument advanced by some friends and put by me . . . deserves consideration if only because so many honestly believe in it and so many followed it out consistently in their conduct in 1921 and 1922,* when thousands went to gaol.

In the first instance, even outside the gaols, embarrassment of the Government is not our goal. We are indifferent if the Government is embarrassed so long as our conduct is right. Our non-co-operation embarrasses the Government as nothing else can. But we non-co-operate as lawyers or Councillors* because it is our duty. That is to say, we will not cease to non-co-operate if we discovered that our non-co-operation pleased the rulers. And we are so indifferent because we believe that, by non-co-operation, we must ultimately benefit ourselves. But there cannot be any such non-co-operation in the gaols. We do not enter them to serve a selfish end. We are taken there by the Government as criminals according to their estimation. Our business, therefore, is to disillusion them by acting in an exemplary (and by them expected) manner, just as our business outside is to disillusion them by avoiding, say, their law-courts, schools or Councils or titles and by showing that we are prepared to do without their doubtful benefits.

Whether all of us realize it or not the method of non-co-operation is a process of touching the heart and appealing to reason, not one of frightening by rowdyism. Rowdyism has no place in a non-violent movement.

I have often likened *satyagrahi* prisoners to prisoners of war. Once caught by the enemy, prisoners of war act towards the enemy as friends. It will be considered dishonourable on the part of a soldier as a prisoner of war to deceive the enemy. It does not affect my argument that the Government does not regard *satyagrahi* prisoners as prisoners of war. If we act as such, we shall soon command respect. We must make the prisons a neutral institution in which we may, nay, must co-operate to a certain extent.

We would be highly inconsistent and hardly self-respecting if, on the one hand, we deliberately break prison rules and, in the same breath, complain of punishment and strictness. We may not, for instance, resist and complain of search and, at the same time, conceal prohibited things in our blankets or our clothes. There is nothing in *satyagraha* that I know whereby we may, under certain circumstances, tell untruths or practise other deception.

When we say that, if we make the lives of prison officials uncomfortable, the Government will be obliged to sue for peace, we either pay them a subtle compliment or regard them as simpletons. We pay a subtle compliment when we consider that, even though we may make prison officials' lives uncomfortable, the Government will look on in silence and hesitate to award us condign punishment so as utterly to break our spirit. That is to say, we regard the administrators to be so considerate and humane that they will not severely punish us even though we give them sufficient cause. As a matter of fact, they will not and do not hesitate to throw overboard all idea of decency and award not only authorized but even unauthorized punishments on given occasions.

But it is my deliberate conviction that, had we but acted with uniform honesty and dignity behoving *satyagrahis*, we should have disarmed all opposition on the part of the Government, and such strictly honourable behaviour on the part of so many prisoners would have at least shamed the Government into confessing their error in imprisoning so many honourable and innocent men. For, is it not their case that our non-violence is but a cloak for our violence? Do we not, therefore, play into their hands every time we are rowdy?

In my opinion, therefore, as *satyagrahis* we are bound, when we become prisoners:

1. to act with the most scrupulous honesty;
2. to co-operate with the prison officials in their administration;
3. to set, by our obedience to all reasonable discipline, an example to co-prisoners;
4. to ask for no favours and claim no privileges which the meanest of prisoners do not get and which we do not need strictly for reasons of health;
5. not to fail to ask what we do so need and not to get irritated if we do not obtain it;
6. to do all the tasks allotted, to the utmost of our ability.

It is such conduct which will make the Government position uncomfortable and untenable. It is difficult for them to meet honesty with honesty for their want of faith and unpreparedness for such a rare eventuality. Rowdyism they expect and meet with a double dose of it. They were able to deal with anarchical crime, but they have not yet found out any way of dealing with non-violence save by yielding to it.

The idea behind the imprisonment of a *satyagrahi* is that he expects relief through humble submission to suffering. He believes that meek suffering for a just cause has a virtue all its own and infinitely greater than the virtue of the sword. This does not mean that we may not resist when the treatment touches our self-respect. Thus, for instance, we must resist to the point of death the use of abusive language by officials or if they were to throw our food at us, which is often done. Insult and abuse are no part of an official's duty. Therefore, we must resist them. But we may not resist search because it is part of prison regulations.

Nor are my remarks about mute suffering to be construed to mean that there should be no agitation against putting innocent prisoners like *satyagrahis* in the same class as confirmed criminals. Only as prisoners we may not ask for favours. We must be content to live with the confirmed criminals and even welcome the opportunity of working moral reform in them. It is, however, expected of a Government that calls itself civilized to recognize the most natural divisions.

'My Jail Experiences—VII'. *Young India*, 5 June 1924

222. The evil of social ostracism

Nevertheless, the issue raised by the correspondent is important and serious. It would be a dangerous thing if, for differences of opinion, we were to proclaim social boycotts.

It would be totally opposed to the doctrine of non-violence to stop the supply of water and food. This battle of non-co-operation is a programme of propaganda by reducing profession to practice, not one of compelling others to yield obedience by violence, direct or indirect. We must try patiently to convert our opponents. If we wish to evolve the spirit of democracy out of slavery, we must be scrupulously exact in our dealings with opponents. We may not replace the slavery of the Government by that of the non-co-operationists. We must concede to our opponents the freedom we claim for ourselves and for which we are fighting. The stoutest co-operationist will bend to the stern realities of practice if there is real response from the people.

But there is a non-violent boycott which we shall be bound to practise if we are to make any impression. We must not compromise with what we believe to be an untruth, whether it resides in a white skin or a brown. Such boycott is political boycott. We may not receive favours from the new Councillors. The voters, if they are true to their pledge, will be bound to refrain from making use of the services of those whom they have declined to regard as their representatives. They must ratify their verdict by complete abstention from any encouragement of the so-called representatives.

The public will be bound, if they are non-co-operationists, to refrain from giving these representatives any prestige by attending their political functions or parties.

I can conceive the possibility of non-violent social ostracism under certain extreme conditions, when a defiant minority refuses to bend to the majority, not out of any regard for principle but from sheer defiance or worse. But that time has certainly not arrived. Ostracism of a violent character, such as the denial of the use of public wells is a species of barbarism which I hope will never be practised by any body of men having any desire for national self-respect and national uplift. We will free neither Islam nor India by processes of coercion, whether among ourselves or against Englishmen.

'Social Boycott'. *Young India*, 8 Dec. 1920

223. The snares of social boycott

Non-co-operation being a movement of purification is bringing to the surface all our weaknesses as also excesses of even our strong points. Social boycott is an age-old institution. It is coeval with caste. It is the one terrible sanction exercised with great effect. It is based upon the notion that a community is not bound to extend its hospitality or service to an excommunicate. It answered when every village was a self-contained unit, and the occasions of recalcitrancy were rare. But when opinion is divided, as it is today, on the merits of non-co-operation, when its new application is having a trial, a summary use of social boycott in order to bend a minority to the will of the majority is a species of unpardonable violence. If persisted in, such boycott is bound to destroy the movement. Social boycott is applicable and effective when it is not felt as a punishment and accepted by the object of boycott as a measure of discipline. Moreover, social boycott to be admissible in a campaign of non-violence must never savour of inhumanity. It must be civilized. It must cause pain to the party using it, if it causes inconvenience to its object. Thus, depriving a man of the services of a medical man, as is reported to have been done in Jhansi, is an act of inhumanity tantamount in the moral code to an attempt to murder.

I see no difference in murdering a man and withdrawing medical aid from a man who is on the point of dying. Even the laws of war, I apprehend, require the giving of medical relief to the enemy in need of it. To deprive a man of the use of an only village-well is notice to him to quit that village. Surely, non-co-operators have acquired no right to use that extreme pressure against those who do not see eye to eye with them. Impatience and intolerance will surely kill this great religious movement. We may not make people pure by compulsion. Much less may we compel them by violence to respect our opinion. It is utterly against the spirit of democracy we want to cultivate.

There are no doubt serious difficulties in our way. The temptation to resort to social boycott is irresistible when a defendant, who submits to private arbitration, refuses to abide by its award. Yet it is easy to see that the application of social boycott is more than likely to arrest the splendid movement to settle disputes by arbitration which, apart from its use as a weapon in the armoury of non-co-operation, is a movement fraught with great good to the country. People will take time before they accommodate themselves to private arbitration. Its very simplicity and inexpensiveness will repel many people even as palates jaded by spicy foods are repelled by simple combinations. All awards will not always be above suspicion. We must therefore rely upon the intrinsic merits of the movement and the correctness of awards to make itself felt.

It is much to be desired if we can bring about a complete *voluntary* boycott of law courts. That one event can bring about *swaraj*. But it was never expected that we would reach completion in any single item of non-co-operation. Public opinion has been so far developed as to recognize the courts as signs not of our liberty but of our slavery. It has made it practically impossible for lawyers to practise their profession and be called popular leaders.

Non-co-operation has greatly demolished the prestige of law courts and to that extent of the Government. The disintegrating process is slowly but surely going on. Its velocity will suffer diminution if violent methods are adopted to hasten it. This Government of ours is armed to the teeth to meet and check forces of violence. It possesses nothing to check the mighty forces of non-violence. How can a handful of Englishmen resist a voluntary expression of opinion accompanied by the voluntary self-denial of thirty crores of people?

I hope, therefore, that non-co-operation workers will beware of the snares of social boycott. But the alternative to social boycott is certainly not social intercourse. A man who defies strong, clear public opinion on vital matters is not entitled to social amenities and privileges. We may not take part in his social functions such as marriage feasts, we may not receive gifts from him. But we dare not deny social service. The latter is a duty. Attendance at dinner parties and the like is a privilege which it is optional to withhold or extend. But it would be wisdom to err on the right side and to exercise the weapon even in the limited sense described by me on rare and well-defined occasions. And in every case the user of the weapons will use it at his own risk. The use of it is not as yet in any form a duty. No one is entitled to its use if there is any danger of hurting the movement.

'Social Boycott'. *Young India*, 16 Feb. 1921

224. Fasting and the *satyagrahi*

New Delhi,
December 10, 1947

QUESTION. Why does Gandhiji resort to a fast when he faces extreme difficulties? What is the effect of this action on the life of the public of India?

ANSWER. Such a question has been put to me before but never, perhaps, precisely in the same terms. The answer, however, is easy.

It is the last weapon in the armoury of the votary of *ahimsa*. When human ingenuity fails, the votary fasts. This fasting quickens the spirit of prayer, that is to say, the fasting is a spiritual act and, therefore, addressed to God. The effect of such action on the life of the people is that when the person fasting is at all known to them their sleeping conscience is awakened. But there is the danger that the people through mistaken sympathy may act against their will in order to save the life of the loved one. This danger has got to be faced. One ought not to be deterred from right action when one is sure of the rightness. It can but promote circumspection. Such a fast is undertaken in obedience to the dictates of the inner voice and, therefore, prevents haste.

'Question Box'. *Harijan*, 21 Dec. 1947

d. Tactics and dilemmas in *satyagraha*

225. Timing and tactics

March 15, 1939

Satyagraha does not begin and end with civil disobedience. Let us do a little more *tapascharya* which is the essence of *satyagraha*. Suspension thus conceived can never do harm to the movement. The opponent will find that his battery is exhausted when we do not act up to his expectations, refuse to have any firework displays or put ourselves at his disposal for brutal assaults of his *goondas*. We must meet all his provocative and repressive measures with a coolness and an exemplary self-restraint even at the risk of being charged with cowardice. If there is no cowardice in us, we are safe; ours will ultimately be reckoned an act of rare bravery.

Meanwhile we should watch how things shape themselves. I am thinking out new plans of conducting the movement in view of the terrorist methods that some [Princely] States seem to have adopted. We have to develop that technique of rendering futile the employment of hired hooligans against peaceful citizens.

An able general always gives battle in his own time on the ground of his choice. He always retains the initiative in these respects and never allows it to pass into the hands of the enemy.

In a *satyagraha* campaign the mode of fight and the choice of tactics, e.g., whether to advance or retreat, offer civil resistance or organize non-violent strength through constructive work* and purely selfless humanitarian service, are determined according to the exigencies of the situation. A *satyagrahi* must carry out whatever plan is laid out for him with a cool determination giving way to neither excitement nor depression.

For a *satyagrahi* there can be only one goal, viz., to lay down his life performing his duty whatever it may be. It is the highest he can attain. A cause that has such worthy *satyagrahi* soldiers at its back can never be defeated.

Harijan, 27 May 1939

226. Personal *satyagraha* in Champaran district, 1917

18 April 1917

With the permission of the Court,* I would like to make a brief statement showing why I have taken the very serious step of seemingly disobeying the order made under Section 144 of the Criminal Procedure Code. In my humble opinion, it is a question of difference of opinion between the local administration and myself. I have entered the country with motives of rendering humanitarian and national service. I have done so in response to a pressing invitation to come and help the *ryots*, who urge they are not being fairly treated by the indigo planters. I could not render any help without studying the problem. I have, therefore, come to study it with the assistance, if possible, of the administration and the planters. I have no other motive and I cannot believe that my coming here can in any way disturb the public peace or cause loss of life. I claim to have considerable experience in such matters. The administration, however, have thought differently. I fully appreciate their difficulty, and I admit too, that they can only proceed upon information they receive. As a law-abiding citizen, my first instinct would be, as it was, to obey the order served upon me. I could not do so without doing violence to my sense of duty to those for whom I have come. I feel that I could just now serve them only by remaining in their midst. I could not, therefore, voluntarily retire. Amid this conflict of duty, I could only throw the responsibility of removing me from them on the administration.

I am fully conscious of the fact that a person, holding in the public life of India a position such as I do, has to be most careful in setting examples. It is my firm belief that in the complex constitution under which we are living, the only safe and honourable course for a self-respecting man is, in the circumstances such as face me, to do what I have decided to do, that is, to submit without protest to the penalty of disobedience. I have ventured to make this statement not in any way in extenuation of the penalty to be awarded against me, but to show that I have disregarded the order served upon me, not for want of respect for lawful authority, but in obedience of the higher law of our being—the voice of conscience.

'Statement Before the Court'. *The Leader*, 22 Apr. 1917. *EWMG*, pp. 331–2

227. Suspending civil disobedience, 1919

Bombay,
April 18, 1919

It is not without sorrow that I feel compelled to advise the temporary suspension of civil disobedience.* I give this advice not because I have less faith now in its efficacy, but because I have, if possible, greater faith than before. It is my perception of the law of *satyagraha* which impels me to suggest the suspension. I am sorry, when I embarked upon a mass movement, I underrated the forces of evil and I must now pause and consider how best to meet the situation. But whilst doing so, I wish to say that from a careful examination of the tragedy at Ahmedabad and Viramgam, I am convinced that *satyagraha* had nothing to do with the violence of the mob and that many swarmed round the banner of mischief raised by the mob, largely because of their affection for Anasuyabai and myself. Had the Government in an unwise manner not prevented me from entering Delhi and so compelled me to disobey their order, I feel certain that Ahmedabad and Viramgam would have remained free from the horrors of the past week. In other words, *satyagraha* has neither been the cause nor the occasion of the upheaval. If anything, the presence of *satyagraha* has acted as a check even so slight upon the previously existing lawless elements. As regards events in the Punjab, it is admitted that they are unconnected with the *satyagraha* movement.

In the course of the *satyagraha* struggle in South Africa, several thousands of indentured Indians had struck work. This was a *satyagraha* strike and therefore entirely peaceful and voluntary. Whilst the strike was going on, a strike of European miners, railway employees, etc., was declared. Overtures were made to me to make common cause with the European strikers. As a *satyagrahi*, I did not require a moment's consideration to decline to do so. I went further and for fear of our strike being classed with the strike of Europeans in which methods of violence and use of arms found a prominent place, ours was suspended and *satyagraha* from that moment came to be recognized by the Europeans of South Africa as an honourable and honest movement—in the words of General Smuts, a constitutional movement. I can do no less at the present critical moment. I would be untrue to *satyagraha*, if I allowed it by any action of mine to be used as an occasion for feeding violence for embittering relations between the English and the Indians. Our *satyagraha* must therefore now consist in ceaselessly helping the authorities in all the ways available to us as *satyagrahis* to restore order and to curb lawlessness. We can turn the tragedies going on before us to good account if we could but succeed in gaining the adherence of the masses to the fundamental principles of *satyagraha*.

Satyagraha is like a banyan tree with innumerable branches. Civil disobedience is one such branch, *satya* (truth) and *ahimsa* (non-violence) together make the parent trunk from which all innumerable branches shoot out. We have found by bitter experience that whilst in an atmosphere of lawlessness, civil disobedience found ready acceptance. *Satya* and *ahimsa*, from which alone civil disobedience can worthily spring, have commanded little or no respect. Ours then is a Herculean task, but we may not shirk it. We must fearlessly spread the doctrine of *satya* and *ahimsa* and then, and not till then, shall we be able to undertake mass *satyagraha*.

My attitude towards the Rowlatt legislation remains unchanged. Indeed, I do feel that the Rowlatt legislation is one of the many causes of the present unrest. But in a surcharged atmosphere, I must refrain from examining these causes. The main and only purpose of this letter is to advise all *satyagrahis* to temporarily suspend civil disobedience, to give Government effective co-operation in restoring order and by preaching and practice to gain adherence to the fundamental principles mentioned above.

Press statement on suspension of civil disobedience. *The Hindu*, 21 Apr. 1919. *EWMG*, pp. 332–3

228. The method of non-co-operation

14 August 1920

I hope then that whatever I say this evening to this vast mass of people will bear fruit in that same sacrifice for which the life of Lokamanya Tilak Maharaj* stands. His life, if it teaches us anything whatsoever, teaches one supreme lesson: that if we want to do anything whatsoever for our country, we can do so not by speeches, however grand, eloquent and convincing they may be, but only by sacrifice at the back of every word and at the back of every act of our life. I have come to ask every one of you whether you are ready and willing to give sufficiently for your country's sake, for your country's honour and for religion. I have boundless faith in you, the citizens of Madras, and the people of this great presidency, a faith which I began to cultivate in the year 1893 when I first made acquaintance with the Tamil labourers* in South Africa; and I hope that, in these hours of our trial, this province will not be second to any other in India, and that it will lead in this spirit of self-sacrifice and will translate every word into action.

NEED FOR NON-CO-OPERATION

What is this non-co-operation about which you have heard much, and why do we want to offer this non-co-operation? I wish to go for the time being into the why. There are two things before this country. The first and the foremost is the Khilafat question.* On this the heart of the Mussulmans of India has become lacerated. British pledges, given after the greatest deliberation by the Prime Minister of England in the name of the English nation, have been dragged into the mire. The promises given to Moslem India, on the strength of which the consideration that was accepted by the British nation was exacted, have been broken and the great religion of Islam has been placed in danger. The Mussulmans hold—and I venture to think they rightly hold—that so long as British promises remain unfulfilled so long is it impossible for them to tender whole-hearted fealty and loyalty to the British connection; and, if it is to be a choice for a devout Mussulman between loyalty to the British connection and loyalty to his Code and Prophet, he will not require a second to make his choice and he has declared his choice. The Mussulmans say frankly, openly and honourably to the whole world that if the British ministers and the British nation do not fulfil the pledges given to them and do not wish to regard with respect the sentiments of 70 millions of the inhabitants of India who profess the faith of Islam, it will be impossible for them to retain Islamic loyalty.

It is a question, then, for the rest of the Indian population to consider whether they want to perform a neighbourly duty by their Mussulman countrymen and, if they do, they have an opportunity of a lifetime which will not occur for another hundred years, to show their goodwill, fellowship and friendship and to prove what they have been saying for all these long years that the Mussulman is the brother of the Hindu. If the Hindu regards that before the connection with the British nation comes his natural connection with his Moslem brother, then I say to you that if you find that the Moslem claim is just, that it is based upon real sentiment, and that at its background is this great religious feeling, you cannot do otherwise than help the Mussulmans through and through so long as their cause remains just and the means for attaining the end remains equally just, honourable and free from harm to India. These are the plain conditions which the Indian Mussulmans have accepted and it was when they saw that they could accept the proffered aid of the Hindus, that they could always justify the cause and the means before the whole world, that they decided to accept the proffered hand of fellowship. It is then for Hindus and Mussulmans to offer a united front to the whole of the Christian powers of Europe and tell them that weak as India is, India has still got the capacity of preserving her self-respect, she still knows how to die for her religion and for her self-respect.

That is the Khilafat in a nutshell; but you have also got the Punjab.* The Punjab has wounded the heart of India as no other question has for the past century. I do not exclude from my calculation the Mutiny of 1857. Whatever hardships India had to suffer during the Mutiny, the insult that was attempted to be offered to her during the passage of the Rowlatt legislation,* and that which was offered after its passage, were unparalleled in Indian history. It is because you want justice from the British nation in connection with the Punjab atrocities, you have to devise ways and means as to how you can get this justice. The House of Commons, the House of Lords, Mr Montagu,* the Viceroy of India, every one of them knows what the feeling of India is on this Khilafat question and on that of the Punjab; the debates in both the Houses of Parliament, the action of Mr Montagu and that of the Viceroy have demonstrated to you completely that they are not willing to give the justice which is India's due and which she demands. I suggest that our leaders have got to find a way out of this great difficulty and unless we have made ourselves even with the British rulers in India, and unless we have gained a measure of self-respect at the hands of the British rulers in India, no connection and no friendly intercourse is possible between them and ourselves. I, therefore, venture to suggest this beautiful unanswerable method of non-co-operation.

IS IT UNCONSTITUTIONAL?

I have been told that non-co-operation is unconstitutional. I venture to deny that it is unconstitutional. On the contrary, I hold that non-co-operation is a just and religious doctrine; it is the inherent right of every human being and it is perfectly constitutional. . . . I do not claim any constitutionality for a rebellion successful or otherwise so long as that rebellion means in the ordinary sense of the term what it does mean, namely, wresting justice by violent means. On the contrary, I have said it repeatedly to my countrymen that violence, whatever end it may serve in Europe, will never serve us in India.

My brother and friend Shaukat Ali* believes in methods of violence; and if it was in his power to draw the sword against the British Empire, I know that he has got the courage of a man and he has got also the wisdom to see that he should offer that battle to the British Empire. But because he recognizes as a true soldier that means of violence are not open to India, he sides with me accepting my humble assistance and pledges his word that so long as I am with him and so long as he believes in the doctrine so long will he not harbour even the idea of violence against any single Englishman or any single man on earth. I am here to tell you that he has been as true as his word and has kept it religiously. I am here to bear witness that he has been following out this plan of non-violent non-co-operation to the very letter and I am asking India to follow this non-violent non-co-operation. I tell you that there is not a better soldier living in our ranks in British India than Shaukat Ali. When the time for the drawing of the sword comes, if it ever comes, you will find him drawing that sword and you will find me retiring to the jungle of Hindustan.

As soon as India accepts the doctrine of the sword, my life as an Indian is finished. It is because I believe in a mission special to India, and it is because I believe that the ancients of India, after centuries of experience, have found out that the true thing for any human being on earth is not justice based on violence but justice based on sacrifice of self, justice based on *yajna* and *kurbani*—I cling to that doctrine and I shall cling to it for ever—it is for that reason I tell you that whilst my friend believes also in the doctrine of violence and has adopted the doctrine of non-violence as a weapon of the weak, I believe in the doctrine of non-violence as a weapon of the strongest. I believe that a man is the strongest soldier for daring to die unarmed with his breast bare before the enemy. So much for the non-violent part of non-co-operation. I, therefore, venture to suggest to my learned countrymen that so long as the doctrine of non-co-operation remains non-violent so long there is nothing unconstitutional in the doctrine.

I ask further, is it unconstitutional for me to say to the British Government, 'I refuse to serve you'? Is it unconstitutional for our worthy chairman to return with every respect all the titles that he has ever held from the Government? Is it unconstitutional for any parent to withdraw his children from a Government or aided school? Is it unconstitutional for a lawyer to say, 'I shall no longer support the arm of the law so long as that arm of law is used not to raise me but to debase me'? Is it unconstitutional for a civil servant or for a judge to say, 'I refuse to serve a Government which does not wish to respect the wishes of the whole people'? I ask, is it unconstitutional for a policeman or for a soldier to tender his resignation when he knows that he is called to serve a Government which traduces its own countrymen? Is it unconstitutional for me to go to the *krishak*, to the agriculturist, and say to him, 'It is not wise for you to pay any taxes, if these taxes are used by the Government not to raise you but to weaken you'? I hold and I venture to submit that there is nothing unconstitutional in it. What is more, I have done every one of these things in my life and nobody has questioned the constitutional character of it. I was in Kaira* working in the midst of seven lakhs of agriculturists. They had all suspended the payment of taxes and the whole of India was at one with me. Nobody considered that it was unconstitutional.

I submit that in the whole plan of non-co-operation there is nothing unconstitutional. But I do venture to suggest that it will be highly unconstitutional in the midst of this unconstitutional Government—in the midst of a nation which has built up its magnificent constitution—for the people of India to become weak and to crawl on their belly—it will be highly unconstitutional for the people of India to pocket every insult that is offered to them; it is highly unconstitutional for the 70 millions of Mohammedans of India to submit to a violent wrong done to their religion; it is highly unconstitutional for the whole of India to sit still and co-operate with an unjust Government which has trodden under its feet the honour of the Punjab; I say to my countrymen: 'So long as you have a sense of honour and so long as you wish to remain the descendants and defenders of the noble traditions that have been handed to you for generations after generations, it is unconstitutional for you not to non-co-operate and unconstitutional for you to co-operate with a government which has become so unjust as our Government has become.'

I am not anti-English; I am not anti-British; I am not anti-any government; but I am anti-untruth—anti-humbug and anti-injustice. So long as the Government spells injustice, it may regard me as its enemy, implacable enemy. I had hoped at the Congress at Amritsar*—I am speaking God's truth before you—when I pleaded on knees before some of you for co-operation with the Government, I had full hope that the British ministers, who are wise as a rule, would placate the Mussulman sentiment, that they would do full justice in the matter of the Punjab atrocities, and, therefore, I said: Let us return goodwill to the hand of fellowship that has been extended to us, which, I then believed, was extended to us through the Royal Proclamation.* It was on that account that I pleaded for co-operation. But today that faith having gone and been obliterated by the acts of the British ministers, I am here to plead not for futile obstruction in the legislative council but for real substantial non-co-operation which would paralyse the mightiest government on earth. That is what I stand for today.

Until we have wrung justice and until we have wrung our self-respect from unwilling hands and from unwilling pens, there can be no co-operation. Our Shastras say and I say so with the greatest deference to all the greatest religious preceptors of India but without fear of contradiction that our Shastras teach us that there shall be no co-operation between injustice and justice, between an unjust man and a justice-loving man, between truth and untruth. Co-operation is a duty only so long as Government protects your honour, and non-co-operation is an equal duty when the government, instead of protecting, robs you of your honour. That is the doctrine of non-co-operation.

NON-CO-OPERATION AND THE SPECIAL CONGRESS

I have been told that I should have waited for the declaration of the special Congress* which is the mouthpiece of the whole nation. I know that it is the mouthpiece of the whole nation. If it was for me, individual Gandhi, to wait, I would have waited for eternity. But I had in my hands a sacred trust. I was advising my Mussulman countrymen and for the time being I hold their honour in my hands. I dare not ask them to wait for any verdict but the verdict of their own conscience. Do you suppose that Mussulmans can eat their own words, can withdraw from the honourable position they have taken up? If perchance—and God forbid that it should happen—the special congress decides against them, I would still advise my countrymen, the Mussulmans, to stand single-handed and fight rather than yield to the attempted dishonour to their religion. It is, therefore, given to the Mussulmans to go to the Congress on bended knees and plead for support. But support or no support, it was not possible for them to wait for the Congress to give them the lead. They had to choose between futile violence, drawing of the naked sword and peaceful non-violent but effective non-co-operation, and they have made their choice.

I venture further to say to you that if there is any body of men who feel as I do, the sacred character of non-co-operation, it is for you and me not to wait for the Congress but to act and to make it impossible for the Congress to give any other verdict. After all what is the Congress? The Congress is the collected voice of individuals who form it, and if the individuals go to the Congress with a united voice, that will be the verdict you will gain from the Congress. But if we go to the Congress with no opinion because we have none or because we are afraid to express it, then naturally we await the verdict of the Congress. To those who are unable to make up their mind, I say, by all means wait. But for those who have seen the clear light as they see the lights in front of them, for them to wait is a sin. The Congress does not expect you to wait but it expects you to act so that the Congress can gauge properly the national feeling. So much for the Congress.

BOYCOTT OF THE COUNCILS

Among the details of non-co-operation I have placed in the foremost rank the boycott of the councils.* Friends have quarrelled with me for the use of the word boycott, because I have disapproved—as I disapprove even now—of boycott of British goods or any goods for that matter. But there, boycott has its own meaning and here boycott has its own meaning. I not only do not disapprove but approve of the boycott of the councils that are going to be formed next year. And why do I do it? The people—the masses—require from us, the leaders, a clear lead. They do not want any equivocation from us. The suggestion that we should seek election and then refuse to take the oath of allegiance would only make the nation distrust the leaders. It is not a clear lead to the nation. So I say to you, my countrymen, not to fall into this trap. We shall sell our country by adopting the methods of seeking election and then not taking the oath of allegiance. We may find it difficult and I frankly confess to you that have not that trust in so many Indians making that declaration and standing by it. Today I suggest to those who honestly hold the view, viz. that we should seek election and then refuse to take the oath of allegiance—I suggest to them that they will fall into a trap which they are preparing for themselves and for the nation. That is my view.

I hold that if we want to give the nation the clearest possible lead and if we want not to play with this great nation, we must make it clear to this nation that we cannot take any favours, no matter how great they may be, so long as those favours are accompanied by an injustice, a double wrong done to India not yet redressed. The first indispensable thing before we can receive any favours from them is, that they should redress this double wrong. There is a Greek proverb* which used to say: 'Beware of the Greeks but especially beware of them when they bring gifts to you.' Today from those ministers who are bent upon perpetuating the wrong to Islam and to the Punjab, I say we cannot accept gifts but we should be doubly careful lest we may not fall into the trap that they may have devised. I therefore suggest that we must not coquet with the councils and must not have anything whatsoever to do with them. I am told that if we, who represent the national sentiment, do not seek election, the Moderates who do not represent that sentiment will. I do not agree. I do not know what the Moderates represent and I do not know what the Nationalists represent. I know that there are good sheep and black sheep among the Moderates. I know that there are good sheep and black sheep amongst the Nationalists. I know that many Moderates hold honestly the view that it is a sin to resort to non-co-operation. I respectfully agree to differ from them. I do say to them also that they will fall into a trap which they will have devised if they seek election. But that does not affect my situation.

If I feel in my heart of hearts that I ought not to go to the councils, I ought at least to abide by this decision and it does not matter if ninety-nine other countrymen seek election. That is the only way in which public work can be done and public opinion can be built. That is the only way in which reforms can be achieved and religion can be conserved. If it is a question of religious honour, whether I am one or among many, I must stand upon my doctrine. Even if I should die in the attempt, it is worth dying for than that I should live and deny my own doctrine. I suggest that it will be wrong on the part of anyone to seek election to these councils. If once we feel that we cannot co-operate with this Government, we have to commence from the top. We are the natural leaders of the people and we have acquired the right and the power to go to the nation and speak to it with the voice of non-co-operation. I, therefore, do suggest that it is inconsistent with non-co-operation to seek election to the councils on any terms whatsoever.

LAWYERS AND NON-CO-OPERATION

I have suggested another difficult matter, viz., that the lawyers* should suspend their practice. How should I do otherwise knowing so well how the Government had always been able to retain this power through the instrumentality of lawyers? It is perfectly true that it is the lawyers of today who are leading us, who are fighting the country's battles, but when it comes to a matter of action against the

Government, when it comes to a matter of paralysing the activity of the Government, I know that the Government always looks to the lawyers, however fine fighters they may have been, to preserve their dignity and their self-respect. I, therefore, suggest to my lawyer friends that it is their duty to suspend their practice and to show to the Government that they will no longer retain their offices, because lawyers are considered to be honorary officers of the courts and, therefore, subject to their disciplinary jurisdiction. They must no longer retain these honorary offices if they want to withdraw co-operation from Government. But what will happen to law and order? We shall evolve law and order through the instrumentality of these very lawyers. We shall promote arbitration courts and dispense justice, pure, simple, home-made justice, *swadeshi* justice to our countrymen. That is what suspension of practice means.

PARENTS AND NON-CO-OPERATION

I have suggested yet another difficulty—to withdraw our children from the Government schools and to ask collegiate students to withdraw from the college and to empty Government-aided schools. How could I do otherwise? I want to gauge the national sentiment. I want to know whether the Mohammedans feel deeply. If they feel deeply, they will understand in the twinkling of an eye that it is not right for them to receive schooling from a Government in which they have lost all faith; and which they do not trust at all. How can I, if I do not want to help this Government, receive any help from that Government? I think that the schools and colleges are factories for making clerks and Government servants. I would not help this great factory for manufacturing clerks and servants if I want to withdraw co-operation from that Government. Look at it from any point of view you like. It is not possible for you to send your children to the schools and still believe in the doctrine of non-co-operation.

THE DUTY OF TITLE-HOLDERS

I have gone further. I have suggested that our title-holders should give up their titles. How can they hold on to the titles and honours bestowed by this Government? They were at one time badges of honour when we believed that national honour was safe in their hands. But now they are no longer badges of honour but badges of dishonour and disgrace when we really believe that we cannot get justice from this Government. Every title-holder holds his title and honours as trustee for the nation, and in this first step in the withdrawal of co-operation from the Government, they should surrender their titles without a moment's consideration. I suggest to my Mohammedan countrymen that, if they fail in this primary duty, they will certainly fail in non-co-operation unless the masses themselves reject the classes and take up non-co-operation in their own hands and are able to fight that battle even as the men of the French Revolution were able to take the reins of Government in their own hands, leaving aside the leaders, and marched to the banner of victory.

I want no revolution. I want ordered progress. I want no disordered order. I want no chaos. I want real order to be evolved out of this chaos which is misrepresented to me as order. If it is order established by a tyrant in order to get hold of the tyrannical reins of Government, I say that it is no order for me but it is disorder. I want to evolve justice out of this injustice. Therefore, I suggest to you the passive non-co-operation. If we would only realize the secret of this peaceful and infallible doctrine, you will know and you will find that you will not want to use even an angry word when they lift the sword at you and you will not want even to lift your little finger, let alone a stick or a sword.

A SERVICE TO THE EMPIRE

You may consider that I have spoken these words in anger because I have considered the ways of this Government immoral, unjust, debasing and untruthful. I use these adjectives with the greatest deliberation. . . . I tell the British people that I love them and that I want their association but I want that association on conditions well defined. I want my self-respect and I want my absolute equality with them. If I cannot gain that equality from the British people, I do not want the British connection. If I have to let the British people go and import temporary disorder and dislocation of national business, I will rather favour that disorder and dislocation than that I should have injustice from the hands of a great nation such as the British nation.

You will find that by the time the whole chapter is closed that the successors of Mr Montagu will give me the credit for having rendered the most distinguished service that I have yet rendered to the Empire, in having offered this non-co-operation and in having suggested the boycott, not of His Royal Highness the Prince of Wales* but of boycott of a visit engineered by the Government in order to tighten its hold on the national neck. I will not allow it even if I stand alone, if I cannot persuade this nation not to welcome that visit, but will boycott that visit with all the power at my command. It is for that reason I stand before you and implore you to offer this religious battle, but it is not a battle offered to you by a visionary or a saint.

I deny being a visionary. I do not accept the claim of saintliness. I am of the earth, earthly, a common gardener man as much as any one of you, probably much more than you are. I am prone to as many weaknesses as you are. But I have seen the world. I have lived in the world with my eyes open. I have gone through the most fiery ordeals that have fallen to the lot of man. I have gone through this discipline. I have understood the secret of my own sacred Hinduism. I have learnt the lesson that non-co-operation is the duty not merely of the saint but it is the duty of every ordinary citizen, who not knowing much, not caring to know much, but wants to perform his ordinary household functions. The people of Europe teach even their masses, the poor people, the doctrine of the sword. But the *rishis** of India, those who have held the traditions of India, have preached to the masses of India the doctrine, not of the sword, not of violence but of suffering, of self-suffering. And unless you and I are prepared to go through the primary lesson, we are not ready even to offer the sword and that is the lesson my brother Shaukat Ali has imbibed to teach and that is why he today accepts my advice tendered to him in all prayerfulness and in all humility and says: 'Long live non-co-operation.'

Please remember that even in England the little children were withdrawn from the schools; and colleges in Cambridge and Oxford were closed. Lawyers had left their desks and were fighting in the trenches.* I do not present to you the trenches but I do ask you to go through the sacrifice that the men, women and the brave lads of England went through. Remember that you are offering battle to a nation which is saturated with the spirit of sacrifice whenever the occasion arises. Remember that the little band of Boers offered stubborn resistance to a mighty nation. But their lawyers had left their desks. Their mothers had withdrawn their children from the schools and colleges and the children had become the volunteers of the nation. I have seen them with these naked eyes of mine.

I am asking my countrymen in India to follow no other gospel than the gospel of self-sacrifice which precedes every battle. Whether you belong to the school of violence or non-violence, you will still have to go through the fire of sacrifice and of discipline. May God grant you, may God grant our leaders the wisdom, the courage and the true knowledge to lead the nation to its cherished goal! May God grant the people of India the right path, the true vision and the ability and the courage to follow this path, difficult and yet easy, of sacrifice.

Speech on non-co-operation, Madras. *The Hindu*, 13 Aug. 1920.
MPWMG, vol. iii, pp. 132–44

229. The need for the right atmosphere for mass civil disobedience

Civil disobedience was on the lips of every one of the members of the All-India Congress Committee. Not having really ever tried it, everyone appeared to be enamoured of it from a mistaken belief in it as a sovereign remedy for our present-day ills. I feel sure that it can be made such if we can produce the necessary atmosphere for it. For individuals there always is that atmosphere except when their civil disobedience is certain to lead to bloodshed. I discovered this exception during the *satyagraha* days.* But even so, a call may come which one dare not neglect, cost what it may. I can clearly see the time coming to me when I *must* refuse obedience to every single State-made law, even though there may be a certainty of bloodshed. When neglect of the call means a denial of God, civil disobedience becomes a peremptory duty.

Mass civil disobedience stands on a different footing. It can only be tried in a calm atmosphere. It must be the calmness of strength not weakness, of knowledge not ignorance. Individual civil disobedience may be and often is vicarious. Mass civil disobedience may be and often is selfish in the sense that individuals expect personal gain from their disobedience. Thus, in South Africa, Kallenbach and Polak* offered vicarious civil disobedience. They had nothing to gain. Thousands offered it because they expected personal gain also in the shape, say, of the removal of the annual poll-tax levied upon ex-indentured men and their wives and grown-up children. It is sufficient in mass civil disobedience if the resisters understand the working of the doctrine.

It was in a practically uninhabited tract of country that I was arrested in South Africa when I was marching into a prohibited area* with over two to three thousand men and some women. The company included several Pathans and others who were able-bodied men. It was the greatest testimony of merit the Government of South Africa gave to the movement. They knew that we were as harmless as we were determined. It was easy enough for that body of men to cut to pieces those who arrested me. It would have not only been a most cowardly thing to do, but it would have been a treacherous breach of their own pledge, and it would have meant ruin to the struggle of freedom and the forcible deportation of every Indian from South Africa. But the men were no rabble. They were disciplined soldiers and all the better for being unarmed. Though I was torn from them, they did not disperse, nor did they turn back. They marched on to their destination till they were, every one of them, arrested and imprisoned. So far as I am aware, this was an instance of discipline and non-violence for which there is no parallel in history. Without such restraint I see no hope of successful mass civil disobedience here.

We must dismiss the idea of overawing the Government by huge demonstrations every time someone is arrested. On the contrary we must treat arrest as the normal condition of the life of a non-co-operator. For we must seek arrest and imprisonment, as a soldier who goes to battle seeks death. We expect to bear down the opposition of the Government by courting and not by avoiding imprisonment, even though it be by showing our supposed readiness to be arrested and imprisoned *en masse*. Civil disobedience then emphatically means the desire to surrender to a single unarmed policeman. Our triumph consists in thousands being led to the prisons like lambs to the slaughter-house. If the lambs of the world had been willingly led, they would have long ago saved themselves from the butcher's knife. Our triumph consists again in being imprisoned for no wrong whatsoever. The greater our innocence, the greater our strength and the swifter our victory.

As it is, this Government is cowardly, we are afraid of imprisonment. The Government takes advantage of our fear of jails. If only our men and women welcome jails as health resorts, we will cease to worry about the dear ones put in jails which our countrymen in South Africa used to nickname His Majesty's Hotels.

We have too long been mentally disobedient to the laws of the State and have too often surreptitiously evaded them to be fit all of a sudden for civil disobedience. Disobedience to be civil has to be open and non-violent.

Complete civil disobedience is a state of peaceful rebellion—a refusal to obey every single State-made law. It is certainly more dangerous than an armed rebellion. For it can never be put down if the civil resisters are prepared to face extreme hardships. It is based upon an implicit belief in the absolute efficiency of innocent suffering. By noiselessly going to prison a civil resister ensures a calm atmosphere. The wrongdoer wearies of wrong-doing in the absence of resistance. All pleasure is lost when the victim betrays no resistance. A full grasp of the conditions of successful civil resistance is necessary at least on the part of the representatives of the people before we can launch out on an enterprise of such magnitude. The quickest remedies are always fraught with the greatest danger and require the utmost skill in handling them. It is my firm conviction that, if we bring about a successful boycott of foreign cloth, we shall have produced an atmosphere that would enable us to inaugurate civil disobedience on a scale that no Government can resist. I would therefore urge patience and determined concentration on *swadeshi* upon those who are impatient to embark on mass civil disobedience.

'Civil Disobedience'. *Young India*, 4 Aug. 1921

230. Civil disobedience requires immense care

The next few weeks should see civil disobedience in full working order in some part of India. With illustrations of partial and individual civil disobedience the country has become familiar. Complete civil disobedience is rebellion without the element of violence in it. An out and out civil resister simply ignores the authority of the state. He becomes an outlaw claiming to disregard every unmoral state law. Thus, for instance, he may refuse to pay taxes, he may refuse to recognize the authority of the state in his daily intercourse. He may refuse to obey the law of trespass and claim to enter military barracks in order to speak to the soldiers, he may refuse to submit to limitations upon the manner of picketing and may picket within the prescribed area. In doing all this he never uses force and never resists force when it is used against him. In fact, he invites imprisonment and other uses of force against himself. This he does because and

when he finds the bodily freedom he seemingly enjoys to be an intolerable burden. He argues to himself that a state allows personal freedom only in so far as the citizen submits to its regulations.

Submission to the state law is the price a citizen pays for his personal liberty. Submission, therefore, to a state wholly or largely unjust
is an immoral barter for liberty. A citizen who thus realizes the evil
nature of a state is not satisfied to live on its sufferance, and therefore
appears to the others who do not share his belief to be a nuisance
to society whilst he is endeavouring to compel the state without
committing a moral breach to arrest him. Thus considered, civil
resistance is a most powerful expression of a soul's anguish and an
eloquent protest against the continuance of an evil state. Is not this
the history of all reform? Have not reformers, much to the disgust of
their fellows, discarded even innocent symbols associated with an
evil practice?

When a body of men disown the state under which they have hitherto lived, they nearly establish their own government. I say nearly,
for they do not go to the point of using force when they are resisted
by the state. Their 'business' as of the individual is to be locked up
or shot by the state, unless it recognizes their separate existence, in
other words bows to their will. Thus three thousand Indians in
South Africa after due notice to the Government of the Transvaal
crossed the Transvaal border in 1914 in defiance of the Transvaal
immigration law and compelled the Government to arrest them.
When it failed to provoke them to violence or to coerce them into
submission, it yielded to their demand. A body of civil resisters is,
therefore, like an army subject to all the discipline of a soldier, only
harder because of want of excitement of an ordinary soldier's life.
And as a civil resistance army is or ought to be free from passion
because free from the spirit of retaliation, it requires the fewest
number of soldiers. Indeed one PERFECT civil resister is enough to
win the battle of Right against Wrong.

Though, therefore, the All-India Congress Committee has
authorized civil disobedience by Provincial Congress Committees on
their own responsibility, I hope they will put due emphasis on the
word 'responsibility' and not start civil disobedience with a light
heart. Every condition must be given its full effect. The mention of
Hindu–Muslim unity, non-violence, *swadeshi* and removal of
untouchability means that they have not yet become an integral part

of our national life. If an individual or a mass have still misgivings about Hindu–Muslim unity, if they have still any doubt about the necessity of non-violence for the attainment of our triple goal, if they have not yet enforced *swadeshi* in its completeness, if the Hindus among that mass have still the poison of untouchability in them, that mass or that individual are not ready for civil disobedience. Indeed it would be best to watch and wait whilst the experiment is being carried on in one area. Reverting to the analogy of the army, those divisions that watch and wait are just as much co-operating actively as the division that is actually fighting.

The only time, whilst the experiment is going on, that individual civil disobedience may be resorted to simultaneously is when the Government obstruct even the silent persecution of *swadeshi*. Thus if an order of prohibition is served upon an expert spinner going to teach or organize spinning, that order should be summarily disregarded and the teacher should court imprisonment. But in all other respects, in so far as I can judge at present, it will be best for every other part of India scrupulously to respect all orders and instructions whilst one part is deliberately taking the offensive and committing a deliberate breach of all the unmoral state laws it possibly can. Needless to add that any outbreak of violence in any other part of India must necessarily injure and may even stop the experiment. The other parts will be expected to remain immovable and unperturbed, even though the people within the area of experiment may be imprisoned, riddled with bullets or otherwise ill-treated by the authorities. We must expect them to give a good account of themselves in every conceivable circumstance.

'The Momentous Issue'. *Young India*, 10 Nov. 1921

231. Retreat—to preserve non-violence

God has been abundantly kind to me. He has warned me the third time that there is not as yet in India that truthful and non-violent atmosphere which and which alone can justify mass disobedience which can be at all described as civil, which means gentle, truthful, humble, knowing, wilful yet loving, never criminal and hateful.

He warned me in 1919 when the Rowlatt Act agitation was started. Ahmedabad, Viramgam and Kheda erred; Amritsar and Kasur erred.

I retraced my steps, called it a Himalayan miscalculation,* humbled myself before God and man, and stopped not merely mass civil disobedience but even my own which I knew was intended to be civil and non-violent.

The next time it was through the events of Bombay that God gave a terrific warning. He made me eyewitness of the deeds of the Bombay mob on the 17th November.* The mob acted in the interest of non-co-operation. I announced my intention to stop the mass civil disobedience which was to be immediately started in Bardoli. The humiliation was greater than in 1919. But it did me good. I am sure that the nation gained by the stopping. India stood for truth and non-violence by the suspension.

But the bitterest humiliation was still to come. Madras did give the warning, but I heeded it not. But God spoke clearly through Chauri Chaura.* I understand that the constables who were so brutally hacked to death had given much provocation. They had even gone back upon the word just given by the Inspector that they would not be molested, but when the procession had passed the stragglers were interfered with and abused by the constables. The former cried out for help. The mob returned. The constables opened fire. The little ammunition they had was exhausted and they retired to the *Thana** for safety. The mob, my informant tells me, therefore set fire to the *Thana*. The self-imprisoned constables had to come out for dear life and as they did so, they were hacked to pieces and the mangled remains were thrown into the raging flames.

It is claimed that no non-co-operation volunteer had a hand in the brutality and that the mob had not only the immediate provocation but they had also general knowledge of the high-handed tyranny of the police in that district. No provocation can possibly justify the brutal murder of men who had been rendered defenceless and who had virtually thrown themselves on the mercy of the mob. And when India claims to be non-violent and hopes to mount the throne of Liberty through non-violent means, mob-violence even in answer to grave provocation is a bad augury. Suppose the 'non-violent' disobedience of Bardoli* was permitted by God to succeed, the Government had abdicated in favour of the victors of Bardoli, who would control the unruly element that must be expected to perpetrate inhumanity upon due provocation? Non-violent attainment of self-government presupposes a non-violent control over the violent elements in the country. Non-violent non-co-operators can only succeed when they have succeeded in attaining control over the hooligans of India, in other words, when the latter also have learnt patriotically or religiously to refrain from their violent activities at least whilst the campaign of non-co-operation is going on. The tragedy at Chauri Chaura, therefore, roused me thoroughly.

'But what about your manifesto to the Viceroy and your rejoinder to his reply?' spoke the voice of Satan. It was the bitterest cup of humiliation to drink. 'Surely it is cowardly to withdraw the next day after pompous threats to the Government and promises to the people of Bardoli.' Thus Satan's invitation was to deny Truth and therefore Religion, to deny God Himself. I put my doubts and troubles before the Working Committee and other associates whom I found near me. They did not all agree with me at first. Some of them probably do not even now agree with me. But never has a man been blessed, perhaps, with colleagues and associates so considerate and forgiving as I have. They understood my difficulty and patiently followed my argument. . . . The drastic reversal of practically the whole of the aggressive programme may be politically unsound and unwise, but there is no doubt that it is religiously sound, and I venture to assure the doubters that the country will have gained by my humiliation and confession of error.

The only virtue I want to claim is Truth and Non-violence. I lay no claim to superhuman powers. I want none. I wear the same corruptible flesh that the weakest of my fellow beings wears and am therefore as liable to err as any. My services have many limitations, but God has up to now blessed them in spite of the imperfections.

For, confession of error is like a broom that sweeps away dirt and leaves the surface cleaner than before, I feel stronger for my confession. And the cause must prosper for the retracing. Never has man reached his destination by persistence in deviation from the straight path.

It has been urged that Chauri Chaura cannot affect Bardoli. There is danger, it is argued, only if Bardoli is weak enough to be swayed by Chauri Chaura and is betrayed into violence. I have no doubt whatsoever on that account. The people of Bardoli are in my opinion the most peaceful in India. But Bardoli is but a speck on the map of India. Its effort cannot succeed unless there is perfect co-operation from the other parts. Bardoli's disobedience will be civil only when the other parts of India remain non-violent. Just as the addition of a grain of arsenic to a pot of milk renders it unfit as food so will the civility of Bardoli prove unacceptable by the addition of the deadly poison from Chauri Chaura. The latter represents India as much as Bardoli.

Chauri Chaura is after all an aggravated symptom. I have never imagined that there has been no violence, mental or physical, in the places where repression is going on. Only I have believed, I still believe and the pages of *Young India* amply prove, that the repression is out of all proportion to the insignificant popular violence in the areas of repression. The determined holding of meetings in prohibited areas I do not call violence. The violence I am referring to is the throwing of brickbats or intimidation and coercion practised in stray cases. As a matter of fact in civil disobedience there should be no excitement. Civil disobedience is a preparation for mute suffering. Its effect is marvellous though unperceived and gentle. But I regarded a certain amount of excitement as inevitable, certain amount of unintended violence even pardonable, i.e., I did not consider civil disobedience impossible in somewhat imperfect conditions. Under perfect conditions disobedience when civil is hardly felt. But the present movement is admittedly a dangerous experiment under fairly adverse conditions.

The tragedy of Chauri Chaura is really the index finger. It shows the way India may easily go if drastic precautions be not taken. If we are not to evolve violence out of non-violence, it is quite clear that we must hastily retrace our steps and re-establish an atmosphere of peace, re-arrange our programme and not think of starting mass civil disobedience until we are sure of peace being retained in spite of mass civil disobedience being started and in spite of Government provocation. We must be sure of unauthorized portions not starting mass civil disobedience.

As it is, the Congress organization is still imperfect and its instructions are still perfunctorily carried out. We have not established Congress Committees in every one of the villages. Where we have, they are not perfectly amenable to our instructions. We have not probably more than one crore of members on the roll. We are in the middle of February, yet not many have paid the annual four-anna subscription for the current year. Volunteers are indifferently enrolled. They do not conform to all the conditions of their pledge.

They do not even wear hand-spun and hand-woven khaddar. All the Hindu volunteers have not yet purged themselves of the sin of untouchability. All are not free from the taint of violence. Not by their imprisonment are we going to win swaraj or serve the holy cause of the Khilafat or attain the ability to stop payment to faithless servants. Some of us err in spite of ourselves. But some others among us sin wilfully. They join Volunteer Corps well knowing that they are not and do not intend to remain non-violent. We are thus untruthful even as we hold the Government to be untruthful. We dare not enter the kingdom of Liberty with mere lip homage to Truth and Non-violence.

Suspension of mass civil disobedience and subsidence of excitement are necessary for further progress, indeed indispensable to prevent further retrogression. I hope, therefore, that by suspension every Congressman or woman will not only not feel disappointed but he or she will feel relieved of the burden of unreality and of national sin.

Let the opponent glory in our humiliation or so-called defeat. It is better to be charged with cowardice and weakness than to be guilty of denial of our oath and sin against God. It is a million times better to *appear* untrue before the world than to *be* untrue to ourselves.

And so, for me the suspension of mass civil disobedience and other minor activities that were calculated to keep up excitement is not enough penance for my having been the instrument, however involuntary, of the brutal violence by the people at Chauri Chaura.

I must undergo personal cleansing. I must become a fitter instrument able to register the slightest variation in the moral atmosphere about me. My prayers must have much deeper truth and humility about them than they evidence. And for me there is nothing so helpful and cleansing as a fast accompanied by the necessary mental co-operation.

I know that the mental attitude is everything. Just as a prayer may be merely a mechanical intonation as of a bird, so may a fast be a mere mechanical torture of the flesh. Such mechanical contrivances are valueless for the purpose intended. Again, just as a mechanical chant may result in the modulation of voice, a mechanical fast may result in purifying the body. Neither will touch the soul within.

But a fast undertaken for fuller self-expression, for attainment of the spirit's supremacy over the flesh, is a most powerful factor in one's evolution. After deep consideration, therefore, I am imposing on myself a five days' continuous fast, permitting myself water. . . . This is the least I must do. . . .

If we learn the full lesson of the tragedy, we can turn the curse into a blessing. By becoming truthful and non-violent, both in spirit and deed, and by making the swadeshi, i.e., the khaddar programme complete, we can establish full swaraj and redress the Khilafat and the Punjab wrongs without a single person having to offer civil disobedience.

Young India, 16 Feb. 1922

232. Planning civil disobedience again—despite the danger of violence

But what is there intrinsically wrong in wanting independence? It is not possible for me to understand this opposition from sober Englishmen to the enunciation of an inalienable right of every nation to be independent except on the supposition that even they, the sober Englishmen, do not want India to be free.

'But you are not fit for independence,' say some. Surely it is for us to judge whether we are fit or not. And granting that we are not, there is nothing wrong or immoral in our aspiring after independence and in the attempt rendering ourselves fitter day by day. We shall never be fit being taught to feel helpless and to rely upon the British bayonet to keep us from fighting among ourselves or from being devoured by our neighbours. If we have to go through the agonies of a civil war or a foreign invasion, it won't be a new thing in the history of nations that have struggled for freedom. England has gone through both the experiences. After all freedom is not a hot-house growth.

It is open to those English friends who are sincerely anxious for India's welfare to assist India in her fight for freedom and on her terms. She knows best what she needs. Complete independence does not mean arrogant isolation or a superior disdain for all help. But it does mean complete severance of the British bondage, be it ever so slight or well concealed. The opposition, therefore, to the demand for immediate independence raises the strongest suspicions about the good intentions of those who have conceived the idea of

the Conference. It must be clearly understood that the largest nationalist party in India will no longer submit to the position of a dependent nation or to the process of helpless exploitation. It will run any
risk to be free from the double curse.

Is it not now intelligible why, notwithstanding its undoubted
risks, I am planning some sort of civil disobedience* so as to get
together all the non-violent forces and see if it stems the tide of
onrushing violence? Hatred and ill-will there undoubtedly are in the
air. They are bound sooner or later to burst into acts of fury if they
are not anticipated in time. The conviction has deepened in me that
civil disobedience alone can stop the bursting of that fury. The
nation wants to feel its power more even than to have independence.
Possession of such power *is* independence.

That civil disobedience may resolve itself into violent disobedience is, I am sorry to have to confess, not an unlikely event. But
I know that it will not be the cause of it. Violence is there already
corroding the whole body politic. Civil disobedience will be but a
purifying process and may bring to the surface what is burrowing
under and into the whole body. And British officials, if they choose,
may regulate civil disobedience so as to sterilize the forces of violence. But whether they do so, or whether, as many of us fear, they
will, directly or indirectly, consciously or unconsciously, provoke
violence, my course is clear. With the evidence I have of the condition of the country and with the unquenchable faith I have in the
method of civil resistance, I must not be deterred from the course the
inward voice seems to be leading me to.

But whatever I do and whatever happens, my English friends will
accept my word, that whilst I am impatient to break the British
bondage, I am no enemy of Britain.

'To English Friends'. *Young India*, 23 Jan. 1930

233. Civil disobedience—a sovereign method

There is no halfway house between active loyalty and active
disloyalty. There is much truth in the late Justice Stephen's* remark
that a man to prove himself not guilty of disaffection must prove
himself to be actively affectionate. In these days of democracy there
is no such thing as active loyalty to a person. You are therefore loyal

or disloyal to institutions. When, therefore, you are disloyal you seek not to destroy persons but institutions. The present State is an institution which, if one knows it, can never evoke loyalty. It is corrupt. Many of its laws governing the conduct of persons are positively inhuman. Their administration is worse. Often the will of one person is the law. It may safely be said that there are as many rulers as there are districts in this country. These, called Collectors,* combine in their own persons the executive as well as the judicial functions. Though their acts are supposed to be governed by laws in themselves highly defective, these rulers are often capricious and regulated by nothing but their own whims and fancies. They represent not the interests of the people but those of their foreign masters or principals. These (nearly three hundred) men form an almost secret corporation, the most powerful in the world. They are required to find a fixed minimum of revenue, they have therefore often been found to be most unscrupulous in their dealings with the people.

This system of government is confessedly based upon a merciless exploitation of unnumbered millions of the inhabitants of India. From the village Headmen to their personal assistants these satraps have created a class of subordinates who, whilst they cringe before their foreign masters, in their constant dealings with the people act so irresponsibly and so harshly as to demoralize them and by a system of terrorism render them incapable of resisting corruption. It is then the duty of those who have realized the awful evil of the system of Indian Government to be disloyal to it and actively and openly to preach disloyalty. Indeed, loyalty to a State so corrupt is a sin, disloyalty a virtue.

The spectacle of three hundred million people being cowed down by living in the dread of three hundred men* is demoralizing alike for the despots as for the victims. It is the duty of those who have realized the evil nature of the system, however attractive some of its features may, torn from their context, appear to be, to destroy it without delay. It is their clear duty to run any risk to achieve the end.

But it must be equally clear that it would be cowardly for three hundred million people to seek to destroy the three hundred authors or administrators of the system. It is a sign of gross ignorance to devise means of destroying these administrators or their hirelings. Moreover they are but creatures of circumstances. The purest man entering the system will be affected by it and will be instrumental in propagating the evil. The remedy therefore naturally is not being enraged against the administrators and therefore hurting them, but to non-co-operate with the system by withdrawing all the voluntary assistance possible and refusing all its so-called benefits. A little reflection will show that civil disobedience is a necessary part of non-co-operation. You assist an administration most effectively by obeying its orders and decrees. An evil administration never deserves such allegiance. Allegiance to it means partaking of the evil. A good man will therefore resist an evil system or administration with his whole soul. Disobedience of the law of an evil State is therefore a duty. Violent disobedience deals with men who can be replaced. It leaves the evil itself untouched and often accentuates it. Non-violent, i.e., civil, disobedience is the only and the most successful remedy and is obligatory upon him who would dissociate himself from evil.

There is danger in civil disobedience only because it is still only a partially tried remedy and has always to be tried in an atmosphere surcharged with violence. For when tyranny is rampant much rage is generated among the victims. It remains latent because of their weakness and bursts in all its fury on the slightest pretext. Civil disobedience is a sovereign method of transmuting this undisciplined life-destroying latent energy into disciplined, life-saving energy whose use ensures absolute success. The attendant risk is nothing compared to the result promised. When the world has become familiar with its use and when it has had a series of demonstrations of its successful working, there will be less risk in civil disobedience than there is in aviation, in spite of that science having reached a high stage of development.

'Duty of Disloyalty'. *Young India*, 27 Mar. 1930

234. Suspending civil disobedience for *swaraj*

2 April 1934

This statement owes its inspiration to a personal chat with the inmates and associates of the Satyagraha Ashram who had just come out of prison and whom at Rajendrababu's* instance I had sent to Bihar. More especially it is due to a revealing information I got in the course of conversation about a valued companion of long standing who was found reluctant to perform the full prison task and preferring his private studies to the allotted task. This was undoubtedly contrary to the rules of *satyagraha*. More than the imperfection of the friend, whom I love more than ever, it brought home to me my own imperfection. The friend said he had thought that I was aware of his weakness. I was blind. Blindness in a leader is unpardonable. I saw at once that I must for the time being remain the sole representative of civil resistance in action.

During the informal conference week at Poona in July last I had stated that while many individual civil resisters would be welcome, even one was sufficient to keep alive the message of *satyagraha*. Now after much searching of the heart I have arrived at the conclusion that in the present circumstances only one, and that myself and no other, should for the time being bear the responsibility of civil resistance if it is to succeed as a means of achieving *purna swaraj*.

I feel that the masses have not received the full message of *satyagraha* owing to its adulteration in the process of transmission. It has become clear to me that spiritual instruments suffer in their potency when their use is taught through non-spiritual media. Spiritual messages are self-propagating. The reaction of the masses throughout the *Harijan* tour has been the latest forcible illustration of what I mean. The splendid response of the masses has been spontaneous. The workers themselves were amazed at the attention and the fervour of vast masses whom they had never reached.

Satyagraha is a purely spiritual weapon. It may be used for what may appear to be mundane ends and through men and women who do not understand its spirituality provided the director knows that the weapon is spiritual. Everyone cannot use surgical instruments. Many may use them if there is an expert behind them directing their use. I claim to be a *satyagraha* expert in the making. I have need to be far more careful than the expert surgeon who is complete master of his science. I am still a humble searcher. The very nature of the science of *satyagraha* precludes the student from seeing more than the step immediately in front of him.

The introspection prompted by the conversation with the Ashram inmates has led me to the conclusion that I must advise all Congressmen to suspend civil resistance for *swaraj* as distinguished from specific grievances. They should leave it to me alone. It should be resumed by others in my lifetime only under my direction unless one arises claiming to know the science better than I do and inspires confidence. I give this opinion as the author and initiator of *satyagraha*. Henceforth, therefore, all who have been impelled to civil resistance for *swaraj* under my advice directly given or indirectly inferred will please desist from civil resistance. I am quite convinced that this is the best course in the interests of India's fight for freedom.

I am in dead earnest about this greatest of weapons at the disposal of mankind. It is claimed for *satyagraha* that it is a complete substitute for violence or war. It is designed, therefore, to reach the hearts both of the so-called 'terrorists' and the rulers who seek to root out the 'terrorists' by emasculating a whole nation. But the indifferent civil resistance of many, grand as it has been in its results, has not touched the hearts of either the 'terrorists' or the rulers as a class. Unadulterated *satyagraha* must touch the hearts of both. To test the truth of the proposition, *satyagraha* needs to be confined to one qualified person at a time. The trial has never been made. It must be made now.

Let me caution the reader against mistaking *satyagraha* for mere civil resistance. It covers much more than civil resistance. It means relentless search for truth and the power that such a search gives to the searcher. The search can only be pursued by strictly non-violent means.

What are the civil resisters, thus freed, to do? If they are to be ready for the call whenever it comes, they must learn the art and the beauty of self-denial and voluntary poverty. They must engage themselves in nation-building activities, the spread of *khaddar* through personal hand-spinning and hand-weaving, the spread of communal unity of hearts by irreproachable personal conduct towards one another in every walk of life, the banishing of untouchability in every shape or form in one's own person, the spread of total abstinence from intoxicating drinks and drugs by personal contact with individual addicts and generally by cultivating personal purity. These are services which provide maintenance on a poor man's scale. Those for whom the poor man's scale is not feasible should find a place in small unorganized industries of national importance which give a better wage. Let it be understood that civil resistance is for those who know and perform the duty of voluntary obedience to law and authority.

It is hardly necessary to say that in issuing this statement I am in no way usurping the function of the Congress. Mine is mere advice to those who look to me for guidance in matters of *satyagraha*.

Statement to the press, 2 Apr. 1934. CW 9137. *MPWMG*, vol. iii, pp. 73–5

235. The requirements of discipline and non-violence

Sevagram,
March 5, 1940

Everybody is asking me not whether but when I am to call the country to civil disobedience. Some of my questioners are the most sober among co-workers. . . . It is proof that the country, or that part of it that has hitherto taken part in the struggle for freedom, is tired of waiting and suspense. It is heartening to think that there are in the country so many persons who count no sacrifice too dear for gaining independence.

While, therefore, I admire the zeal of my questioners, I must warn them against being impatient. There is nothing in the resolution to warrant the belief that the atmosphere is suitable for declaring civil disobedience. It will be suicidal to declare it when there is so much indiscipline and violence within the Congress itself. Congressmen will make a serious mistake if they do not give full weight to my words. I cannot, will not, start mass civil disobedience so long as I am not convinced that there is enough discipline and enough non-violence in Congress ranks. The apathy about the Constructive Programme, i.e., spinning and sales of *khadi*, I take to be positive signs of unbelief. Battle through such instruments is foredoomed to failure. Such persons should know that I am not their man. If there is no hope of attaining the necessary measure of discipline and non-violence, it would be better to let me retire from leadership.

Let it be clearly understood that I cannot be hustled into pre-cipitating the struggle. They err grievously who think that I can ever declare civil disobedience, having been driven thereto by the so-called leftists. I make no such distinction between rightists and leftists.* Both are my co-workers and friends. He will be a bold man who can with any measure of certainty draw the line of demarcation between leftists and rightists. Congressmen and non-Congressmen should also know that, even if the whole country were to turn against me, I must, when the time comes, fight single-handed. The others have or may have weapons besides non-violence. I have no choice. Being the author of non-violent technique in the political field, I am bound to fight when I feel the urge from within.

It is inherent in the technique that I never know the timetable in advance. The call may come at any time. It need not be described as from God. The inner urge is a current phrase easily understood. Everybody sometimes acts upon the inner urge. Such action need not always be right. But there is no other explanation possible for certain actions.

The thought often comes to me that it would be a good thing if the Congress could forget me. I do sometimes feel that with my strange views of life I am a misfit in the Congress. Whatever special qualifications I may possess and for which the Congress and the country may have use can perhaps be better utilized if I were wholly cut off from the Congress. But I know that this severance cannot be brought about mechanically or violently. It will come in its own time, if it has to come. Only Congressmen should know my limitations and should not be surprised or grieved if they find me stiff and unbending. I ask them to believe me when I say that I am incapable of acting without the fulfilment of the conditions laid down for declaring mass civil disobedience.*

'When?' *Harijan*, 9 Mar. 1940

236. Mistaking passive resistance for non-violent resistance

29 November 1947

Coming to my personal experience, whilst we undoubtedly got through passive resistance our political freedom, over which lovers of peace like you and your good husband* of the West are enthusiastic, we are daily paying the heavy price* for the unconscious mistake we made or better still, I made in mistaking passive resistance for non-violent resistance. Had I not made the mistake, we would have been spared the humiliating spectacle of weak brother killing his weak brother thoughtlessly and inhumanly.

I am only hoping and praying and I want all the friends here and in other parts of the world to hope and pray with me that this blood-bath will soon end and out of that, perhaps, inevitable butchery will rise a new and robust India—not warlike, basely imitating the West in all its hideousness, but a new India learning the best that the West has to give and becoming the hope not only of Asia and Africa, but the whole of the aching world.

I must confess that this is hoping against hope, for, we are today swearing by the military and all that naked physical force implies. Our statesmen have for over two generations declaimed against the heavy expenditure on armaments under the British regime, but now that freedom from political serfdom has come, our military expenditure has increased and still threatens to increase and of this we are proud! There is not a voice raised against it in our legislative chambers. In spite, however, of the madness and the vain imitation of the tinsel of the West, the hope lingers in me and many others that India shall survive this death dance and occupy the moral height that should belong to her after the training, however imperfect, in non-violence for an unbroken period of thirty-two years since 1915.

Letter to Madame Edmond Privat. *Harijan*, 2 Dec. 1947

237. *Ahimsa* does not fail

1 January 1948

In any case, whatever I have said does not refer in any way to the failure of *ahimsa*, but it refers to my failure to recognize, until it was too late, that what I had mistaken for *ahimsa* was not *ahimsa*, but passive resistance of the weak, which can never be called *ahimsa* even in the remotest sense. The internecine feud* that is going on today in India is the direct outcome of the energy that was set free during the thirty years' action of the weak. Hence, the proper way to view the present outburst of violence throughout the world is to recognize that the technique of unconquerable non-violence of the strong has not been at all fully discovered as yet. Not an ounce of non-violent strength is ever wasted. I must not, therefore, flatter myself with the belief— nor allow friends like you to entertain the belief—that I have exhibited any heroic and demonstrable non-violence in myself. All I can claim is that I am sailing in that direction without a moment's stop. This confession should strengthen your belief in non-violence and spur you and friends like you to action along the path.

'*Ahimsa* Never Fails'. *Harijan*, 11 Jan. 1948

EXPLANATORY NOTES

I. GANDHI, HIS MISSION, AND THE INFLUENCES ON HIM

1 *Moksha*: salvation or self-realization. In Hindu thought, becoming one with the divine within each individual, and achieving freedom from the bondage of the cycle of lives determined by *karma*.

4 *sannyasi*: Hindu holy person who retreats from ordinary working life in the pursuit of holiness and is often dressed in saffron or ochre clothes. Such a retreat from ordinary life was contrary to Gandhi's vision of the practice of true religion, or the pursuit of truth.

brahmacharya: sexual restraint or celibacy. In Hindu thinking, such a state of life allows the person to generate spiritual energy. Gandhi took a vow of celibacy in 1906: see his *Autobiography*, part IV, chap. XXV, and II. 73 in the present selection.

tapascharya: practices of self-discipline.

5 *swaraj*: self-rule. For Gandhi's understanding of self-rule or freedom for India, see the Introduction and Section IV of this selection. His major exposition of the meaning of *swaraj* for India was a pamphlet written in Gujarati, *Hind Swaraj*. It was published in 1909 and banned the next year in India. The most modern English edition is published by Cambridge University Press, 1997, with an excellent introduction by Anthony J. Parel.

Gita: the *Bhagavad Gita* is a Hindu scriptural text which Gandhi found a major source of spiritual inspiration. It is part of the great Hindu epic, the *Mahabharata*, and deals with major ethical issues which are part of the active human life.

6 *Vinoba*: Vinoba Bhave (1895–1982) was a follower of Gandhi from the time he was a young man and devoted himself to non-violent social and economic reconstruction in India.

bhakti: religious devotion.

Newman: John Henry Newman (1801–90), notable English Christian theologian, writer, and leader. The quotation comes from his well-known hymn, 'Lead Kindly Light', which was one of Gandhi's personal favourites and sometimes sung at his prayer meetings.

bhajan: a devotional song. Many were sung at Gandhi's prayer meetings and in his *ashram* communities.

mukti: spiritual deliverance or freedom from the bondage of the cycle of lives dictated by *karma*.

7 *dharma*: religious duty appropriate to one's age and status in life.

8 *control them*: this was at a stage in Gandhi's career after he had withdrawn the campaign of non-cooperation in 1922 after some Indians had abandoned

non-violence and attacked a police station at Chauri Chaura, killing the Indian policemen within it. He eventually after much heart-searching about the issue of violence started a new campaign of civil disobedience in 1930, focusing initially on the illegal manufacture of salt to ensure non-violence as far as possible.

8 *I cannot name him*: towards the end of his life Gandhi effectively named Jawaharlal Nehru (1889–1964) as his political heir, even though they disagreed on many issues. He became India's first Prime Minister. See Judith M. Brown, *Nehru: A Political Life* (New Haven and London: Yale University Press, 2003).

Brooks: Far Eastern correspondent of the *Chicago Defender*, which published the interview, of which this exchange is a part, on 10 June 1945. Gandhi was observing one of his regular days of silence and jotted his answers down on paper.

ahimsa: non-violence.

book form: Gandhi's autobiography was first published as a series of newspaper articles and then collected into a book: it covered his life until *c*.1921.

9 *Harijan*: 'Child of God', the name given to untouchables by Gandhi (and often much disliked by them as patronizing). It was also the title of a periodical he published in the last decades of his life to further his campaign against untouchability.

Manu Gandhi: Gandhi's grand-niece, who had asked him why he was prepared to correspond with someone who abused him. She was a constant companion in the final months of his life and was supporting him as he walked to his prayer meeting when he was assassinated in January 1948.

The critic: a criticism of him in *East and West*, April 1920.

11 *the conditions of work there*: this speech was on the occasion of a visit to the steelworks in Jamshedpur, Bihar, owned by the Tata family, one of the great industrialist families of modern India. The speech displays the ambiguities in Gandhi's relations with capitalists. He fundamentally disapproved of capitalism and factory production, yet was close to many powerful business people and was supported financially by them. In his thinking on class relations he developed the idea that the rich should see themselves as trustees of their wealth on behalf of the wider society.

Ahmedabad: great industrial city in Gandhi's home region of Gujarat, where his first *ashram* or religious community was established. It had also been the site of one of his earliest movements of non-violent resistance in 1918, on behalf of workers in the cotton industry. He subsequently took much interest in industrial relations there.

12 *Sir Michael O'Dwyer and General Dyer*: General Dyer was the General who ordered the infamous shooting on an unarmed crowd in Jallianwalla Bagh, Amritsar, Punjab, in 1919; and Sir Michael O'Dwyer was Lt.-Governor of the Punjab at the time.

15 *the spinning-wheel*: regular use of the *charkha*, spinning-wheel, was part of Gandhi's prescription for the socio-economic transformation of India. It was part of his larger campaign to persuade people to use *khadi*, locally produced and handmade cloth: and this was in turn part of his belief in *swadeshi*, using items made in one's own place and country.

condemnation: this condemnation was at the heart of Gandhi's pamphlet, *Hind Swaraj*.

16 *Lancashire men*: Gandhi refers here to the Lancashire cotton industry which exported cotton goods to India. When in England in 1931 he made a special point of visiting Lancashire to explain his position to owners of and workers in the cotton mills.

21 *Chaturmas*: a period of four months of fasting during the monsoon rains.

Ramanama: the name of the Hindu God, Ram. Gandhi died with the name of Ram on his lips.

Ramayana: Hindu epic of which Ram is the hero. The highly popular Hindi version was by the poet, Tulsidas, who lived in northern India at the end of the fifteenth and beginning of the sixteenth century AD. He refashioned the epic to portray Ram as the incarnation of the supreme God, and taught the way of *bhakti* as the path to the divine, including the recitation of the divine name.

22 *Narasainyo*: Narasinh Mehta (1414–79), saint poet of Gujarat. This poem was used in the daily prayers of Gandhi's *ashram*.

23 *introduction*: this was among a number of introductions made for Gandhi by a family friend on his return from studying in England in 1891.

24 *vairagya*: disinterestedness, freedom from attachment.

25 *gadi*: in this context, a cushion.

atman: the universal self underlying individual human personality.

26 *Gita*: the *Bhagavad Gita* is one of the most important texts in the practice of modern Hinduism: see above, note to p. 5. The translation of the *Gita*, entitled *The Song Celestial* (1886), was by Sir Edwin Arnold (1832–1904), poet, journalist and sometime Principal of the Deccan Sanskrit College, Poona. He also wrote a verse account of Buddha's life and teaching, *The Light of Asia* (1875), which Gandhi also read with great interest on the recommendation of the same brothers who encouraged him to read *The Song Celestial*.

28 *About the same time*: during his second year as a student in England.

Rajkot recollections: Gandhi's first encounter with Christianity had been in his boyhood home in Rajkot, western India, when he had encountered missionaries who condemned Hinduism. He had also mistakenly understood that converts to Christianity had to adopt European dress, eat beef, and drink alcohol. See *An Autobiography*, part I, chap. X.

your book: Henry Salt (1851–1939), an English classical scholar, socialist, and publicist on social issues, wrote numerous works on vegetarianism. Gandhi probably refers here to *A Plea for Vegetarianism*. Gandhi recounted his growing experiments with and understanding of vegetarianism as a student in England in his *Autobiography*, part I, chap. XVII. Salt wrote a life of Henry Thoreau in 1890.

28 *Thoreau's*: Henry David Thoreau (1817–62), American philosopher and writer. His famous essay, on civil disobedience, was published in 1849, and his account of living in a self-built cabin, *Walden*, was published in 1854.

29 *He*: the friend who lent Gandhi *Unto this Last* in 1904 was Henry Polak (1882–1959). Born in London, he emigrated to South Africa and became a close associate of Gandhi in his struggle for Indian rights in South Africa.

Ruskin's Unto this Last: John Ruskin (1819–1900), English art critic and social critic. His *Unto this Last*, which made the most profound impression on Gandhi, was published in 1862: for a modern edition see C. Wilmer (ed.), *Unto this Last and Other Writings by John Ruskin* (Penguin Classics, 1997). Gandhi made a Gujarati paraphrase of *Unto this Last* in 1908 in a series of articles for readers of his newspaper, *Indian Opinion*. These articles are available in English translation in *The Collected Works of Mahatma Gandhi*, vol. viii (New Delhi: Publications Division of the Government of India, 1962); and in *The Moral and Political Writings of Mahatma Gandhi*, ed. Raghavan Iyer, vol. iii: *Non-violent Resistance and Social Transformation* (Oxford: Clarendon Press, 1987), 410–33.

30 *one book*: i.e. *Unto this Last*; see previous note.

31 *Tolstoy's books*: Leo Tolstoy (1878–1910), Russian novelist and philosopher. The book referred to was published in 1896. Another of Tolstoy's books which greatly influenced Gandhi was *The Kingdom of God is Within You* (1894): see above I. 21. In his *Autobiography* (part II, chap. IV), he wrote that this book 'overwhelmed' him and made an 'abiding impression' on him.

letter: this was Tolstoy's 'Letter to a Hindu', which Gandhi translated into Gujarati and published in 1909 in *Indian Opinion*, the newspaper he ran in South Africa.

32 *satyagrahis*: exponents of *satyagraha*, the name Gandhi began to use in South Africa for non-violent resistance to wrong.

34 *Naoroji*: Dadabhai Naoroji (1825–1917), Parsi academic and politician, founder member of the Indian National Congress. Elected Liberal MP for Central Finsbury, London, in 1902.

Dadabhai's book: an influential book on the economic impact of British rule in India, *Poverty and Un-British Rule in India* (1901).

35 *Ramayana*: see above, note to p. 21.

36 *Mr Gokhale*: G. K. Gokhale (1866–1915), western Indian academic and moderate Congress politician, founder of the Servants of India Society (1905); visited South Africa in 1912 to assist Gandhi's work for Indian rights. Gandhi accepted him as his main political teacher or *guru*.

shlokas: verses.

Shastras: Hindu scriptures.

37 *Shantiniketan*: university founded by Rabindranath Tagore in Bengal, where Gandhi and his immediate associates spent some time on their return from South Africa to India in 1915.

38 *opportunity*: this was the jail sentence following the non-cooperation movement of 1920–2, when Gandhi was in prison from 1922 to 1924. The document continues with a long and very eclectic list of reading. Subsequent prison sentences in the 1930s and 1940s were for Gandhi a time for physical refreshment and intellectual renewal and he recorded his voluminous reading programmes during them.

II. AUTHENTIC HUMAN LIFE AND THE TRANSFORMATION OF THE INDIVIDUAL

39 *A. H. West*: Albert West was a close associate of Gandhi's in South Africa. The context was Gandhi's increasing conviction of the evils of so-called modern civilization, most clearly demonstrated in his pamphlet, *Hind Swaraj*. See below, Section III.

41 *Sir J. C. Bose*: Sir Jagdish Chandra Bose (1858–1937), a famous Indian scientist.

44 *Satyagraha Ashram*: the Satyagraha Ashram was Gandhi's first *ashram* in India, set up in Ahmedabad in 1915 on his return from South Africa. This letter was intended to be read aloud at *ashram* prayer time in Gandhi's absence, as he was in prison during the civil disobedience movement.

47 *Tulsidas*: see above, note to p. 21.

both Gods: this phrase came from Tolstoy: 'There are two Gods. There is the God people generally believe in, a God who has to serve them sometimes in a very refined way; perhaps merely by giving them peace of mind. This God does not exist. But the God whom we all have to serve does exist and is the prime cause of our existence and of all we perceive.' Gandhi had been asked which of these two Gods he believed in.

48 *the fast*: Gandhi had decided early in 1933 to undertake a three-week fast of self-purification to equip him better to combat the evil of untouchability. Many of his colleagues were baffled by this.

'still small Voice': this phrase comes in the English translation of an Old Testament story (1 Kings 19: 12) in which the prophet Elijah perceived God not as wind, earthquake, or fire but as a still, small voice. The phrase was taken up in a popular Christian hymn, 'Dear Lord and Father of Mankind', by the American poet, John Greenleaf Whittier (1807–92). It is not clear from which source Gandhi discovered the phrase; possibly from both.

49 *Rajagopalachari*: C. R. Rajagopalachariar (1879–1972), a prominent south Indian politician, was one of those who was deeply concerned about

Gandhi's decision to undergo a three-week purificatory fast in 1933 (see above, note to p. 48).

51 *Raychandbhai*: see above, I. 21–3.

52 *apprehensions*: this was written at a time of increasing hostility between Hindus and Muslims in India, leading to severe riots.

54 *Brahma satyam jaganmithya*: 'Brahma is real, this world is unreal'.

Dasanudasa: servant of servants.

55 *neti, neti*: 'not this, not this'.

56 *cry for peace*: this was written at a time when many people and world leaders were trying to find ways of preventing another world war. Among the attempts was the foundation of the League of Nations (1919).

58 *every evening*: in the *ashram* prayers.

61 *S.S. Rajputana*: the ship on which Gandhi was sailing to London in 1931 to attend the Second Round Table Conference on the future of India. This was part of a discourse he gave at his evening prayers on the ship, and was subsequently published.

62 *eleven organs*: five of perception, five of action, and the mind.

63 *service of the kind I was rendering*: Gandhi refers to the work of the Indian Ambulance Corps he organized during the Zulu Rebellion of 1906. It was in response to this experience that he finally took the vow of celibacy.

our religious books: in Hindu thinking, sexual abstinence conserves and generates spiritual energy.

non-attachment: disinterestedness, or not being attached to, concerned with, objects or with the fruits of one's action, was significant in Gandhi's thinking. He believed it was a key message of the *Gita*, and had also learned it from Raychandbhai, his Jain mentor: see above, I. 23.

64 *Sir S. Radhakrishnan*: (1888–1975), famous Indian philosopher and academic; President of India, 1961–7.

65 *the suppressed classes*: those at the base of Hindu society, untouchables. See below, Section IV.

III. TRANSFORMING SOCIETIES

67 *catastrophe at Paris*: a fire on the metro in August 1903 which killed 84 people and injured many others.

68 *observations made here*: made by Gandhi in London during a visit there to publicize the problems of Indians in South Africa.

It came off last night: 13 October 1909, when Gandhi spoke at the Friends' Meeting House, Hampstead, at a meeting held under the auspices of the Hampstead Peace and Arbitration Society.

70 *You will be seeing*: Polak was about to go to India to publicize the problems of Indians in South Africa.

READER: Gandhi wrote his 1909 tract on true *swaraj* in the form of a dialogue between himself as a newspaper Editor and his Reader. On this choice of literary genre see *Hind Swaraj*, ed. Parel, pp. l–li; also Gandhi's own explanation in the Preface and Introduction, ibid., pp. 6, 11.

A great English writer: Edward Carpenter (1844–1929), sometime Anglican clergyman, socialist writer, and campaigner for homosexual equality. He experimented with the simple life of manual labour as a market gardener. His book, *Civilization: Its Cause and Cure*, originally a Fabian Lecture, was published in 1889. He considered modern civilization to be a social and moral disease.

74 *W. J. Wybergh*: a Theosophist, a member of the Transvaal Legislature, and Commissioner for Mines in Transvaal. The phrases in quotation marks are from a letter from Wybergh to Gandhi of 3 May 1910.

75 *Bow*: Gandhi was in London for the Second Round Table Conference on India's political future and had elected to stay in the East End of London rather than the West End, as had many other Indian delegates. He stayed at the Kingsley Hall settlement.

The tendency . . . began in Durban: see Gandhi's account of his early attempts at washing his own shirts and cutting his own hair: the results amused his colleagues in court. Gandhi, *An Autobiography*, part III, chap. IX.

Ruskin's teaching: Ruskin's book *Unto this Last* profoundly influenced Gandhi. See above, note to p. 29.

the said settlement: Phoenix Settlement near Durban, where Gandhi and several colleagues settled to experiment with the simple life in 1904, where each person would labour and draw the same living wage. Phoenix was set up after Gandhi had read Ruskin's *Unto this Last*.

Tolstoy and Ruskin: the works of both authors profoundly influenced Gandhi, particularly with their ideas of the value of the simple life and manual labour. See above, I. 29–32. Gandhi named his second experiment with simple communal living Tolstoy Farm.

82 *swadeshi*: literally belonging to one's own country. Gandhi made the use of Indian-made goods one of the planks of his movement for *swaraj* (self-rule) in India.

83 *Bengal*: reference to a *swadeshi* movement in Bengal Presidency in 1905.

86 *Sir William Wilson Hunter*: (1840–1900), member of the Indian Civil Service, authority on Indian finance and also (1871) Director-General of Statistics. He drew up the scheme for the *Imperial Gazetteer of India*, and supervised much of the gathering of information for it, himself authoring the statistical volumes on Bengal and Assam.

'Take no thought for the morrow': a phrase in the English translation of the Bible, taken from Christ's Sermon on the Mount, which appealed to Gandhi: Matthew 6: 34.

87 *'wise, temperate and furious'*: a phrase from Shakespeare's *Macbeth*, II. iii.

89 *lakh*: a hundred thousand.

90 *bread labour*: this was a concept Gandhi drew from Tolstoy, who in turn
elaborated it after drawing on another Russian writer, T. Bonduref.

the well-being of all: sarvodaya, Gandhi's ideal of moral social relations,
and also the title he chose for his Gujarati paraphrase of Ruskin's *Unto
this Last*.

zamindar: landholder, landlord.

ryot: peasant, agricultural labourer.

96 *avatars*: an incarnation of the divine.

tapasya: the practice of *tapas*, austerity.

97 *The past twelve months*: Gandhi refers to the civil disobedience movement he
inaugurated in March 1930 with his march from his Ahmedabad *ashram*
to Dandi on the coast to make salt.

Ahmedabad: industrial city in Gujarat where Gandhi had involved himself
in relations between mill-owners and workers and had tried to create a
new form of trade union.

98 *'Love thy neighbour as thyself'*: Jesus' words, as given in Luke 10: 27.

99 *crore*: ten million.

100 *Princes*: one-third of India remained under indigenous princes, in subordinate alliance with the British.

bighas: a *bigha* is a measurement of land just over an acre.

101 *varna*: caste, in the sense of the idea of a fourfold division of Indian society into Priests, Warriors, Traders, and Labourers.

102 *ganja*: hemp.

103 *Sevagram*: the place where Gandhi created his second *ashram* community
in India in 1936, near Wardha in the Central Provinces.

104 *Maine*: Sir Henry Maine (1822–88), jurist: Legal Member of the council
of the Governor-General of India, 1862–9; Vice-Chancellor of Calcutta
University, 1863–9.

Congress: this was written in the context of Congress politicians becoming
Ministers in the Indian Provinces through electoral success, raising questions as to whether one-time *satyagrahis* should use weapons of control as
the British had done.

goondaism: violent disorder, from *goonda*, violent ruffian.

105 *the method*: non-violent civil resistance, a method Gandhi had developed
in South Africa during the struggle for Indian rights.

108 *Vow against untouchability*: this paragraph and the subsequent one were
added in the third edition of the Constitution, published on 7 November
1915.

varnashram dharma: varnashram is the organization of society into four
castes (*varnas*) each with a distinctive function, and the division of life

into four stages; *dharma* is duty so this means the duty in life to maintain *varnashram*.

110 *consent of their parents*: this clause was replaced in the third edition by the rule that children under 12 would not be admitted if their parents did not join the *ashram* at the same time.

ten years: this clause was omitted in the third edition.

111 *Visitors*: many Indians and non-Indians came to visit Gandhi in this Ahmedabad *ashram* and later at Sevagram. Some were spiritual seekers and some were involved in politics. Sevagram virtually became the headquarters of the Congress Party.

112 *Daily routine*: this section was added in the third edition.

113 *Ashrams like this one*: Gandhi was referring to the *ashram* at Wardha which was a branch of the Ahmedabad *ashram* and was directed by a close associate of Gandhi, Vinoba Bhave. On Bhave, see above, note to p. 6.

A constitution: see above, III. 115, for the draft Constitution.

incarceration: after the non-cooperation movement of 1920–2, Gandhi was imprisoned from 1922 to 1924.

114 *Maganlal's death*: Maganlal was the grandson of Gandhi's uncle, had been with him in South Africa and returned with him to India. He was the driving force in the Satyagraha Ashram when Gandhi was away, either on political work or in prison. Gandhi was devoted to him and felt his death in 1928 very deeply. See Judith M. Brown, *Gandhi: Prisoner of Hope* (New Haven and London: Yale University Press, 1989), 201–2.

Prahlad: a figure in Hindu mythology who had a wicked father.

117 *smritis*: Hindu scriptural authorities which are less sacred than the *Vedas*.

124 *Prayer in the life of the ashram*: this section is taken from an unfinished history of the *ashram* written by Gandhi in 1932 while he was in prison.

126 *Dinabandhu Andrews and the late Mr Pearson*: C. F. Andrews and William Pearson, Englishmen who were friends and identified strongly with India and were concerned for Indian labourers overseas. Pearson spent much time at Tagore's home, Santiniketan, while Andrews was a close friend of Gandhi. See H. Tinker, *The Ordeal of Love: C. F. Andrews and India* (Delhi: Oxford University Press, 1979).

128 *parayan*: regular recitation.

131 *Sevagram*: Sevagram in the Central Provinces was where Gandhi established his second main *ashram* in India and made his home from 1936.

IV. INDIA UNDER BRITISH RULE: MAKING A NEW NATION

133 *Congress*: the Indian National Congress, founded in 1885, the main political party in India and voice of Indian nationalism.

Partition: the partition of Bengal in 1905, which gave rise to a major protest movement among Bengali Hindus.

134 *Englistan*: this is a word fabricated by Gandhi from 'English' and 'stan' (*land*) in opposition to Hindustan, meaning India, land of the Hindus.

Spencer, Mill and others: Herbert Spencer (1820–1903), English political philosopher; John Stuart Mill (1806–73), British philosopher and economist. These were among the authors widely read by the English-educated Indian intelligentsia.

135 *Mr Asquith*: Henry Herbert Asquith (1852–1928), Liberal politician and Prime Minister of Great Britain, 1908–16.

Mr Balfour: Arthur James Balfour (1848–1930), Conservative politician and Prime Minister of Great Britain, 1902–5.

without pay: payment of Members of Parliament in Britain was instituted in 1911.

Carlyle: Thomas Carlyle (1795–1881), author, biographer, and historian.

137 *... day by day*: there follows as Chapter VI a discussion of civilization part of which is given above as III. 80.

the Company Bahadur: the East India Company, which was the earliest vehicle for a British trading presence in India and then for British political control. India only came under the British crown after the Indian Mutiny of 1857. *Bahadur* means powerful or sovereign.

138 *bhang*: an intoxicant.

Mr Gladstone: William Ewart Gladstone (1809–98), Liberal politician who was Prime Minister of Great Britain four times in the later nineteenth century.

139 *Mr Chamberlain*: Joseph Chamberlain (1836–1914), British Secretary of State for the Colonies for part of the time Gandhi was in South Africa.

President Kruger: Stephanus Johannes Kruger (1825–1904), Transvaal statesman and general, President of Transvaal, 1883–1900.

140 *the Thugs, the Pindaris and the Bhils*: warlike groups in India who were seen as a menace to peaceful society.

141 *Macaulay*: Thomas Babington Macaulay (1800–59), essayist, poet, historian, lawyer, and politician; Law Member of the Supreme Council of India, 1835–8.

143 *One of our poets*: Tulsidas; see above, note to p. 21.

neither an extremist nor a moderate: at the time Congress politicians were divided among so-called Moderates and Extremists. Moderates wanted self-government within the Empire, achieved through constitutional means, while Extremists defined self-rule as complete independence and were prepared to use unconstitutional means if necessary.

149 *before long*: the end of British rule came in August 1947.

today: in 1921 Gandhi was leading the first non-cooperation movement against British rule and had said he thought India would gain *swaraj* in a year if Indians followed all the aspects of his programme. At a critical meeting of the Congress in Nagpur in December 1920, where Gandhi's new influence in Congress was clear, the party adopted as its goal *swaraj* by all legitimate and peaceful means. Gandhi himself did not think this automatically meant the end of a connection with Britain. See Judith M. Brown, *Gandhi's Rise to Power: Indian Politics 1915–1922* (Cambridge: Cambridge University Press, 1972), particularly chaps. 8 and 9.

150 *28 December 1926*: Gandhi was speaking on the Independence Resolution in the Subjects Committee at the annual session of Congress.

151 *the resolution*: Gandhi was referring to the recent session of Congress: see previous note for his speech in the Subjects Committee there.

152 *will take care of itself*: this reflects Gandhi's insistence that means and ends were indivisible. See above, II. 65.

resolution of independence: most surprisingly, Congress at its session in December 1927 had passed a resolution calling for independence rather than *swaraj*: this led to a major critique by Gandhi and a confrontation with his younger protégé, Jawaharlal Nehru. On this, see Brown, *Nehru: A Political Life*, 86–7.

Dadabhai Naoroji: Naoroji (see above, note to p. 34) had used the word *swaraj* in his presidential address at the Congress session of 1906.

154 *hide the light under a bushel*: reference to a saying of Jesus recorded in Matthew 5: 15.

Oxford: Gandhi was in England in the autumn of 1931 for the Second Round Table Conference on India's political future, and he visited Oxford several times for private conversations with leading intellectuals. This one was held at the home of his friend, Edward Thompson, and he was responding to the concerns of Gilbert Murray (Classical scholar and internationalist) about the dangers of the Indian nationalist movement. He had been in England a month and was already exhausted. Mrs Thompson had found him asleep over his spinning-wheel in front of their drawing-room fire before the discussion. See M. Lago, *'India's Prisoner': A Biography of Edward John Thompson, 1886–1946* (Columbia, Mo.: University of Missouri Press, 2001), 245. Gandhi also twice stayed at Balliol College and his signature can be seen in the Master's Guest Book, which is still in use.

155 *Constituent Assembly*: Nehru first raised this idea at the Congress Working Committee on 14 September 1939. Serious attention to constitution-making was overwhelmed by the outbreak of war and the renewed conflict between Congress and the British. It only resumed after the war, when the British were planning their departure.

the communal problem: Gandhi was referring to the deepening rift between Congress and the Muslim minority about the future shape of an independent India. See the discussion later in this section on Gandhi's attitude to increasing Hindu–Muslim hostility.

156 *these elections*: Gandhi refers to elections to a new Constituent Assembly held in July 1946 according to the May 1946 Cabinet Mission Plan for the creation of a new government on the subcontinent following the end of British rule.

157 *Deshbandhu Chittaranjan Das and Pandit Motilal Nehru*: C. R. Das and Motilal Nehru (father of Jawaharlal) were two prominent Congressmen who had founded the so-called Swaraj Party in the early 1920s in the aftermath of the collapse of Gandhi's non-cooperation movement, and after a struggle with Gandhi in 1924 had been permitted to be effectively the Congress parliamentary wing of activity, though Gandhi reluctantly accepted that the use of imperial legislative bodies was an appropriate part of the struggle for *swaraj*. He himself remained consistent that 'constructive work' was the surest way to achieve *swaraj*.

159 *State Paper*: Gandhi here refers to the Cabinet Mission Plan of May 1946.

160 *partitioned*: India was partitioned into India and Pakistan at the point of independence in August 1947, by agreement between the British and the main political parties, as the only way of achieving a constitutional formula for independence acceptable to the Muslim League which had become the spokesman for much Muslim political opinion.

this price: the partition of the country at independence.

161 *29 January 1940*: this was the day before Gandhi was assassinated in Delhi: hence the title conventionally given to the document he drafted on the future of Congress.

A.I.C.C.: the All-India Congress Committee.

the following rules: there followed a list of suggestions, including a tiered organization of workers from the village upwards, and work to organize the villages to make them self-supporting through agriculture and handicrafts, to encourage good health and cleanliness, and to provide basic education. Through this Gandhi was trying to build true independence as he visualized it, from the villages upwards.

162 *Rashtrabhasha*: the national language.

164 *Constructive Programme: Its Meaning and Place*: a lengthy pamphlet originally written by Gandhi in December 1941: this is a revised version which appeared in 1945. It is a document which reflects his mature conception of the right path to *swaraj*, and is as significant as *Hind Swaraj* earlier in his life.

167 *sanatanis*: orthodox Hindus.

169 *Jawaharlal Nehru*: Nehru, Gandhi's younger colleague, eventually became India's first Prime Minister.

A.I.S.A.: All-India Spinners' Association, founded by Gandhi in 1925.

170 *mals*: straps.

172 *the Haripura session*: the Congress session of 1938 held at Haripura.

177 *This fight*: when Gandhi wrote the original version in 1941 the Congress was in the middle of a prolonged final struggle against British rule which culminated in the 'Quit India' movement of 1942.

the movement in Champaran: Gandhi's first individual movement of civil disobedience in India, in 1917, on behalf of agriculturalists growing indigo.

178 *Babu Brijkishore Prasad and Babu Rajendra Prasad*: two Bihari lawyers and Congress politicians who first cooperated with Gandhi in the Champaran movement. Rajendra Prasad rose high in Congress politics and eventually became the first President of the Indian Republic.

179 *adivasis*: tribal people.

'*the harvest is rich but the labourers are few*': Matthew 9: 37.

180 *The Chinese Generalissimo*: Chiang Kai-shek, the leader of the Chinese Nationalists.

181 *Vandemataram*: a national song which Muslims found offensively Hindu.

183 *as it was in 1941*: Gandhi refers to a movement of individual civil disobedience which took the form of protesting that it was wrong to help the war effort.

184 *pice*: the smallest denomination of money in India.

185 *Communal relations*: this is a phrase often used in India which refers to the relationship (often fraught) between members of different religions, particularly as the British devolved political power into Indian hands, and minorities feared for their future at the hands of the Hindus who were in a demographic majority on the subcontinent. It particularly means relationships between Hindus and Muslims. Gandhi's insistence on the need for communal unity as a precondition for true *swaraj* was clear in his Constructive Programme: see above IV. 139.

Your last question: at the end of the previous chapter the Reader had asked how India could be one nation, given the religious differences between Hindus and Muslims.

186 *as there are individuals*: for Gandhi's views on true religion as the individual's response to the divine, see above, Section II b.

187 *cow-protection*: killing of cows by Muslims at great festivals such as *Id* had become one of the flashpoints between Hindus and Muslims, as for the Hindu the cow is sacred. In the increasingly charged relations between Hindus and Muslims in India since the later nineteenth century Hindus had set up numerous cow-protection societies.

188 *manners and customs of all peoples*: Gandhi is referring to numerous British writings on India, particularly government collection of information about Indians, as in the decennial census and the district gazetteers. Several members of the Indian Civil Service also turned themselves into amateur ethnographers and anthropologists and wrote voluminous accounts of the peoples of different regions of India. One strand in these writings was the description of difference between members of different religious traditions.

189 *Lord Morley*: John Morley, Viscount Morley of Blackburn (1858–1923), Liberal politician and writer, Secretary of State for India, 1905–11. With the then Viceroy, Lord Minto, he was behind the so-called Morley–Minto Reforms of 1909 which enlarged the Indian representation in the provincial and central legislatures. A deputation of Muslims, to Minto in fact,

388 *Explanatory Notes*

in 1906, asked for protection for Muslims, as a minority, in the forthcoming reforms and received it in the forms of separate electorates. See S. A. Wolpert, *Morley and India 1906–1910* (Berkeley and Los Angeles: University of California Press, 1967).

190 *the Ali Brothers*: leading lights in the Khilafat movement (see next note), Mahomed and Shaukat Ali, who were arrested in 1915.

the Khilafat: the authority of the Khalifah or Sultan of Turkey. Gandhi supported the campaign of Indian Muslims to ensure that at the end of the First World War the defeated Sultan of Turkey would retain sufficient authority to protect the Muslim faith and the Muslim holy places in the Middle East. It became one of the twin planks on which he argued for non-cooperation with the British government in India. The other plank was the protest against military violence in Punjab, particularly the Jallianwalla Bagh massacre in Amritsar in 1919. Congress adopted non-cooperation in 1920, a departure which signalled Gandhi's rise to dominance in the party and in the nationalist movement more broadly. See Brown, *Gandhi's Rise to Power*, particularly chaps. 6–8. Ultimately the Khilafat movement lost its foundations when Turkey became a secular republic in 1923.

193 *as members*: many Muslims became Congress members in 1920 to help push through the non-cooperation programme: see above, note to p. 190.

Bakr-i-Id: a Muslim religious festival at which cows were often sacrificed, in memory of the sacrifice of Ishmael by Ibrahim.

195 *Bharata Mata*: Mother India.

my release: Gandhi's early release from prison on grounds of ill-health in February 1924. He had had to have surgery for appendicitis.

Hindu–Muslim Tension: Its Cause and its Cure: this was the title of a lengthy article in *Young India*, 29 May 1924, which was subsequently reprinted as a pamphlet. It was Gandhi's response to the deteriorating relations between Hindus and Muslims he saw on his release from prison early that year, of which the manifestations were not only controversy but violence. The document is summarized in the following document, IV. 148, and so only extracts are given here indicating Gandhi's core ideas rather than his detailed response to the deterioration of communal relations following the end of the non-cooperation movement and the collapse of the Khilafat campaign.

196 *Chauri Chaura outrage*: the burning of a police station in a village in the United Provinces, killing the Indian policemen inside it. This took place in February 1922, in the course of the non-cooperation movement, and was the occasion for Gandhi calling off the campaign.

199 *Saharanpur*: town in the United Provinces: this province was the most afflicted by the communal violence which increasingly took place in the 1920s.

200 *akhadas*: gymnasia used for practices of body-building, wrestling, etc. Among overtly Hindu nationalists, physical fitness and exercises were (and still are) important as a way of building up the Hindu race in the face of minority communities.

the Prince's day in 1921: violence which broke out the day the Prince of Wales visited Bombay, following a stoppage of work organized by Congress, and left dead and injured among the city's European, Anglo-Indians, and Parsis. Gandhi said at the time that if this was *swaraj* it stank in his nostrils.

202 *Ajmal Khan*: (1863–1928), highly respected Muslim politician from Delhi, founder-member of the Muslim League in 1906, who had been involved with the Khilafat movement but was a moderating influence on Muslim politics and strove to keep an alliance with Congress. He was also a notable *hakim*, or doctor.

203 *Mr Jinnah*: M. A. Jinnah (1876–1948), major Muslim politician from western India. He became leader of the Muslim League and main spokesman in the 1940s for the idea (abhorrent to Gandhi) that there were 'two nations' in India, one of which was Muslim and needed its own homeland, Pakistan. When Pakistan was created by the partition of India in 1947 he became its first Governor-General. He is revered as the father of the nation.

that one black sin: the observance of untouchability. This thought of divine punishment for Hindus for this observance re-surfaced after the terrible earthquake in Bihar in 1934, which Gandhi took to be a divine punishment.

204 *the long statement*: his lengthy statement on Hindu–Muslim tension, which appeared in *Young India*, 29 May 1925: see above, IV. 147.

the Moplah rebellion: an uprising by the Moplahs, an agricultural community on the south-west coast of India, which occurred in 1921 during the non-cooperation campaign and was associated with it, but during which Muslim labourers turned on their Hindu landlords.

Mr Fazl Hussain: Fazli Husain, prominent Muslim Punjabi politician, at the time Minister for Education and Local Self-government in the Punjab.

shuddhi: Hindu movement of purification and reintegration into the Hindu fold.

205 *arati*: Hindu mode of worship making circular movements with lights.

Ajmal Khan: see above, note to p. 202.

tabligh: Muslim purificatory movement, like the Hindu *shuddhi* movement.

206 *recent events*: Gandhi decided to undergo a three-week fast for communal unity following a communal disturbance in Kohat on the North-West Frontier in early September. More than 150 people were killed or injured and the whole Hindu population fled in terror.

210 *our lamps well trimmed*: a reference to the parable Jesus told of the wise and foolish virgins waiting for the bridegroom on his way to the wedding feast. The foolish ones did not have enough oil to trim their lamps, and so had to go to the oil vendors, and when they returned the doors to the feast were shut on them: Matthew 25: 1–13.

the proposed partition: on 23 March 1940 the Muslim League meeting at Lahore had resolved that no constitution for a free India was acceptable to Muslims unless they gained autonomous states in the north-west and north–east of the country, where they were a majority. The details of such a partition were vague. For Gandhi's anguish when a precise scheme for partition was worked out and accepted in 1947, see above, IV. 135 and 136.

210 *the other day*: Gandhi must be referring to those Indian Muslims who were, many centuries earlier, converts to Islam rather than Muslim incoming migrants, such as the majority of the lowly Muslims in Bengal during the time of Muslim rule in India.

untouchability: the practice of treating those at the base of Hindu society as untouchable, ritually polluting. They did the dirtiest jobs for the rest of society, like cleaning latrines and removing the carcases of dead animals. The abolition of the practice was part of Gandhi's Constructive Programme: see above, IV. 139.

211 *Puja*: Hindu worship.

old dame: Gandhi appears to be referring to his nurse, as described in his *Autobiography*; see above, I. 19.

213 *would not countenance untouchability*: this was written into one of the early drafts of the *ashram* constitution: see above, III. 115 and 118.

216 *Yudhishthira*: a saintly figure in the *Mahabharata*.

Dyer and O'Dwyer: see above, note to p. 12. Reference here is to the 'crawling order' under martial law, when Indians were told to crawl in the presence of Europeans.

217 *Sahebs*: Saheb/Sahib was the honorific term used by Indians for European men.

to remove the mote from that of our masters: here Gandhi echoes Christ's words recorded in Matthew 7: 3.

Dyerism and O'Dwyerism: see above, notes to pp. 12 and 216.

218 *'Do unto others . . . do unto you'*: Christ's words, recorded in Matthew 7: 12.

the Punjab and Khilafat: martial law in the Punjab in 1919 and the treatment of the Khalifah, the Sultan of Turkey after the First World War, were the two issues on which Gandhi had campaigned and persuaded Congress to adopt non-cooperation in 1920.

the opening of a particular temple: because untouchables were considered polluting they were forbidden entry into temples used by higher-caste Hindus. So temple-entry became a major issue in attempts to end untouchability. This was particularly important in southern India, where temple worship was far more important than in the practice of Hinduism in northern India.

219 *Harijan Sevak Sangh*: literally, Society for the Service of Harijans, also known in English as the All-India Anti-untouchability League, which Gandhi founded in 1932 after his famous fast against the provision of separate electorates for untouchables in a Communal Award by the British Government in preparation for forthcoming constitutional reforms, and after Congress and the minorities had not been able to reach agreement in a series of Round Table Conferences in London. It was meant to be

non-political and separate from Congress. Its President was G. D. Birla, a prominent businessman and supporter of Gandhi's social reform movements. It was from this time that Gandhi really threw himself into work for untouchables, both in prison and when he was a free man.

220 *Satyagraha*: this was a civil resistance movement, which Gandhi supported, to permit untouchables access to the roads around a temple, in 1924. Significantly, he did not think that the time was ripe to undertake *satyagraha* to force the broader issue of temple-entry for untouchables, and never adopted this mode of action in his work against untouchability.

221 *The fast*: Gandhi undertook a fast in protest against the award of separate electorates to untouchables by the British government in 1932 after Indians had failed to achieve an agreement among themselves at a series of Round Table Conferences in London about the representation of minorities. Gandhi believed passionately that untouchables were not a minority, but part of the Hindu population. In response to his fast, untouchable and Hindu representatives worked out a method of representation for untouchables with reserved seats rather than separate electorates, which became known as the Poona Pact, as Gandhi was in prison in Poona at the time. A conference in Bombay ratified the pact and passed a resolution which Gandhi had drafted, that no Hindu should be regarded as untouchable because of his birth, and that all those who were once untouchables would now have access to all public institutions, including wells, roads, and schools. See Brown, *Gandhi: Prisoner of Hope*, 265–8.

224 *Yeravda Pact*: the Poona Pact: see previous note. Gandhi was in Yeravda jail at the time.

Dr Ambedkar, Rao Bahadur Raja: B. R. Ambedkar (1891–1956) and M. C. Raja (1883–1943) were both untouchable spokesmen, though opposed to each other, who had been involved in negotiating the Poona Pact. Ambedkar was bitterly critical of Gandhi's attitudes and methods of approach to untouchability, and wrote a book in 1945 called *What Congress and Gandhi have done to the Untouchables*.

The (impending) fast: Gandhi did in fact undertake a three-week fast in May 1933. He maintained that this was one of purification to generate inward power to fight an evil of incomparable proportions. He was released from prison to undertake this fast as the British could not risk his death in prison.

225 *last September*: see above, note to p. 221.

I.P.C: the Indian Penal Code.

227 *Harijan*: Gandhi not only began to call untouchables by this name but started a new journal with the same name early in 1933.

228 *a true companion*: see above, IV. 139, for the important position Gandhi gave to the necessary 'revolution' in the role of women in the Constructive Programme (Point 9).

the Sarda Bill: the Child Marriage Restraint Act, which had just been passed in early October 1929 by the central legislature, and was known informally after the name of the man who proposed it in 1927. After much discussion and controversy, it set the minimum age of marriage as 14 for females and 18 for males.

235 *Sir Pherozeshah*: Sir Pherozeshah Mehta (1848–1915), Parsi and prominent moderate politician from Bombay.

236 *Maritzburg*: an old name for Pietermaritzburg in Natal.

237 *Ramarajya*: the rule of Ram, God.

Sita: the great mythical heroine of the *Ramayana* whom Gandhi held up as the role model for Indian women for her courage, purity, and wifely devotion. She was the wife of King Rama and was abducted by the wicked King Ravana, but later rescued by Rama.

239 *chauth*: one-quarter of farm produce, formerly collected as land revenue.

Antyajas: untouchables.

for some time: presumably referring to the temporarily polluted state of women in childbirth or during menstruation, from which caste Hindu women could be ritually purified.

Bhangis: sweepers who remove polluting substances.

242 *the time of my marriage*: in 1882, when he was 13.

243 *Kathiawad*: the area of western India Gandhi came from (modern spelling is Kathiawar).

244 *Margaret E. Cousins*: (1878–1954), Irish Theosophist and feminist who spent much of her life in India. She was important in numerous campaigns for the reform of women's status in India and in several women's organizations, such as the All-India Women's Conference.

245 *Legislation*: see above, note to p. 228. There was much discussion on the issue of the age of marriage, and several failed bills before the Sarda bill became legislation.

246 *Basanti Devi*: widow of 'Deshbandhu', C. R. Das, who had died in 1925. See above, note to p. 157.

249 *In this case*: a correspondent had asked Gandhi to say whether he thought Hindu widows should spend their lives in educating themselves and young girls.

250 *Mirabehn*: the Hindu name given to Madelaine Slade, an English devotee of Gandhi.

the profession of nursing: high-caste Hindu women did not go into nursing as this involved doing tasks which were considered ritually polluting. The Indian nursing profession was (and to a large extent still is) largely made up of Christians, for example from what is now Kerala.

252 *a sister*: Mrs Margaret Sanger, a protagonist of artificial birth-control.

253 *Sita*: see above, note to p. 237.

the Conference: of Rajputs from Kathiawar; probably convened to discuss social reform.

pandal: tent.

254 *purdah*: the custom of veiling women, in Muslim and some Hindu communities.

255 *Mr Brayne's book*: F. L. Brayne (1882–1952), member of the Indian Civil Service and expert on rural reconstruction, wrote numerous books on the subject including *Village Uplift in India* (1927), *The Gurgaon Experiment* (1928), and *The Remaking of Village India* (1929), published before Gandhi noted reading his work. Brayne felt that gold and silver ornaments were symbols of peasant extravagance.

256 *darshan*: viewing—often of a divine image.

258 *swadeshi*: Gandhi made this one of the planks of his movement for what he saw as true *swaraj*. For earlier documents indicating this, see III. 88; III. 115 and 118 on *swadeshi* observance in the Ahmedabad *ashram*; and IV. 139 for the section on Khadi in the 1941 Constructive Programme.

at the present moment: Gandhi's exposition of the meaning of a *swadeshi* vow occurred in the middle of his first pan-Indian movement of non-cooperation, in 1919, on the issue of the Rowlatt bills, which were intended to suppress sedition. He called off the campaign when violence erupted in the Punjab.

259 *Kabir*: a fifteenth-century poet and saint, who taught the path of devotion to God.

265 *Sir William Wilson Hunter*: see above, note to p. 86.

Sir Dinshaw Wacha's: (1844–1936), Indian Parsi politician and President of Congress, 1901.

yogis: those following a spiritual discipline.

266 *Naoroji*: see above, note to p. 34.

267 *Principal Paranjapye*: Principal, Fergusson College, Poona.

268 *Kamadhenus*: or Kamadhuks; mythical cows which bestow everything one wishes for.

Ruskin: see above, note to p. 29.

269 *artha*: material welfare.

270 *Dhaulagiri peak*: Dhaulagiri (8,167 metres) is the seventh highest mountain in the world and is located in the Annapurna mountain range of the Himalaya of north-central Nepal.

The Congress resolution: the resolution calling for non-cooperation, passed at the Nagpur session of the Congress in December 1920.

273 *the calling*: here Gandhi refers to the fact that the Punjab was the primary recruiting ground for Indian soldiers.

julahis: weavers.

278 *The parliamentary programme*: in late 1936 and early 1937 Congress was contesting elections to the new legislatures set up by the 1935 Government of India Act.

280 *Jawaharlal*: see above, note to p. 8.

280 *Lord Linlithgow*: 2nd Marquess of Linlithgow (1887–1952), Viceroy of India, 1935–43.

281 *Macaulay's ideas on Indian education*: for Macaulay, see above, note to p. 141. In 1835, as Law Member of the Supreme Council of India Macaulay was the author of a famous Minute on Education which proposed supporting English education in India rather than traditional forms of education. He felt the latter to be far inferior.

EDUCATION: see above, IV. 139, for Gandhi's Constructive Programme and in it his views on Basic and Adult education.

282 *Professor Huxley*: Thomas Huxley (1825–95), biologist and science educationalist; the quotation is from an 1869 essay on a liberal education.

283 *Kamadhuk*: see above, note to p. 268.

284 *Mr Lloyd George*: David Lloyd George (1863–1945), reforming Chancellor of the Exchequer at the time Gandhi visited London in 1909. As a Welshman, he wanted Welsh children to learn Welsh.

285 *The Mullas, the Dasturs and the Brahmins*: the religious teachers of Muslims, Parsis, and Hindus.

287 *a national school*: Gandhi had called this 'a big educational scheme' in a letter to K. Mehta, 18 January 1917, *CWMG*, vol. xiii, p. 331. A more elaborate version of the scheme, published in October 1917, can be found in *CWMG*, vol. xiv, pp. 37–42.

289 *carried on at the Ashram*: Gandhi refers to the *ashram* he established in Ahmedabad on his return to India. See above, III. 115 and 118 on the constitution and work of the *ashram*; III. 118 shows how the educational work in the *ashram* was elaborated over subsequent years.

291 *Lord Curzon's*: Curzon (1859–1925) was Viceroy from 1899 to 1905.

Macaulay's: see above, note to p. 141.

294 *National School*: see above, note to p. 287.

295 *Shri Malabari*: B. M. Malabari (1854–1912), poet, journalist, and social reformer.

298 *doli*: seat slung from a pole carried by two or more people on their shoulders.

300 *pathshala*: indigenous school.

301 *the Gujarat Vidyapith*: the National School Gandhi was closely involved with in Ahmedabad. See above, III. 118, and note to p. 287.

the conference: a conference on education planned for later in October 1937 under Gandhi's presidency.

primary education: for Gandhi's views on primary education, see also three articles written in May 1928: *CWMG*, vol. xxxvi, pp. 316–17, 327–9, 343–5.

302 *gur-making*: gur is a syrup made from crushed sugar cane.

303 *propositions*: the ideas Gandhi had put forward before the conference: see previous extract.

Kallenbach: Hermann Kallenbach (1871–1945), close Jewish friend of Gandhi in South Africa, who gave him the land on which Tolstoy Farm was built.

304 *takli-spinning*: using a spinning-wheel.

the Congress Ministries: Congress had formed the provincial government in the majority of provinces after the 1936/7 elections under the new constitution provided for in the 1935 Government of India Act. Education was therefore an urgent issue for them, and their Education Ministers were present at this conference.

307 *this plan of education*: as a result of the conference a committee was appointed to work out the details of the scheme Gandhi had sketched out and the conference had accepted. It was known as Basic Education and was subsequently endorsed by the Congress.

V. NON-VIOLENCE AS POLITICAL ACTION

309 *The birth of non-violent action*: this section deals with Gandhi's experiments with non-violent action in the realm of politics. For his underlying belief in non-violence as essential in the search for truth see above, Section II d.

310 *Asiatic Act of 1907*: Act requiring Indians in Transvaal to register if they wished to live and work legally there—a provision which did not apply to other citizens of the British Empire. This was one of the major grievances on which Gandhi led Indians into non-violent resistance in South Africa. For his own account of this see M. K. Gandhi, *Satyagraha in South Africa,* trans. from Gujarati by V. G. Desai (Ahmedabad: Navajivan, 1928); and for modern historical analyses, see M. Swan, *Gandhi: The South African Experience* (Johannesburg: Ravan Press, 1985); R. A. Huttenback, *Gandhi in South Africa: British Imperialism and the Indian Question, 1860–1914* (Ithaca and London: Cornell University Press, 1971).

311 *my departure to India*: Gandhi finally left South Africa in July 1914, reaching India via England in January 1915.

312 *victory at Mafeking*: the relief of Mafeking, where a British garrison had been besieged for 217 days, 17 May 1900. The news reached London on the evening of 18 May. Many towns in Great Britain were immediately caught up in huge impromptu celebrations. This gave birth to the verb, to 'maffick', in the English language, meaning to celebrate boisterously with public demonstrations.

314 *Mr Gokhale*: see above, note to p. 36.

Lord Hardinge: (1858–1944), diplomat and Viceroy of India (1910–16). Just before his appointment as Viceroy he had been Under-Secretary of State at the Foreign Office.

315 *A Gujarati-speaking gentleman*: Maganlal Gandhi. See next extract.

316 *a sanguinary war*: a reference to the First World War, as this discussion dates from 1917.

   this self-purification: Gandhi here refers to his vow of *brahmacharya*, celibacy, taken in 1906. See above, II. 72 and 73.

317 *Maganlal Gandhi*: a close relative, who worked closely with Gandhi in South Africa and India. See above, note to p. 114.

   Tulsidas: see above, note to p. 21.

318 *'It so happened'*: the Gujarati word, transliterated, is *itihas*.

   '. . . shall perish by the sword': reference to the Gospel account of Jesus Christ's betrayal. One of his followers struck off the ear of one of those who came to take him, but Jesus rebuked him for using his sword: Matthew 26: 52.

319 *a new-fangled notion*: reference to nineteenth-century Utilitarian philosophy, which saw utility as the basis of law. Utilitarianism became a strong force in British thinking about India. See E. Stokes, *The English Utilitarians and India* (Oxford: Clarendon Press, 1959).

324 *the present movement*: Gandhi refers to his first all-India *satyagraha* movement in 1919 against the Rowlatt legislation. See above, note to p. 258.

327 *The satyagraha campaign in the Transvaal*: see above, note to p. 310.

329 *'. . . and a dagger under the arm'*: a Hindi saying.

330 *as this is a satyagraha campaign*: these instructions were issued during the *satyagraha* Gandhi led in Kaira district of Gujarat in 1918 against the land revenue demand in a time of economic hardship. See Brown, *Gandhi's Rise to Power*, 83–111.

333 *salaam*: to greet, normally with folded hands.

   Sarkar: the government.

335 *in 1921 and 1922*: Gandhi here refers to the 1920–2 movement of non-cooperation which he led with the full backing of the Congress. Nearly 16,000 people were convicted for activities which laid them open to prosecution during this movement. See Brown, *Gandhi's Rise to Power*, chap. 9. Gandhi himself was in prison between 1922 and 1924.

   Councillors: those who had not followed the Congress policy of boycotting the new legislatures set up in the provinces by the 1919 Montagu–Chelmsford reforms, and had contested the elections in November 1920. A total of 637 seats were up for election and in only 6 were there no candidates.

342 *organize non-violent strength through constructive work*: see above, IV. 139, Gandhi's Constructive Programme, which concludes with the quite limited role of civil disobedience in the struggle for freedom, compared with the constructive programme as a whole. The final sentence indicates that he felt his 'handling of civil disobedience without the constructive programme will be like a paralysed hand attempting to lift a spoon'.

the Court: the court of the District Magistrate of Champaran district, Bihar. This was Gandhi's first exercise of *satyagraha* in India after he had returned from South Africa, when he refused to obey the order to leave the district where he was investigating the problems of peasants who grew indigo. On this, see Brown, *Gandhi's Rise to Power*, 52–83.

343 *temporary suspension of civil disobedience*: this was during *satyagraha* against the Rowlatt legislation. See above, note to p. 258. Violent disturbances had occurred in Ahmedabad and Viramgam, after Gandhi had been removed from the train in which he was travelling to Delhi to promote *satyagraha*, and sent back to Bombay. Subsequent violence, particularly in the Punjab, led him to admit that he had made a 'Himalayan miscalculation' in calling on people to undertake civil disobedience before they were prepared for it: Gandhi, *An Autobiography*, part V, chap. XXXIII. On the Rowlatt *satyagraha*, see Brown, *Gandhi's Rise to Power*, 160–89.

345 *Lokamanya Tilak Maharaj*: B. G. Tilak (1856–1920), famous western Indian politician.

Tamil labourers: Tamil-speaking indentured labourers from southern India, which was the main region of India from which labourers were recruited in the nineteenth century, particularly to work on the sugar plantations.

the Khilafat question: see above, note to p. 190.

346 *the Punjab*: reference to the shooting of an unarmed crowd by soldiers at Amritsar in 1919: see above, note to p. 190.

347 *the Rowlatt legislation*: see above, note to p. 258.

Mr Montagu: E. S. Montagu (1879–1924), Secretary of State for India, 1917–22.

Shaukat Ali: brother of Mahomed Ali; both men were allies of Gandhi in the Khilafat movement.

348 *kurbani*: sacrifice of a sheep or cow by Muslims at the *Id* festival.

349 *Kaira*: the site of Gandhi's local *satyagraha* in 1918. See above, note to p. 330.

the Congress at Amritsar: the Congress meeting at Amritsar in December 1919, when Gandhi had still hoped that Indians could cooperate with the British, in particular by working with the proposed new legislative councils created under the 1919 Montagu–Chelmsford reforms.

the Royal Proclamation: this Proclamation, in December 1919, accompanied the constitutional reforms described in the previous note. This called for a new era of cooperation in India between rulers and ruled.

350 *the special Congress*: scheduled to take place in Calcutta in September 1920, well before the regular annual session which was always held in December at Christmas time.

351 *boycott of the councils*: refusal to stand for elections late in 1920 to the new legislatures created under the 1919 Montagu–Chelmsford reforms.

351 *a Greek proverb*: in fact what Gandhi alludes to is not a proverb, and certainly not a Greek proverb. It is a sentence translated from the Latin of Virgil's *Aeneid*, Book 2: *Quidquid id est, timeo Danaos et dona ferentes*: 'Whatever it is, I fear the Greeks, even when they bring gifts'. It refers to the wooden horse by which the Greeks tricked their way into the city of Troy.

352 *the lawyers*: Gandhi's advice here to lawyers echoes his critique of Indian lawyers in his *Hind Swaraj*, chap. XI. He believed lawyers aggravated disputes between Indian compatriots, and that their work enabling courts to function tightened the English grip on India. He wrote, 'If pleaders were to abandon their profession, and consider it just as degrading as prostitution, English rule would break up in a day.'

355 *the Prince of Wales*: a visit to India by the heir to the British throne, and thus one who would become Emperor of India, was being planned. For the violence which broke out in November 1921 when he visited Bombay, and Gandhi's horror at this, see above, note to p. 200.

rishis: seers.

the trenches: reference made to the disruptions in Britain in order to fight the First World War and to find men to fight on the Western Front, where trench warfare was prolonged, bloody, and destructive of human life.

356 *the satyagraha days*: presumably a reference to the Rowlatt *satyagraha* and the violence which broke out when Gandhi was stopped from visiting Delhi. See above, note to p. 343.

Kallenbach and Polak: Hermann Kallenbach and Henry Polak were two of Gandhi's closest European friends and allies in his work in South Africa.

357 *marching into a prohibited area*: in November 1913 Gandhi was arrested for leading a group of Indians into the Transvaal illegally.

361 *a Himalayan miscalculation*: Gandhi here refers to the instances of violence during the Rowlatt *satyagraha*, which made him suspend civil disobedience and admit to a huge miscalculation. See above, note to p. 343.

the deeds of the Bombay mob on the 17th November: reference to the violence in Bombay during the boycott of the visit of the Prince of Wales. See above, note to p. 200.

Chauri Chaura: the massacre of twenty-two policemen in Chauri Chaura, UP, in February 1922, which caused Gandhi to suspend civil disobedience.

Thana: police station.

Bardoli: the area in Gujarat where Gandhi had envisaged that civil disobedience would first take place in February 1922.

366 *I am planning some sort of civil disobedience*: this was the prelude to the second great *satyagraha* campaign in India, which lasted, with a break in 1931, from 1930 to 1934. Gandhi started it with civil resistance to the government salt monopoly by marching from the Ahmedabad *ashram* to the coast at Dandi to make salt illegally in March–April 1930. He hoped this issue would unite Indians and avoid violence.

the late Justice Stephen's: presumably a reference to Sir James Fitzjames Stephen (1829–94), judge and writer. He was Legal Member of the Viceroy's Council, 1869–72, and responsible for some major legislation: an Evidence Act, a Contract Act, and a revised Code of Criminal Procedure.

367 *Collectors*: officers of the Indian Civil Service who were in charge of districts. The title was in use in some parts of India and reflected the essential governmental role of collecting revenue.

three hundred men: there were far more than 300 Europeans in senior positions in the administration of India. In 1929 there were 894 Europeans and 367 Indians in the Indian Civil Service, for example, and 564 Europeans and 128 Indians in the Indian Police Service. Even so, these were tiny numbers to rule a subcontinent and as Gandhi rightly saw they were dependent on a very large number of subordinate Indian allies who helped to perpetuate British rule.

368 *Rajendrababu's*: Rajendra Prasad (1884–1963), Bihari politician, leading Congressman, and ally of Gandhi since the Champaran *satyagraha* of 1917.

371 *rightists and leftists*: by the late 1930s a vocal left-wing element had emerged in Congress which was impatient with Gandhi's leadership and his reservations about mass political action, and his apparently conservative reaction to issues of class.

372 *declaring mass civil disobedience*: in fact, when Gandhi did decide on civil disobedience in 1940–1 during the war it was initially 'individual' civil disobedience by hand-picked people proclaiming hostility to the war. Far more important to him was the Constructive Programme which he had elaborated in December 1941 (see above, IV. 139). It was only later in 1942, after much inner struggle, that he envisaged a final mass struggle, the 'Quit India' movement, which the government had no compunction in squashing firmly, compared with its measured response to his campaigns of 1920–2 and 1930–4. See Brown, *Gandhi: Prisoner of Hope*, chap. 9.

your good husband: Edmond Privat (1889–1962) was a journalist, writer, academic, and pacifist.

the heavy price: the partition of India in August 1947 at the time of independence, the appalling violence which occurred both before and afterwards, and the displacement of thousands of people who trekked across the new international borders to the side where they considered they would be safest.

373 *the internecine feud*: violence accompanying the partition of India at independence, which saw Muslims pitted against Hindus and Sikhs, and vice versa.

GLOSSARY

adivasis tribal people

ahimsa non-violence

arati Hindu worship with a lighted lamp

artha material welfare

ashram religious community, gathered round a *guru*

ashramas four stages of life in Hindu thinking

atman the universal self underlying individual personality

avatar incarnation of the divine

bhajan devotional song

bhakti religious devotion

bhangi sweeper

bigha measurement of land just over an acre

brahmachari one who practises *brahmacharya*

brahmacharya sexual restraint, celibacy

charkha spinning-wheel

Chaturmas period of four months of fasting

chopais quatrains

crore ten million

darshan view, or sight, of a holy person or image

dharma religious duty appropriate to one's age and station in life

dohas couplets

doli seat slung between poles carried by people on their shoulders

fakir Muslim or Hindu religious mendicant

gadi cushion, throne

ganja hemp

goonda violent ruffian (and from this *goondaism*)

gur syrup made from sugar cane

guru revered teacher, guide

Harijan lit. 'Child of God', Gandhi's name for untouchables: also the name of one of his periodicals

haveli Vaishnava temple

himsa violence

julahis weavers

khadi/khaddar hand-spun cloth

kisan peasant

lakh a hundred thousand

Mahatma Great Soul: used as an honorific title for Gandhi

moksha salvation; freedom from the cycle of birth and death

mukti spiritual deliverance or freedom

pan a delicacy to chew

panchayat local council: from *panch*, five

pandal tent

pathshala indigenous school

prarthana prayer

purdah the veiling and seclusion of women

Ramanama the name of God, Ram

Ramarajya literally the rule of Ram, God; often used by Gandhi to denote true *swaraj*

Rashtrabhasha national language

rishis seers

rotlis bread

ryot peasant

salaam to greet, normally with folded hands

sanatani orthodox Hindu

sannyasi in Hinduism, one who retreats from ordinary life in pursuit of holiness

sarkar government

sarvodaya the welfare of all

satya truth

satyagraha the practice of non-violent resistance to wrong

satyagrahi one who practises *satyagraha*

shastras Hindu scriptures

shastri teacher

shloka verse

shuddhi purification

smritis Hindu scriptural authorities which are less sacred than the Vedas

swadeshi use of things belonging to one's own country

swaraj self-rule, independence (*purna swaraj* is full/complete independence)

takli spinning-wheel

tapascharya practices of self-discipline

tapasya the practice of *tapas*, austerity

thana police station

tika an ornamental mark on the forehead

vairagya disinterestedness, freedom from attachment

varna caste (in the sense of a fourfold division of Hindu society)

varnashram organization of society into four castes (*varnas*) each with a distinctive function, and the division of life into four stages

varnashrama dharma one's duty in life in order to maintain *varnashram*

yajna sacrifice

yogi one who follows spiritual discipline

zamindar landholder, landlord

INDEX

A SELECTION OF   OXFORD WORLD'S CLASSICS

Bhagavad Gita

The Bible Authorized King James Version
   With Apocrypha

Dhammapada

Dharmasūtras

The Koran

The Pañcatantra

The Sauptikaparvan (from the
   Mahabharata)

The Tale of Sinuhe and Other Ancient
   Egyptian Poems

The Qur'an

Upaniṣads

ANSELM OF CANTERBURY	The Major Works
THOMAS AQUINAS	Selected Philosophical Writings
AUGUSTINE	The Confessions On Christian Teaching
BEDE	The Ecclesiastical History
HEMACANDRA	The Lives of the Jain Elders
KĀLIDĀSA	The Recognition of Śakuntalā
MANJHAN	Madhumalati
ŚĀNTIDEVA	The Bodhicaryàvatàra

	Late Victorian Gothic Tales
JANE AUSTEN	Emma
	Mansfield Park
	Persuasion
	Pride and Prejudice
	Selected Letters
	Sense and Sensibility
MRS BEETON	Book of Household Management
MARY ELIZABETH BRADDON	Lady Audley's Secret
ANNE BRONTË	The Tenant of Wildfell Hall
CHARLOTTE BRONTË	Jane Eyre
	Shirley
	Villette
EMILY BRONTË	Wuthering Heights
ROBERT BROWNING	The Major Works
JOHN CLARE	The Major Works
SAMUEL TAYLOR COLERIDGE	The Major Works
WILKIE COLLINS	The Moonstone
	No Name
	The Woman in White
CHARLES DARWIN	The Origin of Species
THOMAS DE QUINCEY	The Confessions of an English Opium-Eater
	On Murder
CHARLES DICKENS	The Adventures of Oliver Twist
	Barnaby Rudge
	Bleak House
	David Copperfield
	Great Expectations
	Nicholas Nickleby
	The Old Curiosity Shop
	Our Mutual Friend
	The Pickwick Papers

CHARLES DICKENS	A Tale of Two Cities
GEORGE DU MAURIER	Trilby
MARIA EDGEWORTH	Castle Rackrent
GEORGE ELIOT	Daniel Deronda
	The Lifted Veil and Brother Jacob
	Middlemarch
	The Mill on the Floss
	Silas Marner
SUSAN FERRIER	Marriage
ELIZABETH GASKELL	Cranford
	The Life of Charlotte Brontë
	Mary Barton
	North and South
	Wives and Daughters
GEORGE GISSING	New Grub Street
	The Odd Women
EDMUND GOSSE	Father and Son
THOMAS HARDY	Far from the Madding Crowd
	Jude the Obscure
	The Mayor of Casterbridge
	The Return of the Native
	Tess of the d'Urbervilles
	The Woodlanders
WILLIAM HAZLITT	Selected Writings
JAMES HOGG	The Private Memoirs and Confessions of a Justified Sinner
JOHN KEATS	The Major Works
	Selected Letters
CHARLES MATURIN	Melmoth the Wanderer
JOHN RUSKIN	Selected Writings
WALTER SCOTT	The Antiquary
	Ivanhoe

HONORÉ DE BALZAC	**Père Goriot**
CHARLES BAUDELAIRE	**The Flowers of Evil**
DENIS DIDEROT	**Jacques the Fatalist** **The Nun**
ALEXANDRE DUMAS (PÈRE)	**The Count of Monte Cristo** **The Three Musketeers**
GUSTAVE FLAUBERT	**Madame Bovary**
VICTOR HUGO	**The Essential Victor Hugo** **Notre-Dame de Paris**
J.-K. HUYSMANS	**Against Nature**
PIERRE CHODERLOS DE LACLOS	**Les Liaisons dangereuses**
GUY DE MAUPASSANT	**Bel-Ami** **Pierre et Jean**
MOLIÈRE	**Don Juan and Other Plays** **The Misanthrope, Tartuffe, and Other** **Plays**
ABBÉ PRÉVOST	**Manon Lescaut**
ARTHUR RIMBAUD	**Collected Poems**
EDMOND ROSTAND	**Cyrano de Bergerac**
JEAN-JACQUES ROUSSEAU	**Confessions**
MARQUIS DE SADE	**The Crimes of Love**
STENDHAL	**The Red and the Black** **The Charterhouse of Parma**
PAUL VERLAINE	**Selected Poems**
VOLTAIRE	**Candide and Other Stories**
ÉMILE ZOLA	**L'Assommoir** **The Kill**

The Oxford World's Classics Website

www.oup.com/uk/worldsclassics

- Information about new titles
- Explore the full range of Oxford World's Classics
- Links to other literary sites and the main OUP webpage
- Imaginative competitions, with bookish prizes
- Articles by editors
- Extracts from Introductions
- Special information for teachers and lecturers

www.oup.com/uk/worldsclassics